Refining AND Reminding

A Devotional Study of Numbers and Deuteronomy

Warren Henderson

All Scripture quotations are from the New King James Version of the Bible, unless otherwise noted. Copyright © 1982 by Thomas Nelson, Inc. Nashville, TN

Refining and Reminding – A Devotional Study of Numbers and Deuteronomy

By Warren Henderson
Copyright © 2018

Cover Design by Benjamin Bredeweg

Published by Warren A. Henderson
3769 Indiana Road
Pomona, KS 66076

Editing/Proofreading:
    Randy Amos, Brian Gunning,
    Marilyn MacMullen, Dan Macy,
    and David Lindstrom

Perfect Bound ISBN: 978-1-939770-48-6
eBook ISBN: 978-1-939770-49-3

Available through many online retailers.

Other Books by the Author

Afterlife – What Will It Be Like?
Answer the Call – Finding Life's Purpose
Be Holy and Come Near– A Devotional Study of Leviticus
Behold the Saviour
Be Angry and Sin Not
Conquest and the Life of Rest – A Devotional Study of Joshua
Door of Hope – A Devotional Study of the Minor Prophets
Exploring the Pauline Epistles
Forsaken, Forgotten, and Forgiven – A Devotional Study of Jeremiah
Glories Seen & Unseen
Hallowed Be Thy Name – Revering Christ in a Casual World
Hiding God – The Ambition of World Religion
In Search of God – A Quest for Truth
Infidelity and Loyalty – A Devotional Study of Ezekiel and Daniel
Knowing the All-Knowing
Managing Anger God's Way
Mind Frames – Where Life's Battle Is Won or Lost
Out of Egypt – A Devotional Study of Exodus
Overcoming Your Bully
Passing the Torch – Mentoring the Next Generation For Christ
Relativity and Redemption – A Devotional Study of Judges and Ruth
Revive Us Again – A Devotional Study of Ezra and Nehemiah
Seeds of Destiny – A Devotional Study of Genesis
Sorrow and Comfort – A Devotional Study of Isaiah
The Beginning of Wisdom – A Devotional Study of Job, Psalms, Proverbs, Ecclesiastes, and Song of Solomon
The Bible: Myth or Divine Truth?
The Evil Nexus – Are You Aiding the Enemy?
The Fruitful Bough – Affirming Biblical Manhood
The Fruitful Vine – Celebrating Biblical Womanhood
The Hope of Glory – A Preview of Things to Come
The Olive Plants – Raising Spiritual Children
Your Home the Birthing Place of Heaven

Table of Contents

Preface	1
Numbers	3
Overview of Numbers	5
Devotions in Numbers	7
Deuteronomy	261
Overview of Deuteronomy	263
Devotions in Deuteronomy	267
Endnotes	477

Preface

The Pentateuch is one continuing storyline which ultimately reaches its typological climax in the subsequent book of Joshua. Notice how the following prepositions and adverbs form a mini-outline of these six books. In Genesis, sin brought man *down*. In Exodus, he is redeemed by blood and brought *out* of the world. In Leviticus, man is permitted to come *near* (but not too close) to God in worship by substitutional sacrifices. In Numbers, man is guided *through* trials and is refined for service. In Deuteronomy, which means "Second Law," man is brought *back* to remember his responsibility to the Lord and the consequences of rebellion. In Joshua, the redeemed people are led by Joshua through the Jordan River *into* victorious living as they seize their inheritance.

Numbers records the wilderness experience of God's covenant people, who are moving towards receiving the promises of God in Canaan, despite their failures and unbelief. It is a humbling story as far as man is concerned, but also a blessed and beautiful account of God's exhaustless patience and mercy, as He works to refine His people. The book of Numbers clearly unfolds to us what man is and also what God is through practical experience.

Deuteronomy is quite distinct from the other Pentateuch books, as God's covenant people are viewed as in the Promised Land, and yet the book repeatedly orders them to enter into the place where God would place His name. Deuteronomy has more occurrences of the expression *"the Lord our God"* than any other book in the Bible. The frequency of this phrase and the prevalent occurrences of the words "law," "love," "land," and "possession" combine to declare Deuteronomy's central message: First, through faithful obedience to God's Law, the Israelites would properly recognize Jehovah as their God among the nations. Second, Jehovah's love for Israel would also be evident to the nations when the Jewish nation miraculously possessed Canaan as His

Refining and Reminding

inheritance for them. Deuteronomy is a book of practical directives to ensure that Israel both experiences and affirms covenantal love.

Refining and Reminding is a "commentary style" devotional which upholds the glories of Christ while exploring the books of Numbers and Deuteronomy within the context of the whole of Scripture. I have endeavored to include in this book some of the principal gleanings from other writers. *Refining and Reminding* contains dozens of brief devotions. This format allows the reader to use the book either as a daily devotional or as a reference source for deeper study.

— Warren Henderson

Numbers

Overview of Numbers

The Author
Both Jewish and Christian traditions credit Moses with being the author of the Pentateuch. The Lord Jesus affirmed that Moses was the author of the books of the Law (Luke 24:27, 44). Moses led the Israelites out of Egypt and was then the principal human instrument God used to communicate with His people and guide them through several wildernesses to the border of Canaan. Moses spoke directly with the Lord and was an eyewitness of all the events occurring during this forty-year period.

Date
Biblical scholars have placed the date of the Exodus from as early as 1580 B.C. to as late as 1230 B.C. Archeological evidence has been used to bolster various dates in this range. Recognizing that the Exodus occurred 480 years before Solomon began constructing the temple (1 Kgs. 6:1) and that the temple work was initiated in about 960 B.C., a date in the mid-fifteenth century B.C. for the Exodus seems appropriate. Note: The 1 Kings 6:1 reference may include 93 years in which Israel was in service to foreigners during the era of the judges (Acts 13:18-21). An Exodus date of 1446 B.C. is approximately placed.[1] The completion date of the book of Numbers would be approximately forty years later, just prior to the death of Moses, or 1406 B.C.

Theme
A little over a year after the Exodus, God commanded Moses to number the people, excluding the Levites, to establish Israel's army. Then, thirty-eight-plus years later, the people were numbered again in order to determine the size of their tribal inheritance in Canaan. Firstborn males and Levite males a month and older are also counted to

Refining and Reminding

transition into Levite-led worship on behalf of the Jewish nation. It is from these numberings of the people that the book derives its name. Nevertheless, the lessons of the book center in their thirty-eight-year wilderness journey after receiving the Law at Mount Sinai, but before arriving at Canaan's border.

The Hebrew mode of referring to books was to cite the first word in each book. For example, the first Hebrew word in Numbers is *dabar* which means "to properly arrange by words," or by implication, "to teach or command order." Following this custom, the book of Numbers sets forth the pilgrim walk of the child of God while serving God in a strange land. The book of Leviticus focused on how the people could have access and communion with holy Jehovah, who dwelled among them in a tabernacle. Following Leviticus, Numbers speaks of the refining work of God in His people's lives as they journey with Him through successive wilderness experiences. The book could be thus titled, "Walking, Working, and Warring in the Wilderness."

Outline
Preparations to Leave Sinai (1:1-10:10)
Journeying to Kadesh-Barnea (10:11-14:45)
Wilderness Wanderings (15:1-22:1)
The Moabites and Balaam (22:2-25:18)
Preparations for Entering Canaan (26:1-36:13)

Devotions in Numbers

Legitimate Lineage
Numbers 1

The book commences thirteen months after Israel's departure from Egypt. The Jewish nation had been encamped before Mount Sinai for about a year when Jehovah instructed Moses and Aaron to number the army:

> *Now the Lord spoke to Moses in the Wilderness of Sinai, in the tabernacle of meeting, on the first day of the second month, in the second year after they had come out of the land of Egypt, saying: "Take a census of all the congregation of the children of Israel, by their families, by their fathers' houses, according to the number of names, every male individually, from twenty years old and above – all who are able to go to war in Israel. You and Aaron shall number them by their armies. And with you there shall be a man from every tribe, each one the head of his father's house"* (vv. 1-4).

Numbers 1 pertains to recognizing the **lineage** of those in the camp, and Numbers 2 to the proper placement of **standards** to order the camp. Moses and Aaron recognized one leader, by name, from each of the tribes to assist in numbering the people (vv. 5-16). Aaron already represented the tribe of Levi, who were exempt from warfare; they were set apart to God to attend to the tabernacle and offer sacrifices on behalf of the nation (vv. 47-51). For this reason, the Levites were not to be numbered as soldiers.

Jacob had twelve sons, but there were literally thirteen tribes, as Ephraim and Manasseh were fathered by Joseph (Rachel's firstborn son) who received the double portion of the birthright instead of Reuben (Leah's firstborn son) because he sinned with Jacob's concubine. Nonetheless, Scripture always speaks of the Jewish nation

Refining and Reminding

as having twelve tribes, not thirteen. The number thirteen represents rebellion throughout God's Word, but the number twelve symbolizes completeness or perfection in administration, which is a central theme in Numbers. All that was necessary in God's mind to bring His people into proper order is conveyed in the number twelve, not thirteen.

For non-Levitical tribes, families and clans associated by birth with a particular tribal leader were to gather behind that leader's pole or standard. Men twenty years and older were then numbered as warriors by the recognized tribal head. Concerning the numbering of Israel's warriors, C. A. Coates observes:

> This is not a numbering of the redeemed or of believers as such, but of those who are competent to take up military service.... Ceasing from warfare is not contemplated in this chapter, nor such decline as would unfit us for it. It is one of the perfections of Scripture that it should be said here repeatedly "from twenty years old and upward" without any mention of an age when exemption would be granted. In relation to "the wars of the Lord" there is no retiring age; we are to be soldiers to the end.[2]

About thirty-eight years into the future, Caleb would be a great example of warring for the Lord and in His strength even at the age of eighty-five (Josh. 14). Indeed, no one retires from the Lord's army until the Lord releases His soldiers. Then, the shield of faith, the sword of the Spirit, and the helmet of salvation will suddenly fall to the ground and the discharged believer will be in the dear Savior's presence forever (2 Cor. 5:8).

Every male who was a true Israelite was officially counted as a member of a specific tribe and validated as being a part of the Jewish nation (vv. 17-45). As each leader is mentioned, the meaning of their names merits consideration.

The order of the tribes in this chapter does not follow birth order but rather introduces the nation's encampments about the tabernacle in the next chapter. Verses 52-53 command families of a particular tribe to camp by their tribal standard and for the Levites to *"camp around the tabernacle of the Testimony, that there may be no wrath on the congregation of the children of Israel."*

Tribe	Tribal Leader	Meaning of Leader's Name	Number of Warriors
Reuben	Elizur	God is my strength or rock	46,500
Simeon	Shelumiel	A friend of God	59,300
Gad	Eliasaph	The Lord increases	45,650
Judah	Nahshon	One who foretells	74,600
Issachar	Nethanel	Given of God	54,400
Zebulun	Eliab	My God is Father	57,400
Ephraim	Elishama	God of hearing	40,500
Manasseh	Gamaliel	God's recompense or reward	32,200
Benjamin	Abidan	Father of a judge	35,400
Dan	Ahiezer	Brother of help	62,700
Asher	Pagiel	Prayer of God	41,500
Naphtali	Ahira	Brother of sin or of the shepherd	53,400
Total			**603,550**

The total number of non-Levite men who were twenty years of age or older was 603,550 (v. 46). This meant that the overall population of the Jewish nation was likely between two and three million people. Moses had originally estimated the size of the group departing Egypt at *"about six hundred thousand men on foot, besides children ... a mixed multitude went up with them also"* (Ex. 12:37-38). The official census now would legitimize the number of warriors in Israel's army. This ensured that no one of "the mixed multitude" (i.e., those who were not God's people) could represent Jehovah before the nations, especially in warfare. Only those formally validated as God's people could engage His enemies.

Similarly, in the Church Age, only those who have become *"sons of God through faith in Christ Jesus"* (Gal. 3:26; 1 Jn. 3:2) can be led into victorious warfare: *"For as many as are led by the Spirit of God, these are sons of God"* (Rom. 8:14). Only a true child of God can put on the whole armor of God, wield the sword of the Spirit (the Word of God), and pray in the Spirit (Eph. 6:11-18). Believers today do not trace their spiritual pedigree to men, but directly to Jesus Christ who was raised up from the dead and ascended into glory.

In ordering the camp, Jehovah designated **warrior**s (non-Levites), **workers** who were put in charge of the sanctuary (Levites, less the priests), and **worshippers** who would offer worship on behalf of the entire Jewish nation (Aaron and his sons). F. B. Hole observes a similarity between these three callings in Israel to those of believers today:

> Though the three callings were separate in Israel, the Christian of today finds them coalesced in himself, though the occasions of their exercise be separate. The Apostle Paul was called to be the pattern saint, and we certainly see in him the worshipper, the worker, and the warrior, as the occasion suited.[3]

The Lord Jesus is the head of His Church. He also has a precise order and a full life for those who are His to enjoy now. The life Christ lived qualified Him for the death He died – and the death He died qualifies the believer for the life we are to live. May all those who stand in faith under His banner be faithful warriors, workers, and worshippers.

Meditation

> All God's plans have the mark of the cross on them, and all His plans have death to self in them.
>
> — E. M. Bounds

> That is why He warned people to "count the cost" before becoming Christians. "Make no mistake," He says, "if you let Me, I will make you perfect. The moment you put yourself in My hands, that is what you are in for. Nothing less, or other than that."
>
> — C. S. Lewis

Proper Order and Standards
Numbers 2

It was first necessary for all Jews to be identified by their tribal lineage (see the previous chapter), so that the Lord could put their encampment in order in this chapter. In anticipation of the long journey ahead and frequent movements of a large number of people, God gave instructions to efficiently organize His people. We would expect no less of God, for regardless of what dispensation He establishes, His glory is declared by the order of what He calls into being (Rom. 1:19-20). Paul affirms this truth in the Church Age: *"For God is not the author of confusion but of peace, as in all the churches of the saints"* (1 Cor. 14:33). God's peace is enjoyed through willing submission to His order.

God's arrangement for the camp consisted of four groups of three tribes. These four groups were to camp on each side of the Levites who were directly around the tabernacle. Although each tribe would have its own distinct flag or banner of identification (v. 2), a single standard was to mark each of the four groups of three tribes (v. 3). These non-Levite tribes were to camp some distance from the tabernacle to allow sufficient room for the Levites to pitch their tents around it. Alfred Barnes suggests that the "standard" spoken of in verse 3 was probably a solid figure or emblem mounted on a pole.[4]

Issachar and Zebulun were to identify with Judah's standard. They were to camp to the east of the tabernacle (vv. 3-9). Being the fourth, fifth, and sixth sons of Jacob through Leah, these tribes had maternal ties. Judah's leader, Nashon, the son of Amminadab, was in the lineage of Christ (Ruth 4:20; Matt. 1:4). These three tribes would be the first group to depart when the trumpets sounded the command.

Reuben and Simeon, the first and second sons of Jacob through Leah, along with Gad, the oldest son of Leah's handmaiden, compose the southern group (vv. 10-17). When traveling, the Levites followed this group, which was under Reuben's standard. Instructions as to the specific placement and order of the three Levitical clans and priests are provided in the next chapter (3:21-28).

The three tribes tracing their lineage through Rachel – Ephraim, Manasseh and Benjamin – gathered under Ephraim's standard to the west of the tabernacle (vv. 18-24). As previously mentioned, Rachel's oldest son Joseph received the birthright blessing instead of Reuben who sinned with his father's concubine. Hence, Joseph fathered two Jewish tribes, Ephraim and Manasseh. These three tribes followed the Levites in the tribal procession when journeying.

Finally, to the north, were the tribes of Dan, Asher, and Naphtali. These were sons born to Rachel's and Leah's handmaidens (vv. 25-34). These three tribes would be under Dan's standard.

Ancient Hebrew tents were usually made of long goat-hair panels secured together and then suspended on poles to create two, sometimes three, compartments. The section directly behind the tent door was the men's section. The other section separated by a curtain wall was the women's and children's section. The only males allowed into the women's section was the father of the tent and male children. Tent sizes varied and panels could be added to lengthen the tent to accommodate growing families.

It is difficult to estimate the actual size of the Hebrew camp. If we figure twenty square yards per person (which is 40 percent of the standard figure used for ancient city population densities)[5] to accommodate a family's tent, goods, and animals, that would result in a camp size of about four miles by four miles. Later, Balaam was unable to see the entirety of the Israelite camp from two different summits, which means that the camp was probably no smaller than four miles across. The overall tribal arrangement of the camp is depicted below.

Devotions in Numbers

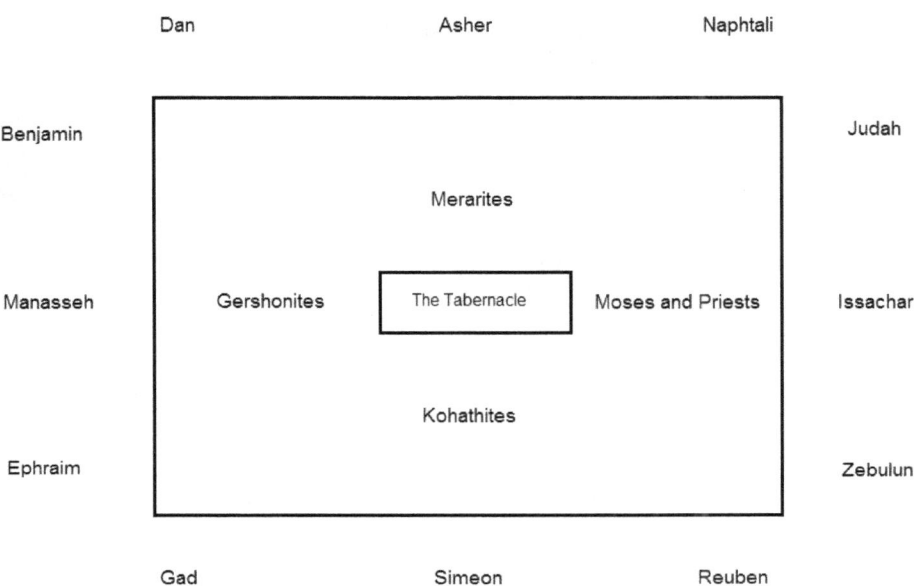

The position of the various tribes at a distance from the tabernacle would be a constant reminder that wrath would beset anyone who infringed on God's holy place (1:53). It is observed that whether they marched in procession or rested in their tents, God's people were to adhere to His order always. Their arrangement and procedures as His people were not left to their own discretion or whims. Any other order, even one which might seem to be better, would merely be disorder (i.e., rebellion against God).

May the Church learn this lesson and adhere to Christ's headship under His standard and yield in every way to His order and purpose for His Church! Indeed, Christians have historically fought and languished under many banners, but only Christ holds the Church's proper standard and He demands our full allegiance.

Meditation

> There's a royal banner given for display
> To the soldiers of the King;
> As an ensign fair we lift it up today,
> While as ransomed ones we sing.

Refining and Reminding

    Though the foe may rage and gather as the flood,
    Let the standard be displayed;
    And beneath its folds, as soldiers of the Lord,
    For the truth be not dismayed!

    When the glory dawns 'tis drawing very near –
    It is hastening day by day;
    Then before our King the foe shall disappear,
    And the cross the world shall sway!

                          — D. W. Whittle

Devotions in Numbers

God's Order for His Servants
Numbers 3

The Levitical Priesthood Affirmed (vv. 1-4)

Before Moses discusses the service of the priests and census of the Levites, he mentions two matters. First, the Lord had decreed that only Aaron and his descendants were to offer sacrifices in His tabernacle (Ex. 28-29). Second, the previous judgment of two of Aaron's four sons (Lev. 16):

> *Now these are the records of Aaron and Moses when the Lord spoke with Moses on Mount Sinai. And these are the names of the sons of Aaron: Nadab, the firstborn, and Abihu, Eleazar, and Ithamar. These are the names of the sons of Aaron, the anointed priests, whom he consecrated to minister as priests. Nadab and Abihu had died before the Lord when they offered profane fire before the Lord in the Wilderness of Sinai; and they had no children. So Eleazar and Ithamar ministered as priests in the presence of Aaron their father* (vv. 1-4).

Jehovah had selected Aaron and his four sons Nadab, Abihu, Eleazar, and Ithamar to be the official ministers in the tabernacle on behalf of the nation. But shortly after their consecration at Mount Sinai, Nadab and Abihu, Aaron's oldest two sons, were judged and killed for intruding into God's presence with "strange fire" (Lev. 16:1-5).

We know Aaron's younger sons, Eleazar and Ithamar, were not yet twenty years of age when the Jewish adults were judged the following year at Kadesh-Barnea (Num. 14). This indicates Eleazar and Ithamar were teenagers at this time when they began assisting their father Aaron, the high priest, in the tabernacle. Later, when the Israelites were in the Promised Land, Eleazar replaced his father as high priest. Future priests, after this initial period, had to be thirty years of age to enter the tabernacle or to offer sacrifices on the Bronze Altar (4:3).

Servants in the Tabernacle (vv. 5-10)

Levi had three sons, Gershon, Kohath and Merari. Moses and Aaron were Kohathites. To each of these three Levitical clans was allotted a special service in connection with the tabernacle. Furthermore, each group was to pitch their tents in a specified location around the tabernacle.

The Levites were responsible for moving and caring for the various components of the tabernacle and its furnishings, but only the priests could approach the sanctuary and offer sacrifices: *"So you shall appoint Aaron and his sons, and they shall attend to their priesthood; but the outsider who comes near shall be put to death"* (v. 10). As we see in the following verses, the Lord ordered every detail of their service and nothing was left to their own devising.

The Census and Levitical Order (vv. 11-39)

Through the blood of the Passover lamb, Jehovah had spared the lives of firstborn Jews and their livestock during the tenth plague in Egypt. God claimed these surviving people and animals as His own (v. 13). But now, the tribe of Levi was to be substituted for the firstborns that had been preserved from wrath. This substitution required the census of souls to be accurate and legitimate (v. 14). Hence, the Levite males one month of age and older had to be tallied. The numbering of the tribes in chapter 1 was to establish warriors for the army, but this census was for the purpose of setting aside the Levites as workers and worshippers on behalf of Israel. C. H. Mackintosh comments on God's design for the Jewish nation revealed in Numbers and what we should learn from it:

> Now, in all these things, the camp of Israel was a type – a vivid, striking type. A type of what? A type of the Church of God passing through this world. The testimony of Scripture is so distinct on this point, as to leave no room and no demand for the exercise of imagination. *"All these things happened to them for ensamples; and they are written for our admonition, upon whom the ends of the world are come"* (1 Cor. 10:11). ... Look at that mysterious camp in the desert, composed, as we have said, of warriors, workers, and worshippers! What separation from all the nations of the world! What utter helplessness! What exposure! What absolute dependence upon God! They had nothing – could do nothing – could know nothing. ...

Such is the Church of God in the world – a separated – dependent – defenseless thing, wholly cast upon the living God.[6]

In the wilderness, Israel had no morsel of food for the next day (except on Fridays); they lived expectantly by the hand of God day by day as they journeyed to the Promised Land. There were no storehouses or markets from which to purchase necessities; they were alone with God in the wilderness and completely dependent upon Him for everything. History has shown that when God's people are so spiritually disposed, they are invincible. Israel's order and reliance on God as they journeyed to Canaan presents a valuable pattern for the Church to follow. The Israelites camped alone with God in the desert, and the Church possesses Christ alone in the world.

As ambassadors of Christ, we too, as Israel did long ago, journey with God through a wicked and dangerous world. Ours is a spiritual pilgrimage heavenward, where Israel's course was a physical journey to the Promised Land. May the Church yield to Christ's order and be completely dependent upon Him for all things. Our time, resources, and abilities have value to God only when sanctified by and for Christ as empowered by the Holy Spirit. The Lord warned His disciples, *"For without Me you can do nothing"* (John 15:5) but yet Paul states, *"I can do all things through Christ who strengthens me"* (Phil. 4:13). Apart from Christ, no one has any suitable sacrifice or service to offer God, nor an acceptable means in which to offer it – we must therefore remain completely dependent upon Him.

The duties of the three Levite clans will be more thoroughly discussed in the next chapter, but their number (males a month old or older) and their camp locations around the tabernacle are given in verses 18-37:

Levite Clan	Number	Location
Gershon (vv. 18-26)	7500	West
Kohath (vv. 27-32)	8600	South
Merari (vv. 33-37)	6200	North

The priests were to camp near the only entrance to the tabernacle courtyard located on its east side. This meant the tabernacle was surrounded by Levites on all four sides. God's order for the Levites,

Refining and Reminding

even the location of their encampments, was an expression of what "Levi" meant, says C. A. Coates:

> Levi means "united" and no family of his sons served independently of the other families, nor were any or all of them to serve apart from the priests who appointed them "every one to his service and to his burden" (4:19). In the divinely ordered system there are no gaps and no overlapping; every needed service is adequately provided for, and though there is great variety in the nature of the service, it constitutes one whole, all directed in spiritual intelligence and contributing to a complete result. Each Levite would be conscious that he was doing something that was necessary to further the whole tabernacle system and its service. However small his bit might be, he would do it as having the universal thought before him, and as realizing that he was one with all his brethren in the service.
>
> There could be no movement of the testimony apart from the activity of all three branches of Levitical service. The priests take the lead, and the Levites do nothing save under their direction, but the service of each family is essential to every movement.[7]

Similarly, Paul reminds the believers at Corinth that all members in the body of Christ have been spiritually equipped and divinely called to serve the Body in a prescribed way (1 Cor. 12). All members of the Body are needed and important in the unified working of the Body to fully accomplish all that God desires. All must do their part under the headship of Christ and none should despise any other member of the Body or the ministry which God chose him or her to fulfill.

The total number of Levite males one month and older according to verse 39 was 22,000. Some have argued that this number is too small as compared to other tribal figures recorded in chapter 1 and therefore must be in error. In response to this challenge, it is first noted that the number of men twenty years old and upwards was 32,200 for Manasseh. If those under twenty years of age are removed from Levi's figure, then Levi would be about half the size of Manasseh. Though clearly the smallest tribe at this juncture, this number would still be reasonable. Second, the number of Levite men from thirty to fifty years of age was 8,580 (4:8) and therefore agrees well with the 22,000 males one month old or older. Third, the Lord accepted the 22,000 total as is (i.e., not a rounded figure) since the number of firstborns in verse 43 numbered 22,273 and thus outnumbered the Levites by 273 (v. 46). Fourth, when the same census was repeated thirty-eight years later, there were only 23,000 Levite males one month old and older (26:62).

Another numerical anomaly in the text is that the summation of the Levitical clans in verses 22, 28, and 34 equal 22,300, not 22,000 as stated in verse 39. While a slight numerical error in the Hebrew text for one of the Levitical clans is a possibility, the supposed discrepancy is best explained in that 300 firstborn sons in Levi (born during the last year since the exodus) were excluded from the count because they were the Lord's already (Ex. 13:11-13).

Levites Dedicated Instead of Firstborn (vv. 40-51)

The census showed that the number of the firstborn in Israel (born after the Exodus) exceeded the number of the Levite males by 273. This meant there were not enough Levites to redeem all the firstborn males. We might understand the transaction this way: Why would God trade more of anything for less of the same thing? That would not be an equitable exchange. However, the Lord claimed these 273 equally with the 22,000 for whom a Levite was found as a substitute, and thus five shekels of silver had to be paid for each of the 273 needing to be redeemed. To acknowledge His ownership, the Lord required all the firstborns of men and beasts to be redeemed at birth (Ex. 13:13). However, the principle of redemption in this chapter is not positional, but provisional for service, for all Israel had been positionally redeemed by blood in Egypt. The firstborns who had survived the tenth plague were a constant reminder of the positional redemption that the nation had already received.

The redemption money was collected by Aaron the high priest to illustrate God's acceptance and claim on the redeemed Levites to serve and worship Him on behalf of the nation. Considering the deplorable behavior of Levi in Genesis 34, this is a wonderful testimony of what can be accomplished by God's grace through redemption. By nature, Levi had been an instrument of cruelty, but by grace he was a vessel serving in God's sanctuary!

It is important to understand that redemption in this chapter pertains to the opportunity to serve God; it is not speaking of the initial act of positional recovery. What God redeems, He further sanctifies for His glory. Not only were the Levites redeemed, but they now had the opportunity to come near God in service and to worship. J. N. Darby relates the pattern of redemption in this chapter to its spiritual implications for believers in the Church Age:

> Service is rendered in dependence on Christ, and in the communion of the Lord: it is linked to the priesthood and flows from and is connected with Himself, and the place where He is, and with which He has connected our hopes, our lives, and the affections of our hearts. We serve from and in view of that: *"to present every man perfect in Christ Jesus."* Service appears to be limited to the tabernacle, that is, to be exercised in the midst of God's people and in connection with their drawing near to God.[8]

Today, all profitable spiritual exercise begins by drawing near to Christ in heavenly places and resting in Him (Eph. 1:3, 2:6). Only in Him and through Him can believers be equipped to properly serve each other, enjoy fellowship with each other, war against spiritual wickedness in high places, and worship God. The prosperity of our walk, our work, our warfare, and our worship are all connected with how closely we commune with Christ. This spiritual reality is pictured in the arrangement of Israel around the tent of meeting. Only those who draw near to God in holiness will experience the fullness of His presence and the abundance of His power.

Meditation

> *How lovely are your tents, O Jacob!*
> *Your dwellings, O Israel!*
> *Like valleys that stretch out,*
> *Like gardens by the riverside,*
> *Like aloes planted by the Lord,*
> *Like cedars beside the waters.*
> *He shall pour water from his buckets,*
> *And his seed shall be in many waters.*
>
> — Num. 24:5-6

The Pattern for the Church

The first three chapters of Numbers record the precise pattern Jehovah desired the Israelite camp to display before the nations. When the pagan prophet Balaam peered down from a high mountain to behold Israel's camp, the Spirit of God moved him to prophesy about the beauty of Jacob's tents (24:5). Israel's submission to God's order honored Him among the nations, though they were a *"congregation in the wilderness"* (7:38). Besides its precise layout, the Israelite camp was composed of three distinct elements: a nation of warriors, a tribe of workers, and a family of priests.

Similarly, the Lord has also set a pattern in place for His Church to follow today. As in the Old Testament, the Lord is honored today among the nations when His people heed His order. God is using the Church to instruct creation about His glory, His character, His attributes, as well as the appropriate response of creation to all of this (Eph. 3:10). Regrettably, much of Christendom has departed from the divine pattern and is, in fact, representing something quite different from what God intended.

Christ's sevenfold pattern for His Church is as follows:

1. **Christ is the Head and Center of the Church (Eph. 1:22-23; Col. 1:18; Acts 20:7).** By breaking bread each week in remembrance of Christ, the Church declares to all who observe that Christ is the gathering focus of the Church (Luke 22:19; Acts 2:42, 20:7). God the Father is honored when the Church worships His Son: *"For the Father judges no one, but has committed all judgment to the Son, that all should honor the Son just as they honor the Father. He who does not honor the Son does not honor the Father who sent Him"* (John 5:22-23). The Church is to worship God, and to adore Christ as its Head.

Refining and Reminding

2. **The Unity of All Believers (1 Cor. 12:13; Eph. 4:3-4; John 17:21-23; Heb. 10:25).** The Lord affirmed the oneness and equal-standing of all believers when He told His disciples, *"But be not ye called Rabbi: for one is your Master, even Christ; and all ye are brethren"* (Matt. 23:8, KJV). Christians are identified by biblical names such as Christians, believers, saints, and brethren. No denominations, cliques, or separate followings should be found in the body of Christ. Paul asked the Corinthians, who were bestowing special honors to particular preachers instead of following Christ, *"Is Christ divided?"* (1 Cor. 1:13). The act of identifying with anyone or any organization instead of with Christ is completely unbiblical. Harry A. Ironside's response to the question to what denomination he belonged stresses this point. He answered, "I belong to the same denomination that David did," and then quoted Psalm 119:63, *"I am a companion of all them that fear Thee and of them that keep Thy precepts."*[9]

3. **The Priesthood of All Believers (Rev. 1:6; Heb. 10:22; 1 Pet. 2:5, 10).** All believers should engage in Spirit-led worship and service (Eph. 5:18-20). All believers are equipped with spiritual gifts to serve and edify the body of Christ (1 Cor. 12:4-7). Paul proclaimed this truth to the Church at Ephesus:

> *Speaking the truth in love, may grow up in all things into Him who is the head -- Christ -- from whom the whole body, joined and knit together by what every joint supplies, according to the effective working by which every part does its share, causes growth of the body for the edifying of itself in love* (Eph. 4:15-16).

Only when all believers use their spiritual gifts with the full measure of faith that God gives will the Church be fully functional (see also Rom. 12:3 and 1 Pet. 4:10). The New Testament reveals ministries and offices that individuals were associated with, but no believer was given a personal title as part of his or her fulfillment of these. For example, there were apostles, elders, deacons, evangelists, pastor-teachers, etc. in the early Church, but no disciple of Christ was referred to by a title before his or her name. However, for centuries it has been the practice of the Church to ascribe to men names and labels that they ought not to have; one of the most prevalent of these is the title "Pastor" as applied to an individual leader of a local church. In truth, all believers have been equipped to serve Christ. Accordingly, all believers in Christ have common designations and should not seek titles or use terminologies that elevate themselves to unbiblical roles in the Church or that displace Christ's supreme position over the Church.

> A church which bottlenecks its outreach by depending on its specialists – its pastors and evangelists – to do its witnessing is living in violation of both the intention of its Head and the consistent pattern of the early Christians.
>
> — Leighton Ford

Although the Lord provides elders to shepherd (i.e. to pastor) local assemblies, these men are not referred to as the pastors of that particular church (e.g. "Pastor Bob" or "Pastor Jim"). Those in local church leadership have a ministry to the Chief Shepherd, not an elevated position above fellow-believers. Whatever authority the elders have springs forth from lives of godliness and subjection to the Lord, and not from human ambition, certificates, or titles.

4. **Family Life of the Church, the Household of God (Eph. 2:19; 1 Tim. 3:15).** We read in Acts 2:42 that the New Testament Christians continued in activities such as teaching, prayer, fellowship, and the Lord's Supper. In the Greek text, there is a definite article before the word "fellowship" in this verse, meaning that there was one particular fellowship that the Church enjoyed – Christ's fellowship. The Church is a living body composed of many members who enjoy divine fellowship with each other. Such body life will be manifested chiefly within the local assembly, but it is not restricted to it. The Lord's Table, mentioned in 1 Corinthians 10, is a place where all believers enjoy communion with each other and with Christ, and receive from Him what is needed to serve Him. Local churches were commanded to receive other believers who desired to take part in the privileges and responsibilities of church fellowship (Rom. 15:7) and those received into the local church fellowship were instructed not to neglect it (Heb. 10:25).

Refining and Reminding

Each individual church fellowship is a local manifestation of Christ's fellowship with the Church as a whole.

Believers, including new converts, relocating Christians, and traveling workers, who desired to be an active part of a local church were added to the fellowship in various ways. For example, we read that Barnabas provided a word of testimony to the saints in Jerusalem on Paul's behalf so that he would be received by them (Acts 9:27). New converts, after being water baptized, were received into church fellowship. As believers moved from one location to another, they carried with them letters of introduction from their home church meeting in order to be received into this fellowship with another assembly (Acts 18:26-27; Rom. 16:1; Col. 4:7-8). However, a believer who was known to have a good testimony, such as Paul, would not need a letter of introduction to be received as he would already be well-known to the gathering (2 Cor. 3:1-2). Letters not only introduced believers to other meetings, but affirmed their faithfulness to their profession of faith and their moral integrity. Such believers could be welcomed into the family life of the assembly without reservation. This biblical practice safeguards the assembly against wolves who want to secretly enter into the meeting, and provides a huge blessing to those who desire Christian fellowship.

5. **Sanctity of the Genders (Gen. 1:27, 2:24; 1 Tim. 2:11-14).** God instituted creation order over the genders when He fashioned the first man and then created the first woman from that man. Genesis 2 informs us that the woman came from the man, was made for the man, and was brought to the man by God to be his helper. The general principle in creation is that men are to lead and women are to support. God's creation order is further depicted in biblical authority structures for other spheres such as home order, civil order, and church order. In marriage, husbands are to love and care for their wives and wives are to submit to and respect their husbands (Eph. 5:22-33). In the realm of civil authority, it is notable that nowhere in the Bible do we find any example of God appointing a woman to lead His people. For example, although Deborah was a wise prophetess who provided personal counsel to the people (Judg. 4:4), she would not lead Israel's army into battle against the Canaanites because she knew that would be

inappropriate (Judg. 4:6). The same pattern for gender roles is also witnessed in the Church; only men were called to be apostles of the early Church, only men served as church elders (Tit. 1:6; 1 Tim. 3:1-2), and only men are to be appointed as deacons in the local church (1 Tim. 3:11-12; Acts 6:3). Likewise, there are also ministries reserved for women, into which men cannot intrude. The Bible is full of examples of godly women who served and assisted others through various means and methods. For example, the sisters, like the Kohathites of old, have been entrusted with the ministry of the coverings within the house of God. They are to cover and conceal all glories that compete with God's glory.

As the assembly gathers in the presence of the Lord Jesus, each woman who covers her head ensures that she (the glory of man, 1 Cor. 11:7) and her long hair (her own personal glory, 1 Cor. 11:15) do not compete with God's glory, as symbolically portrayed in the man's uncovered head (1 Cor. 11:7). This earthly activity patterns the heavenly reality where only God's glory is observed and where even the cherubim and the seraphim use their wings to cover their own intrinsic glories in His presence. As Lucifer (a covering cherub) learned, God does not tolerate any competing glories in His presence (Ezek. 28:12-17).

The Church faithfully obeyed this command for nearly two millennia, but the practice was widely rejected in the 20th century as a result of the feminist movement, although even today most men still remove their hats to pray. The practice of the head covering is a visible salute by believers to show submission to God's authority and order for the Church. It is like a soldier who salutes a commanding officer who has come into his or her presence; the salute indicates to all present that the soldier is in agreement with the authority over him or her. The same Scripture that commands the head covering practice also explains its application: it is to be used when God's people come into His presence to talk with Him in prayer or to learn from Him through the teaching of His Word. The uncovered head of the man and the covered head of the woman indicate to God and to all who observe (including the angels, see 1 Cor. 11:10) their willing submission to God's authority. God wants

6. **The Plurality of Leadership (Tit. 1:5; Acts 14:23).** There is no example (i.e. no God-honoring example) of one individual overseeing a specific local church in the New Testament. Rather, just the opposite was true; the oversight of each local gathering was to be plural in nature. God revealed a similar leadership structure for Israel to follow (11:16-25); He was to rule over them as their God, and there were also to be seventy elders who would oversee His people by enforcing His written Law. The Jews later demanded a king to rule over them so that they could be like other nations (1 Sam. 8:19-22). Though God saw this as a rejection of His own administration, He granted their request in order to teach them about the consequences of following a man instead of Himself. God's model for Church order is similar to the one given to Israel: Christ is head of the Church and elders are to oversee local churches. As with Israel, the men (1 Tim. 3:1-2; Tit. 1:6) who led a local church were normally referred to as "elders." The New Testament clearly indicates that a plurality of qualified men was to share the spiritual leadership of a local church:

- There were elders in the church at Jerusalem (Acts 15:6, 22).
- The sick were instructed to call for the elders of the church (Jas. 5:14).
- Paul and Barnabas recognized "elders in every church" on their missionary journeys (Acts 14:23).
- In 1 Peter 5:1, Peter refers to the elders among a particular local church.
- Paul instructed Titus to appoint elders in every city (i.e. every church; Tit. 1:5).
- There were multiple elders within the church at Ephesus (Acts 20:17, 28).
- Paul mentions that there were elders (overseers) and deacons in the church at Philippi (Phil. 1:1).

The New Testament mainly applies two Greek words in conjunction with men who are in the office of leadership in their respective local churches: *presbuteros* and *episkopos*. These two words (including their verb forms) relate to a church position which was not given at spiritual rebirth, but was gained as a result of spiritual maturity, divine calling, and public recognition. A man may serve as a *presbuteros* and *episkopos* in one assembly, but if he relocates he may not be in the leadership of another church. A third word, *poimen,* is normally used to speak of the shepherding work in which both elders and non-elders engage. It is also mentioned in a list of five spiritual gifts that Christ bestows to individuals in the Church at their conversion (Eph. 4:11-12). Thus, the pastoral gift remains within the recipient throughout his or her entire lifetime, regardless of where he or she may take up residence. The gift *poimen* is not gender-specific, nor can it be equated directly with the office of elder, though certainly many elders will have this spiritual gift. It is noted that the only instances in which *poimen* is used in the New Testament to describe a specific person is when it is applied to the Lord Jesus. He is the Good *Poimen* (John 10:11), the Chief *Poimen* (1 Pet. 5:4), and the Great *Poimen* (Heb. 13:20). Men should not be called by a title that is attributed only to Christ in Scripture.

In summary, elders (a plurality of godly men called *presbuteros* and *episkopos*) are to govern each assembly; they are to pastor those whom God puts into their care, though they may not have received the pastoral spiritual gift. All the elders of a meeting have equal authority, but they do not necessarily have equal gifts or equal administrations of a gift – this is what brings strength and balance to a plurality of church leadership. Several brothers serving in unity with the mind of Christ is a lovely representation of the triune nature of God at work!

7. **The Great Commission – Reaching the Lost for Christ (Matt. 28:18-20).** Believers are to be witnesses for Christ in the world and the Church is to send out workers to do the same. These workers are sent out, not from mission boards or parachurch organizations, but from a local church. The elders of the particular church are responsible for overseeing their missionaries. The missionaries of the book of Acts did not raise funds in order to be sent; rather, they *were* sent, and the Lord provided for them as they went (Acts 13:1-5, 14:26, 15:40). They were to live by faith and, when necessary, to work with their own hands so that their motives for service would

not be questioned by the people they were trying to reach (Acts 18:3; 2 Cor. 11:7-9). The Great Commission demonstrates God's great love for the lost and the fact that He wants to see as many as possible redeemed by the blood of His dear Son (2 Pet. 3:9).

What is God declaring about Himself through this sevenfold pattern that the Church is to portray today?
1. That Christ is the center of attention in heaven; the Father is honored when His Son is honored.
2. Just as God is one, all believers are one in Him.
3. God alone is to be worshipped and all believers are able priests who are to worship Him.
4. God is the source of all good things; only those in God's family will bask in His goodness forever.
5. In heaven, God's glory, and its reflection in others, will be the only glory seen.
6. God is masculine, plural in persons, and perfectly unified in all that He does.
7. God is merciful and no respecter of persons; He desires heaven to be full of redeemed people from every kindred.

Meditation

Alas! Much has been done of late to promote the production of dwarfish Christians. Poor, sickly believers turn the church into a hospital, rather than an army. Oh, to have a church built up with the deep godliness of people who know the Lord in their very hearts, and will seek to follow the Lamb wherever He goes!

— Charles H. Spurgeon

The Duties of the Levites
Numbers 4

The Duties of the Kohathites (vv. 1-20)

Aaron and his two sons had the crucial task of lowering the veil between the holy and most holy places in the tabernacle and carefully placing it over the Ark of the Covenant (or Testimony) to ensure no human would gaze on it and die. Then they were to put *"on it a covering of badger skins, and spread over that a cloth entirely of blue; and they shall insert its poles"* (v. 6). When the Kohathites arrived to carry the Ark, they would find it covered with a blue cloth and with its carrying poles already in place. This meant that the Kohathites had to do nothing but lift up the Ark and place the poles on their shoulders to carry it. Although the Gershonites and Merarites could use carts or wagons to transport the components of the tabernacle and its curtain wall, the Kohathites were to carry the tabernacle's holy furnishings and vessels.

The other furnishings of the tabernacle were covered in a similar fashion and the carrying poles were also inserted. The priests were to cover the Table of Showbread with a blue cloth, then put all the dishes, pans, bowls, and pitchers on top of the blue cloth and then cover everything with a scarlet cloth and then a covering of badger skins (vv. 7-9). All the components of the Lampstand were to be covered with a blue cloth and then its utensils were to be put with it and covered with badger skins and put on carrying beams (vv. 9-10). A blue cloth was to be placed over the Golden Altar of Incense and then it was to be covered with badger skins (v. 11). All the utensils of service in the sanctuary were to be placed in a blue cloth, which was also to be covered with a badger skin covering and put on a carrying beam (v. 12).

The priests were also to clean out the ashes of the Bronze Altar and cover it with a purple cloth, then place its implements (i.e., the firepans, the forks, the shovels, the basins, and the utensils) on top of the altar and cover it with badger skins, and insert its carrying poles (vv. 13-14). The Bronze Laver is not mentioned because it was not entrusted to the Kohathites to carry. The Laver did not have carrying sockets, nor was it to be covered.[10] It was likely transported on a cart with the other heavier metal items of the tabernacle. C. H. Mackintosh explains why the Laver did not need to be carried:

> The reason may be found in the double fact of what that laver was made from, and what it was made for. The laver was made of the looking-glasses of the women who assembled at the door of the tabernacle of the congregation (Ex. 38:8). This was its material. And, as to its object, it was provided as a means of purification for man. Now, in all those things which formed the special burden and charge of the Kohathites, we see only the varied manifestations of God in Christ, from the Ark in the holiest of all, to the Brazen Altar in the court of the tabernacle; and, inasmuch as the laver was not a manifestation of God, but a purification for man, it is therefore not found in the custody and charge of the Kohathites.[11]

Eleazar, Aaron's third son, was in charge of packing up the oil for the lampstand, the sweet incense, the daily grain offering, and the anointing oil (v. 16). He was also to oversee all the packing and unpacking of the tabernacle's furnishings that the Kohathites were to carry. This was an incredible responsibility for a young man, likely 18 to 19 years of age. If all was not done appropriately as Jehovah decreed, Kohathites could perish while fulfilling their responsibility (vv. 15, 17-20).

Although various furnishings of the tabernacle had colorful coverings, none would be seen except the blue cloth over the Ark of the Covenant, as the remaining furnishings were outwardly covered with badger skins. J. N. Darby acknowledges the lovely typology of Christ exhibited in the coverings over the Ark of the Covenant:

> The Ark of the Covenant represented the throne of God in heaven, the holiness and the justice which are there manifested in God. It was first of all covered with the veil of the humanity of Christ, such as He was here below in His Person; that is, that divine holiness and righteousness have clothed themselves in humanity. Over this were the badgers' skins. We have seen, in these skins, that practical and watchful holiness down here which keeps itself from the evil to which we are liable in passing through the wilderness. However, when there

is an immediate connection with what God is in heaven itself (and it is thus that He Himself was manifested in Christ), the entirely heavenly character, which results therefrom, manifests itself outside.[12]

The covering of the Ark of the Covenant was unique because the veil which separated the most holy place from the holy place was draped over it. When the tabernacle was pitched, this veil of separation prevented the Ark from any intrusion; when being transported, the Ark was completely covered, the significance of which is alluded to by the writer of Hebrews:

Therefore, brethren, having boldness to enter the Holiest by the blood of Jesus, by a new and living way which He consecrated for us, through the veil, that is, His flesh (Heb. 10:19-20).

But over the veil was a covering of badger skins, and over all, a cloth of blue. Badger skins were rough and durable and would protectively shield the holy thing beneath. Yet, the blue cloth, the heavenly color, represents the part of Christ's deity observable to the human eye. In the humanity of the Lord Jesus was the protective element, His impeccability, which repelled any evil suggestion or temptation. This intrinsic and essential covering protected the honor of His divine essence, beneath the surface, so to speak. Thus, His outward manner, which man witnessed for over thirty-three years, displayed the character of His heavenly origin. The wood in the Ark's composition expressed Christ's humanity, and the gold, His deity, but the outward holy and heavenly ramifications of His incarnation were witnessed by men only when He journeyed from His abode into ours. Hence, the Ark, journeying through the wilderness, pictures God's moral excellence demonstrated in Christ after He departed from heaven and sojourned among spiritually barren men on Earth.

The Duties of the Gershonites (vv. 21-28)

The Gershonites were responsible for transporting the non-wooden and non-metal portions of the tabernacle and the curtain wall surrounding its courtyard. This included the ten four-color fine linen curtains, and the layers of goats' hair, ram skins, and badger skins above the ten curtains which form the tabernacle and other coverings within the tabernacle, and all related securing ropes.

Refining and Reminding

The Duties of the Merarites (vv. 29-33)

The Merarites were in charge of transporting all that was remaining: the tabernacle's baseplates, boards, metal securing rods, pillars, sockets, and cords. There were many components to transport, so the priests were to *"assign to each man by name the items he must carry"* (v. 32). All was under priestly control, everyone worked in unity, and all was done according to God's order, so that the task of setting up and taking down God's dwelling place was accomplished with great efficiency.

The following table summarizes the duties and census results for each of the three Levitical clans.

Levitical Clan (age 30 to 50 years)	Clan Duties	Clan Number
Kohath (vv. 1-20)	Carrying the most holy things of the tabernacle (its furnishings and associated vessels) once covered by the priests.	2750
Gershon (vv. 21-28)	Curtains, coverings, hangings of the tabernacle and the outer court wall, excluding the inner veil which covered the Ark of the Covenant and the tabernacle.	2630
Merari (vv. 29-33)	The boards, the bars, the pillars, and the socketed baseplates of the tabernacle, and the pegs and cords for securing it.	3200

It was critical that the Kohathites worked in cooperation with Aaron and his son Eleazar who oversaw the tabernacle furnishings, lest they die (vv. 17-20). In contrast, the duties of the Gershonites and Merarites were under the authority of Ithamar, Aaron's fourth son (vv. 28, 33). This was an incredible responsibility for one person, especially for a young man of only 16 to 18 years of age.

Census and Age Restrictions (vv. 34-49)

The total number of Levites between the ages of thirty and fifty who would be given to the work of setting the tabernacle up, taking it down and transporting it to a different location was 8,580 (vv. 46-49).

However, we learn in Numbers 8 that a Levite could begin training as an apprentice at the age of twenty-five:

> *Then the Lord spoke to Moses, saying, "This is what pertains to the Levites: From twenty-five years old and above one may enter to perform service in the work of the tabernacle of meeting; and at the age of fifty years they must cease performing this work, and shall work no more. They may minister with their brethren in the tabernacle of meeting, to attend to needs, but they themselves shall do no work. Thus you shall do to the Levites regarding their duties"* (8:23-26).

There was no under-age apprenticeship for the priests, who had to be thirty years of age to offer sacrifices and enter the tabernacle as worshippers. The only exception, initially, was Aaron's two teenage sons who assisted him, as discussed in the previous chapter. In God's design, all Levites had to retire from laboring at the age of fifty; however, this did not end their privilege of serving the Lord, but rather altered how they did so. These veterans were to be available to direct the younger men and to answer questions so that all the affairs of the tabernacle would be accomplished as God intended by the next generation of servants. The value of mentoring is upheld throughout Scripture (e.g. 1 Tim. 2:2), but unfortunately is a much neglected aspect of Church life today.

The walk of the Israelites in the wilderness consisted of three qualities: warfare, working, and worship. It is interesting to notice the level of maturity required for each of these facets of service to God. Those men twenty and older were enlisted in the army as soldiers, while men of twenty-five could assist in the setting up, transporting, and dismantling of the tabernacle, but the descendants of Aaron had to be thirty to engage in worship on behalf of the nation. The principle is that worship requires more spiritual maturity than service, which requires more than warfare. C. A. Coates highlights the implications of this principle for believers in the Church Age:

> All saints are called to the defense of the testimony against hostile attacks to which it may be exposed in an evil world, but they are also called to maintain the testimony as in relation to the holy pleasure of God, and in doing so they render Levitical service. It is not that any saints are precluded from being Levites; they may all be wholly for

Refining and Reminding

> God, and separated to His service in relation to "the tabernacle of testimony," but, viewed as Levites, they are in a nearer and holier place and service than when they are viewed as the children of Israel generally, and numbered for military service. We are all called to be warriors in the Lord's host, and to stand against infidelity and evil teachings of all kinds, but this is not such a profound and heart-searching exercise, nor does it call for such intense separation or holiness, as seeking to carry out all the service connected with the testimony.[13]

The application is sound – all believers are to be witnesses for Christ and to defend the gospel, but they are also to be worshippers of God. Yet, the latter occupation requires deeper reflection and spiritual understanding. True worshippers of God must labor in His Word to understand what God has revealed about Himself – that is, His character, nature, attributes, and what He has done and what He promises to do. What God does is an extension of who He is – God is good and does good (Ps. 85:12, 100:5).

The value of our service relates directly to having fellowship with God in spirit and in truth (John 4:23-24). In the Church Age, those who have been born again through the gospel message have the Holy Spirit within them and are thus able to worship God through their human spirit according to the truth of Scripture. The Holy Spirit guides believers into a deeper understanding of truth concerning the Lord Jesus and the overall greatness and goodness of God (John 16:13-14). Only through Spirit-led worship, which will be completely founded in divine truth, can the believer offer any acceptable sacrifice of praise unto God. If we become satisfied with the goodness of God's blessings and yet lose sight of who He is and what He desires for us, we will become feeble and powerless. God strengthens those who want to be guided into the knowledge of Himself and the purposes of His grace.

It is also observed from Numbers 4 that the Lord wants His people to give Him their best years for service. They were to be old enough to not be controlled by youthful passions, but young enough to be energetic and zealous for God. On this point, Matthew Henry writes:

> The middle-aged men of the tribe of Levi, all from thirty years old to fifty, were to be employed in the service of the tabernacle. The service of God requires the best of our strength, and the prime portion of our time, which cannot be better spent than to the honor of Him

who is the First and Best. And the service of God should be done when we are most lively and active. Those do not consider this who put off repentance to old age, and so leave the best work to be done in the worst time.[14]

God's Calling

In surveying this chapter, we are awestruck by the way in which the Lord ordered every detail concerning His tabernacle. Nothing was left to human choice. F. B. Hole reminds us that God has done the same in setting up His house during the Church Age:

> God ordered everything in connection with His wilderness house, leaving nothing to man's preference. It reminds us at once of 1 Corinthians 12 and 14, where we learn that in God's present house, which is *"the Church of the living God"* (1 Tim. 3:15), the Spirit of God is sovereign, acting under the lordship of Christ, and that He divides *"distributing to each one individually as He wills"* (1 Cor. 12:11). We are only right as we serve under the direction of the Spirit of God. It is not for us to pick and choose.[15]

Just as the men of war had their lineage (Num. 1) and their standard to adhere to (Num. 2), the Levites had their clan assignments and dwelling place about the tabernacle. The soldiers had to do their part and the Levites theirs in God's order of things. For a Levite to put his hand to anything besides what God had prescribed would be to deny his divine calling and insult God. "Just so is it with Christians now," writes C. H. Mackintosh.

> Their exclusive business – their one grand work – their absorbing service is Christ and His belongings. They have nothing else to do. For a Christian to think of putting his hand to anything beside is to deny his calling, to abandon his divinely-appointed work, and fly in the face of the divine commandments.[16]

Christians who do not pursue their divinely appointed roles in the body of Christ will not benefit from the Holy Spirit's enabling power. This normally results in harm to the body and the disdain of Christ's name! May we instead, for the Glory of God, bestow on Him our best years, our best resources, our best abilities, and our spiritual gifts under His control so that we can fulfill His best intentions for us (Eph. 2:10).

Refining and Reminding

Meditation

    Give of your best to the Master;
    Give of the strength of your youth;
    Throw your soul's fresh, glowing ardor
    Into the battle for truth.

    Jesus has set the example,
    Dauntless was He, young and brave;
    Give Him your loyal devotion;
    Give Him the best that you have.

    Give of your best to the Master;
    Naught else is worthy His love;
    He gave Himself for your ransom,
    Gave up His glory above.
    Laid down His life without murmur,
    You from sin's ruin to save;
    Give Him your heart's adoration;
    Give Him the best that you have.

                              — Howard B. Grose

Uncleanness, Restitution, and Jealousy
Numbers 5

This chapter has three main sections: First, the corporate responsibility of removing an unclean person from the camp; second, the self-judgment, confession, and restitution for personal offenses; and third, the necessity of removing jealous emotions among God's people whether they are legitimate or not. In the latter section, the Lord shows that He will not tolerate even the suspicion of evil among His people. The fullness of His communion is enjoyed when His people are holy in their thoughts, affections, and in all their doings.

The Ceremonially Unclean (vv. 1-4)

Leviticus chapters 11-15 record the laws pertaining to cleanliness. When the word "clean" is used in this context, we are not speaking of good hygiene or even the absence of filth, but rather of a state of ritual purity that the general population of Israel was to maintain. While some laws within these chapters do promote good personal hygiene and a healthy diet, this is not their primary focus. Rather, the Lord wanted His people to be consistently thinking about His holiness and the necessity of maintaining "cleanliness" in order to have communion with Him. His desire was for them (and for us too) to strive for holiness in all areas of their lives.

In the things pertaining to God, there were only three ceremonial classifications: holy, clean, and unclean. For example, the priests, their garments, the sacrifices, and the things of the tabernacle were specifically cleansed by blood and anointed with special oil in order to be declared "holy" before the Lord. The Israelites could not participate in any of the feasts or sweet-smelling sacrifices unless they were "clean." If "unclean," they were required to take specific actions to remedy the situation and become ceremonially "clean" again. For major issues, offerings were required, but for lesser and more common matters of uncleanness, one simply washed and remained isolated until evening.

"Holy" status could be gained by only divine imputation, usually by means of blood purification and anointing oil. What God deemed holy was holy. Likewise a "clean" status was obtained only through the means which God set forth; this typically involved washing and waiting, or, depending on the type of uncleanness, blood purification. God labors to keep His people holy and clean, but man pollutes what God has accomplished (i.e., making that which is holy, unholy, and that which is clean, unclean).

After ordering the Jewish nation into warriors, workers, and worshippers, organizing their encampment, and providing procedures for properly moving His tabernacle, the Lord reminds His people of their need to be holy and clean before Him. Lepers, and those defiled by touching a dead body or having some bodily issue, were to dwell outside the camp and no partiality was to be shown in the judgment of such matters (vv. 1-2). These men and women were still part of the Jewish nation and had claims to the commonwealth of Israel, but because of uncleanness must not be permitted to remain in the camp. The reason is explained in verse 3, *"that they may not defile their camps in the midst of which I dwell."* A holy God cannot remain among an unclean people. Thus, their constant need for purification and blood atonement was asserted, which pointed to their ultimate need of a Savior (Gal. 3:24). God's presence among them demanded holiness on their part.

The same principle exhibited in Numbers 5 is true today in the local assembly. Christ has promised to be wherever two or more are gathered in His name (Matt. 18:20). Because of His promised presence, His people must be holy before Him, that is, they must have their sins confessed and cleansed away before gathering in His name (1 Jn. 1:9). If there is unrepented sin amongst the Lord's people, it must be dealt with (1 Cor. 5:1-5), lest Christ's fellowship with and blessing of His people be hindered. When those in willful sin are properly judged (i.e., put out of the assembly, the camp so to speak), Paul tells us that the leaven that would have defiled the entire assembly is nullified (1 Cor. 5:6-7). If God's people want to enjoy Christ in their midst, they must first remove those in ongoing sin, and ensure that their own sins have been confessed to Christ and cleansed away.

Often the rebel will quote Matthew 7:1-2 in an attempt to avoid church reproof or discipline: *"Judge not, that you be not judged. For with what judgment you judge, you will be judged; and with the measure you use, it will be measured back to you."* However, the context, as explained in the verses that follow, relates to judging with unChrist-like attitudes and motives. We cannot help others until we think and speak as Christ would. The fact that the Lord goes on to say that believers should "beware of" false teachers clearly shows that there are things that must be judged (evaluated), namely, sinful behavior and doctrine. On this point, C. H. Mackintosh writes:

> Christian reader, the truth is as simple as possible. God's assembly is responsible to judge the doctrine and morals of all who claim entrance at the door. And why, we may ask, was this separation demanded? Was it to uphold the reputation or respectability of the people? Nothing of the sort. What then? *"That they defile not their camps in the midst whereof I dwell."* And so is it now. We do not judge and put away bad doctrine in order to maintain *our* orthodoxy; neither do we judge and put away moral evil in order to maintain our reputation and respectability. The only ground of judgment and putting away is this, *"Holiness becomes Thine house, O Lord, forever."*[17]

Those naming Christ who embrace false doctrine or who continue in sin should be promptly rebuked by those who love. However, we must be careful not to judge the value of someone's ministry, or someone's motives or someone's liberty in engaging in questionable things, or even someone's salvation – the Lord alone judges these things. As witnessed by the positional redemption in the first Passover (Ex. 12) and in the redemption of the Levites for service (Num. 4), redemption was the basis for permitting God to dwell with His people. But then the redeemed had to maintain proper discipline resulting in holiness for Him to remain among them.

Confession and Restitution (vv. 5-10)

Turning from the subject of uncleanness in the camp (i.e., in God's presence), He reminds His people of the necessity of confessing their trespasses against others and Himself. Legitimate confession wants to make past wrongs as right as possible through restitution. Under Levitical Law this was accomplished through the trespass offering (Lev. 5:14-19, 6:1-7, 7:1-10). The sin offering (Lev. 4:1-35, 5:1-13,

Refining and Reminding

6:24-30) was required for the *offense of sin*, but the trespass offering was commanded for the *damages of sin*. The sin offering pertained to the guilt of sin; Christ's blood purges the believer's conscience of that. The trespass offering deals with the damage that sin causes and seeks to offer restitution. The sin offering targets who we are by nature, while the trespass offering highlights what we have done (sinful acts). Through Christ's sin and trespass offering, full restoration of the sinner to God is permitted.

Neither the sin offering nor the trespass offering were designated as "sweet savor" offerings; each was demanded by God. They could be used only for sins of ignorance towards God (there were no personal offerings which atoned for willful sin) and for trespasses against one's neighbor. On a national level, all sin, including willful sin, was atoned for on the annual Day of Atonement. Through these two personal offerings, God was practically teaching His people that they were sinners by nature and that to properly deal with their offenses they needed to offer atonement to God, to confess their sins, and to make restitution to those wronged.

When it came to restitution for these wrongs, the offender was to restore what had been wrongfully appropriated plus twenty percent of its intrinsic value (vv. 5-7). Moses had already revealed to the Israelites what restitution was required for *willful* offenses against others in the matter of property rights (Ex. 22:1-15). Accordingly, the Jews were already familiar with the concept of restitution – that true remorse over sin is shown by the offender's desire to right a wrong. In fact, true repentance is shown by a desire to over-compensate for the damage that was done by sin, if possible. If there was no person to make restitution to, then the compensation went to the Lord (v. 8).

The Lord reminded the people that their sin and trespass offerings were considered "most holy" and therefore portions of these were to be eaten by the priests, but only in the tabernacle courtyard (v. 9; Lev. 6:25-27, 7:6, 10:17). This was the Lord's Table for His serving priests and illustrates the efficacy of Christ dealing with both the penalty and damage of sin so that the redeemed can enjoy God's fellowship and His bountiful provisions.

Resolving Jealousy (vv. 11-31)

The final section deals with a jealous husband who suspects the unfaithfulness of his wife, but has no proof of the matter. This section naturally affronts our modern sense of justice as there was no provision for a jealous wife who suspected the unfaithfulness of her husband. Yet we must remember that, under the Law, the punishment for proven adultery was death, for both sinning parties. The focus of this section, then, is to highlight the need for God's people to quickly address inner thoughts and feelings which would hinder them from serving the Lord. The bare suspicion of unfaithfulness would be intolerable in a marriage. Not only would marital companionship not be possible, but those with jealous hearts would be unable to serve the Lord as they should. Such emotional snares must be removed one way or another! C. A. Coates explains why a spirit of jealousy arises and why testing is necessary to resolve it:

> The spirit of jealousy comes in when the rights of divine love have been owned, where a covenant has been entered into, but cause has been given to suspect that some corrupting influence is at work. How often is the conduct of God's people such as to provoke Him to jealousy! We see this both in the Old Testament and the New (see 1 Corinthians 10:22). And when this is the case, a divine testing will search the inward parts and discover the true state of the affections. At the present time it is always possible that there may be unfaithfulness, and therefore both the faithful and the unfaithful are constantly being brought under a process of testing which is searching enough to penetrate to the most secret thoughts and intents of the heart.[18]

To alleviate this jealous condition, a husband who suspected his wife's infidelity could bring her and a prescribed offering to the tabernacle. The fact that it would cost him something to publicly pursue his suspicions should eliminate petty feelings from the situation. The priest was then to remove the woman's veil and reveal her hair as a token of shame. This was to signify the serious nature of adultery (but not necessarily her guilt). The wife was then to be brought before the Lord at the Bronze Altar.

After the priest acknowledged the righteous demands of the Law concerning adultery and the nature of the test, she was to confess, *"Amen, so be it"* (v. 22). The curses for guilt and her words affirming innocence were recorded on a scroll, but then the ink, once dried, was scraped off and added to holy water in the earthen vessel. This symbolized that the curses associated with adultery were in the woman's drink. She would have to eat her own words either way, suffering the consequences of deception, if guilty, or being shown to be as virtuous as her testimony, if innocent. Apparently, this holy vessel was set aside for this purpose, although there is no record in Scripture of it being used. Additionally, dust from the floor of the holy place in the tabernacle was mixed into the water. The overall idea was that she would be judged by God's Law according to her own testimony, as there was no public proof of her infidelity.

The priest would then take the grain offering from her hands, wave it before the Lord and place it on the Bronze Altar. This was to acknowledge that adultery offended God and that the guilty would be punished (v. 15; Ex. 20:14). Afterwards, the priest gave the wife the holy water from the holy vessel to drink. There was nothing magical about this concoction, but the sheer terror of the ceremony was designed to cause the guilty conscience to convulse, for God already knew whether the woman was guilty or not. As Albert Barnes supposes, that since there is no record of this ceremony ever being performed, its real benefit was that the procedure served as a deterrent against unfaithfulness (i.e., you may be able to enjoy your sin in secret, but you cannot hide from God's eye or escape His justice):

> Of itself, the drink was not noxious; and could only produce the effects here described by a special interposition of God. We do not read of any instance in which this ordeal was resorted to: a fact which may be explained either (with the Jews) as a proof of its efficacy, since the guilty could not be brought to face its terrors at all, and avoided them by confession; or more probably by the license of divorce tolerated by the law of Moses. Since a husband could put away his wife at pleasure [i.e., for some perceived uncleanness, per Deut. 24], a jealous man would naturally prefer to take this course with a suspected wife rather than to call public attention to his own shame by having recourse to the trial of jealousy.[19]

Returning to the ceremony, if nothing happened to her, the wife was proven innocent. In this case the husband's spirit of jealousy would be proven false and the wife would be publically proclaimed innocent that she *"may conceive children"* (v. 28). In the Jewish culture, child-bearing was associated with God's favor and was greatly desired among women. For this reason, barren women were often despised and mocked (e.g., 1 Sam. 1). No doubt the sexual relations of this couple had been hindered by an unjust spirit of jealousy, but that would no longer be present. If the wife was guilty, her abdomen would swell and her thigh would waste away (v. 27). This probably meant that she would become sterile and thus be cursed among her people.

Although our modern culture would view this entire proceeding as a bit bizarre, C. H. Mackintosh explains why it was a mercy of God to have such a perfect method of settling suspicions of infidelity:

> Suspicion is the death blow to all loving intimacy, and God would not have it in the midst of His congregation. He would not only have His people collectively to judge evil, and individually to judge themselves; but where there was even the suspicion of evil, and no evidence forthcoming, He Himself devised a method of trial which perfectly brought the truth to light. The guilty one had to drink death, and found it to be judgment. The faithful one drank death, and found it victory.[20]

If our hearts be not true to Christ, we will not be able to stand the searching power of His Word, which exposes the true nature of all things (Heb. 4:12). But if truth resides in our inner man, the more we are searched and tried, the more we are blessed. An innocent woman had nothing to fear, but rather would be rewarded by God for her purity. She could stand before the Lord confident of His blessing.

While the last section clearly had a practical implication for Israel, it also presents a dispensational perspective: Later, Jehovah would be rightly jealous over adulterous Israel, who, in figure, had become His wife by covenant (Ezek. 16). Hosea, Jeremiah, and Ezekiel frequently refer to this covenant relationship, to Israel's idolatry, and His judgments to purify and to restore her, the object of His love, to Himself. This will occur ultimately at the conclusion of the Tribulation Period, when a refined remnant of the Jewish nation will receive the Lord Jesus Christ (Zech. 12:10; Rom. 11:25). The point in this chapter is that Israel would be wise to remain loyal to Jehovah to avoid being forced to drink His holy retribution.

F. B. Hole nicely summarizes the content of this chapter and explains why it is necessary for God's people to deal with uncleanness, trespasses, and jealousy to remain in communion with Him:

> First, the removal of persons who may be defiled by leprosy, or by bodily issue, or by contact with death. Leprosy is a type of that "sin in

> the flesh," of which Romans 8:3 speaks. The "issue" reminds us of the words of our Lord, "that which comes out of the mouth, this defiles a man" (Matt. 15:11). Man being corrupted by sin, everything that comes out of him is defiled and defiling; and then "sin when it is finished, brings forth death," as the Apostle James tells us. A second source of defilement meets us in verses 5-10. Trespass against the Lord and one's neighbor is contemplated. Thirdly, we have, from verse 11 to the end of the chapter, what is spoken of as "the law of jealousies." The camp was to be holy as the dwelling place of God, and if jealousy as to his wife entered the mind of a man, it was not to be left to rankle there but to be tested, whether based on fact or fancy. If true, judgment fell on the woman; if false, she was free, and demonstrated to be so. We may see here a type of that which marked Israel and Jerusalem, indicated for instance, in Ezekiel 16 [where God was jealous over His idolatrous wife, and promised to judge her].[21]

Jehovah is a jealous God, and in His presence, Israel must ever be conscious of their holiness and their necessity of dealing with trespasses against the Lord and each other. In the Church Age, we too must remember that the Lord Jesus is likewise jealous of our affections and our care of His saints. This is why with holy zeal Paul rebukes the Corinthians for being unequally yoked with children of the devil and defiling themselves with temple harlots (1 Cor. 6).

After this, we read of the church at Ephesus, which, though they had good works and sound doctrine, lost their lampstand (their church testimony) because over time their love for Christ had waned (Rev. 2:2-5). He no longer had first place in their affections. No doubt, these saints continued in form for some time, but they did not have the joy and power of His presence among them – this is a deathblow to any local church. May we endeavor to remain a loyal, a holy, a confessing and a restoring people – Christ's continuing presence is worth it! God is right to be jealous when His people stray from Him; may our love for Him not be sidetracked by carnal emotions.

Meditation

> When there are dissensions, and jealousies, and evil speaking among professors of religion, then there is great need of a revival. These things show that Christians have got far from God, and it is time to think earnestly of a revival.
>
> — Charles Finney

Personal Consecration
Numbers 6

Numbers 4 conveyed God's order for Levitical service and for moving and setting up His tabernacle. Numbers 5 addressed the removal of anything that would defile those dwelling near to God. In Numbers 6, the focus shifts from the need for corporate examination and for the removal of what was unclean to the matter of personal holiness. What has been cleansed for God should be consecrated to God! Hence, the meaning of Nazarite is "a separated one." Those entering into the Nazarite vow were placing themselves in the most holy and separated position that a non-Levitical Jew could enter.

The Nazarite Vow (vv. 1-21)

A man or woman entering into the Nazarite vow was agreeing to strictly maintain a threefold obligation for the entire time of his or her separation (vv. 1-2). The Rabbinical writings of the Mishna indicate that this separation could last for one hundred days, but the typical duration of the vow was thirty days. The three constraints of the Nazarite vow are listed in verses 3-6:

> *He shall separate himself from wine and similar drink; he shall drink neither vinegar made from wine nor vinegar made from similar drink; neither shall he drink any grape juice, nor eat fresh grapes or raisins. All the days of his separation he shall eat nothing that is produced by the grapevine, from seed to skin* (v. 3-4).

> *All the days of the vow of his separation no razor shall come upon his head; until the days are fulfilled for which he separated himself to the Lord, he shall be holy. Then he shall let the locks of the hair of his head grow* (v. 5).

> *All the days that he separates himself to the Lord he shall not go near a dead body* (v. 6).

Refining and Reminding

The vow prohibited eating or drinking anything from the grapevine, cutting one's hair, and touching a corpse, even the body of a close family member during *"all the days of his separation."* The fruit of the vine, in every form, was forbidden. This included eating grapes, raisins, or cakes made from the grape skins, or drinking grape juice, vinegar, wine, liquor from the grapes (a strong drink made from grape skins macerated in water), or a sour drink made from the seeds of unripened grapes.[22]

We might wonder why God required the Nazarite to let his hair grow. John J. Stubbs suggests this requirement should be linked with Paul's explanation in 1 Corinthians 11:14: *"Does not even nature itself teach you that if a man has long hair, it is a dishonor to him?"* The uncut hair of the Nazarite represents separation from the rights and dignity of manhood. Long hair is a sign of subjection to another, and that is not God's order for the man who represents the image and glory of God.[23]

Number 6 specifies two sets of procedures and offerings required for the vow: first, if failure of the vow occurred (vv. 9-12), and second, when the vow had been fulfilled (vv. 13-21). For the former situation, the earlier days of his vow were lost, and he had to begin all over again. So, if a man under a Nazarite vow accidentally touched a dead body, he had to first undergo the seven-day cleansing process described in Numbers 9. Afterwards, his head was to be shaved and he was to bring two turtledoves or two pigeons for a burnt offering and a sin offering, and a yearling male lamb as a trespass offering to the tabernacle. Then he would start his days of separation again.

Upon the completion of his vow, he would bring a yearling male lamb for a burnt offering, a ewe lamb for a sin offering, and an unblemished ram for a peace offering. He would also bring a basket containing unleavened bread (made with fine flour and oil), cakes anointed with oil, a grain offering, and a drink offering. His head was to be shaved and the hair of his consecration burnt on the Bronze Altar with his peace offering. The hair was a token of the Nazarite's consecration and was a testimony of his faithfulness to complete the vow. The burnt offering symbolized the total surrender of the Nazarite to God, the sin offering provided atonement for any sins committed during the Nazarite's time of consecration, and the peace offering spoke of the communion the Nazarite enjoyed with God during his consecration.

It is unknown how often Jewish men and women entered into the Nazarite vow, as the Old Testament records only one actual case, that of Samson, who was called from his birth by God into life-long consecration (Judg. 13:5). He did not choose to be a Nazarite, but his supernatural strength depended on his willingness to obey his calling, which, as we know, he was seduced into compromising by Delilah.

The Nazarite vow was likely what Paul entered into after returning to Jerusalem in the latter years of his ministry. Paul, a Christian and an apostle to the Gentiles, erred in making a Jewish vow. F. B. Hole writes, "Acts 21:20-26 indicates a lapse in consecration to Christ on Paul's part, but his years of separation and devotion to his Lord before that were not treated as a lost thing."[24]

Figuratively speaking, wine symbolizes earthly joy, as what cheers the heart was derived from the earth. Such enjoyments are not necessarily wrong or evil in themselves (though drunkenness is prohibited in Scripture), but represent what the human heart often clings to. The Beloved in the Song of Solomon illustrates this tendency when he tells his lover that his love for her is *"better than wine"* (Song. 1:2). This means that it is better to enjoy what deeply satisfies and remains rather than enjoy what is short-lived and shallow.

Charles Spurgeon understood the Song of Solomon primarily as a poetic description of the love relationship between Jesus Christ and His redeemed people. In his 1872 sermon entitled *Better Than Wine* (drawn from Song. 1:2), he explained why Christ's love is better than wine:

Christ's love is better than wine because of what it is not:
- It is totally safe, and may be taken without question - you can't take too much.
- It doesn't cost anything.
- Taking more of it does not diminish the taste of it.
- It is totally without impurities and will never turn sour.
- It produces no ill effects.

Christ's love is better than wine because of what it is:
- Like wine, the love of Christ has healing properties.
- Like wine, the love of Christ is associated with giving strength.
- Like wine, the love of Christ is a symbol of joy.
- Like wine, the love of Christ exhilarates the soul.

Refining and Reminding

Indeed, the refreshing and exhilarating communion of the Lord Jesus is better than wine. Fleeting passions and temporary gratification in earthly things can never satisfy the human spirit's intrinsic need for God. As the object of His love, may we maintain our purity and reserve our affections for Him (Col. 3:1-2). The consecrated Nazarite yearned for God and the full satisfaction found only in Him.

Though this spiritual aspiration is indeed praiseworthy, there has only been one true and perfect Nazarite to sojourn on this earth. He maintained, from the first to the last of His days, the most complete separation from earthly enjoyments and carnal amusements in order to maintain the deepest communion with God. From the moment He entered into His public work, the Lord Jesus kept Himself apart from all that was worldly, yet He presented God's message to the world.

C. H. Mackintosh reminds us the heart of the Lord Jesus was fixed upon God and His work with devotion which could not be shaken:

> We see how the perfect Nazarite carried himself throughout. He could have no joy in the earth, no joy in the nation of Israel. The time had not come for that, and therefore He detached Himself from all that which mere human affection might find in association with His own, in order to devote Himself to the one grand object which was ever before His mind. The time will come when He, as the Messiah, will rejoice in His people and in the earth; but, until that blissful moment arrives, He is apart as the true Nazarite, and His people are united with Him. *"They are not of the world, even as I am not of the world. Sanctify them through Thy truth: Thy word is truth. As Thou hast sent Me into the world, even so have I also sent them into the world. And for their sakes I sanctify Myself, that they also might be sanctified through the truth"* (John 17:16-19).[25]

The Lord Jesus enjoyed the deepest sense of significance and satisfaction during His earthly sojourn because He was completely consecrated to God and enjoyed unhindered communion with God. To the fullest extent possible on this side of glorification, the Lord desires believers today to experience this kind of living revival as we labor for Him. Sadly, few Christians enter into the intense power of complete consecration, because they cannot fully separate themselves from the excitement of natural things and of temporary pleasures – the wines of the world.

However, the Nazarite typifies one who embarks on a special path of devotedness or consecration to Christ. The power and ecstasy to continue on that path is derived from a believer's secret communion with God. J. N. Darby highlights the practical implications that the Nazarite vow holds for believers today:

> The Nazarite presents to us another character connected with the walk of the Spirit down here – special separation and devotedness to God. They separated themselves unto Him. Christ is the perfect example of this. The church ought to tread in His footsteps. Cases of special call to devote oneself to the Lord come under this class.[26]

When our blessed fellowship with God is interrupted, our joy and strength for serving Him quickly dissipate too. If you are spiritually dry and powerless today, there is a solution: Freshly consecrate yourself to the Lord and seek Him with all your heart.

The Priestly Blessing (vv. 22-27)

The priests were to pronounce God's favor upon His people by uttering a prescribed blessing. Similarly, the Lord Jesus taught His disciples a model prayer to guide their praying, not a religious utterance of dead rote (Matt. 6:7-9). The idea was not for the priests to repeat vain words, but they were to freshly proclaim God's delight in His people and His desire to bless them. Eugene H. Merrill says the meaning of the pronounced blessing was clear:

> The blessing communicates the desire of the Lord to invest His people with His name. The name of the Lord is tantamount to the Lord Himself so that this blessing becomes a petition that God might live among His people and meet all their needs. He alone can bless His people, keep them, look on them with favor (make His face shine and turn His face toward them), be gracious to them, and give them peace.[27]

Blessing the people in the name of the Lord meant that the people were under His protection, would have their sins forgiven, and would enjoy His favor as long as they continued walking with Him in the wilderness. Matthew Henry comments on the mysterious nature of the priest's three-part blessing for the people (vv. 22-27):

Refining and Reminding

> In so rich a list of mercies, worldly joys are not worthy to be mentioned. Here is a form of prayer. The name Jehovah is three times repeated. The Jews think there is some mystery; and we know what it is, the New Testament having explained it. There we are directed to expect the blessing from the grace of our Lord Jesus Christ, the love of the Father, and the communion of the Holy Ghost (2 Cor. 13:14); each of which Persons is Jehovah, and yet they are not three Lords, but one Lord.[28]

Indeed, a triune God yearns to commune with His redeemed people and this fact likely explains why the blessing is located at the end of Numbers 6. In the previous five chapters God has explicitly expressed His order for His people to follow and in this chapter, the purity and devotion He demands from them. Where there is obedience, purity, and devotion among God's people, His blessing will be upon them also.

For Israel, there is a day nearing when the Jewish nation will receive the full ramifications of this magnificent benediction. After acknowledging Christ as their Messiah, and receiving the Holy Spirit, the nation will have achieved their spiritual destiny – full maturity and irrevocable communion with God. They will know the Lord, His faithfulness, and abiding presence in a new way. In fact, Jerusalem itself will be referred to as *Yahweh-Shammah*, meaning "the Lord is present" or "the Lord is there" (Ezek. 48:35). In that day, Israel shall be purified from all their defilements, and be consecrated to God in the power of true Naziriteship.

Meditation

> Take my life, and let it be
> Consecrated, Lord, to Thee;
> Take my moments and my days,
> Let them flow in ceaseless praise,
> Let them flow in ceaseless praise.
>
> Take my love; my Lord, I pour
> At Thy feet its treasure-store.
> Take myself, and I will be
> Ever, only, all for Thee,
> Ever, only, all for Thee.

— Frances R. Havergal

Offerings of Tribal Leaders
Numbers 7

In Numbers 6 we saw that personal consecration leads to communion with God and results in His blessings. Those experiencing God in this way then yearn to show their appreciation by offering back to Him what He appreciates. Numbers 7 is a lengthy record of personal offerings from each tribal leader to the Lord. Much space could have been saved by lumping all the offerings together and only noting the final amount (vv. 84-88), but the text indicates that God looks beyond what was given, to appreciate the sentiment of the individual giver. C. H. Mackintosh explains why God delights in acknowledging the selfless sacrifices of His people, no matter how small:

> Nothing could satisfy Him but the fullest and most detailed account of each man's name, of the tribe which he represented, and of the offering which he made to the sanctuary of God. Hence this long chapter of eighty-nine verses. Each name shines out in its own distinctness. Each offering is minutely described and duly estimated. The names and the offerings are not huddled promiscuously together. This would not be like our God; and He can only act like Himself, in whatever He does, and speak like Himself, whatever He says. Man may pass hastily or carelessly over gifts and offerings; but God never can, never does, and never will. He delights to record every little act of service, every little loving gift. He never forgets the smallest thing; and not only does He not forget it Himself, but He takes special pains that untold millions shall read the record. How little did those twelve princes imagine that their names and their offerings were to be handed down, from age to age, to be read by countless generations! Yet so it was, for God would have it so.[29]

This chapter, in retrospect, records the offerings given by tribal leaders a few weeks earlier (when the Bronze Altar was dedicated after Moses first set up the tabernacle; vv. 1, 10). Besides sacrificial animals, supplies, and precious metals, the leaders provided Moses with six covered carts (perhaps wagons) and twelve oxen to transport the tabernacle and its curtain wall (vv. 2-3). Each leader provided an ox and two leaders jointly provided a cart. The tribal princes understood that the things of the Lord should be protected and therefore they provided "covered" carts. C. A. Coates explains the spiritual implication of this important detail:

> The things carried were not to be exposed; they were to be protected from the surrounding influences of the wilderness. The things connected with the testimony of the Lord are not for public display. The word "mystery" is very characteristic of the present period; it means that divine things are only known to those who are initiated; they are never to be regarded as things which can be brought within the range of the natural man. They are holy things, and they are to be preserved inviolate while they are being carried through a scene which is everywhere marked by what is unholy, and defiling.[30]

Moses distributed two carts and four oxen to the Gershonites and four carts and eight oxen to the Merarites for this purpose (vv. 4-8), *"but to the sons of Kohath he gave none, because theirs was the service of the holy things, which they carried on their shoulders"* (v. 9). The Merarites required more carts than the Gershonites, because they were charged with transporting the heavier wood and metal components of the tabernacle.

Then, for the next twelve days, one leader from each tribe presented a gift to the Lord consisting of a silver plate and silver sprinkling bowl (each filled with flour), a gold ladle (filled with incense), a young bull, a ram, and a yearling male lamb for burnt offerings, and a male goat for a sin offering, and two oxen, five rams, and five male goats, and five yearling male lambs for peace offerings (vv. 12-83). Each of these tribal leader's names are recorded and agree with the listing of Numbers 1, except the order is different. Elizur from Reuben, Jacob's firstborn son, heads the first list, but Nahshon of Judah, the prophesied royal tribe, is the first to present gifts to the Lord.

Day	Tribe	Tribal Leader	Numbers 7
1	Judah	Nahshon	vv. 12-17
2	Issachar	Nethanel	vv. 18-23
3	Zebulun	Eliab	vv. 24-29
4	Reuben	Elizur	vv. 30-35
5	Simeon	Shelumiel	vv. 36-41
6	Gad	Eliasaph	vv. 42-47
7	Ephraim	Elishama	vv. 48-53
8	Manasseh	Gamaliel	vv. 54-59
9	Benjamin	Abidan	vv. 60-65
10	Dan	Ahiezer	vv. 66-71
11	Asher	Pagiel	vv. 72-77
12	Naphtali	Ahira	vv. 78-83

It is evident from the text that the principle of godly leadership must be present for God's order to be followed and that God provides such leaders for His people. This is a blessing that we also observe in the Church Age, as Christ gave apostles to the Church (Eph. 4:11) and raised up elders to oversee local assemblies (Acts 20:28). There are many today who would lead God's people astray, but those whom God appoints can be safely followed and it is our privilege to do so (Heb. 13:17). As seen in this chapter, godly leadership promotes a spirit of unity and cooperation and ensures God gets what He is supposed to receive. This was accomplished no matter what size any particular tribe might be. May such godly leadership mark our churches today, whether small or great in number – God should get what He deserves!

To this end C. A. Coates summarizes the spiritual significance of this long chapter to believers in the Church Age:

> "The dedication-gift of the altar" is most important; the account of it fills no less than seventy-nine verses. The Spirit of God had pleasure in detailing what each prince offered on each of the twelve days. There was precisely the same kind of gift given on each day; every tribe had a prince who brought what was equal to what the other eleven princes brought. The divine thought being that in every local assembly the spontaneous response should come up to the same measure, so that there might be in each an offering worthy of the

anointed altar. There was not only unity in offering, but uniformity, and this is spiritually important. The saints are all to *"say the same thing"* in teaching (1 Corinthians 1:10); the customs of the assemblies are to be uniform (1 Corinthians 11:16); and we learn here that as regards approach and offering at the altar it is pleasurable to God that there should be uniformity amongst all His people.[31]

The final verse of the chapter states that Moses went into the tabernacle and that God spoke to him from above the Mercy Seat on the Ark of the Covenant (v. 89). Although not a priest per se (i.e., a descendant of Aaron), Moses enjoyed a unique relationship with God that permitted him to have direct access to the Lord: *"The Lord spoke to Moses face to face, as a man speaks to his friend"* (Ex. 33:11). Although further instructions on the affairs of the tabernacle and His people are recorded in the next chapter, it seems likely that Jehovah would have acknowledged His delight in the giving spirit of the people at this time. Obviously, this record has been preserved that we might appreciate the sacrificial giving of others to the Lord. True giving to God is selfless and should never prompt envy or pride, but rather our excitement that God is getting the worship He deserves from those who owe Him everything.

It is quite appropriate, then, that the personal sacrifice in Numbers 7 naturally follows the personal consecration of Numbers 6. Willing daily self-sacrifice and devotion to God cannot be sustained without full separation from secular pulls and worldly philosophies. Little in one's life has value to God after a man or a woman has become mesmerized by earthly things which must ultimately be lost and burnt up! This is why the Lord Jesus exhorted His disciples:

> *Do not lay up for yourselves treasures on earth, where moth and rust destroy and where thieves break in and steal; but lay up for yourselves treasures in heaven, where neither moth nor rust destroys and where thieves do not break in and steal. For where your treasure is, there your heart will be also* (Matt. 6:19-21).

Only what is invested for eternity has value to the Lord. On judgment day all else will be shown to be worthless and will be incinerated by the brilliance of God's holy presence (1 Cor. 3:11-15).

Devotions in Numbers

Meditation

He is no fool who gives what he cannot keep to gain what he cannot lose.

— Jim Elliot

Cleansing and Dedication
Numbers 8

Two things had to occur prior to the cleansing and dedication of the Levites so they could commence tabernacle service – the dedication of the Bronze Altar and the lighting of the Golden Lampstand. These activities symbolize the proper attitude and provision that God's people must possess to engage in ministry which pleases Him. First, there must be a willingness of heart to give to God without reservation – this was observed in the dedication of the Altar in the previous chapter. Second, only ministry which is enabled by the Holy Spirit and projects the glory of Christ has value to God. The latter truth is put before us now in the lighting of the Lampstand.

The Light of the Lampstand (vv. 1-4)

The abrupt appearance of the tabernacle's Lampstand in the narrative would seem misplaced, if it were not for its typological meaning associated with the cleansing, the sanctification, and the dedication of the Levites that followed:

> *And the Lord spoke to Moses, saying: "Speak to Aaron, and say to him, 'When you arrange the lamps, the seven lamps shall give light in front of the lampstand.'" And Aaron did so; he arranged the lamps to face toward the front of the lampstand, as the Lord commanded Moses* (vv. 1-3).

Previously, Moses had discussed the Lampstand's blue covering when being transported, but at this juncture the Lampstand is fully functional before the Lord in the holy place. The Lampstand was made from a single piece of beaten gold and was the only source of light in the tabernacle. The Lampstand's light represents the Holy Spirit's perfect testimony of truth centered in Christ (2 Cor. 1:20; Rev. 4:5, 19:10). The flowing olive oil supplied to each of the seven burning wicks represents the perfect enabling power of the Holy Spirit to accomplish the will of God (Zech. 4:6). The Lampstand typifies the Person and work of Christ; consequently, each of the seven lamps was to be positioned in such a way as to cast their full light before the Lampstand (v. 4).

The Holy Spirit's work in the Church now, as in Israel then, was and is completely dependent on Christ. Every ray of light that radiates God's glory in the life of believers today flows from Christ as empowered by the Holy Spirit. Therefore, the appearance of the Lampstand just prior to the cleansing and dedication of the Levites reminds us of what God values in service to Him – that which is Christ-exalting and Spirit-enabled.

C. H. Mackintosh highlights the practical implications of this truth for Christians desiring to live for God today:

> The very finest evidence which can be afforded of true spiritual work is that it tends directly to exalt Christ. If attention be sought for the work or the workman, the light has become dim, and the minister of the sanctuary must use the snuffers. It was Aaron's province to light the lamps; and he it was who trimmed them likewise. In other words, the light which, as Christians, we are responsible to yield, is not only founded upon Christ, but maintained by Him, from moment to moment, throughout the entire night. Apart from Him we can do nothing. The golden shaft sustained the lamps; the priestly hand supplied the oil and applied the snuffers. It is all *in* Christ, *from* Christ, and *by* Christ. And more, it is all *to* Christ. Wherever the light of the Spirit – the true light of the sanctuary – has shone, in this wilderness world, the object of that light has been to exalt the name of Jesus Christ. Whatever has been done by the Holy Spirit, whatever has been said, whatever has been written has had for its aim the glory of that blessed One.[32]

It was fitting then that the light of the Lampstand be mentioned before the Levites were dedicated to the Lord for service. Only that service which God enables to reflect His glory will please Him. In the wilderness, the only light in the sanctuary came from the seven burning wicks of the Lampstand. Likewise, spiritual darkness today is dispelled by the illuminating testimony of Christ in Spirit-filled believers (Eph. 5:18).

This is why the Lord Jesus taught His disciples, before commissioning them, that they must shine out life-changing truth for others to see: *"Let your light so shine before men, that they may see your good works and glorify your Father in heaven"* (Matt. 5:16). They were to imitate Christ's own Spirit-enabled ministry. The Lord had been previously anointed and empowered by the Holy Spirit to accomplish His appointed ministry: *"The Spirit of the Lord is upon Me"* (Luke 4:18) and *"Jesus returned in the power of the Spirit to Galilee"* (Luke 4:14). As Paul summarizes, the spiritual darkness in the world is overcome today by the illuminating Spirit-supplied ministry of God's Son through His people:

> *But we have renounced the hidden things of shame, not walking in craftiness nor handling the word of God deceitfully, but by manifestation of the truth commending ourselves to every man's conscience in the sight of God. But even if our gospel is veiled, it is veiled to those who are perishing, whose minds the god of this age has blinded, who do not believe, lest the light of the gospel of the glory of Christ, who is the image of God, should shine on them. For we do not preach ourselves, but Christ Jesus the Lord, and ourselves your bondservants for Jesus' sake. For it is the God who commanded light to shine out of darkness, who has shone in our hearts to give the light of the knowledge of the glory of God in the face of Jesus Christ* (2 Cor. 4:2-6).

This statement proves that Zacharias' prophetic announcement concerning Christ just prior to His birth has been fulfilled. Through Christ, God promised *"to give light to those who sit in darkness and the shadow of death, to guide our feet into the way of peace"* (Luke 1:79). Simeon also foretold Christ's illuminating message just eight days after His birth: *"A light to bring revelation to the Gentiles, and the glory of Your people Israel"* (Luke 2:32). Years later, the Lord Himself declared, *"I am the light of the world. He who follows Me shall not walk in darkness, but have the light of life"* (John 8:12). He was *"the true Light which gives light to every man coming into the world"* (John 1:9). The Lord Jesus was God's perfect Lampstand, casting His light before fallen humanity in the power of the Holy Spirit. All those who desire to serve the Lord must follow His example and be His light in a dark world also.

Cleansing and Dedication of Levites (vv. 5-26)

Numbers contains progressive revelation as to the privileges and responsibilities pertaining to the Levites, but it all hinged on the Levites first being ceremonially purified and set apart for the Lord. Moses was to cleanse the Levites, but both he and the Levites had obligations to accomplish this (vv. 5-7).

The Levites were to shave their entire bodies, wash themselves, and launder their clothes. Moses was to sprinkle them with the water of purification (probably referring to 19:1-22). There is a sharp contrast between the Levites washing with water and Moses sprinkling them with holy water of purification. One could be made clean by washing with water (e.g. Ps. 51:7), but under Levitical rite, sprinkling something with either blood or holy water (water containing the ashes of the red heifer) brought it under the value of what was sprinkled (Heb. 9:19-22). Thus, the Levites were not only clean, but were considered holy – they were set aside for the Lord.

Likewise, believers in the Church Age experience cleansing and regeneration by the Holy Spirit after trusting the gospel message (Tit. 3:5). They also are positionally removed from the world and are consecrated as a holy priesthood to serve Christ (Gal. 6:14; Col. 2:20; 1 Pet. 2:9; Rev. 1:6). We have been, spiritually speaking, sprinkled by the blood of Christ, and not only have been brought under its power, but we also receive the value of what it is worth to God (i.e., positional holiness). This is only possible because the precious blood of God's Lamb was without blemish or spot (1 Pet. 1:19). Given the moral cleansing and spiritual purification that believers have undergone to be called into service, may we also serve the Lord as fully consecrated holy priests.

After the ceremonial acts of washing, shaving, and sprinkling were complete, the Levites were to offer a young bull with fine flour mingled with oil for a burnt offering and a second young bull for a sin offering. As discussed in the first seven chapters of Leviticus, these offerings present to us, in type, two different aspects of Christ's death.

> The Burnt Offering – Literally, this was the ascending offering which was completely for God's pleasure. It was a freewill offering that was totally consumed, excluding the skins (Lev. 7:8). The burnt offering pictures Christ's absolute devotion and

submission to the Father's will in being a sacrifice for humanity's sin.

Sin Offering – At His death, Christ bore in His body our sin, taking the place of the sinner (1 Pet. 2:24). We are inherently fallen, sinful creatures deserving judgment. Christ as the sin offering satisfied God's righteous demand for justice concerning human sin.

After the Levites completed the ceremonial cleansing and purification and had their burnt and sin sacrifices ready to offer, the full assembly was to gather at the tabernacle before the Lord (v. 8). The Levite dedication service was as follows:

So you shall bring the Levites before the Lord, and the children of Israel shall lay their hands on the Levites; and Aaron shall offer the Levites before the Lord like a wave offering from the children of Israel, that they may perform the work of the Lord. Then the Levites shall lay their hands on the heads of the young bulls, and you shall offer one as a sin offering and the other as a burnt offering to the Lord, to make atonement for the Levites. And you shall stand the Levites before Aaron and his sons, and then offer them like a wave offering to the Lord. Thus you shall separate the Levites from among the children of Israel, and the Levites shall be Mine (vv. 10-14).

Two important matters were accomplished through this dedication service: First, the Levites now represented the entire Jewish nation, and would act on their behalf in executing their duties. In the same way that the children of Israel had laid their hands on the heads of the Levites, they put their hands on the heads of the sacrifices. This act publicly symbolized the transference of representation. Second, the Levites were now fully separated unto the Lord. The Lord relinquished his claim on the firstborns who had been spared in the first Passover and now accepted the tribe of Levi instead (vv. 15-18).

Interestingly, the Lord viewed the Levites *"as a gift to Aaron and his sons from among the children of Israel, to do the work for the children of Israel in the tabernacle of meeting, and to make atonement for the children of Israel, that there be no plague among the children of Israel when the children of Israel come near the sanctuary"* (v. 19). Initially, there were only three priests, so the Levites were essential helpers in accomplishing all that the Lord had prescribed (vv. 20-22).

In all these proceedings it is important to observe that this section on cleansing and dedication begins and ends with "after that" (vv. 15, 22). F. E. Stallan writes concerning these phrases:

> The two mentions of the words "after that" are very significant. They come between two conditions, showing that service for the Lord was not acceptable without the necessary preliminaries. Even after washing, clean clothing had to be worn; there was to be no perpetuation of any aspect of defilement. The break with the past had to be made and *after that* service for the Lord could begin.[33]

Verses 23-26 reveal two more clarifications to the thirty- to fifty-year age restriction levied in Numbers 4: First, those who were twenty-five could begin serving in the tabernacle as apprentices. The help of younger men loading and unloading the heavy components of the tabernacle into carts certainly would have been appreciated by the older men. Second, those Levites over fifty years of age were no longer permitted to assist in the laborious tasks of moving the tabernacle (v. 25). However, their expertise was considered valuable and, if they desired, they could continue to *"minister with their brethren in the tabernacle of meeting, to attend to needs, but they themselves shall do no work"* (v. 26). "Attend to needs" would include providing counsel and directing affairs, but not actually taking part in the burdensome tasks.

God's order for proper worship had been revealed previously and now those appointed to represent the nation in worship in the tabernacle had been dedicated to the Lord and were ready to serve (vv. 20-22). What was at the center of God's Law, and pictured what would be later accomplished by His Son, was ready to commence. The dispensation of the Law would continue for centuries to come until it would be put away forever by the New Covenant established at Calvary. What could neither fully redeem nor save sinners was replaced with what could – the blood of the Lord Jesus Christ.

Meditation

> A forgiven sinner is quite different from an ordinary sinner, and a consecrated Christian is quite different from an ordinary Christian.
>
> — Watchman Nee

Refining and Reminding

Jesus Christ has bought us with His blood, but, alas, He has not had His money's worth! He paid for ALL, and He has had but a fragment of our energy, time and earnings. By an act of consecration, let us ask Him to forgive the robbery of the past, and let us profess our desire to be henceforth utterly and only for Him - His slaves, owning no master other than Himself.

— F. B. Meyer

The Second Passover and the Cloud
Numbers 9

The Second Passover (vv. 1-14)

Although the Passover, the redemption-feast of Israel, was celebrated annually, we find three distinct mentions of it in the course of Israel's history: in Egypt at their deliverance (Ex. 12), in the wilderness while enduring trials (Num. 9), and in Canaan to commence the conquest of the land (Josh. 5). Whether addressing their deliverance from the bondage of sin, or their challenging trials, or seizing their God-given inheritance by faith, redemption is the basis for what God accomplishes in His people.

Consequently, there was to be no neglect of keeping the Passover in the dispensation of the Law. To do so would show contempt for all the blessings and benefits God's people had received through redemption.

The appointed time to eat the Passover was at twilight on the fourteenth day of the first month in the Hebrew calendar (vv. 1-5). Understanding the Passover's importance, Moses was asked about certain men who had become unclean, not because of sin, but because of attending to a dead body at the time of the Passover (vv. 6-7). Their dilemma was that they could not eat the Passover because they were ceremonially unclean, yet they were commanded to do so by the Law.

Moses knew that he had no authority to answer the matter and wisely told the inquirers, *"Stand still, that I may hear what the Lord will command concerning you"* (v. 8). This is a wise course of action for believers to follow today, suggests F. B. Hole:

> Have we ever sighed for guidance in our pilgrim way, wishing we had some visible sign to direct? We have to remember what the Epistle to the Hebrews was written to enforce; namely, that the outward and visible things of Judaism were but shadows, which have given place to the realities that have reached us in Christ, and are known to faith. We have His Spirit and His Word, and if we have that meekness, of

which Psalm 25:9 speaks, we shall not lack the overruling guidance that we need.[34]

Indeed, if the path ahead is not clearly affirmed by God's Word, it is best to stop where we are and seek counsel from the Lord. He promises to guide those who leave life's decisions to Him. To venture forward in the absence of faith-rooted direction is sin (Rom. 14:23).

Moses did receive guidance from the Lord concerning this situation and told his inquirers that an allowance for those unclean at the time of the first Passover would be permitted. They could observe the Passover the following month (i.e., the fourteenth day of the second month). This provision highlights the overall significance that God puts on His people memorializing the Passover annually. With this observation in mind, C. H. Mackintosh highlights the importance of believers continually participating in the Lord's Supper today:

> The Christian reader should understand the immense importance and deep interest of the ordinance [the Lord's Supper in view of the Passover ordinance] as viewed on the double ground of subjection to the authority of Scripture, and responsive love to Christ Himself. Furthermore, we are anxious to impress the seriousness of neglecting to eat the Lord's Supper, according to the scriptures. We may depend upon it; it is dangerous ground for any to attempt to set aside this positive institution of our Lord and Master. It argues a wrong condition of soul altogether. It proves that the conscience is not subject to the authority of the word, and that the heart is not in true sympathy with the affections of Christ. Let us therefore see to it that we are honestly endeavoring to discharge our holy responsibilities to the table of the Lord – that we forbear not to keep the feast – that we celebrate it according to the order laid down by God the Holy Spirit.[35]

A Jew genuinely desiring to keep the Passover under Law then or a Christian observing the Lord's Supper under grace proves the integrity of one's heart. Any Jew who could contentedly pass over the Passover year after year only proved that his heart was far from the Lord. Likewise, any professing believer in the Church Age who can carelessly ignore the Lord's dying request to remember Him through the breaking of the bread suffers from coldness of heart towards the Lord.

The text shows that God understands that at times we will be hindered by legitimate duties from remembering the Lord, but to do so out of carelessness or while enjoying secular amusements is a great travesty resulting in spiritual loss and may prompt the chastening hand of God. Similarly, it would be offensive to God for any Jew enjoying the blessings of redemption to willfully ignore God's annual ordinance memorializing how He had accomplished their redemption. Those Jews who neglected observing the Passover were to be put out from the camp and therefore could not enjoy the commonwealth of Israel (Ex. 12:14-15). In a manner of speaking, they would be disowned by Jehovah. Even strangers, living among the Jews (as proselytes) and enjoying the blessings of Israel's redemption, were to keep the Passover feast (v. 14).

Through the blood of a lamb Jehovah had delivered His people from the harsh bonds of slavery and out of Egypt (a symbol of the worldly influence), and then from the threat of annihilation at the Red Sea. How could any true Jew not appreciate that! Likewise, how could any true Christian not appreciate what God accomplished through the redemptive blood of His Lamb, that is, the death of His own Son. Believers have been set *"free from the law of sin and death"* (Rom. 8:2), have been positionally carved out of the world by the cross of Christ (Gal. 6:14), and have been saved from experiencing God's righteous wrath and eternal punishment in hell for sinners (Rom. 5:9). There is much to remember and celebrate!

The Cloud and the Fire (vv. 15-23)

After the tabernacle was set up and dedicated to the Lord, we read that His visible presence among His people was seen as a cloud over the tabernacle by day and a pillar of fire by night (also see Ex. 40:34).

> *Now on the day that the tabernacle was raised up, the cloud covered the tabernacle, the tent of the Testimony; from evening until morning it was above the tabernacle like the appearance of fire. So it was always: the cloud covered it by day, and the appearance of fire by night. Whenever the cloud was taken up from above the tabernacle, after that the children of Israel would journey; and in the place where the cloud settled, there the children of Israel would pitch their tents* (vv. 15-17).

Refining and Reminding

God overshadowed His people with a cloud after delivering them from bondage in Egypt (Ex. 13:21-22). The ever-present cloud was a constant token of Jehovah's kind parental care; the cloud would reassure the Jews of God's abiding presence. God would accompany His covenant people through the best of times and the worst of times to ensure that they entered the Promised Land.

While in the desert, the cloud would illuminate their camp at night and its shadow would protect them from excess solar radiation during the day. It is not likely that the cloud changed in appearance throughout the day; the upper portion appeared as a pillar of fire, while its base flattened out and spread over the entire camp (Ex. 14:24). The cloud would safely guide the Israelites through the wilderness if its movements were observed and heeded. Hence, the phrase *"the command of the Lord"* occurs seven times in this chapter to affirm God's guidance and blessing, if His people will obey His commands.

So, when the cloud moved, the Israelites pulled up their tent pegs and followed it. When the cloud lingered in a particular location over the tabernacle, the Israelites were to tarry under its shadow – whether for days, weeks, or even months (vv. 18-23). When the cloud moved, those closest to the Lord, the priests, were the first to be aware of it; they were then to ensure that all of God's people knew His will. Praise the Lord for those who can quickly discern the will of God and can convey it accurately to others who need help to understand it.

Today, God does not, per se, use a cloud by day or a pillar of fire by night to lead His people along, but, Matthew Henry points out, He still leads them on by His Word and by His Spirit.

> This cloud was appointed to be the visible sign and symbol of God's presence with Israel. Thus we are taught to see God always near us, both night and day. As long as the cloud rested on the tabernacle, so long they continued in the same place. There is no time lost while we are waiting God's time. When the cloud was taken up, they removed themselves, however comfortably they were encamped. ... It is very safe and pleasant going when we see God before us, and resting where he appoints us to rest. The leading of this cloud is spoken of as signifying the guidance of the blessed Spirit. We are not now to expect such tokens of the Divine presence and guidance; but the promise of God's guidance is sure. ... All the children of God shall be led by the Spirit of God (Rom. 8:14). He will direct the paths of those who in all their ways acknowledge Him (Prov. 3:6).[36]

The cloud was a daily, visible reminder that Jehovah had not forsaken His people, but was in fact dwelling with them. Today, the Holy Spirit takes up eternal residence within new believers and then daily guides them towards Christ-likeness and enables them to represent Christ before the lost. This is why the Lord Jesus promises those that are His, *"I will never leave you nor forsake you"* (Heb. 13:5). Going through life without the Lord is like wandering aimlessly through a vast, arid desert, but under the shadow of His wing there is peace and security despite life's unknowns: *"O God, be merciful to me! For my soul trusts in You; and in the shadow of Your wings I will make my refuge, until these calamities have passed by"* (Ps. 57:1).

Meditation

> Under His wings I am safely abiding,
> Though the night deepens and tempests are wild,
> Still I can trust Him; I know He will keep me,
> He has redeemed me, and I am His child.
>
> Under His wings, what a refuge in sorrow!
> How the heart yearningly turns to His rest!
> Often when earth has no balm for my healing,
> There I find comfort, and there I am blessed.
>
> — William Cushing

The Silver Trumpets
Numbers 10

Two months after departing from Egypt, the Israelites arrived in the wilderness of Sinai and camped before the Mount of God (Ex. 18:5, 19:1-2). God had kept His promise to Moses, fulfilling the sign presented to him during their first meeting: *"This shall be a sign to you that I have sent you: When you have brought the people out of Egypt, you shall serve God on this mountain"* (Ex. 3:12).

The Israelites would remain at this location for approximately a year, until the twentieth day of the second month in the following year (v. 11). During this time, Moses received the Law and many other instructions which would govern the nation's worship and conduct. A large portion of the Pentateuch (from Exodus 19 to Numbers 10) record God's dealings with Israel during this time. Verse 11 marks the beginning of the second major division in the book of Numbers – the Israelites were leaving Sinai and moving towards the Promised Land.

Two Silver Trumpets (vv. 1-28)

In this chapter we are introduced to two silver trumpets which were to be constructed and blown by the priests for various reasons, but chiefly to declare the mind of God to His people (vv. 3-8). The trumpets were also to be blown when man made a crucial appeal to God, such as on the eve of a battle (vv. 9-10). The former situation occurred in the wilderness only, and the latter usage permitted the people to ceremonially summon God's help while warring in "the land" (i.e., Canaan). John J. Stubbs observes:

> The trumpets when used in the wilderness were to bring God in remembrance before the people, but when used in the land against their enemy they were to bring the nation before God for remembrance. There are at least two occasions of warfare in their history where there is direct reference to the silver trumpets being used. The first time is in (31:1-6). This is the avenging war against the

Midianites. The other is the battle between King Abijah of Judah and King Jeroboam of Israel in (2 Chron. 13:12). The trumpets in the land would have been used in a ceremonial way. They were no longer used for guidance as in the wilderness, but possibly still had a practical use. But at the very sounding of these trumpets, Israel's army would be greatly strengthened in heart in the time of battle knowing that God was for them and would give them the victory.[37]

As already seen in Numbers 3, silver is associated with redemption throughout Scripture (e.g., Ex. 30). While traversing the wilderness, these two trumpets sounded out God's call to the redeemed to be heard and responded to. Jehovah was careful to ensure that the trumpets' sound was distinct so all could discern His intentions and so no family would pitch their tent too far away as to not hear the trumpet sound.

Although later, the trumpets were to be blown over sacrifices (v. 10), on feast days (29:1; Lev. 23:24), and when kings were anointed (1 Kgs. 1:34), the main focus of their use in this chapter is to call the people together, to move them out (v. 2), or to sound an alarm (v. 9). (The *showphar,* the ram's horn, was traditionally blown in the year of Jubilee, not the silver trumpets; Lev. 25:9.)

Given their intended purpose, the two silver trumpets represent God's ability to gather His people to Himself and then cause them to move forward in faith, that is, to go on with Him. In fact, every moment of the camp, whether festive, religious, hostile, or for journeying was directed by signals from one or both trumpets. The movement of the cloud over the camp conveyed a general sense of God's will (i.e., that it was time to go and the direction to go), but the trumpets blown by the priests communicated specific guidance for the camp's activities.

If both trumpets sounded a summons, then the entire congregation was to come promptly before the Lord at the tabernacle, but if only one trumpet was blown, only the leaders needed to respond (vv. 3-4). In a spiritual sense, the Lord continues to direct the affairs of His redeemed today as He once did by two silver trumpets. John even likens the sound of the Lord's voice to that of a trumpet (Rev. 1:10, 4:1). In this sense, the Lord summons the local assembly together on the first day of the week (Acts 20:7; 1 Cor. 14:23). This is a call that must not be ignored (Heb. 10:25). The Lord beckons all the redeemed to remember Him often through the breaking of the bread (Luke 22:19-20; 1 Cor. 11:23-25). Furthermore, believers today are waiting for the blast of the trumpet that will signal the Lord's coming for them. Then they will move out, so to speak, in an upward direction, and ever be with Him (1 Thess. 4:13-18).

The journeying of the camp was to be marked by precise order (vv. 5-8). This traveling protocol did not change throughout the Israelites' wilderness journey (vv. 13, 28). When the trumpets sounded the advance, the three tribes on the east side under Judah's standard moved forward (vv. 14-16). After the Gershonites and Merarites had finished dismantling the tabernacle and loading it onto covered carts they followed those under Judah's standard (v. 17).

The priests then blew the trumpets to signal the three southern tribes to move forward under Reuben's standard (vv. 18-20). Following them were the Kohathites carrying the holy articles of the tabernacle which had been previously covered by the priests for the journey (v. 21). This meant that the Gershonites and Merarites would arrive at the next camp site sufficiently ahead of the Kohathites to have the tabernacle set up to receive its furnishings. The next blast from the trumpets (the third and fourth signals are mentioned in the Septuagint, but not in the Hebrew text) caused the three tribes to the west under Ephraim's standard to move forward (vv. 22-24). The last signal from the trumpets caused the northern tribes under Dan's standard to join the long procession (vv. 25-27).

On the twentieth day of the second month in the second year (and just after the second Passover was completed) the cloud above the tabernacle moved from Mount Sinai – it was time to relocate the camp (vv. 11-12). Apparently, the cloud still sheltered the Israelites from the sun while traveling, but also stretched out ahead to point the way they should go (v. 34). Another possibility is that the tall pillar portion of the cloud situated over the tabernacle moved forward while the base portion of the cloud continued to shield the Israelites from the sun. After three days' journey, the cloud ceased to move and marked the new campsite, which was in the wilderness of Paran (vv. 12, 34).

Moses' Brother-in-Law (vv. 29-32)

A year earlier, not long after the Israelites first arrived at Mount Sinai, Moses father-in-law Jethro (Ex. 18:27) or Reuel (v. 29) and his son Hobab came to visit Moses. Jethro also brought Moses' wife Zipporah and their sons, Gershom and Eliezer, whom Moses had not seen in several months while in Egypt and while leading the Israelites to Mount Sinai. Jethro returned to Midian soon after delivering Moses' family to him (Ex. 18:27). Now, a year later, Hobab was also ready to return to his home. However, Moses petitioned Hobab to come with them to the Promised Land, saying that he would receive an inheritance there with Israel (v. 29). Hobab initially refused this offer (v. 30), but Moses pleaded with him more earnestly to remain with them.

Besides Hobab gaining an inheritance in Canaan, Moses also sought to benefit from Hobab's familiarity with the desert routes ahead of them (vv. 31-32). But was not Jehovah's cloud sufficient to guide the Jewish nation through the wilderness? This petitioning of Hobab is the first warning sign of the despair that will overtake Moses in the next chapter. When we begin to rely on human fortitude, instead of on God's wherewithal, it will not be long before we become burdened in His work and become self-focused. Jehovah did not need Hobab's insights to guide His people, and neither did Moses.

Moses did not record whether Hobab accepted his second offer or if he returned home. However, the book of Judges twice records the presence of Midianites in Canaan and states that they were descendants of Hobab and Moses' father-in-law (Judg. 1:16, 4:11).

The Battle Cry (vv. 35-36)

The chapter closes with Moses calling out a charge, a battle cry of sorts, at the beginning of the day's journey when the Ark was picked up by the Kohathites: *"Rise up, O Lord! Let Your enemies be scattered, and let those who hate You flee before You"* (v. 35). When the Ark rested at the end of the day's journey, Moses called out: *"Return, O Lord, to the many thousands of Israel"* (v. 36). These daily charges well characterize the years of warfare ahead for the Israelites after their wilderness experience concluded.

The two silver trumpets were blown by the priests to direct the affairs of the Jewish nation. Although Christians today are not under Law, they also enjoy priestly communion with God, which means they should not move or act apart from the divine testimony of God's Word and the prompting of His Spirit. God has shown us in Scripture how those in the Church Age should assemble together, and how to walk, to war, and to worship effectively. Consequently, F. B. Hole suggests that God is no less concerned today about the movement and resting of His people than He was during the original wilderness journey of the Israelites: "The church was 'scattered abroad,' in Acts 8:1, but in Acts

Refining and Reminding

9:31 we read, *'Then had the churches rest,'* and both things were under the control of the Lord."[38]

When the Lord seems to be silent, we must wait for His marching orders, and when He clearly says "go," we must rise up and move forward with Him. He put His people in proper order to be a testimony of Himself to onlookers. This also required that He put them under orders that He might accomplish all His purposes for them.

It is a great privilege to go on with the Lord and to face the unknowns and the challenges of the next day with confidence. The believer's union with Christ means that He meets every trial His redeemed encounter. This is why the Lord Jesus keenly felt Saul's attack on His Church (Acts 9:4). In Christ, we have resources to overcome whatever challenge we enter: *"For as the sufferings of Christ abound in us, so our consolation also abounds through Christ"* (2 Cor. 1:5). The Israelites enjoyed God's presence as they chose to walk with Him, but believers today are indwelt by God forever! What confidence the believer has then: Wherever I am – the Lord is there with me.

Meditation

> Just as a servant knows that he must first obey his master in all things, so the surrender to an implicit and unquestionable obedience must become the essential characteristic of our lives.
>
> — Andrew Murray

> Rest in this – it is God's business to lead, command, impel, send, call or whatever you want to call it. It is your business to obey, follow, move, respond, or what have you.
>
> — Jim Elliot

Murmuring, the Mixed Multitude, and Manna
Numbers 11:1-9

Fourteen months after being delivered from slavery in Egypt, and about a year after arriving at Mount Sinai, the Israelites were finally on their way to the Promised Land. They traveled three days before the cloud stopped to mark their new campsite. However, the tent pegs were barely pounded in the ground before the people's murmuring and complaining were heard by the Lord. The three-day march was physically exhausting and as we all know, the worst part of us just oozes out when we get fatigued.

This is a sorrowful chapter marked throughout by human failure. First, Moses, weary under the burden of leadership, complains to God. Second, in his jealousy for Moses, Joshua behaves rashly. Third, the people became contemptuous and doubted God's goodness to them. Despite these human failings and God's daily care of the nation, He is immediately prompted to assist His beloved servant who has slumped into despair. Be encouraged, dear believer, the Lord knows how to reach us where we are and how to get us to where we need to go!

Murmuring and Complaining (vv. 1-3)

Now when the people complained, it displeased the Lord; for the Lord heard it, and His anger was aroused. So the fire of the Lord burned among them, and consumed some in the outskirts of the camp. Then the people cried out to Moses, and when Moses prayed to the Lord, the fire was quenched. So he called the name of the place Taberah, because the fire of the Lord had burned among them (vv. 1-3).

Months earlier fire from the Lord devoured Nadab and Abihu, the two oldest sons of Aaron who had offered strange fire and incense to the Lord (Lev. 16:2). God is holy, and man can approach Him only in the way He deems as holy; two of Aaron's sons ignored God's revealed way. Now, the complainers, living as far from God as possible (on the

Refining and Reminding

fringes of the camp), were burnt by God's fire. We learn from these two instances that to live apart from God is death and to approach Him in our own way also results in death, or separation, *"for the wages of sin is death"* (Rom. 6:23). To experience His goodness we must approach Him through Christ's finished work alone and then remain near Him in purity and through confession of sin (1 Jn. 1:9).

God wants us to come near, but the only option is to do so in practical holiness and through His holy Way – the Lord Jesus Christ. The writer of Hebrews warns us that God has not changed, that *"we may serve God acceptably with reverence and godly fear. For our God is a consuming fire"* (Heb. 12:28-29). Coming out of Egypt, the Israelites did not have the Law, and therefore they were not punished for their earlier complaining (Rom. 5:13). But now they were under its judicial authority and the Lord would teach them about the consequences of sin and the necessity of their reverence and godly fear.

Yet, God is longsuffering, and His judgments against His people are tempered with mercy as shown in verse 1, in that God's anger had to be "aroused" or "kindled" (KJV) before it came forth in righteous indignation. The Hebrew word translated as "kindled" in the above verses is *charah*, which means "to grow warm." It is normally applied in a figurative sense, "to blaze up." The word describes the igniting of combustible materials and the nursing of the initial spark into the desired conflagration. Not only is God slow to be angry, but once provoked to anger, His anger fully develops before action is rendered. God's anger requires sufficient kindling before flaming vengeance is released. God shows us that righteous provocation and a period of anger development are necessary before proper action is discharged.

We must understand that God is not angry by nature but must be provoked to anger (Deut. 4:25, 9:18). As we see from the text, His anger has a building up time before causing Him to act (v. 1; Ex. 4:14). Thankfully, our God is slow to anger (Ps. 103:8-9, 145:8) and He is quick to forgive (Ps. 86:5). We would do well to imitate God's example when we become angry for a righteous cause!

Living a Christ-centered and disciplined life will reduce the number of occasions on which we feel inappropriately and unnecessarily angry. While in close fellowship with the Lord, the power of the Holy Spirit will effectively control and mold our anger to accomplish the righteousness of God – *"for the wrath of man does not produce the righteousness of God"* (Jas. 1:20). However, God's wrath does uphold

His righteousness: *"For the wrath of God is revealed from heaven against all ungodliness and unrighteousness of men, who suppress the truth in unrighteousness"* (Rom. 1:18). And as Paul confirms, *"the wrath of God is coming upon the sons of disobedience"* (Col. 3:6). Accordingly, may we not be numbered with or imitate rebellious complainers who burden God's heart.

The murmuring of the people greatly displeased the Lord, which aroused His anger and His chastening hand. However, the humble intercessor, Moses, cried out to the Lord on behalf of those under judgment and God's indignation was stayed. Because God's wrath had burned among them Moses called the place *Taberah*.

The Mixed Multitude (vv. 4-6)

But the smoke rising from smoldering bodies had barely been extinguished when "the mixed multitude" among the Israelites began to lust after the staples of Egypt. Their lusting stirred up others in the camp to complain against the Lord also. They lamented, *"Why did we ever come up out of Egypt?"* (v. 20).

Who was this "mixed multitude?" The supernatural feats of Jehovah in Egypt had inspired many Egyptians to depart with the Jews. Why did these pagans leave their homes, their people, and their way of life to venture into a desert with their liberated slave population? Perhaps it was because Egypt had been decimated by plagues and there was nothing left to live for in Egypt. Exodus 12:43 forbade any foreigner from eating the Passover, which meant the Egyptians traveling with the Israelites had not been redeemed by a lamb's blood, and therefore they had suffered the death of the firstborn among them.

Perhaps there were some Egyptians who became Jewish proselytes (these would be permitted to eat the Passover), but that fact is not recorded in Scripture. Rather, this group of foreigners is referred to as "rabble" (v. 4 NASV). They complained against Jehovah despite His goodness to them in the wilderness (because they were with the Israelites), and they stirred up the Jews to voice dissatisfaction also. The carnal man longs to feed on the things of the world and this mixed multitude lusted for the fancies of Egypt; they were not humbled by Jehovah's magnificent presence or satisfied with His simple provisions.

The mixed multitude caused the Israelites to crave what God had determined was not necessary for their diet and to loathe what He had provided to sustain them. He had given them manna, but they still had the taste of the world in their mouths. They craved the flesh pots, the fish from the Nile, and fresh vegetables they had enjoyed in Egypt:

> *Now the mixed multitude who were among them yielded to intense craving; so the children of Israel also wept again and said: "Who will give us meat to eat? We remember the fish which we ate freely in Egypt, the cucumbers, the melons, the leeks, the onions, and the garlic; but now our whole being is dried up; there is nothing at all except this manna before our eyes!"* (vv. 4-6).

F. B. Hole observes that Satan's tactic of mixing his people with God's people for the purpose of corrupting them and thwarting the work of God is a common ploy by the enemy:

> To corrupt by introducing a mixture is a very common and very successful device of Satan. Directly God called a people out of Egypt to Himself, the "mixed multitude" appears. The same thing we see in principle in Matthew 13 [in the parable of the wheat and the tares].[39]

C. H. Mackintosh also highlights the crippling influence of the mixed multitude on those who would seek to follow the Lord:

> There is nothing more damaging to the cause of Christ or to the souls of His people than association with men of *mixed* principles. It is very much more dangerous than having to do with open and avowed enemies. Satan knows this well, and hence his constant effort to lead the Lord's people to link themselves with those who are only half and half; or, on the other hand, to introduce spurious materials – false professors – into the midst of those who are seeking, in any measure, to pursue a path of separation from the world.[40]

Many of our failures in life can be attributed to having the wrong view of what a wilderness experience is all about. If new converts would realize that they are destined for disappointments, hardships, and persecution because of their identification with Christ, then every provision of God's grace in the wilderness would be answered with joyful praise. But if the new believer starts out on his or her wilderness journey expecting ease and rest in the world, the relentless hardships to follow will be overwhelming. The book of Numbers is a slap in the face to the *Prosperity Gospel* message often preached today by those desiring the benefits of the cross, but denying its demands (Luke 9:23-26).

Every devoted Christian is destined for trouble, but not for despair: *"Yes, and all who desire to live godly in Christ Jesus will suffer persecution"* (2 Tim. 3:12). It is a promise of God that if you live to serve Christ, you will suffer for it. Dear believer, do not expect anything less and you will not be disappointed (1 Pet. 1:13). Prepare your mind for the struggles ahead, and don't get bogged down in self-pity, grappling with despair when those forecasted storms of life do arrive. Every Christian who righteously suffers for the cause of Christ will be rewarded: *"If we suffer, we shall also reign with Him"* (2 Tim. 2:12, KJV).

Murmuring and complaining must be replaced by thanksgiving and contentment, which are closely related. Paul informed the Christians at Philippi what he had learned about these two virtues:

> *For I have learned in whatever state I am, to be content: I know how to be abased, and I know how to abound. Everywhere and in all things I have learned both to be full and to be hungry, both to abound and to suffer need. I can do all things through Christ who strengthens me* (Phil. 4:11-13).

Paul instructed Timothy, *"Now godliness with contentment is great gain ... having food and clothing, with these we shall be content"* (1 Tim. 6:6-8). Verse 10 of that chapter speaks of those who were neither content nor thankful for what God had provided. They coveted money and erred from the faith. If God wanted us to have more than what we have, He would have bestowed it upon us. Being thankful defeats dissatisfaction.

The most common cause of sin seems to be dissatisfaction, with selfishness and pride trailing close behind. When we are not content with what we have, we murmur against God. Murmuring is half-uttered complaints that God fully hears anyway. It results from looking backwards instead of Godward. The nation of Israel grumbled and complained the whole time they were in the Sinai Peninsula. Why? It was because they were always comparing what they presently had to that which they once had in Egypt – in slavery!

We complain and grumble today because our expectations are not met in comparison to what we had the previous month, whereas last month we complained because our expectations were not satisfied

Refining and Reminding

when compared to the preceding month. Looking backwards to that which once was and comparing it to our wanton desires leads to complaining. The spiritual response to life's difficulties should be to ponder potential God-honoring outcomes, to be thankful in all things, and to cease bemoaning our current predicament. We will find this mindset much easier to grasp if we do not peer back into history to compare where we once were to someone else's circumstances, or our previous ones to our present situation.

> *Every good gift and every perfect gift is from above, and comes down from the Father of lights, with whom there is no variation or shadow of turning* (Jas. 1:17).

The children of Israel were being led by God into consecutive wilderness experiences – this was for the purpose of testing and perfecting them. His provision of bread from Heaven (manna) was all they needed to be sustained through it.

Manna (vv. 7-9)

The Israelites would soon learn that the world's diet is not what the child of God should want to eat, that is, what the world offers the believer will never strengthen him, spiritually speaking. The Lord has a diet and a training program to mature His people and properly prepare them for warfare and what He would have them do. Moses describes God's provision of manna for the Israelites:

> *Now the manna was like coriander seed, and its color like the color of bdellium. The people went about and gathered it, ground it on millstones or beat it in the mortar, cooked it in pans, and made cakes of it; and its taste was like the taste of pastry prepared with oil. And when the dew fell on the camp in the night, the manna fell on it* (vv. 7-9).

An immense supply of food was needed to sustain two million people in a desolate wilderness. The main item on the menu was something never before seen by human eyes; the people called it manna, which literally means, "What is it?" Manna was small in size (similar to a hoar frost), white in color (like a coriander seed), round in shape, and tasted like a wafer made with honey (Ex. 16:14, 31). A year earlier, Jehovah said that He would furnish a normal portion of manna

Devotions in Numbers

six days each week, with a double portion on Fridays to supply Saturday's Sabbath Day needs. Without fail, for over a year, God delivered manna from heaven to His people as promised.

The Lord Jesus spoke of Himself being the Bread of Life which came down from heaven, and then explained what it meant to feed upon Him. He likened the Israelites, who fed daily upon the manna in the wilderness for physical survival, to a believer who feeds daily upon Him in order to have the spiritual strength to live for Him.

> *Then Jesus said to them, "Most assuredly, I say to you, Moses did not give you the bread from heaven, but My Father gives you the true bread from heaven. For the bread of God is He who comes down from heaven and gives life to the world." Then they said to Him, "Lord, give us this bread always." And Jesus said to them, "I am the bread of life. He who comes to Me shall never hunger, and he who believes in Me shall never thirst"* (John 6:32-35).

To eat of the Bread of Life is the same as to trust Christ for salvation (John 6:35, 50-57). His redemptive work at Calvary would then be appropriated by all those who would personally exercise faith in Him. Then believers are to continually feed on Him, that is, those who read and mentally digest His Word will find help and guidance for each day. Those who spend time with the Lord learn of Him and of His will; Christ speaks to believers in the quietness of His presence. The main reason the Church is spiritually weak and frail today is not because it lacks spiritual food and drink, but because many of her members refuse to be strengthened by that which Christ has provided for them.

Physically, we are what we eat; spiritually speaking, we are what we think upon: *"For as he thinks in his heart, so is he"* (Prov. 23:7). What we spend our time thinking upon will ultimately determine if our inner man (Eph. 3:16) or our flesh is being strengthened, and which nature will likely triumph when we are tested or tempted.

Eating of the Bread of Life confers eternal salvation, and continuing to feed on Him is the only spiritual food which satisfies the human soul and strengthens the inner man for spiritual conflict. Just as the Israelites had to eat manna in the wilderness to live, the believer will be destitute of spiritual vigor unless he or she consistently feeds on the Bread of Life. The manna of Exodus and the Bread of Life of John 6 have a

Refining and Reminding

number of specific typological correlations and contrasts. Both the manna to the Israelites and Christ to the world:

1. Were a supernatural gift from God (rained down from heaven vs. directly from heaven's throne).
2. Were supplied where the people were (in the wilderness vs. in the world).
3. Were to be eaten (to sustain physical life vs. to obtain spiritual life in Christ).
4. Were to be gathered daily (each morning vs. throughout each day).
5. Were obtained by labor (going out to gather vs. meditation on God's Word).
6. Were not to be neglected (turned to worms vs. lost opportunities to know and serve).
7. Were incomprehensible to the natural man (not natural vs. obviously supernatural).
8. Were despised by the mixed multitude (hated by the Egyptians vs. despised by the world).
9. Were preserved for future generations (placed in the ark vs. the eternal Word).
10. Were supplied until the destination was reached (ceased at Canaan vs. grace received by faith will no longer be needed in heaven).[41]

Personally appropriating the finished work of Christ by faith is the only means of gaining Christ's life, and obeying His Word the only means of living it out for Him. His Word is our spiritual food for each day! No believer can gather another's manna; each one must personally meditate on the Word of God to obtain his or her provision of grace for the day.

Christ alone is the true "bread from heaven" which brings life and deliverance – He is all we need for daily living. But, like the Israelites of old after the first joy of our spiritual deliverance is past, we also are prone to lust for the carnal things of Egypt which we relished in our unconverted state. This is especially true when our spiritual walk with the Lord is difficult.

Meditation

> Adore and tremble, for our God is a consuming fire!
> His jealous eyes His wrath inflame, and raise His vengeance higher.

Yet, mighty God, Thy sovereign grace sits regent on the throne;
The refuge of Thy chosen race when wrath comes rushing down.

— Isaac Watts

Stumbling, the Seventy, and the Quail
Numbers 11:10-35

Moses Stumbles (vv. 10-15)

The "mixed multitude" caused the Israelites to murmur against the Lord and to doubt His goodness, but that was not the only effect of their carnality. Verses 10-15 reveal how deeply Moses, burdened by the leadership of an obstinate people, was affected also. He complained to the Lord about the immense responsibility he had as Israel's leader:

> *Why have You afflicted Your servant? And why have I not found favor in Your sight, that You have laid the burden of all these people on me? Did I conceive all these people? Did I beget them, that You should say to me, "Carry them in your bosom, as a guardian carries a nursing child," to the land which You swore to their fathers? Where am I to get meat to give to all these people? For they weep all over me, saying, "Give us meat, that we may eat." I am not able to bear all these people alone, because the burden is too heavy for me. If You treat me like this, please kill me here and now – if I have found favor in Your sight – and do not let me see my wretchedness!"* (vv. 11-15).

Moses felt that he could not go on "carrying," so to speak, all the Israelites to the Promised Land. If the Lord was not going to offload his responsibility, he asked the Lord to kill him. It is not wise to give *if-then* ultimatums to the Lord – for these elevate our reasoning above His providential care and pre-determined prerogatives. Being overwhelmed by the sense of endless burden, Moses had forgotten that all of his responsibility really rested upon God rather than himself. E. L. Bevir provides this insightful assessment of Moses' mental state at this juncture:

> Moses in this chapter feels that the burden is too much for him, and ends his first discourse in verse 15 with a petition to be "killed out of hand." He appears, all through the passage, to great advantage as a

noble and disinterested soul, but, occupied with himself and his own resources, he felt himself unable to accomplish the task of leading the people through the wilderness. It is a very remarkable thing that the two grand figures of the Old Testament, Moses and Elijah, both begged to be allowed to die in peace. Death is a sovereign remedy for an energetic person, whose task is too hard for him; and surely neither Moses nor Elijah were wanting in energy; but they had to learn that it was not *their* power or energy that could accomplish their tasks, though they never could have known what the great Apostle to the Gentiles speaks of in 2 Corinthians; that is, the power of the resurrection, and the full and perfect mistrust of all that is of the natural man.

The word "I" is found very frequently in Moses' speeches in this chapter, and when this (I, me) becomes the object of our thoughts, we generally find words to express them. Moses had said, *"I am not eloquent.... I am slow of speech, and of a slow tongue"* (Ex. 4:10); but he becomes eloquent when "Moses" is the theme of his discourse (vv. 21-22); he finds the use of his tongue in describing his own difficulty; and that is natural to all men.

But the great and blessed lesson to be learnt in this remarkable passage is the faithfulness of God whilst chastening His rebellious and lusting people, and the boundless resources of Jehovah in the wilderness when, to all appearance, everything had come to a dead stop, and the mere energy of man is proved to be nothing worth. Nothing could be more interesting to us at the present time, when the enlightened leaders of the nineteenth century, leaving God out of their calculations, assure us that it was physically impossible for Israel to cross the desert, and when not a few may be found following the mixed multitude in all manner of worldliness and self-seeking.[42]

Depressed people rarely think straight, and clearly Moses' anger, despair, and prayer are all misplaced. The unbelief, murmuring, and demands of the people had prompted Moses' emotional breakdown; in striking contrast is the Lord's kindness to encourage and strengthen His fainting servant. It was neither the Lord's plan to take Moses' life nor to remove him from his responsibility. Yet, no condescending words or rebuke are heard; instead the Lord immediately provides seventy Spirit-empowered helpers to assist His servant in guiding the people.

The Seventy Elders (vv. 16-30)

The number seventy is associated with the nation of Israel in a special way throughout Scripture (Ex. 1:5). Genesis 46 provides the first roster of the nation, which includes the names of those in Jacob's family who traveled with him to Egypt. In all, twelve sons, fifty-three grandsons, four great-grandsons, one daughter Dinah, and one granddaughter Serah are named. Although Jacob had four wives, other daughters and granddaughters (Gen. 46:7) they are not included in this number, nor were his son's wives or grandson's wives. As women were not included in any Israelite census, it seems likely that Dinah and Serah are only mentioned as substitutes for the two sons of Judah, Er and Onan, who were judged by God in Canaan. Hence the symbolism of seventy as representing Israel is preserved. Counting Joseph and his two sons, who were already in Egypt, and Jacob himself, the total number of persons composing the nation of Israel at this time was stated to be seventy, though clearly there were dozens of females beyond this figure (Gen. 46:5).

God now appointed seventy elders to shepherd His people for centuries to come (v. 16). During New Testament times, there were seventy members of the Sanhedrin and seventy witnesses sent out to Israel by Christ (Luke 10:1). This thread of seventy and Israel can also be seen in the books of Jeremiah and Daniel where it relates to the regathering of the Jewish people to their homeland (i.e., in the seventieth week).

Although these seventy men would be a help to Moses in judging the people in the future, it is important to understand that more men did not mean more spiritual power. The same Spirit of God who had come upon Moses to empower his leadership was also given to the seventy elders. So more men could never mean more power from God's perspective; it was only what His Spirit accomplished through them that mattered to Him. So in retrospect, although the seventy would assist Moses, his complaining and the repercussion of it cost him a measure of dignity. A similar consequence had happened at his commissioning at the burning bush less than two years earlier. His excuses caused God to place Aaron at Moses' side, and thus some of the honor God wanted to bestow on Moses was transferred to Aaron.

In His letter to the vibrant and evangelical church at Philadelphia, the Lord Jesus said, *"Behold, I am coming quickly! Hold fast what you have, that no one may take your crown"* (Rev. 3:11). There was no

Devotions in Numbers

rebuke for this church, but the Lord knows our human tendency to pull back when things get tough; thus, the warning. The meaning of the message is that if you are not willing to do the Lord's bidding, He will find someone else to do it; then, that person will get the reward that could have been yours.

Though Moses had stumbled by complaining to the Lord, we also see the humility of the Lord's servant after the Holy Spirit came upon the seventy elders God had appointed. This was a one-time event during the dispensation of the Law that initially confirmed God's chosen leaders to the people, as the Israelites heard them all prophesying. Two of the seventy elders (Eldad and Medad) were not before the Lord at the tabernacle, but were still in the camp when this occurred. It was not appropriate for them to still be in the camp – they should have been standing with Moses after being summoned. But God overlooked this infraction and poured out His Spirit on all the chosen – His gift to Moses.

Joshua heard Eldad and Medad prophesying in the camp and wanted these two men silenced because of their indiscretion, but Moses forbad him from doing so. He responded that he would desire all God's people to be controlled by the Holy Spirit and to acknowledge God's word, and to this we add our "Amen."

Moses' humble response to Joshua's request stands in sharp contrast to Joshua's misplaced jealousy. F. B. Hole and C. H. Mackintosh both applaud Moses' meek character, respectively:

> Envy might have found a place in the heart of Joshua but it had no place in the heart of Moses. The desire for preeminence, which is so rooted in the mind of the natural man, had no place with him. He displayed very clearly that meekness which is attributed to him in verse 3 of the next chapter. When 40 years old, he was *not very meek* (Ex. 2:12); now after the 40 years' discipline from God in Midian, he is *very meek* though he had become *very great* (Ex. 11:3) in the eyes of the world.[43]

> This is perfectly beautiful. Moses was far removed from that wretched spirit of envy which would let no one speak but himself. He was prepared, by grace, to rejoice in any and every manifestation of true spiritual power, no matter where or through whom. He knew full well that there could be no right prophesying but by the power of the

Refining and Reminding

Spirit of God; and wherever that power was exhibited, who was he that he should seek to quench or hinder?[44]

Moses experienced what David later would find out to be true: *"The Lord is near to those who have a broken heart, and saves such as have a contrite spirit"* (Ps. 34:18). Truly, on this particular occasion, the Lord saved Moses from Moses.

On this side of glory, God's servants are not perfect and will experience failures in their doings and attitudes. Thankfully, failures are never final unless we make them so – God wants us to succeed. *"For a just man falls seven times and rises up again"* (Prov. 24:16). It is not falling that makes one a failure; it is remaining submersed in our failures and wallowing in our self-pity that makes us a failure. Moses stumbled, but he did not stay down. May we also learn from our mistakes and failures, rise up in grace, and go on humbly with the Lord.

The Quail (vv. 31-35)

The Lord had a practical lesson in mind to confront His people's lusting; He was going to provide them with so much meat that in time they would detest it. Moses told the people to sanctify themselves because on the next day they would receive enough meat for an entire month (vv. 18-29). As far as the Lord was concerned, they could gorge themselves until it came out their nostrils (v. 20). This, of course, was a satirical hyperbole to express what God wanted them to learn from the experience: those who reject His best for an alternative will later realize that what they thought was more desirable to have – was not.

Moses response to the Lord's promise is another indication that he was suffering from spiritual distress. As Elijah experienced centuries later, this crippling mental condition can beset any of the Lord's servants when their expectation for ministry is not realized. The same one who had commanded Jehovah's ten plagues in Egypt, had opened the Red Sea by lifting his rod, had witnessed His awesome presence at Mount Sinai, and had eaten His provision of manna for over a year now doubted God's ability to provide sufficient meat for His people in the wilderness (v. 21).

From a rational standpoint, Moses knew there was not enough livestock in all of Israel, nor fish to be taken from the sea, to set meat before 600,000 men (in addition to their families) for an entire month (v. 22). No doubt Moses remembered how the Lord provided quail for the Israelites to eat in the evening and manna in the morning just after they departed from Egypt (Ex. 16:13), but that was meat for an evening, not for an entire month. Furthermore, they were now camped in the Wilderness of Paran in the northeastern portion of the Sinai Peninsula – far away from where the quail had been provided previously.

Moses's lapse of faith, however, did confirm that there was no obvious solution to accomplish what God promised to do. This meant that what God intended to do was beyond any natural explanation – a miracle by definition! Without proper understanding of natural order, we would not recognize a miracle if it were staring us in the face, but through science we can understand our surroundings sufficiently to notice what cannot be explained, naturally speaking.

The Lord's retort to Moses' doubting was terse, *"Has the Lord's arm been shortened? Now you shall see whether what I say will happen to you or not"* (v. 23). Moses needed spiritual strengthening, so not only would Jehovah teach His people about the ills of lusting for what was outside His will, but He would also reinvigorate Moses' faith by fulfilling His word quickly. So after the Lord put His Spirit on the seventy chosen elders, He was determined to fulfill His promise concerning the quail the very next day:

> *Now a wind went out from the Lord, and it brought quail from the sea and left them fluttering near the camp, about a day's journey on this side and about a day's journey on the other side, all around the camp, and about two cubits above the surface of the ground. And the people stayed up all that day, all night, and all the next day, and gathered the quail (he who gathered least gathered ten homers); and they spread them out for themselves all around the camp. But while the meat was still between their teeth, before it was chewed, the wrath of the Lord was aroused against the people, and the Lord struck the people with a very great plague. So he called the name of that place Kibroth Hattaavah, because there they buried the people who had yielded to craving* (vv. 31-34).

Psalm 78:26 indicates that God used a strong southeast wind to provide the quail. That would mean the Lord blew quail migrating northward along the Gulf of Aqaba into the camp. Actually, the flight path of the quail covered several miles (a day's journey) on either side of the camp. This meant that the Israelites could spread out over a vast region to harvest the birds. Quail are heavy birds in respect to their short wingspan and usually fly low to the ground. The text says that they were flying about three feet off the ground, which meant the people could easily net the birds or even club them, if they preferred. For two days and a night, the Israelites took advantage of the overflight and the least of them gathered ten homers. A homer is the equivalent of about sixty gallons and there are 9.3 gallons to a bushel. This meant that each person gathered at least sixty-four bushels of quail.

It is likely that the bird associated with this miracle was the *Cotumix-cotumix* or the common quail. These birds winter in African lands and migrate north into Europe during the months of March and April. Adult birds would be about eight inches in height and weigh about 5 ounces. If we assume the volume of eight birds would be equivalent to a gallon, that would mean that a minimum of 4,800 birds were harvested by each person. It is likely that women and children assisted in the gathering process and then helped lay birds out to dry in the sun. But even if only the 600,000 men gathered the birds, that would still mean that about 3 billion quail were collected! That would be about 1,500 birds for every man, woman, and child in the camp, or about fifty birds a day for each person for a month.

Obviously, this was more meat than could possibly be consumed no matter how hearty someone's appetite might be. It was more than anyone would ever want to consume and that was the point of the lesson. The people had disdained the Lord's provision of plain manna and wanted what they thought was better – meat. And when He did provide them with meat, the people, carried away by lust, killed far too many birds. From a practical standpoint, they probably killed four or five times the number of birds they could ever consume in a month.

Our carnal whims loathe moderation and on this day the Israelites were clearly ruled by their stomachs. Consequently, their own obsessive gratification would determine the measure by which God would punish Israel's ingratitude and greed. *"He gave them their request, but sent leanness into their soul"* (Ps. 106:15). Though the supply of birds was abundant, the providential care of God ensured that what His people lusted for would be shown to never satisfy their souls. C. A. Coates reminds us that indulging in permissible things can easily become evil and can war against our soul if we crave more than what is prudent or lawful:

The "flesh" which the people craved was what would suit the taste of men as men. Not necessarily bad things, as men would judge, but things that minister to natural tastes. It is figurative of all the things that have been introduced to attract people, and to keep them together. They have, to a large extent, got what they want, but oh! what spiritual leanness goes with it![45]

There are times that we should not ask God for what we want, but it will always be profitable for us to ask Him what He wants us to have and to help us want only that! Moses learned that even when he prayed outside of God's best for him, the Lord still did what was most profitable for him. Our aspiration should be to always pray in the Spirit (Eph. 6:18), but when we do not, we know that our blessed heavenly Father will do only what is best for us, for *"every good gift and every perfect gift is from above, and comes down from the Father of lights, with whom there is no variation or shadow of turning"* (Jas. 1:17).

Because the Israelites rejected God's best for them and were rather given over to out-of-control craving, He sent a plague on them and many died (vv. 33-34). Not only were there many corpses throughout the camp that needed to be buried, but the stench of so much unconsumed flesh and the innards of the dressed birds would have created a nauseating environment to live in. Yet, the Lord kept them immersed in it for an entire month. This would cause them to appreciate the cost of lusting for what God disapproved of. It also caused them to anticipate journeying again with a bit more enthusiasm than their first excursion.

Paul reminds us that this narrative and others like it were recorded for *"our examples, to the intent that we should not lust after evil things as they also lusted. ... Now all these things happened to them as examples, and they were written for our admonition"* (1 Cor. 10:6, 11). May we heed God's disciplinary dealings with Israel who lusted for what was beyond God's will for them, lest we also invite God's chastening hand for our own carnality.

After a month, the Lord moved the Israelites from Kibroth Hattaavah (meaning "the graves of lust") to Hazeroth (v. 35).

Meditation

I have been learning all along my pilgrim journey that the more my heart is taken up with Christ, the more do I enjoy practical

Refining and Reminding

deliverance from sin's power, and the more do I realize what it is to have the love of God shed abroad in that heart by the Holy Spirit given to me, as the earnest of the glory to come.

— H. S. Ironside

Aaron and Miriam's Dissent
Numbers 12

The Challenge (vv. 1-2)

In Numbers 1, the Lord confronted murmuring, complaining, envy, and despair among His people through various means. In this chapter, the serious offense of dissension against Moses, His chosen leader, occurred shortly after departing Mount Sinai:

> *Then Miriam and Aaron spoke against Moses because of the Ethiopian woman whom he had married; for he had married an Ethiopian woman. So they said, "Has the Lord indeed spoken only through Moses? Has He not spoken through us also?" And the Lord heard it. (Now the man Moses was very humble, more than all men who were on the face of the earth.)* (vv. 1-3).

This entire scene is an interruption in Israel's journey to the Promised Land. Two questions should be answered before exploring the text in order to better understand the situation before us. First, why did Moses, at the age of 81 or 82, abruptly marry an Ethiopian (a Cushite) woman when he already was married to Zipporah (Ex. 2:21)? Second, why would Aaron and Miriam suddenly challenge their younger brother's leadership in Israel seeing all that God had done through him the last two years?

The most likely answer to the first question is that Zipporah, his wife of nearly forty years, had died. She was not an old woman, for she probably had just weaned Eliezer, who had been circumcised just fourteen months earlier. When Moses had initially set out for Egypt, he had set Zipporah and both their sons, Gershom and Eliezer, on one donkey (Ex. 4:20). So if Zipporah had died suddenly, that would make Moses solely responsible for the care of his two children, one of whom was a toddler. Certainly, Moses loved his sons and would want to take good care of them, but he had a dilemma. He also was God's appointed leader of the Jewish nation, a task that consumed much of his time.

Refining and Reminding

Marrying a second wife (a nanny, so to speak) was a natural solution to ensure none of his obligations were neglected.

If this reasoning is correct, it may help explain Moses' despair in the previous chapter; he may have been grieving over Zipporah's death, which had likely been unexpected. Being nomadic from her birth and accustomed to frequent desert journeys, and not an Egyptian, it seems doubtful that Zipporah would have been judged with the complainers in the previous chapter. This may also explain why Hobab wanted to depart to his Midianite home – his sister and only close relative still residing with the Jews had died.

But why did Moses marry an Ethiopian woman and not a Hebrew woman? Being a devoted Jehovah-worshipper, Moses would never have married a pagan, so his new wife must have been a proselyte (a converted Jew, so to speak). Even Zipporah was a Midianite – a descendant of Abraham through Keturah, Abraham's second wife after Sarah died (Gen. 25:1-2). Coming from Abraham, the Midianites were, generally speaking, monotheistic in their beliefs, although some, as we shall see, were influenced by the paganism of Moab and Canaan (Num. 25).

Because Moses' new wife was not a Hebrew, there would be no concern of her trying to assume any authority among the Jews, for she, a foreigner, would have no social status. The marriage does not seem to be for the purpose of producing children, at least none are recorded in Scripture from this union. That would also prevent possible issues later of rights and inheritance matters, as tribes were not to intermarry to ensure no tribal inheritance would be lost in the Promised Land. Moses' marriage to a Cushite was not prohibited, although marriages later with those in Canaan were (Ex. 34:11-16). It seems likely that Moses married the Ethiopian woman to care for his young sons so that no future power struggles or inheritance issues would arise.

Albert Barnes suggests that Zipporah's death is the correct answer to the first question, which then answers the second inquiry, as to why Aaron and Miriam chose this particular time to challenge Moses' leadership:

> It is likely that Zipporah was dead, and that Miriam in consequence expected to have greater influence than ever with Moses. Her disappointment at his second marriage would consequently be very great.[46]

Miriam was a prophetess, and had led the women in jubilant singing of Moses' song after Pharaoh's army was wiped out in the Red Sea. The prophet Micah lists her name with Moses and Aaron as important individuals whom God had sent to benefit Israel (Mic. 6:4). However, her calling as a prophetess did not authorize Miriam to usurp Moses' leadership. Miriam appears to be the instigator of this sibling rivalry, as her name appears first and the Hebrew verb *dabar* translated "spoke" is feminine singular. The text could be rendered, "she spoke against." Miriam persuaded her brother Aaron to her way of thinking, and he merely went along with Miriam in this insurrection, rather than driving it. Her seeking more influence over Israel and being the inciter of the challenge partially explains why she was judged more severely than Aaron.

Furthermore, Aaron was Israel's high priest. He represented the nation to God, and if he had been struck with leprosy, he would have been unable to offer worship to Jehovah on behalf of the people. It would not be fitting for the sin of two people to hinder two million Jews from worshipping their God in the way He had commanded.

As we review how Miriam, Aaron, and Moses were called to serve God, J. N. Darby suggests that we find a helpful application in Miriam and Aaron's error for the Church to consider today:

> When the members of the church, in the thought of making themselves spiritual, take advantage of their glory and position as prophets and priests (characters which do indeed belong to them) to disown the rights of Christ, as king in Jeshurun, having authority over the house of God, there is room for considering whether they are not guilty of the rebellion here spoken of. For my part, I believe they are.[47]

F. B. Hole also highlights the importance of heeding the lesson to be learned from the narrative:

> Aaron and Miriam made the bold claim that Jehovah had equally spoken by them – that their utterances should be accepted as an inspired revelation from Him. ... During the church's history, sad to say, similar false claims have been made all too frequently; and are even made today by men who claim that what they say is to be received as a word inspired of God.[48]

Refining and Reminding

Indeed, any proclamation of God's word or intercession to God on the behalf of others today must always remain under the headship and priesthood of Christ. We are not to proclaim as truth what He has not endorsed as being so, and we are not to request Him to do what His character rejects. Matters of obedience should never be prayed about, just surrendered to. The Lord Jesus will honor only what honors Himself, and further proclaims the glory of God.

From a dispensational standpoint, notice that Moses' first marriage to a Midianite and his second marriage to an Ethiopian foreshadow the future extension of God's blessings to the Gentiles through His New Covenant with Israel (Ps. 45:9; Heb. 8:8). Although the Lord Jesus told several parables hinting at this future reality (e.g., Luke 20:9-18), it was not fully revealed until the time of the apostles. Paul was chosen to explain this wonderful mystery which had been concealed since the beginning of the world in the far recesses of God's own mind:

> *You have heard of the dispensation of the grace of God which was given to me for you, how that by revelation He made known to me the mystery (as I have briefly written already, by which, when you read, you may understand my knowledge in the mystery of Christ), which in other ages was not made known to the sons of men, as it has now been revealed by the Spirit to His holy apostles and prophets: that the Gentiles should be fellow heirs, of the same body, and partakers of His promise in Christ through the gospel* (Eph. 3:2-6).

So Miriam and Aaron's discontent represents, in type, Jewish resentment of their promised blessings in Christ being made available to Gentiles because of their unbelief at His first advent (Rom. 11:13-25).

Two Responses to the Challenge (vv. 3-12)

Miriam and Aaron were permitted to voice only two questions against Moses' authority before the Lord, who knew what was in their hearts, intervened to end their revolt. Moses, being a meek man (v. 3), did not answer their defiance; he did not need to, for *"the Lord lifts up the humble and He casts the wicked down to the ground"* (Ps. 147:6).

> Humility is perfect quietness of heart. It is to expect nothing, to wonder at nothing that is done to me, to feel nothing done against me. It is to be at rest when nobody praises me, and when I am blamed or

despised. It is to have a blessed home in the Lord, where I can go in and shut the door, and kneel to my Father in secret, and am at peace as in a deep sea of calmness, when all around and above is trouble.

—Andrew Murray

The Lord summoned the three to the tabernacle and appeared before them in a pillar of cloud at its entrance (v. 4). He commanded Aaron and Miriam to step forward, before He charged them (v. 5):

Hear now My words: If there is a prophet among you, I, the Lord, make Myself known to him in a vision; I speak to him in a dream. Not so with My servant Moses; He is faithful in all My house. I speak with him face to face, even plainly, and not in dark sayings; and he sees the form of the Lord. Why then were you not afraid to speak against My servant Moses? (vv. 6-8).

It should have been evident to everyone, that Jehovah had a special and unique relationship with Moses, whom He spoke with face to face. The logic of the Lord's argument is, of course, sound: Seeing that Moses enjoyed such close communion with the Lord, who would dare speak against him? God's question is a direct rebuke of Aaron and Miriam's two questions.

Furthermore, Moses' special relationship and ministry (though not perfect) typified Christ's calling and His communion with His Father during His earthly sojourn. Hence, as J. N. Darby explains, an attack on Moses quickly prompted God's rebuke:

Miriam and Aaron speak against Moses. It is the prophetess and the priest (one who has the word from God and access to God, the twofold character of the people of God) who rise up against him who is king in Jeshurun, with whom God speaks as unto His friend. In this Moses is in all respects a type of Christ, who stands personally outside the rights which grace has conferred upon the people. Faithful in all the house of God, he enjoys close intercourse with Him. Miriam and Aaron ought to have been afraid.[49]

God was angry with them and when He finished speaking, the cloud departed, and Miriam was struck with leprosy (v. 9). "When God goes," says Matthew Henry, "evil comes: expect no good when God departs."[50] As a priest, Aaron was to be the judge of leprosy; it is therefore ironic that his very first pronouncement of "unclean" was likely against his own sister (v. 10; Lev. 13). Being equally as guilty as she, he could not have declared her uncleanness without trembling before the Lord in fear and shame for himself.

Aaron, being the High Priest, was in a position to petition God on behalf of his sister, but instead, he shows repentance and contrition by requesting Moses to intervene on her behalf: *"Oh, my lord! Please do not lay this sin on us, in which we have done foolishly and in which we have sinned. Please do not let her be as one dead, whose flesh is half consumed when he comes out of his mother's womb!"* (vv. 11-12). Aaron asked Moses not to permit their sister to be like a stillborn child, whose flesh is partly decomposed at birth.

Miriam and Aaron had exhibited self-assertiveness, the opposite of meekness. If Moses had not excelled in meekness, he also may have been tempted to violate God's prophetic office by introducing his own words and misrepresenting God to others. But Moses was a faithful servant and would not intrude into what would have certainly invoked God's anger, harmed God's people, and resulted in his own shame. Moses chose to speak to God in humble faith, rather than to speak for God with carnal motives. Oh that the people of God would heed this example!

Moses' response to the challenge was one of meekness, forgiveness, and intercession. He chose not to defend himself, for he knew that his God was quite able to protect and vindicate him!

Moses Intercedes (vv. 13-14)

Moses quickly reacted to Aaron's confession and plea: *"Please heal her, O God, I pray!"* (v. 13). It was a short, but powerful and effectual prayer. Through his intercession, Moses shows us the forgiving heart of our Savior, who from the cross cried out to His Father not to judge those who were harming and blaspheming Him – *"Father, forgive them"* – literally "Father, let it be" (Luke 23:34). Peter summarizes the Lord's humility while being abused on the cross: *"He was reviled, did not revile in return; when He suffered, He did not threaten, but committed Himself to Him who judges righteously"* (1 Pet. 2:23). This was the type of behavior the Lord wanted His disciples to exhibit as a testimony of God's mercy to others: *"But I say to you, love your enemies, bless those who curse you, do good to those who hate you, and pray for those who spitefully use you and persecute you"* (Matt. 5:44).

In praying for Miriam's healing, Moses showed that he had accepted Aaron's contrite acknowledgement of sin and had forgiven him. "This was victory – the victory of a meek man – the victory of grace. A man who knows his right place in the presence of God is able to rise above all evil speaking,"[51] writes C. H. Mackintosh. Praise God for all those who can rightly suffer for righteousness' sake and still beseech God on behalf of their oppressors because they understand what great things God might accomplish through intercession. How indebted Miriam now was for the prayers of the man she had terribly wronged.

The Lord honored Moses' prayer and spoke to him, not to Aaron or Miriam: *"If her father had but spit in her face, would she not be shamed seven days? Let her be shut out of the camp seven days, and afterward she may be received again"* (v. 14). Spitting in one's face was a gesture of contempt (Deut. 25:9) and Miriam's unruly behavior had drawn God's contempt – He smote her with leprosy and made her unclean.

Under the law, the spittle of an unclean person made a clean person unclean for the day (Lev. 15:8). But the Lord reminds Moses that if her natural father had expressed such repugnance towards her, she would have felt the humiliation for a long time, not just for a day. How much more appropriate then for Miriam to experience the shame of being smitten by God with leprosy for a period of time. The Lord's statement implied that even though He would heal Miriam as Moses had requested, she should suffer this minimum period of shame and isolation given the magnitude of her offense.

An Example to Learn From (vv. 15-16)

Leviticus 14 details a week-long process to ceremonially cleanse a healed leper. Apart from Miriam, there is no other example of a Jew being healed of leprosy after the Law was given. This means that the Leviticus 14 text would have been applied here first and not likely again until Christ sent a steady stream of healed lepers to the temple to be examined by the priests.

It seems likely that Miriam was forced to feel the terrible pain of the disease for only a short time before being healed, but then had to suffer the shame of her offense for a full week. Her punishment and

Refining and Reminding

resulting uncleanness halted the entire camp's progression to Canaan (v. 15). This episode indicates how much God hates evil speaking against His appointed leaders and how such conduct impedes the spiritual growth of those in their care. John J. Stubbs suggests that the spiritual health of many local churches has been adversely affected by those verbally assaulting the Lord's servants:

> Scripture says that *"one sinner destroys much good"* (Eccl. 9:18). How solemnly illustrated this is in the case of Miriam's sin. Israel could make no progress at all while the sin of Miriam had to be dealt with. There have been assemblies of the Lord's people which have ceased to make spiritual progress because of one or more who have spoken evil of some of God's servants. No company of Christians can possibly prosper until such an evil is repented of. Is it not an alarming thought that the wrong behavior of a believer, especially the sin of evil speaking, can seriously hamper God's work in the midst of His assembly and bring to a halt furtherance in the things of God? Let not this terrible evil be underestimated, and let there be a great regard for the preciousness of the assembly to God so that one's attitude to others does not bring any harm.[52]

We should never think that our sin, no matter how small or secret it is, does not negatively affect the Body of Christ or hinder our pilgrim journey heavenward. With this said, C. A. Coates reminds us of the practical benefit that the seven days of isolation had for Miriam and for the entire camp:

> A working of evil may be truly judged, and owned in confession, and yet a moral work may require to be perfected in the soul. The "seven days" come in here. Time is required, not for God to forgive, but for the saint who has given place to the flesh to go through the moral exercises that are essential if one is to "be received in again" as established in the gain and deliverance which divine grace has brought. The "seven days" deepen the conviction of what has been already admitted before God.
>
> The whole assembly was detained to get the gain of this exercise. The working of flesh was exposed and judged in two prominent members of the congregation, but all had to learn by it. The same flesh was in every one of them, and seeing it judged in Miriam, they had an

opportunity to judge it in themselves. It was a solemn "seven days" for all Israel.[53]

So Miriam was shut out of the camp seven days, but after she was cleansed and restored, the Israelites journeyed to Hazeroth in the Wilderness of Paran (v. 16). We may regard Miriam, who was shut out of the camp, as a figure of the present spiritual condition of the Jewish nation. Yet, during the Tribulation Period, Israel will suffer intense cleansing and isolation which will cause a remnant to receive Christ and ask Him for forgiveness. With this understanding in mind, C. H. Mackintosh summarizes the typological portrait of future things presented to us in this chapter:

> In "the Ethiopian woman," we have a type of that great and marvelous mystery, the union of the Church with Christ her Head. ...The type is complete and most striking. The Jews have not believed in the glorious truth of mercy to the Gentiles, and therefore wrath has come upon them to the uttermost. But they will be brought in, by and by, on the ground of simple mercy, just as the Gentiles have come in.[54]

Moses' example of meekness and immediate intercession for those who had offended him typifies the character and ministry of the Lord Jesus, which we would do well to emulate in our own lives. Moses' marriage to an Ethiopian woman and his dealings with Aaron and Miriam wonderfully prefigure Christ's taking a Gentile bride, the Church (Eph. 5:23-32), and also His future work of refining and restoring the idolatrous wife of Jehovah, the nation of Israel, to Himself (Rom. 9:25-27).

Mercy flows down from heaven throughout this chapter. Praise the Lord that He is able to reach us where we are and then bring us closer to Himself – that is mercy indeed!

Meditation

> When a Christian shows mercy, he experiences liberation.
>
> — Warren Wiersbe

Refining and Reminding

God never withholds from His child that which His love and wisdom call good. God's refusals are always merciful – "severe mercies" at times but mercies all the same. God never denies us our heart's desire except to give us something better.

— Elisabeth Elliot

Spies Sent to Canaan
Numbers 13

The Spies Selected (vv. 1-16)

The Israelites arrived at Kadesh-Barnea (probably camping at the great oasis of Ein el-Qudeirat) in the far northern portion of the Wilderness of Paran (v. 26). Kadesh means "consecrated," but as we will soon see, the Israelites failed to live up to the meaning of the place where they were camped.

The Lord commanded Moses to *"send men to spy out the land of Canaan, which I am giving to the children of Israel; from each tribe of their fathers you shall send a man, everyone a leader among them"* (vv. 1-2). The names of the men selected from each tribe to spy out Canaan are noted in verses 3-15. All these men would abruptly perish in divine judgment shortly after returning from Canaan, except Caleb from the tribe of Judah and Hoshea (whom Moses called Joshua) from the tribe of Ephraim (v. 16).

The Symbolism of Canaan

Before exploring the narrative further, it behooves us to understand what Canaan represented to Israel and to us in type. Some hymns liken physical death to crossing the Jordan River and the land of Canaan to heaven, but this is not correct. Redemption brought the Israelites out of Egypt, through the Red Sea, and into the wilderness as a nation, but when each one passed through the Jordan, they experienced death, practically and individually. "When one is dead and risen (in spirit)," says J. N. Darby, "one enters into the heavenly places (in spirit). For us, death is life. Jordan is not the sign of natural death, because afterwards they met with fighting. It is death practically, death in us spiritually."[55] William MacDonald explains why Canaan does not represent heaven (speaking of God's peaceful spiritual abode):

Refining and Reminding

> There was conflict in Canaan, whereas there is no conflict in heaven [for the believer]. Actually the land of Canaan pictures our present spiritual inheritance. It is ours, but we must possess it by obeying the Word, claiming the promises, and fighting the good fight of faith."[56]

Warren Wiersbe elaborates on the symbolism of Canaan and then expounds its practical meaning for Christians today:

> What does Canaan represent to us as Christians today? It represents our spiritual inheritance in Christ (Eph. 1:3, 11, 15-23). ... Since Canaan was a place of battles, and even of defeats, it is not a good illustration of heaven! Israel had to cross the river by faith (a picture of the believer as he dies to self and the world, Rom. 6) and claim the inheritance by faith. They had to "step out by faith" (Josh. 1:3) and claim the land for themselves, just as believers today must do. Now we understand that the wilderness wanderings represent: the experiences of believers who will not claim their spiritual inheritance in Christ, who doubt God's Word and live in restless unbelief. To be sure, God is with them, as He was with Israel; but they do not enjoy the fullness of God's blessing. They are "out of Egypt" but they are not yet "in Canaan."[57]

Canaan represents all of the believer's inheritance in Christ who is seated in heavenly places (Eph. 1:3; Heb. 1:3). In Christ, believers will find an infinite treasury of spiritual resources which enable them to powerfully represent the Lord while on earth, but these provisions must first be possessed to do so. Certainly, there are future aspects of our inheritance in Christ that believers will enjoy after glorification. For example, believers will rule and reign with Christ once He returns to claim His inheritance and establish His kingdom (2 Tim. 2:12; Rev. 21:7). Yet, Canaan does not represent what we will enjoy with Christ later, but rather the benefits of possessing much of our inheritance in Christ now.

In summary, the Canaan rest for Israel illustrates the spiritual rest we have in Christ when we, by faith, submit to His Word (Heb. 4:11-12). Salvation rest is experienced when we respond in faith to Christ's kind invitation (Matt. 11:28); through His gospel message we obtain peace with God (Rom. 5:1). As we learn of Him and yield to His will (as expressed in His Word), we enjoy the peace of God (Phil. 4:6-8).

Devotions in Numbers

By faith we enter into God's salvation rest (Heb. 4:3), and, by continuing in faith and obedience, His rest enters into us.

When faithful believers depart from their mortal bodies, they depart from Canaan rather than enter it. Their fighting days will be behind them and they will reside with Christ in heavenly bliss (2 Cor. 5:8).

Spying Out the Land (vv. 17-26)

Moses directed the twelve spies to first go southward, and then climb the mountains heading northward (v. 17). There are two possible understandings of these instructions. First, their campsite was far enough north (on the southern fringe of what would later become Judah's territory) that they first had to travel south around the southern shore of the Dead Sea to then survey the Eastern Plateau (which would later be their route into Canaan). The spies then ventured all the way north to Hamath (which is in modern Lebanon) and then traveled southward through Canaan (v. 21). The spies were strangers in the land, but the fact that they were moving through Canaan from the north to the south would not arouse suspicion that they were Israelites.

The second possibility is that the spies were to go to the southern end of the Negev (which means "South") and work their way north through Beersheba along the central highland to pass through Canaan. However, the first possibility seems more likely as the mountains to the east of the Dead Sea were much more pronounced and we know that the spies' route through the highlands, where Hebron is situated, was on their return route to camp. In other words, it seems doubtful that the spies would have departed from Canaan the same way they entered Canaan.

The spies were tasked with discovering how vast the population of Canaan was and whether or not the people lived in fortified cities or in open camps. They were also to assess the fertility of the land, including what forests there might be, and to bring back fruitful gleanings of the land (vv. 19-20). Moses noted that it was the start of the grape harvest, so the spies were sent out in either July or August (v. 20). Their scouting expedition discovered that giants (the sons of Anak) lived in the fortified city of Hebron (v. 22).

Their forty-day reconnaissance mission concluded with the cutting down of a huge branch of grapes in the Valley of Eshcol (just northwest of Hebron) which had to be carried on a pole between two men, and the picking of some figs and pomegranates (vv. 23-25). Clearly, the land

Refining and Reminding

was characterized by fertility and the enormous cluster of grapes, as discussed in Numbers 6, symbolized joy. Of course, the spiritual antitype of this scene is pictured in Christ, the unifying, satisfying, and sustaining grapevine (John 15:1, 11, 16:24). With this understanding, C. A. Coates explains the figurative meaning for Israel of what the spies found in Canaan:

> "One bunch" sets forth a complete unity, made up of a number of different parts. I have no doubt it was a figure of what was in the mind of God in regard to His people. His thought was that, as in "the land," they should be an expression in unity of the joy into which He had brought them.[58]

The spies collected the fruit last so it would still be somewhat fresh when they brought it into camp. Hebron lay some fifty miles northeast of Kadesh-Barnea. This meant that the spies had at least a two-day journey back to camp after cutting the grape branch.

The Report (vv. 27-33)

The spies reporting back to Moses and Aaron exhibited the fruit of the land they had gathered and stated their findings to the entire congregation:

> *We went to the land where you sent us. It truly flows with milk and honey, and this is its fruit. Nevertheless the people who dwell in the land are strong; the cities are fortified and very large; moreover we saw the descendants of Anak there. The Amalekites dwell in the land of the South; the Hittites, the Jebusites, and the Amorites dwell in the mountains; and the Canaanites dwell by the sea and along the banks of the Jordan* (vv. 27-29).

The spies did confirm that Jehovah had kept His word – Canaan was a fertile land, flowing with milk and honey, so to speak. Yet, there were obstacles, many of the inhabitants of the land dwelt in large fortified cities and there were even giants living in Hebron. Sensing the disheartening effect this latter information had on the people, Caleb quickly interjected: *"Let us go up at once and take possession, for we are well able to overcome it"* (v. 30). This was the voice of faith, the declaration of a man who knew his God.

However, the other spies, excluding Joshua, had no thought of God in their reports. Such men, as C. H. Mackintosh surmises, will always add a "nevertheless" to what God makes available to them by faith:

> There is always sure to be a "nevertheless" where man is concerned, and when unbelief is at work. The unbelieving spies saw the difficulties – great cities, high walls, tall giants. All these things they saw; but they did not see Jehovah at all. They looked at the things that were seen, rather than at the things that were unseen. Their eye was not fixed upon Him who is invisible. Doubtless, the cities were great, but God was greater. The walls were high, but God was higher. The giants were strong, but God was stronger.[59]

The carnal spies countered: *"We are not able to go up against the people, for they are stronger than we"* (v. 31). This was a true statement; the Israelites were weaker than the opposition facing them in Canaan. Without the Lord, they could not take the land. Unfortunately, the favorable report of the land's fertility was soon forgotten because the ten spies convinced the people that they would be slaughtered if they invaded Canaan (v. 32). They said that the Israelites would be like grasshoppers before the taller Canaanites, especially when faced with the giants (v. 33).

In effect, they were saying that God had kept His Word concerning Canaan, but that He was not able to give them the land. Apparently, they believed that the Canaanites were more powerful than Jehovah, the One who had decimated Egypt to loosen their bonds of slavery and had brought them all the way to Canaan. How demeaning it is to God when we shut our eyes of faith; instead of joyfully feasting with Him, we are content to grovel in despair for a leaner portion of His goodness.

Meditation

> Faith reasons from God to the difficulties: it begins with Him. Unbelief, on the contrary, reasons from the difficulties to God: it begins with them. This makes all the difference. It is not that we are to be insensible to the difficulties; neither are we to be reckless. Neither insensibility nor yet recklessness is faith.
>
> — C. H. Mackintosh

Rebellion, Intercession, Pardon, and Death
Numbers 14

Unbelief and Unrest (vv. 1-10)

Although the Canaan spies all agreed that Jehovah had kept His promise and had brought His people to fertile land, ten spies caused the people to believe that the giants and fortified cities in Canaan were too big for Him to overcome. Instead of praising God for honoring His Word, the people mourned and complained before Him. Besides assuming a degrading view of God, they also rejected His appointed leaders, and began to make plans to return to Egypt:

> *So all the congregation lifted up their voices and cried, and the people wept that night. And all the children of Israel complained against Moses and Aaron, and the whole congregation said to them, "If only we had died in the land of Egypt! Or if only we had died in this wilderness! Why has the Lord brought us to this land to fall by the sword, that our wives and children should become victims? Would it not be better for us to return to Egypt? So they said to one another, "Let us select a leader and return to Egypt"* (vv. 1-4).

Faith that was rooted in God's attributes, character, and promises had been replaced with unbelief. No wonder the people wept. All they could see with their carnal eyes were giants, great cities with high walls, and an immense host of fierce people. Those who will not trust God vex themselves! Their unbelief led them to murmur against God without cause, to reject His appointed leaders, and to turn back into a terrible wilderness whether God came with them or not. Carnality will always abound when craving for Egypt and its charms displaces devotion to the Lord.

The Israelites had obeyed God when they kept the first Passover, entered a dry passageway through the Red Sea, and followed His Law and His order for the camp, but they utterly failed by not entering Canaan. Their ingratitude and rebellion at Kadesh-Barnea was so offensive that the Lord inspired various writers to refer to it in Scripture as a lesson to learn from. For example, the writer of Hebrews (chp. 3) reiterates what the psalmist wrote centuries earlier about this rebellion and its consequences:

> *Today, if you will hear His voice: "Do not harden your hearts, as in the rebellion, as in the day of trial in the wilderness, when your fathers tested Me; they tried Me, though they saw My work. For forty years I was grieved with that generation, and said, 'It is a people who go astray in their hearts, and they do not know My ways.' So I swore in My wrath, 'They shall not enter My rest'"* (Ps. 95:7-11).

Then the apostle explains why Israel failed: *"they could not enter in [to Canaan] because of unbelief"* (Heb. 3:19). As C. H. Mackintosh suggests, believers in the Church Age can also fail to enter God's rest because of unbelief:

> We fail to enter upon our heavenly inheritance – fail to take possession, practically, of our true and proper portion – fail to walk, day by day, as a heavenly people, having no place, no name, no portion in the earth – having nothing to do with this world save to pass through it as pilgrims and strangers, treading in the footsteps of Him who has gone before, and taken His place in the heavens.[60]

To summarize, the Israelites failed to obtain God's ongoing rest in Canaan for the same reason believers today do not experience God's rest, because of disbelief (Heb. 4:4-6). Thirty-eight years later, the Israelites did enter into God's rest in Canaan (Josh. 1:13-15, 11:23), but then, as shown in the book of Judges, they failed to go on with the Lord in faith to secure their inheritance after receiving it (Josh. 13:1). Consequently, the rest Jehovah had for them was never fully realized and, in time, was lost. The writer of Hebrews uses their failure as an exhortation, *"Let us therefore be diligent to enter that rest, lest anyone fall according to the same example of disobedience"* (Heb. 4:11-12). The matter of victorious living has not changed; continued faith and obedience ultimately translate into obtaining divine possessions and rest. Labor without faith or faith without labor will never translate into divine conquest and spiritual peace, but will rather conclude in human failure and emotional anxiety.

Refining and Reminding

This is the message conveyed to us in the words "possession" and "rest" in the book of Joshua. By faith and obedience, God's people did later enter Canaan – their inheritance. But they could not engage in conquest until they entered the land, they could not possess the land without conquest, and they could not enter God's rest in the land without first possessing it. In the Church Age, believers do not labor for a *place* of rest; our rest and inheritance are in a *Person* – *"Christ in heavenly places"* (Eph. 1:3). Thus, Paul prayed for fellow believers, *"The Lord of peace Himself give you peace in every way"* (2 Thess. 3:16) and he shared his life's aspiration with them:

> *Not that I have already attained, or am already perfected; but I press on, that I may lay hold of that for which Christ Jesus has also laid hold of me. Brethren, I do not count myself to have apprehended; but one thing I do, forgetting those things which are behind and reaching forward to those things which are ahead, I press toward the goal for the prize of the upward call of God in Christ Jesus* (Phil. 3:12-14).

Christ is the believer's inheritance and resting place. The practical blessing of these present possessions granted the believer in Christ will be experienced through faith and obedience as one engages in active conquest, enabled by resurrection power.

No crisis since the incident of Aaron's fashioning a golden calf at Mount Sinai had gravity equal to this situation. Though not as crude as worshipping an idol, the rejection of God's appointed leaders and the refusal of His command to enter Canaan was a denunciation of God nonetheless. C. H. Mackintosh connects these two offenses as equal expressions of the same unbelief:

> There are two melancholy phases of unbelief exhibited in Israel's history in the wilderness: the one at Horeb, the other at Kadesh. At Horeb they made a *calf,* and said, *"These be thy gods, O Israel, that brought thee up out of the land of Egypt."* At Kadesh, they proposed to make a *captain* to lead them back into Egypt. The former of these is the *superstition* of unbelief; the latter, the willful *independence* of unbelief; and, most surely, we need not marvel if these who thought that a calf had brought them out of Egypt should seek a captain to lead them back.[61]

Devotions in Numbers

Sadly, there were only four men of faith to side with the Lord that day. Moses and Aaron fell on their faces before the congregation, likely in prayer. This demonstrated a spirit of utter meekness, as their necks were exposed in this completely defenseless position (v. 5). One blow of a sword would end their lives. Moses and Aaron were publicly demonstrating their complete dependence on God to deliver them out of this threatening situation.

Caleb and Joshua sought to reason with the faithless, hostile crowd (vv. 6-9): *"If the Lord delights in us, then He will ...if the Lord be with us there is nothing to fear... only do not rebel against the Lord, nor fear the people of the land, for they are our bread."* Their point was that there was nothing to fear because Jehovah was with them! In fact, they viewed the giants and fortifications of Canaan as God's food to grow their faith. God had set before them an opportunity for faith to feed on what caused most of them to tremble in unbelief. Genuine faith founded in truth brings God into every situation and He is able to overcome all that opposes His people, including high walls and giants. What are such things in comparison to Almighty God?

This was all sound reasoning, but it would not be heeded. There were two voices upholding God's glory among 600,000 giant-fearing dissenters, who were now ready to silence the Lord's servants with stones. But the glory of the Lord suddenly appeared at the tabernacle, which, of course, stunned the mutineers and preserved the faithful (v. 10).

Moses Intercedes (vv. 11-19)

It does not appear that the people heard the conversation between Moses and the Lord (v. 39), as even Aaron was not made aware of it until afterwards (v. 26). This shows the private and personal nature of prayer for those who love the Lord and desire His presence. However, the people did see the glory of God at the tabernacle and Moses standing directly before the Lord. The Lord told Moses:

> *How long will these people reject Me? And how long will they not believe Me, with all the signs which I have performed among them? I will strike them with the pestilence and disinherit them, and I will make of you a nation greater and mightier than they* (vv. 11-12).

Refining and Reminding

About a year earlier, Moses had interceded on behalf of the Israelites after the golden calf incident, and although three thousand souls died in judgment for that offense, the nation as a whole was spared (Ex. 32). Now, at Kadesh-Barnea, Israel's offense of unbelief was so grave that again the Lord threatened to destroy the entire nation and raise up a new nation through Moses. In other words, God would cut them all off, but would maintain the posterity of Abraham as promised, by starting afresh through Moses, just as He had previously preserved the posterity of Adam through Noah after destroying mankind with a flood. Practically speaking, however, flesh is flesh, and those in the flesh cannot please God (Rom. 8:8). A nation derived from Moses would have fared no better, spiritually speaking. In fact, we see Jonathan, the grandson of Moses through Gershom, engaged in gross idolatry a few years later in Canaan (Judg. 18).

Moses boldly and passionately pleads for God to be merciful to His people (vv. 13-19). He reminds the Lord that His character will be doubted and His name tarnished among the nations if His people perish in the wilderness. The nations would think Jehovah was not strong enough to bring His people into the land He had promised them. Knowing his God, Moses affirms both the holy, righteous character of God that must judge sin, and also His gracious attributes often witnessed in pardoning the condemned:

The Lord is longsuffering and abundant in mercy, forgiving iniquity and transgression; but He by no means clears the guilty, visiting the iniquity of the fathers on the children to the third and fourth generation. Pardon the iniquity of this people, I pray, according to the greatness of Your mercy, just as You have forgiven this people, from Egypt even until now (vv. 18-19).

This reminds us of Moses' intercession on Mount Sinai for the Israelites down below who were dancing about the golden calf that Aaron had made. Moses was a successful mediator on both occasions and immediate judgment was averted. Of the former account we read, *"The Lord relented from the harm which He said He would do to His people"* (Ex. 32:14). Seeing that God yielded to Moses' intercession on both occasions begs the question, Whose "will" was accomplished in these matters – Moses' or God's?

Both Moses and God received what they desired; certainly God's will was fully achieved by dealing with the sin and yet showing mercy. God did not change His mind in the way He planned to punish Israel, but rather, it was the will of God for Moses to intercede for His wayward people so that He could extend them mercy. God longs for a person with a righteous standing to stand in the gap between Himself and the unrighteous in order to plead for grace and mercy on their behalf. God does not change His mind in such matters, but from man's perspective, it may seem as though He does. Both the declaration of God's anger over sin and the punishment deserved by the offenders were stated before Moses was given the opportunity to make intercession in both situations.

John J. Stubbs suggests that Moses' character exhibited while engaging in this critical intercessory work typifies that of the Lord Jesus Christ and His ongoing priestly work in heaven for His people:

> One cannot avoid seeing in this a precious picture of the Lord Jesus Christ, who not only intercedes now in heaven for His people, but also, as the Mediator, pleads for their pardon. In Psalm 106:23 it is mentioned that had it not been for Moses, God's chosen, standing before Him in the breach, then the nation would have been destroyed. This passage refers to the time of the apostasy in Exodus 32, which is also referred to in Deuteronomy 9:25-26. Moses again at Kadesh stands like a warrior in the breach of the city wall repelling the oncoming force at the risk of his life. His intercession not only shows his intense love for the nation, but also his great courage in coming before such a mighty and great God. [62]

As a result of Moses' intercession, the Lord did what He had planned to do all along – show mercy to Israel. God's nature is gracious and merciful, but when confronted by unrepentant sin, God desires a mediator to plead the case of those deserving His indignation, that He may be shown to be merciful. Faithful Moses who enjoyed communion with God fulfilled this role. Praise God for all those who, being in joyful communion with God, can plead for those who are not.

A Pardoning God (vv. 20-25)

The Lord heeded Moses' request to refrain from destroying the nation, but sin always has a bitter consequence eventually:

Refining and Reminding

> *I have pardoned, according to your word; but truly, as I live, all the earth shall be filled with the glory of the Lord – because all these men who have seen My glory and the signs which I did in Egypt and in the wilderness, and have put Me to the test now these ten times, and have not heeded My voice, they certainly shall not see the land of which I swore to their fathers, nor shall any of those who rejected Me see it. But My servant Caleb, because he has a different spirit in him and has followed Me fully, I will bring into the land where he went, and his descendants shall inherit it. Now the Amalekites and the Canaanites dwell in the valley; tomorrow turn and move out into the wilderness by the Way of the Red Sea* (vv. 20-25).

Moses had asked God to pardon Israel and the Lord affirms that He had pardoned Israel as requested; otherwise Israel would have not entered Canaan at all. However, God's pardon did not overlook their guilt; rather, He chose to act differently than swift justice demanded. This pardon did not accomplish for the Israelites what confession and forgiveness by atonement could have. The Israelites had requested death in the wilderness and God was going to grant them that request as punishment (vv. 29, 35). A holy God could *"by no means clear the guilty"* (Ex. 34:7) – the guilty must be punished.

But, instead of suffering immediate executions, the Israelites would be under forty years of camp-arrest, until all the unfaithful generation had perished. Centuries later, Paul would refer to this as an example of what can happen when believers continue to lust for what is out of God's will: *"But with most of them God was not well pleased, for their bodies were scattered in the wilderness"* (1 Cor. 10:5). As witnessed with our first parents in Eden, unchecked lusting eventually results in doubting God's goodness.

God's judgment in the matter would preserve His holy character and also honor His word to Moses. Only those who were twenty years of age and older would be judged. This older generation, aside from Joshua and Caleb, would expire while wandering in the wilderness during the next forty years (less the months they had already been out of Egypt; v. 33).

From this text we notice that God has a great concern for children. The Lord even threatens those who abuse them with dire consequences (Matt. 18:6). Children have guardian angels to provide a certain level of protection against the forces of evil which work to prevent them from understanding divine truth and turning to God (Matt. 18:10). Just as a shepherd with one hundred sheep is concerned about one lamb that strays from the fold, God is concerned about each child and desires that none be lost (Matt. 18:14).

The failure of the older, unbelieving generation is astounding; they were able to get their little ones out of the slavery of Egypt, but failed to get them into the promised blessings of Canaan: *"But your little ones, whom you said would be victims, I will bring in, and they shall know the land which you have despised. But as for you, your carcasses shall fall in this wilderness"* (vv. 31-32). In effect God was saying, "Your children will get the land that you have despised, but you shall die in this wilderness as you requested because of your unbelief."

Just seeing our children saved from the Lake of Fire is not the full salvation God wants them to experience in His Son. He wants them to experience resurrection power and to enjoy the invigorating life of Christ now. Clearly, prying the leeks and garlic from our children's mouths is only the first step in a journey to enabling them to enjoy the figs and grapes of God's promises. They need to be taught the promises and blessings of Christ at an early age. Then we must help them grow in their faith by encouraging the reading of good devotional books and biographies, by having personal quiet times and family devotions, and engaging in prayer and ministry. They need to see the glory of God as a real and tangible outcome of their faith too!

The Consequences of Sin (vv. 26-45)

The sentence that the Lord had determined against Israel, already made known to Moses, was confirmed to Aaron also (v. 26). God always honors genuine faith (Heb. 11:6); hence, Joshua and Caleb were rewarded for their diligence in speaking for God when so many opposed them (vv. 29-32). Their message was one of complete confidence in God and, for that reason, their feet would be striding over the vine-clad hills and fertile valleys of Canaan long after the bodies of their brethren had decayed in the desert.

However, true faith is patient and willing to suffer long, even as the result of the unbelief of others. Joshua and Caleb would live outside their inheritance for forty years, but in grace they waited for the coming day of God's promise (Josh. 14). Then, too, they had to return and live among their unbelieving brethren destined to die in the wilderness. They watched their friends and relatives perish one by one, month after month, and year after year, until none of the rebellious generation remained.

After the Lord affirmed the punishment of the people to Moses and Aaron, the Lord smote the ten spies with a plague and they died immediately (vv. 36-38). Then Moses informed the congregation of their long-term punishment. Sadly, God's judicial decree caused feelings of disgust among His people rather than genuine remorse.

They rose up early in the morning and told Moses that they had sinned and would now go up into the land that God had promised them (vv. 39-40). Although they had acknowledged their sin, they also were quite keen on escaping its consequences. Instead of going back into the wilderness with God and under His verdict, they decided it was better to push forward into Canaan without Him. A few hours earlier they had concluded that even with Jehovah, they would not be able to overcome Canaan's giants and strongholds. So, what sense did it make for them to charge the enemy without Jehovah? Surely this would result in many casualties as Moses warned:

Now why do you transgress the command of the Lord? For this will not succeed. Do not go up, lest you be defeated by your enemies, for the Lord is not among you. For the Amalekites and the Canaanites are there before you, and you shall fall by the sword; because you have turned away from the Lord, the Lord will not be with you (vv. 41-43).

But they disregarded Moses' admonition. Though the Ark of the Covenant remained in the camp, they went out to face the Amalekites and Canaanites and were driven back to Hormah (vv. 44-45). Hormah was the Canaanite city thought to be less than ten miles east of Beersheba. Its name means "cursed for destruction." But that is not what happened in the Israelites' first encounter with Hormah because the Lord was not with them.

The words of the Lord Jesus to His disciples resound forcibly in this outcome: *"For without Me you can do nothing"* (John 15:5). The overconfident and rebellious Israelites went into battle without the Lord and were soundly defeated. We too will always suffer loss if we face the enemy in our own strength (Eph. 6:10-13). Thankfully, thirty-eight years later, the Lord would be with His people and they would defeat the Canaanites at Hormah (21:3). We conclude that, with the Lord,

Devotions in Numbers

victory is possible in every encounter with the enemy. Paul puts the matter this way: *"I can do all things through Christ who strengthens me"* (Phil. 4:13).

But without the Lord's help, human lust, conceit, and unbelief will always result in flawed reasoning. There is an insanity to sin and the sorrowful irony of this truth is quite evident in the text: the Jews had chosen to die as criminals under divine justice, rather than to live as blessed conquerors under God's favor. C. H. Mackintosh reminds us that any child of God acting in the flesh can stoop to this same level of stupidity:

> How often is this the case with us! We fail; we take some false step; we get into trying circumstances in consequence; and, then, instead of meekly bowing down under the hand of God, and seeking to walk with Him, in humbleness and brokenness of spirit, we grow restive and rebellious; we quarrel with the circumstances instead of judging ourselves; and we seek, in self-will, to escape from the circumstances, instead of accepting them as the just and necessary consequence of our own conduct.[63]

Unfortunately, the Israelites did not accept God's pardon granting them life with Him in the wilderness instead of immediate death. May we learn from this situation: sin has painful consequences, but despite past failures, holding on to God's promises and going on with Him in grace is still a life worth living. Though true believers in the Church Age cannot experience eternal death for such failures, they can still suffer the painful consequences of severed communion with God.

Meditation

> Ye fearful saints, fresh courage take;
> The clouds ye so much dread
> Are big with mercy and shall break
> In blessings on your head.
>
> Judge not the Lord by feeble sense,
> But trust Him for His grace;
> Behind a frowning providence
> He hides a smiling face.
>
> Blind unbelief is sure to err
> And scan His work in vain;

Refining and Reminding

> God is His own interpreter,
> And He will make it plain.
>
> — William Cowper

Various Offerings, Laws, and the Blue Tassel
Numbers 15

After the people's rebellion at Kadesh-Barnea, the Lord decreed, *"they certainly shall not see the land"* (14:23), but in this chapter, He says, *"when you have come into the land"* (15:2). This is truly one of the most remarkable phrases in the entire book of Numbers and reaffirms a central theme throughout the Bible – salvation is completely of the Lord. When all seems lost – God saves the day! God rises above human failures to find a way to make good on all He has promised to do.

"When you have come into the land" conveys two key ideas: first, that a number of years had passed between chapters 14 and 15, and second, that though the previous generation did not have the faith to enter God's wonderful promises, the next generation, by God's grace, would. This meant that, before Israel entered Canaan, the nation needed to be reminded of the offerings and sacrifices commanded by God on Mount Sinai.

Various Offerings (vv. 1-21)

Just before the Israelites enter the land, Moses will provide a thorough review of God's Law (the book of Deuteronomy) to the new generation. The offerings described in this section (largely grain and drink offerings) were what were to be brought voluntarily to the Lord in Canaan with various sacrifices (vv. 1-16). These grain and drink offerings were therefore supplementary to the sweet savor offerings already discussed in Leviticus chapters 1-3.

Various meal offerings of flour and oil and drink offerings of wine were to be added to the burnt and peace offerings. These contributions expressed personal satisfaction in the Lord and thankfulness for His blessings to the degree the offerer understood and appreciated them. This same correlation should be observed in the Church Age, suggests C. A. Coates:

Refining and Reminding

> But it is encouraging and stimulating to see that the measure contemplated here is an increasing one. It rises from one tenth part to two and then to three. This is how things go normally in "the land." We become increasingly possessed of the perfections of Christ Godward, and have thus spiritual material for offerings. All those perfections attach to One whom God values in the very highest degree – His beloved Son in whom He has found His delight. And as in "the land," the saints, through grace, value those perfections so as to be able to bring them to God in a profound sense of how pleasurable they are to Him. All here is "a sweet odor." As we learn Christ, we increase in the apprehension of what is spiritual. This is conveyed to us typically in the bringing of the "fourth part of a hin of oil" with a lamb; "a third part" with a ram; "half a hin" with a bullock. This suggests that, as in the land, we approach God with an ever increasing measure of apprehension of what is spiritual as seen in Christ.[64]

Regardless of their spiritual understanding or social status, everyone identifying with Israel, native Jew or alien living in the Promised Land, was to participate in these offerings. Likewise, all believers today, regardless of their spiritual maturity, should be occupied with Christ and should show their appreciation for Him through genuine worship and selfless offerings.

Moses also reminded the people that the firstfruits of the land, whether the firstborn of man or beast, or the first sheaves of the harvest, were always to be the Lord's (vv. 17-19; Ex. 22:29; 34:20; Lev. 23:15). Therefore, firstborns should be redeemed by an offering and the firstfruits of the harvest should be presented to the Lord on an ongoing basis. A special cake baked from the ground meal derived from the first sheaves of the harvest was also to be heaved (or waved) before the Lord by a priest (vv. 20-21). This cake was then likely eaten by the offering priest as part of the Lord's provision to sustain him.

Unintentional and Intentional Sins (vv. 22-31)

Among the offerings mentioned, there is a special emphasis on those for unintentional sins committed by the congregation (vv. 22-26) or by individuals (vv. 27-29). Though generally described here, the specifics of offering a bull (for congregational sins) or a goat (for sins committed by leaders) are recorded in Leviticus 4. See the discussion in Numbers 5:5-10 for more specifics on the sin and trespass offerings. Concerning atoning for these sins of ignorance, Matthew Henry writes:

Though ignorance will in a degree excuse, it will not justify those who might have known their Lord's will, yet did it not. David prayed to be cleansed from his secret faults, those sins which he himself was not aware of. Sins committed ignorantly shall be forgiven through Christ the great Sacrifice, who He offered up Himself once for all upon the cross.[65]

The people were then reminded that there were no personal offerings for willful sin (vv. 30-31). These two verses supply a preface for understanding the next section about a man violating the Sabbath. Malicious rebels were to be cut off from the people, which meant that offenders at a minimum would be excommunicated, but could be put to death depending on the infraction (vv. 35-36). Sins not settled by the personal sin and trespass offerings were atoned for on the annual Day of Atonement.

The Sabbath Breaker (vv. 32-26)

To illustrate an example of severely punishing someone for defiant sin, Moses records the story of a man found gathering sticks on the Sabbath Day. He was placed under arrest until Moses obtained direction from the Lord as to what should be done with him.

Moses' example of patience is a good one for us to follow. When a crisis demands that a decision be made, we should wait for clear direction from the Lord (i.e., unless His Word already defines what should be done). God will provide more light for those willing to seek Him for guidance:

> *But let patience have its perfect work, that you may be perfect and complete, lacking nothing. If any of you lacks wisdom, let him ask of God, who gives to all liberally and without reproach, and it will be given to him* (Jas. 1:4-5).

While it is true that God promises to grant wisdom to those who ask Him for it, we first must realize that we need His wisdom. Moses sought the Lord for counsel and the Lord provided him with His wisdom.

For this situation, the Lord had already commanded: *"You shall keep the Sabbath, therefore, for it is holy to you. Everyone who profanes it shall surely be put to death; for whoever does any work on it, that person shall be cut off from among his people"* (Ex. 31:14). But

Refining and Reminding

such a blatant act of defiance against God's Law had not likely been anticipated, so the gravity of the infraction and the means of punishment needed to be specified by God. The verdict was death by stoning which was immediately carried out by the congregation outside the camp.

We are not told whether the man was a Jew or not. However, given that the Jews rested in camp on the Sabbath and they were in the wilderness (isolated from the nations), it seems likely that this man was encamped with Israel and therefore would have been aware of God's laws for His Sabbath. Perhaps he was part of the mixed multitude. However, being associated with the camp, it did not matter to the Lord whether he was a Jew or not. Foreigners living among Jehovah's people partook of the same blessings as they did, but that also meant that foreigners became subject to Jehovah's laws for His people (e.g., Ex. 12:48; Lev. 16:29).

C. H. Mackintosh suggests that one of the reasons that this man was judged so severely is what his rebellion symbolized to others:

> This man had no heart for God's rest. To kindle a fire on the Sabbath Day was not only a positive breach of the law, but it evidenced the most complete alienation from the mind of the Lawgiver, inasmuch as it introduced into the day of *rest* that which is the apt symbol of *judgment*. Fire is emblematic of judgment, and as such it was wholly out of keeping with the repose of the Sabbath. Nothing therefore remained but to visit the Sabbath-breaker with judgment, for *"whatsoever a man sows, that shall he also reap."*[66]

This understanding then would explain why God had expressly forbidden kindling a fire in the camp on the Sabbath Day (Ex. 35:3). There were to be no symbols of wrath among Jehovah's people while they were enjoying His rest of salvation.

The Blue Tassel (vv. 37-41)

Not only were foreigners living among the Jews to honor Jehovah, the Jews living in the Promised Land were to be a testimony to foreigners. Besides honoring Jehovah's Law, the Jews were to add a blue tassel or cord to the fringes of their garments. John J. Stubbs explains the addition to their attire:

Fringes or tassels were to be placed on the four wings or corners of their garments (Deut. 22:12). "The ordinary outer Jewish garment was a quadrangular piece of cloth like a modern plaid, to the corners of which, in conformity with this command, a tassel was attached. Each tassel had a conspicuous thread of deep blue, this color being doubtless symbolic of the heavenly origin of the commandments of which it was to serve as a memento" (*The Speaker's Commentary*). The Jew regarded the tassels on the borders of the garment with much sanctity.[67]

The blue tassel would publicly identify themselves as Jehovah-worshippers and would also serve to remind them of their covenant with Him. They must remain holy before the Lord (v. 40)! Blue, the heavenly color, represented where God's covenant came to them from – heaven. Believers in the Church Age, as Paul exhorts, should also be a heavenly-minded people (Col. 3:1-3).

The Pharisees in Christ's day had enlarged the borders of their garments and set aside this specific commandment of the Lord (Matt. 23:5). When human traditions replace God's commands, it is not superior spirituality that is demonstrated, but vain piety. Likewise, we should remember that while evangelical methods and the particulars of church meetings may change over time, we should never set aside God's order for the Church for what seems more profitable or spiritual to us. We are creatures of rote, so let us guard against making our worship a mindless activity, but rather let our worship be a fresh declaration of love and thankfulness to God.

Meditation

Well did Isaiah prophesy of you hypocrites, as it is written: "This people honors Me with their lips, but their heart is far from Me. And in vain they worship Me, teaching as doctrines the commandments of men." For laying aside the commandment of God, you hold the tradition of men! (Mark 7:6-8).

— The Lord Jesus Christ

Rebellion Against God's Appointed
Numbers 16

In Numbers 14 we observed what is in the heart of man by nature and his carnal ways. In the previous chapter, we witnessed God and His righteous ways, but in this chapter, we are back to man and his fallen ways again. The flames of revolt that blazed up in Numbers 14 had been extinguished by the Lord, but smoldering resentment still lingered, resulting in a fresh flare up of rebellion in this chapter. No longer did the people desire a captain to lead them back to Egypt, but rather someone who would lead them into their inheritance in Canaan (v. 14).

God's Leaders Challenged (vv. 1-7)

Some in the congregation challenged God's appointed leader, Moses, and the anointed high priest, Aaron:

> *Now Korah the son of Izhar, the son of Kohath, the son of Levi, with Dathan and Abiram the sons of Eliab, and On the son of Peleth, sons of Reuben, took men; and they rose up before Moses with some of the children of Israel, two hundred and fifty leaders of the congregation, representatives of the congregation, men of renown. They gathered together against Moses and Aaron, and said to them, "You take too much upon yourselves, for all the congregation is holy, every one of them, and the Lord is among them. Why then do you exalt yourselves above the assembly of the Lord?"* (vv. 1-3).

Understanding who the protagonists are will enable us to better discern what may have motivated their behavior. Levi had three sons, Gershon, Kohath, and Merari (Ex. 6:16). Kohath had Amram, Izhar, Hebron, and Uzziel (Ex. 6:18). Amram was the father of Aaron and Moses (Ex. 6:20), and Korah, one of the main characters of this story, was born to Izhar (Ex. 6:21). This meant that Moses, Aaron, and Korah had the same grandfather and were therefore cousins. Besides Moses and Aaron being in the limelight, so to speak, Albert Barnes suggests another reason why Korah felt slighted and why Dathan and Abiram joined the conspiracy:

> Though being a Kohathite, he was of that division of the Levites which had the most honorable charge, yet Elizaphan was made *"chief of the families of the Kohathites"* (Num. 3:30); he belonged to the youngest branch descended from Uzziel (Num. 3:27). Korah probably regarded himself as injured; and therefore took the lead in this rebellion. ... Dathan and Abiram were Reubenites; and were probably discontented because the birthright had been taken away from their ancestor (Gen. 49:3), and with it the primacy of their own tribe among the tribes of Israel. The Reubenites encamped near to the Kohathites (Num. 2:25), and thus the two families were conveniently situated for taking counsel together.[68]

The pretext for this rebellion would then be to reassert the firstborn leadership rights of the tribe of Reuben against Moses, to reject Uzziel as head of the Kohathites, and to replace the priesthood of Aaron and his sons. In all, Korah, Dathan, Abiram, and two hundred fifty men of renown rose up to defy God's prescribed order and appointed leaders. As we shall soon see, their rebellion cost them their lives.

Moses' response to this challenge is astounding. For a second time (14:5), he humbly falls on his face before his opponents (v. 4). He says to Korah and his company:

> *Tomorrow morning the Lord will show who is His and who is holy, and will cause him to come near to Him. That one whom He chooses He will cause to come near to Him. Do this: Take censers, Korah and all your company; put fire in them and put incense in them before the Lord tomorrow, and it shall be that the man whom the Lord chooses is the holy one. You take too much upon yourselves, you sons of Levi!* (vv. 5-7).

By being on his face, Moses was standing aside and permitting the Lord to respond to the situation. Being in close communion with God, Moses already knew what the Lord would do, and he was willing to wait for the Lord to judge these rebels, rather than to take matters into his own hands. William Kelly extols Moses' behavior as evidencing true humility:

Refining and Reminding

> It is a good thing when the haughtiness that Satan knows so well how to excite brings out nothing but lowliness and humiliation of our souls before God. Haughtiness is apt to provoke haughtiness, and flesh to irritate flesh; but it was not so with Moses.[69]

Moses' example is one we desperately need in the Church today. We expect opposition from the lost, but often the most grievous wounds are from disgruntled believers acting in the flesh. When God's people go wrong, do not go wrong with them. Do not jump on the devil's side to get even; it is not the Lord's way.

Shepherding work is most difficult when stubborn sheep are under conviction, as that is when they are most likely to bite those caring for them. Rather than yielding to truth, some will resort to fault-finding to justify their carnality. It is important that at such times we do not respond carnally, but rather provide an example to follow. What we say and do at such times is more important than asserting the facts (1 Cor. 11:19). Moses merely warned his counterparts, and then rested in the Lord to properly judge the situation as He determined best. It is good to remember that even when we are in the right, *"the wrath of man does not produce the righteousness of God"* (Jas. 1:17). If we derive one ounce of satisfaction, instead of grieving with God over His punishment of the guilty, then our own carnality becomes self-evident.

Sonship vs. Headship (vv. 8-19)

Moses reminds Korah of the privileged role in the tabernacle that God had assigned him as a Kohathite and warns him not to rebel against it by seeking the priesthood (vv. 8-11). C. H. Mackintosh suggests that Korah's response to Moses revealed the sin within his own heart:

> What then was Korah? He was a Levite, and, as such, he was entitled to minister and to teach: *"They shall teach Jacob Thy judgments, and Israel Thy law."* ... But Moses, by the Spirit of God, unmasks the man, and shows that, under the plausible pretext of standing up for the common rights of the congregation, he was audaciously seeking the priesthood for himself. It is well to note this. It will most generally be found that loud talkers about the liberties, rights, and privileges of God's people are, in reality, seeking their own exaltation and advantage. Not content with doing their proper work, they are seeking an improper place.[70]

Korah used the truth of *sonship* (i.e., all God's people are sanctified and thus equal) to argue against God's order of *headship*. God made us, redeemed us, called us, and equipped us to serve Him the way He determines best – end of story. It is a terrible blunder to suppose that all believers in the body of Christ are called to positions of prominence or that we can select our role within His Body.

Rather, Christ alone is to have preeminence in the Church – He is the head! Furthermore, every believer's role in the Body is appointed by Him (Eph. 2:10, 4:11) and all must adhere to His order for the Church (1 Cor. 14:33-34). Every Christian is therefore responsible to act in accordance with this divine principle, and to testify against everything that practically denies it. On this point, C. H. Mackintosh writes:

> The fact of the ruin of the professing Church is no reason whatever for abandoning the truth of God, or sanctioning any denial of it. The Christian is always solemnly bound to submit himself to the revealed mind of God. To plead circumstances as an excuse for doing wrong, or for neglecting any truth of God, is simply flying in the face of divine authority, and making God the Author of our disobedience.[71]

Korah was called into Levitical ministry, but not to the Levitical priesthood. Korah did not want to minister in his calling, but sought what he could not be, a priest. While today all believers are ministers to Christ (1 Pet. 4:10) and believer-priests to God (Rev. 1:6), there is but one Great High Priest, who is the mediator between God and man – the Lord Jesus Christ (1 Tim. 2:5; Heb. 4:14). Woe to those who intrude on His priestly office and assume a position before men that is not theirs. Such pomposity will surely result in God's condemnation.

Moses summoned Dathan and Abiram to come to the tabernacle, but they would not (v. 9). Instead they asserted that new leadership was needed because Moses had failed to lead them into a land of milk and honey, and that he rather wanted them to die in the wilderness (vv. 10-14). This sharp accusation was followed up with an equally sarcastic question, *"Will you put out the eyes of these men?"* Dathan and Abiram were insinuating that Moses had sought to blind the people from his true intentions, but they would make sure everyone knew about his secret agenda.

Refining and Reminding

These were hurtful words against Moses, but he did not personally confront them or stoop to their carnality. Rather, he turned the matter over to the Lord to judge: *"Do not respect their offering. I have not taken one donkey from them, nor have I hurt one of them"* (v. 15). As these rebels did not come to the tabernacle, Moses informed Korah that the Lord would show the congregation tomorrow who was approved by Him. Each of the two hundred and fifty princes challenging Aaron's position as high priest were to come to the entrance of the tabernacle with fire and incense upon each of their censors (vv. 16-18).

The next day, Korah not only gathered all the princes with their censers of burning incense to the tabernacle, but he also stirred up the congregation to gather there against Moses and Aaron. However, the Lord restrained this insurrection by suddenly showing His glory to the congregation (v. 19). The challenge of the congregation greatly angered the Lord, who told Moses and Aaron, *"Separate yourselves from among this congregation, that I may consume them in a moment"* (vv. 20-21). Moses and Aaron humbly fell on their faces before the Lord and pleaded for mercy, *"O God, the God of the spirits of all flesh, shall one man sin, and You be angry with all the congregation?"* (v. 22). Indeed, because the Lord is the Creator and Sustainer of all living things, He fully knows what is in the heart of each person (Col. 1:16-17).

The Call of Separation (vv. 20-27)

The Lord responded favorably to their intercession and issued a call of separation – only the guilty would perish, not the entire nation. The message was short and simple: *"Get away from the tents of Korah, Dathan, and Abiram"* (vv. 23-24). In other words, all that pertained to these rebels would be under God's wrath. Clearly, the revolutionaries had a corrupting effect on the entire camp, but murmuring and complaining is not the same as denying God's lordship. There were only two possible responses to the call of separation: stay with the rebels or stand with Moses. The question that everyone had to answer, simply put, was: "Who is on the Lord's side?"

On, the son of Peleth, also a Reubenite, chose rightly when he heard the call of separation. Although initially he was among the rebels (v. 1), On reconsidered his involvement in this uprising and chose to side with Moses, as did most of the people.

Devotions in Numbers

As one's response to the call was a matter of life and death, Moses went to the tents of the rebels (with Israel's elders following) to ensure it was conveyed accurately: *"Depart now from the tents of these wicked men! Touch nothing of theirs, lest you be consumed in all their sins"* (v. 26). Many heeded the call of separation and departed from the tents of Korah, Dathan, and Abiram to stand with Moses, but more importantly to stand with the Lord. The text states that Dathan and Abiram did not budge. They chose to defiantly remain in the doorways of their tents with their families (v. 27).

God's Chosen Confirmed (vv. 28-40)

The line of demarcation was now established. Each person had made their own choice – to stand with Moses and God or those opposing them. Moses then explained the terms of the contest to the people:

> *By this you shall know that the Lord has sent me to do all these works, for I have not done them of my own will. If these men die naturally like all men, or if they are visited by the common fate of all men, then the Lord has not sent me. But if the Lord creates a new thing, and the earth opens its mouth and swallows them up with all that belongs to them, and they go down alive into the pit, then you will understand that these men have rejected the Lord* (vv. 28-30).

Those who died of unnatural causes would be the ones God had rejected and those remaining alive would be God's chosen. The outcome of the contest would show who had God's approval and who had invoked His displeasure.

While Moses was still speaking, the ground opened up and swallowed everything and everyone associated with the rebels (including their tents), and then it closed up again (vv. 31-33). This closing showed that here was no naturally occurring sinkhole, but that the earth was in direct obedience to God's leader, Moses. It suffices to say that the rebels did not die of old age, but, as Moses decreed, by a new phenomenon. This proved decisively that Moses was God's chosen leader for His people.

Some people were afraid that the earth would swallow them too and fled for their lives (v. 34). Then fire came out from the Lord and slew the two hundred and fifty princes standing before the Lord with burning

Refining and Reminding

incense (v. 35). All Aaron's challengers had been rejected; only Aaron with his censor remained. This also emphatically proved to everyone that Aaron alone was chosen to represent the nation before Jehovah as High Priest.

The Lord wanted His people to learn from this painful lesson, so he commanded Moses to have Eliezer gather up the holy censors of the men who had perished and to scatter their fire outside the camp (vv. 36-37). Although the men holding the censors were not holy, the bronze censors themselves had been set aside for worship and therefore were holy. These censors were then to be beaten flat and combined into a covering for the Bronze Altar. Thus they would become holy before the Lord again. The bronze cover would serve as a constant memorial that only Aaron and his sons could offer incense before the Lord (vv. 38-39).

Given the gravity of Korah's sin, F. B. Hole suggests an additional message was also symbolized by this bronze cover:

> There was to be a perpetual reminder of Korah and his company's sin by their censers being made into a covering of the altar, composed of broad plates. For so long as the altar was thus covered, no sacrifice for sin could be offered, and evidently the gainsaying of Korah, which was sin of a most willful kind, had placed him beyond the reach of a sin offering.[72]

Willful rebellion puts man beyond the mercy obtained through God's sin sacrifice on His Altar. The writer of Hebrews identifies God's ultimate sacrifice and altar, both being Christ, who was offered outside the camp of Judaism and thus beyond the limitations of the old covenant (Heb. 13:10-13). In Christ alone is propitiation for sin achieved and mercy granted to those seeking it through repentance. Those who propose another way, another priesthood, another sacrifice, and another altar have no access to God's way of mercy. As the Lord Jesus said, *"I am the way, the truth, and the life. No one comes to the Father except through Me"* (John 14:6).

Complaining Resumes (vv. 41-50)

Reason would dictate that such a powerful display of God's power in judging rebels would cause the people to cease from contention and to humbly walk with Him. Yet, rebellion was still lurking in their hearts, and, despite observing God's spectacular glory and marvelous feats the day before, the people complained against Moses and Aaron the next morning (v. 41). This time they insinuated that Moses and Aaron were the ones responsible for killing the Lord's people (i.e., the rebels who perished the previous day).

This indictment was interrupted by another sudden appearance of God's glory over the tabernacle (v. 42). Moses and Aaron immediately departed to hear what the Lord would say (v. 43). The Lord's message was concise – He was again ready to destroy the nation: *"Get away from among this congregation, that I may consume them in a moment"* (vv. 44-45). For the third time in this chapter we find Moses falling on his face; twice he did so with Aaron to petition God, and once to plead with the opposition.

Moses must have realized that the Lord's judgment was already moving through the camp, for he urged Aaron to quickly take his censor with fire from the Bronze Altar upon it and hurry into the host to offer incense (vv. 46-50). Incense, in Scripture, often symbolizes the offering of prayers to God (Ex. 30:8; Ps. 141:2; Rev. 5:8). By igniting incense on his censor in the midst of the camp, Aaron was symbolizing his intercession on behalf of the dying. But prayers alone without the means of blood atonement cannot avert God's judgment for sin (Heb. 9:22); thus, Moses realized the necessity of igniting the incense with the fire from the Bronze Altar, which was connected with blood atonement.

A similar association can be witnessed on the Day of Atonement. Aaron was to put burning coals from the Bronze Altar and finely beaten incense in a special gold censer and place it before the Lord in the most holy place (Heb. 9:4). The blood of the sin offering was put on the horns of the Bronze Altar where it was then burnt and Aaron also sprinkled the blood on the Mercy Seat of the Ark of the Covenant. The incense was then carried into the most holy place on the basis that atonement had been made by the death of the sin offering. The coals in Aaron's censer from the Bronze Altar in this situation were likewise connected with atonement and therefore the incense he offered outside the tabernacle to stop the plague was honored in that way.

Aaron and his censor alone survived the judgment of fire that brought death to others. Now Aaron and his censor would be the only remedy to stop death from claiming those still alive in the camp. Aaron's successful intercession again showed whom God had endorsed

Refining and Reminding

as the high priest of Israel. Ironically, the one the people wanted to remove was the only one who could save them from death that day. In this respect, Aaron symbolizes Israel's unfounded rejection centuries later of Jesus Christ, God's chosen High Priest for Israel.

The wages of sin is death, and sadly, about 15,000 people in Numbers 16 needlessly perished in a plague, in fire, or buried in the earth because they continued in sin. Those dying in the plague were still defiant, even after seeing the glory of the Lord twice, the earth swallowing men and their families alive, and fire shooting out from the Lord to consume their princes. What a ridiculous sway our flesh has over sound reason. However, nearly 14,700 sudden funerals had a sobering and purifying effect on the congregation; there were no more challenges against Moses and Aaron's leadership.

Meditation

> Be careful, dear friends, that you do not misrepresent God yourselves. You who murmur, you who say that God deals hardly with you, you give God an ill character; when you look so melancholy, worldlings say, "The religion of Jesus is intolerable," and so you stain the honor of God.
>
> — C. H. Spurgeon

Aaron's Rod Buds
Numbers 17

One might think that the tragic events of Numbers 16 would have been sufficient to affirm Aaron's priesthood and to dissuade any more challengers. But the Lord sought to do more than just approve Aaron as high priest. He wanted to reveal the abundant life available to all those willing to yield to His way of forgiveness and acceptance, which would ultimately be revealed in Jesus Christ.

To this end, the Lord commanded Moses (v. 1):

> *Speak to the children of Israel, and get from them a rod from each father's house, all their leaders according to their fathers' houses – twelve rods. Write each man's name on his rod. And you shall write Aaron's name on the rod of Levi. For there shall be one rod for the head of each father's house. Then you shall place them in the tabernacle of meeting before the Testimony, where I meet with you. And it shall be that the rod of the man whom I choose will blossom; thus I will rid Myself of the complaints of the children of Israel, which they make against you"* (vv. 2-6).

As branches severed from living trees, each of the twelve rods was quite dead. It did not matter how beautifully the name of the tribe was carved into the wood or how each rod was decorated or esteemed – these rigid emblems of honorary prominence simply did not possess life.

Moses did as the Lord said and put twelve dead rods, one for each tribe, in the tabernacle (v. 7). Apparently, one rod representing the two tribes through Joseph (Ephraim and Manasseh; Deut. 27:12) was put in the tabernacle to constitute a total of twelve, thus, all thirteen tribes were represented in this test.

The tabernacle was where the priests ministered before the Lord. Therefore, the Lord would cause the rod of the man He had chosen to lead Israel's priesthood to blossom while in the tabernacle. This

Refining and Reminding

symbolized that the priesthood is founded upon that grace of God which alone is able to bring life out of death.

The rod for the tribe of Levi was to have Aaron's name carved into it, not Moses' name. C. H. Mackintosh explains why this was appropriate:

> What about Moses' rod? Why was it not amongst the twelve? The reason is blessedly simple. Moses' rod was the expression of power and authority. Aaron's rod was the lovely expression of that grace that quickens the dead. ... The rod of *authority* could take away *the murmurers,* but the rod of *grace* could take away the *murmurs*.[73]

When Moses went into the tabernacle the next morning, eleven rods were unchanged, but the twelfth, Aaron's rod, was alive (v. 8). When Moses brought the rods out to the people for inspection, they found that Aaron's rod had budded, bloomed, and yielded ripe almonds, but all the other rods were still quite dead (v. 9).

Aaron's budding rod, which had been laid the night before with other dead rods, superbly typifies the resurrection of Christ. The Lord Jesus lay in death and silence in a garden tomb, but during the night He also became alive. Furthermore, what the rod was before, a living branch of an almond tree, is what it became again as evidenced by its fruit-bearing. Likewise, the Lord Jesus, although now in a glorified body, was the same person He was before He experienced death, as evidenced by fulfilling His promises made before His death – after His resurrection.

Additionally, Paul proclaimed that Christ was the firstfruits from the dead (i.e., He was the first man to have experienced glorification). Hence, Christ is likened to a wave sheaf presented before the Lord to represent the great harvest of souls to come, who would also experience the first resurrection (1 Cor. 15:20). Interestingly, almonds were among the earliest fruit to ripen and to be harvested each year (Jer. 1:11-12) – the firstfruits of the harvest to come so to speak. All who have been redeemed by Christ will experience resurrection (1 Thess. 4:13-18). The full fruitfulness of Christ's priestly ministry is clearly beyond anything that we can imagine.

The other eleven dry dead rods were then collected by their owners; this expresses man's barren and worthless condition apart from God's grace. However, the fruit of Aaron's rod testified of the life-giving power that could be received through God's ordained priestly ministry.

The authority and power of Moses' rod could enforce the Law and punish the guilty, but it could not energize the congregation in the wilderness or make them triumphant in Canaan. Efficacious grace, founded in the priesthood alone, was needed for that, as pictured in Aaron's living rod. By God's grace, what was naturally dead could be made alive and fruitful. Of course, as C. A. Coates acknowledges, such life through priestly intercession has its fulfillment in Christ's death, burial and resurrection (1 Cor. 15:3-4):

> Priestly grace and intercession in Christ is the source and sustainment of everything of which God can take account as being in living relation to himself. It is only that which differs from murmuring and rebellious flesh, and only that which has any moral suitability to go through into the land which God has in view for His people.[74]

C. H. Mackintosh also acknowledges the typological similarity between the life-preserving Levitical priesthood and the life-giving priesthood of the Lord Jesus:

> Thus it was as to priesthood of old; and thus it is as to ministry now. All ministry in the Church of God is the fruit of divine grace – the gift of Christ, the Church's Head. There is no other source of ministry whatsoever. From apostles down to the very lowest gifts, all proceed from Christ. The grand root principle of all ministry is embodied in those words of Paul to the Galatians in which he speaks of himself as "an apostle, not of man, neither by man, but by Jesus Christ, and God the Father, who raised Him from the dead" (Gal. 1:1).[75]

In Christ alone, as pictured in Aaron's budding rod, is their eternal life. Through resurrection power, God confirmed that His Son, the Lord Jesus, is *"the resurrection and the life"* (John 11:25; Eph. 1:19-21). Amidst all the other dead rods on the planet (speaking of world religions), resurrection life and power are found only in Christ.

Centuries later, God moved several Old Testament prophets to declare more information about His Son as the living Branch. Four distinct presentations were given, each of which aligns prophetically with the unique vantage points of Christ in the four Gospels:

Refining and Reminding

> "Behold, the days are coming," says the Lord, "that I will raise to David **a Branch of righteousness; a King** shall reign and prosper, and execute judgment and righteousness in the earth" (Jer. 23:5; also see Isa. 11:1).

> Hear, O Joshua, the high priest, you and your companions who sit before you, for they are a wondrous sign;
> for behold, I am bringing forth **My Servant the Branch** (Zech. 3:8).

> Then speak to him, saying, "Thus says the Lord of hosts, saying: 'Behold, **the Man whose name is the Branch**! From His place He shall branch out, and He shall build the temple of the Lord'" (Zech. 6:12).

> In that day **the Branch of the Lord** shall be beautiful and glorious; and the fruit of the earth shall be excellent and appealing for those of Israel who have escaped (Isa. 4:2).

The four divine titles of the Lord perfectly align with the four Gospel presentations of Christ:

> Unto David a Branch ... a King – the Gospel of Matthew speaks of Christ's Jewish royalty.
> My Servant, the Branch – the Gospel of Mark expresses Christ's lowly servanthood.
> The Man ... the Branch – the Gospel of Luke addresses Christ's sinless humanity.
> The Branch of the Lord – the Gospel of John declares Christ's deity.

F. B. Hole summarizes the wonderful allusions to Christ's character and work as expressed by each of these Old Testament prophets when speaking of "the Branch":

Twice in Jeremiah do we get the Lord Jesus alluded to as the Branch, or Sprout (Jer. 23:5, 33:15); but there what is emphasized is righteousness. It is the character He displays rather than the Source from whence He springs. Again in Zechariah the expression occurs twice (Zech. 3:8, 6:12). There the emphasis lies on the fact that though He springs forth from Jehovah, He is to take the place of the Servant, and enter into Manhood to serve. Reading the five occurrences in the fuller light of the New Testament, we see how full these early predictions were as to our blessed Lord. The one in Isaiah 4:2 is the first and deepest of them all.[76]

"The Branch of the Lord" (Isa. 4:2) is indeed the deepest of the "Branch" expressions because it proclaims Christ's essential, divine glory, and His sovereign rule over the earth and over His people, and that He alone is the source of resurrection life and blessing.

Given all these future prophetic expressions that God would inspire in Scripture, it had to thrill the Father's heart to bring life and fruitfulness to Aaron's dead rod. Aaron's rod was the first of many forthcoming branch analogies that would point Israel to His life-giving Son. Apart from Christ, there is nothing but death, but in Him is the abundant and eternal life of God (John 5:24, 10:10).

This would explain why the Lord then instructed Moses to *"bring Aaron's rod back before the Testimony, to be kept as a sign against the rebels, that you may put their complaints away from Me, lest they die"* (v. 10). Moses did as the Lord commanded (v. 11). It was not yet time for the One symbolized by the rod to leave His Father's presence and come into the world. It was appropriate then for Aaron's rod to be with and before the Lord in the most holy place of the tabernacle. Later, we learn that Aaron's rod was actually placed in the Ark of the Covenant, with a golden pot containing manna, and the stone tablets of the Law (Heb. 9:4).

Indeed, what Israel had rebelled against previously was to be remembered, that is, God's provision of manna (Num. 11); His priesthood (Num. 16); and His Law (Ex. 32). But more importantly, Israel was to remember how God was able to overcome their failures in these things: All was placed under the mercy seat which was sprinkled with atoning blood from the sacrifice that was burning on the Bronze Altar. The Ark of the Covenant reminded Israel that a holy God can overcome man's wickedness and show mercy because an innocent and unblemished substitute was judged for the guilty. This pictures God's grand solution to human sin – Calvary. There God judged His own perfect, holy Son in place of the condemned – us! To show His complete satisfaction with His Son's redemptive work, God then raised Christ up from the grave and highly exalted Him in heaven.

Hence, Aaron's fruit-bearing rod, which typifies the resurrection of Christ, was also given as *"a sign against the rebels."* The Lord Jesus

Refining and Reminding

challenged a group of Jewish sign-seekers, by prophesying His own resurrection:

> *So the Jews answered and said to Him, "What sign do You show to us, since You do these things?" Jesus answered and said to them, "Destroy this temple, and in three days I will raise it up"* (John 2:18-19).

> *Then the Pharisees and Sadducees came, and testing Him asked that He would show them a sign from heaven. He answered and said to them, "When it is evening you say, 'It will be fair weather, for the sky is red'; and in the morning, 'It will be foul weather today, for the sky is red and threatening.' Hypocrites! You know how to discern the face of the sky, but you cannot discern the signs of the times. A wicked and adulterous generation seeks after a sign, and no sign shall be given to it except the sign of the prophet Jonah." And He left them and departed* (Matt. 16:1-4).

> *For as Jonah was three days and three nights in the belly of the great fish, so will the Son of Man be three days and three nights in the heart of the earth* (Matt. 12:40-41).

Yet, when Christ did raise up from His grave, the Pharisees and Sadducees, generally speaking, rejected God's sign and continued in their rebellion against Him. They denied that an extraordinary miracle had occurred and rejected their Messiah. This had devastating consequences for the Jewish nation even unto this day.

Aaron's rod was kept in the most holy place of the tabernacle as a memorial of the miracle Israel witnessed that day and as a warning to those who would challenge God's leadership and priestly order. Following the resurrection and ascension of Christ, God the Father and the Son enjoyed communion again in their heavenly abode. Presently, the Son, God's Lamb, sits with His Father on His Father's throne waiting the day of His vindication and rule on earth (Rev. 3:21).

All the events of Numbers 16 and 17 served to cleanse the people. The chapter ends with the congregation expressing to Moses a reverence and fear for God and those things that pertained to Him (vv. 12-13). They realized that any intrusion on what God had deemed holy meant death for them, but through Aaron's ministry in the tabernacle they could live before God in peace.

Meditation

How bright appears the morning star,
With mercy beaming from afar!
The host of Heaven rejoices!
O righteous Branch! O Jesse's Rod!
Thou Son of Man, and Son of God!
We too will lift our voices,
Jesus! Jesus! Holy, holy! Yet most lowly!
Draw Thou near us:
Great Emmanuel! Stoop and hear us!

— Philip Nicolai

Levitical Duties and Support
Numbers 18

The Duties of the Priests and Levites (vv. 1-7)

This chapter summarizes the place of the priesthood and the ministry of the Levites in assisting the priests. The content is somewhat redundant to the opening chapters of the book, but is placed here in response to human challenges against the Aaronic priesthood in Numbers 16 and God's affirmation of it in Numbers 17.

In verses 1-24, the Lord spoke directly to Aaron, and not through Moses, because Aaron and his sons had to *"bear the iniquity related to the sanctuary"* (v. 1). Only they could enter God's holy place situated in the midst of His people. Only what had been deemed holy by God was permitted to come into God's presence. This meant that the priests bore the responsibility of keeping the tabernacle free from defilement, including preventing anyone else from entering it, lest God's wrath fall on the intruder.

The ministry of the Levites and the Levites themselves were a gift from God to the priests (v. 6) – *"they may be joined with you and serve you"* (v. 2). The priesthood itself was His gift to Aaron and his sons (v. 7). The Levites were God's designated tribe of workers to maintain His tabernacle, but all of its affairs were under Aaron's supervision (vv. 3-4). Because of the priests' anointing, the most holy things related to the sacrifices were given to them to eat. This was God's special privilege and provision to sustain His priests.

All of this, of course, pictures the present spiritual ramifications of the Church in association with her Great High Priest – the Lord Jesus Christ. Believer-priests are anointed by the Holy Spirit, and are to remain undefiled and near to their High Priest as they render service to Him in complete submission to His authority. As typified in Numbers 16, there have been many challenges to Christ's headship and priesthood down through the ages. But there is a day coming when all true believers will be gathered to Christ in holiness, brokenness, and

Devotions in Numbers

with genuine spiritual sacrifices in a heavenly sanctuary which cannot be defiled – then the pattern before us will have its fulfillment. Indeed, during the Millennial Kingdom, the Jewish nation will also rejoice to see this priestly pattern, with Christ at its center, complete on the earth.

The Lord's Provision for His Priests (vv. 8-20)

Sin and trespass offerings were considered "most holy" and therefore portions of these (i.e., what was not God's portion burnt on the altar) were to be eaten by the priests, but only in the tabernacle courtyard (vv. 8-10; Lev. 6:25-27, 7:6, 10:17). For most of these offerings, God's portion was only the fat and kidneys of the animals, so the priests (but not their families) actually received all of the meat of the animal for food. C. H. Mackintosh derives a practical application from the limitation of only the males (i.e., not the priests' families) being able to eat the sin and trespass offerings before the Lord:

> To eat the sin offering or the trespass offering is, in figure, to make another's sin or trespass one's own. This is very holy work. It is not everyone who can, in spirit, identify himself with the sin of his brother. To do so in fact, in the way of atonement, is, we need hardly say, wholly out of question. Therefore, the daughters of Aaron were not to eat of the sin offerings or the trespass offerings. They were provided for according to the utmost limit of their capacity; but there were certain functions which they could not discharge – certain privileges which lay beyond their range – certain responsibilities too weighty for them to sustain. It is far easier to have fellowship with another in the presentation of a thank offering than it is to make his sin our own.[77]

Indeed, to identify in prayer with another believer in sin and to confess that sin in the spirit of humble intercession as our own – as failure of the Church to represent Christ – is a much harder priestly work than to enjoy fellowship with those walking with the Lord. However, as shown later by the prophets Isaiah and Daniel and the priest Ezra, this is an important ministry. They did not hold back from confessing the sins of the nation as their own. For example, though grieved by his fellow countrymen's sin, Isaiah does not assume a lofty superiority looking down his nose at them. Rather, he humbly applies the pronouns "we," "us," and "our" to identify himself with his corrupt

Refining and Reminding

nation deserving divine judgment (Isa. 59:9-12). This is difficult intercessory work, but so needful in the Church today.

The burnt offerings were wholly for the Lord, and could not be eaten by the priests, though the offering priest did receive the hide of the animal offered (Lev. 7:8). For the meal offerings, a memorial portion was burned on the altar as a sweet aroma to the Lord, but the remaining portion belonged to Aaron and his sons who were to eat it in the Holy Place (Lev. 6:16). The fact that the priests could eat these offerings before the Lord, illustrates the efficacy of Christ in dealing with both the penalty and damage of sin so that the redeemed can enjoy God's fellowship and His bountiful provisions.

Additionally, the priests and their families (who were clean) would receive a portion of the peace offerings waved before the Lord (v. 11). These free-will offerings symbolized the fellowship God wanted to enjoy with His people. While only the priests could eat of the *most holy* things in the tabernacle, their families could enjoy what was *holy* and associated with the priesthood. John J. Stubbs suggests there is a good application for us to consider in this:

> The sons of the priests would suggest spiritually those who have the capacity to take in the "most holy things," but the daughters, while they cannot function as priests, yet belonging to the priestly family are provided with those things that will sustain. The provision the daughters are given, while not as high as "the most holy things" of the sons, is still viewed as "holy" (v. 19). The "daughters" would refer to the domestic sphere. How good it is that the Christian family is linked with the Christian priesthood. Christ should be fed upon and enjoyed in the home. It is a good thing when that which has been presented in thanksgiving and praise to God willingly from His people is taken up and assimilated by the family. Far too often that which is heard when the saints worship is forgotten or not conversed about when in the home. That this is so is sad.[78]

The priests and their families also received the firstfruit offerings (i.e., wine, olive oil, or grain) that were waved before the Lord, but not burnt on the altar (vv. 12-13). Anything devoted to the Lord was also given to the priests (v. 14; Lev. 27:1-33). The meat from the firstborn of the clean animals dedicated to the Lord was for the priests and their families, as was the redemption money associated with the firstborn of men and unclean animals (vv. 15-18).

Having described His provisions for His priests, the Lord affirms a covenant with Aaron and his descendants:

> *"All the heave offerings of the holy things, which the children of Israel offer to the Lord, I have given to you and your sons and daughters with you as an ordinance forever; it is a covenant of salt forever before the Lord with you and your descendants with you."* Then the Lord said to Aaron: *"You shall have no inheritance in their land, nor shall you have any portion among them; I am your portion and your inheritance among the children of Israel"* (vv. 19-20).

Salt was added to all the meal offerings (Lev. 2:1-16), and when burned it created white smoke. Salt adds flavor to what is eaten, and also serves as a food preservative. Salt then stands in contrast with leaven, which corrupts. This is why Paul used salt as a metaphor to speak of uncompromised truth (Col. 4:6), and why the Lord Jesus exhorted His disciples to have a "salty" testimony (Matt. 5:13). The Gospels confirm that the entire life of the Lord Jesus was marked by dedication to living and declaring truth – His testimony was thus pure (salty) and appreciated by God.

Not only did salt represent a pure testimony, but Albert Barnes asserts that "a covenant of salt" also spoke of perpetuity: "Covenants were ordinarily cemented in the East by the rites of hospitality; of which salt was the obvious token, entering as it does into every article of diet. It indicates perpetuity (see Lev. 2:13)."[79] Hence, the priests were to faithfully attend to their office because the Lord, who is pure, had covenanted with them to meet their every need forever. Indeed, He would always be their portion! After noting the connection between the priest's purity and enjoying the Lord's portion, Matthew Henry exhorts believer-priests today to live consecrated lives to the Lord, for He is their portion too:

> As Israel was a people not to be numbered among the nations, so Levi was a tribe to be distinguished from the rest. Those who have God for their Inheritance and their Portion forever ought to look with holy contempt and indifference upon the possessions of this world![80]

The Lord's Table

As mentioned in Numbers 5, all the above provisions constituted the Lord's Table for His serving priests and represented both the

Refining and Reminding

communion and partaking God wanted His servants to continue enjoying in His presence. *The Lord's Table* is an expression that is used in both the Old and New Testaments to convey this concept of divine provision and fellowship described in this text (Ps. 23:5, 78:19; Mal. 1:7, 12; 1 Cor. 9:13, 10:18). Both the Levitical priests under the old covenant of the Law (Lev. 6:16, 26, 7:6, 31-32) and believer-priests under the new covenant of grace (1 Cor. 10:20-21) have been invited to abide at the Lord's Table.

Often today, the biblical term "the Lord's Table" (which speaks of a spiritual table where believers receive blessing and fellowship in Christ – see 1 Corinthians 10) is confused with the biblical term "the Lord's Supper" (which refers to the remembrance meeting of the local church – see 1 Corinthians 11). Consequently, most of Christendom refers to the Lord's Supper with the non-scriptural term "the communion service." There is *communion with Christ* at the Lord's Table, but more specifically, there is a *remembrance of Christ* at every Lord's Supper – the value of His death is proclaimed afresh. The Lord's Table is spiritual and is set by Him, whereas the table at the Lord's Supper is physical and is set by us; at the former we receive provisions from the Lord, but at the latter we worship and remember Him.

The Lord's Table speaks of the sum total of the spiritual blessings we have in Christ, while the Lord's Supper refers to the remembrance meeting of the Church. In the sense that the souls of believers are refreshed through Spirit-led worship, the Lord's Table probably includes the Lord's Supper, but the distinct terminology and significance of each should not be lost. It is a great privilege to remember and refresh the Savior during the Lord's Supper, and it is a blessing to the heart of every believer to commune with and receive from the Savior at His Table.

Paul thus exhorts the believers at Corinth not to remove themselves from the Lord's Table to partake of the world's resources; to do so is to fellowship with demons:

> *I do not want you to have fellowship with demons. You cannot drink the cup of the Lord and the cup of demons; you cannot partake of the Lord's table and of the table of demons. Or do we provoke the Lord to jealousy? Are we stronger than He?* (1 Cor. 10:20-22).

Devotions in Numbers

When ordering the priesthood and sacrifices, God wonderfully provided for the needs of His priests, through the offerings just reviewed. While atoning blood was being applied to the altar to sanctify it, the priest also appropriated the offering by eating it. This repeats the same idea of Exodus 12 where the blood of a victim (the Passover lamb) was applied to sanctify the one who ate the victim's flesh. The themes of blood atonement, substitutional death, and sanctification to God are all interconnected in Scripture and, ultimately, have their typological climax and fulfillment at Calvary.

The Bronze Altar would be God's Table to supply His priests' needs, but the priests had to eat what was provided by the Lord before Him in the tabernacle. May each believer realize the importance of eating at the Lord's Table and, accordingly, choose to abide with Him there. Failure to do so will provoke the Lord's jealousy and His chastening hand. Why would a believer ever want to sever his or her communion with the Lord? It is a great privilege and honor to sup at His Table!

Tithes for God's Servants (vv. 21-32)

Besides the various offerings to supply the needs of His priests, the Lord also would provide for the Levites as a tribe, for He was their inheritance. In short, the people were to give one-tenth of what God had blessed them with to the Levites (vv. 21-24). The Levites, having collected a tithe from the entire nation, would then deliver one-tenth of it to the priests (vv. 25-32).

Because the tithe of the Levites was to be waved before the Lord before being presented to the priests, it was to be of the highest quality (vv. 26, 28-30). This offering consisted of grape juice and grain (v. 27). What the Levites received, less the tenth given to the Lord on behalf of the priests, could be eaten anywhere, for it was theirs (v. 31). The Levites were then warned with the penalty of death not to profane what the people had given to them by neglecting to give the best of it as a tithe to the Lord (v. 32).

Although believers today are not constrained by the Law to give a tenth of our income to God, the reality of offending Him by not giving back our best is true throughout Scripture. As we have seen, the Law demanded a tithe, but under grace an individual is requested to give proportionately as God has blessed him and as each one purposes in his heart (2 Cor. 9:7).

Refining and Reminding

Additionally, Paul instructed the church at Corinth: *"On the first day of the week let each one of you lay something aside, storing up as he may prosper, that there be no collections when I come"* (1 Cor. 16:2). Clearly, our giving should be **periodic** (on the first day of the week), a **personal** matter requiring thoughtful **preparation**, and **proportional**, as God had prospered the believer.

The Levites were to give their firstfruits to the Lord. Likewise believers today should give the best of what they have to the Lord. This would include, but not be limited to, the following resources:

- Your harvest (Num. 15:19-21; Lev. 23:10)
- Your flocks (Gen. 4:4; Ex. 12:5)
- Your time and attention (Ps. 63:1; Matt. 6:33)
- Your personal purity (Rom. 12:1)
- Your money (Matt. 6:19-21)

The support of the priests depended on the faithfulness of the Levites to give to the Lord what He requested. The support of the Levites depended on the faithfulness of the other tribes giving to the Lord what He requested. Obedience to the Lord in these matters meant that God's worshippers and workers could remain with Him while having all their needs met. This typifies the blessed position and privilege that is also afforded to the Lord's servants of every age. C. H. Mackintosh writes:

> Nothing can be more lovely than the picture here presented. The children of Israel were to bring their offerings, and lay them down at the feet of Jehovah, and He, in His infinite grace, commanded His workers to pick up these precious offerings – the fruit of His people's devotedness – and feed upon them, in His own blessed presence, with thankful hearts.[81]

If all believers enjoying sweet communion with God were faithful to give back to the Lord His due, His workers and ministries around the globe would be adequately supported. Obviously, the support basis for the Lord's servants commanded in this chapter is Jewish in nature, but what a wonderful pattern to follow in principle!

Meditation

You can give without loving, but you cannot love without giving.

— Amy Carmichael

Do not think me mad. It is not to make money that I believe a Christian should live. The noblest thing a man can do is just humbly to receive, and then go amongst others and give.

— David Livingstone

Purification Is Available
Numbers 19

After reviewing the content of this chapter, it would be natural for us to wonder, Why is the sacrifice of the red heifer divulged now and in the book of Numbers, instead of earlier in Leviticus? The first seven chapters of Leviticus reveal to us the five main offerings to be regularly repeated and then, in Leviticus 23, the offerings associated with seven annual feasts are specified, yet nothing is ever said about the sacrifice of a red heifer. C. H. Mackintosh suggests a reason this ordinance was reserved for Numbers:

> The red heifer is, preeminently, a wilderness type. It was God's provision for defilements by the way, and it prefigures the death of Christ as a purification for sin, to meet our need in passing through a defiling world, home to our eternal rest above. It is a most instructive figure, and unfolds a most precious and needed truth. May the Holy Ghost, who has penned the record, be graciously pleased to expound and apply it to our souls![82]

There are several notable differences between the Levitical offerings and the burning of the red heifer before us. First, there was no command to repeat the latter sacrifice. Second, the heifer was not offered on an altar. Third, it was wholly burned outside the camp where its ashes were collected and then remained.

Another distinction is that "the water of purification" is mentioned specifically five times in this chapter and again in Numbers 31:23, but nowhere else in Scripture. What is highlighted in this chapter then, and indeed in the entire book, is the necessity of purification during Israel's wilderness experience (this same consecration would also be necessary in Canaan later). A provision to cleanse away the effects of sin's defilement, rather than blood atonement for offenses, is the main focus.

The children of Israel had yet to learn that the sin and trespass offerings, and those on the Day of Atonement, had not so completely dealt with their sin that they did not need to be concerned about daily defilement. This principle of keeping short accounts with the Lord should be a timeless concern for all God's people. However, such thinking is offensive to the Prosperity Gospel or Easy-Beliefism messages bantered about today. These erroneous ideals emphasize the blessings in Christ, but neglect the believer's crucial need for personal consecration and continued holiness.

What God redeems by the blood of His Son is holy to Him and should be to us also! So while redemption and cleansing of the conscience are accomplished for a believer through Christ's blood, that is not all that is required to live for Christ. Believers also need further and repetitive purification in their wilderness journey through a sin-infested world (e.g. 1 Pet. 1:1-2, 14-16). As we daily walk through a defiled world, some of its influences dirty our hands and feet, which then need to be cleansed. The Lord Jesus illustrated this truth by washing the dirty feet of His disciples the night before His crucifixion (John 13). He told them that they needed only one spiritual bath, speaking of regeneration, but afterwards would need to repeatedly wash the filth from their feet after trudging through the world. John speaks of this type of personal spiritual hygiene in 1 John 1:9.

William Kelly further examines the typological meaning of the red heifer:

> We are justified by His blood; yea more, with Christ we have died to sin; and we are alive to God in Him. But though this is all quite true, such grace is the strongest motive why we cannot tamper with what is defiled. The very fact that we are cleansed perfectly before God is a loud call to us not to endure a blot before men. It was to guard His people from soils by the way that God gave here a provision so remarkable. "A red heifer" was to be brought *"without spot, wherein is no blemish, and upon which never came yoke,"* a striking picture of Christ, but of Christ in a way not often spoken of in Scripture. The requirement supposes not only the absence of such blemishes as was indispensable in every sacrifice; but here expressly also it must have never known the yoke, that is, the pressure of sin. How this speaks of the antitype! Christ was always perfectly acceptable to God. *"And ye shall give her to Eleazar the priest that he may bring her forth without the camp, and one shall slay her before his face."* [83]

Refining and Reminding

This is why the red heifer was not spoken of in Leviticus, which relates to the offense, guilt, and damage of sin through blood atonement. The benefit of these offerings permitted God's people to worship and to commune with Him. Numbers, however, addresses the wilderness experience of God's people. As God's pilgrims trek through a sin-contaminated world, the devil's lair, so to speak, they must remain strangers to its defilements and have a provision for cleansing when they do not. John J. Stubbs summarizes why the practical aspects of this chapter are important for believers today:

> The law of the red heifer shows how the believer can be saved from two extremes: presumption, which says sin does not matter, and despair, which says it cannot be cleansed. In the chapter, the holiness of God is emphasized and the serious nature of the contagious defilement of sin is most solemnly illustrated. God's people were a people separated to Him, and because of this the Israelite had to avoid ceremonial defilement of different kinds, particularly contamination from dead bodies, death, of course, being the most visible outcome of sin. There may well have been hygienic factors in connection with this law, but mainly it would have taught the people to avoid anything that would defile the Camp in which God dwelt.[84]

The types of Christ and His work of purging defilement from His people abound in this chapter. With the Lord's help we will endeavor to understand what the Spirit of God has impressed into the Scripture to enhance our appreciation of Him and His work.

The Offering of the Red Heifer (vv. 1-10)

The Lord commanded Moses to instruct the people concerning the slaughtering and burning of a red heifer and the gathering of its ashes for purification (v. 1). The red heifer had to be without blemish or defect and an animal *"on which a yoke has never come"* (v. 2). Eleazar, the priest, was to take the heifer outside the camp, but someone else was to slaughter it in his presence (v. 3). Eleazar was then to collect some of the heifer's blood and sprinkle it with his finger seven times in front of the tabernacle (v. 4). Then the heifer (every part of it) was to be burned while Eleazar watched (v. 5). A priest, apparently not Eleazar, was to cast cedar wood, hyssop, and scarlet into the fire also (v. 6).

This priest and the one burning the heifer were to wash their clothes and bathe in water before returning to camp, but both would remain unclean until evening (vv. 7-8). Then a man who was ceremonially clean was to gather up the ashes of the heifer, and store them outside the camp in a clean place so they could be added to *"the water of purification"* for the congregation as needed (v. 9). The one who gathered up the ashes of the heifer was to wash his clothes; he was unclean until evening (v. 10). God's provision of purification by the ashes was to be a perpetual statute for the children of Israel.

Several observations of the text highlight various aspects of Christ's sacrifice at Calvary and His continuing ministry of purification in heaven:

First, notice that the red heifer was without blemish or defect. Such an animal, without even one black or white hair would have been rare. Then the animal had to be without any physical abnormalities. This portrays just how unique the Lord Jesus was in character from the normal populace of humanity. The Lord looked like everyone else, but He did not act like everyone else. His life was unique, for *"in Him is no sin"* (1 Jn. 3:5), He *"knew no sin"* (2 Cor. 5:21), and He *"did no sin"* (1 Pet. 2:22). He was God's spotless Lamb without blemish.

Second, in contrast with the sin offering which could only be a male (Lev. 4:14), the animal to be slaughtered and burnt for purification purposes had to be a female. As John J. Stubbs suggests, this feminine aspect likely typifies the subjection of the Lord Jesus to His Father at Calvary:

> The female speaks of subjection and would link with the touching words of the prophet Isaiah relative to our blessed Lord: *"And as a sheep before her shearers is dumb, so He openeth not His mouth"* (Isa. 53:7). He was subject to the Father's will and was passive in the hands of wicked men as they led Him all the way to the death of the cross. The female gender in the type of the red heifer is a precious aspect of the Savior to meditate upon. She is seen in Scripture as affectionate, dependent, and passive. These thoughts of affection, dependence, and passivity are beautifully and perfectly expressed in Christ's person and nowhere more so than at Calvary when He was crucified and yet still so dependent on His Father and affectionate to others.[85]

Third, the heifer had never borne a yoke. A yoke was placed upon beasts to restrain their wild nature and to command subjection, but Christ never needed or was under such a yoke. Not only was the Lord

Refining and Reminding

Jesus sinless, but He was One who never bore the yoke of sin – there was no wild nature within Him that might suddenly come out. This speaks of His impeccability. Christ was fully tested, but not in sin (literally, "sin apart"; Heb. 4:15). To think of Christ as bearing the yoke of sin in His life would diminish our estimation of His fitness to be God's propitiation for our sin. There was nothing evil in Him that could respond to anything outside of God's will or that would give an offense to His holy character.

Fourth, the heifer was to be slaughtered outside the camp. Likewise, Christ did not suffer in heaven for sin, or in the confines of Judaism, but rather in the world and by the hands of those He came to save. Christ was of the tribe of Judah and completely separate from the Levitical priesthood and its constraints. Christ sojourned in a putrid world, and yet was not defiled by it, so that He could legitimately and willingly give His life for a ransom. Like the ashes for purification, He and His provision of cleansing continue to reside outside of Judaism.

In all of this, Christ is our example to follow of purity and through Him alone we can be cleansed from defilement. Just as Israel had to go outside the camp to obtain the water of purification (which contained some ashes from the red heifer), we must go outside the camp to identify with Christ: *"Therefore Jesus also, that He might sanctify the people with His own blood, suffered outside the gate. Therefore let us go forth to Him, outside the camp, bearing His reproach"* (Heb. 13:12-13).

Fifth, Eleazar watched the slaughter and burning of the heifer, but he did not actually participate in it. In type, then, the death of Christ is not presented as an ordinary act of the priesthood (although the priests did watch Him die). What transpired at Calvary was not brought about through any earthly ministry, but rather within the sphere of Christ's heavenly priesthood. The Levitical priests offered animal sacrifices to atone for sin, but they had no power to cleanse away any actual defilement. They could shed the blood of animals for atonement, and declare people ceremonially clean, but they could not do anything about the actual defilement within a person. This requires supernatural cleansing and regeneration (Tit. 3:5) which is possible only through the resurrection power of Christ. Without this new birth, no one can receive eternal life in Christ (John 3:3).

Indeed, centuries later, the priests would be responsible for having Christ crucified for the supposed sin of blasphemy. God permitted them to do this, but it was the Son who surrendered His life and brought it back again: *"I lay down My life that I may take it again. No one takes it from Me, but I lay it down of Myself. I have power to lay it down, and I have power to take it again"* (John 10:17-18). So when it came to Christ's resurrection, the priests could do nothing against it; they could only observe the aftermath of His resurrection power. Thankfully, many Levitical priests did observe, consider, and choose to be cleansed by Christ (Acts 6:7).

Sixth, notice that, other than the bit of blood Eleazar collected to be sprinkled before the entrance of the tabernacle, the heifer was totally consumed by fire and burnt to ashes. In all other animal sacrifices the animal was slain on the north side of the Bronze Altar and the blood was collected. Depending on the specific sacrifice, the blood was then sprinkled, smeared, or poured out, but never burnt on the altar with the animal or its parts, or outside the camp in a clean place. This reminds us of the incredible cost of our redemption and purification – no part of Christ was exempt from being consumed by the full wrath of God for our sin. Christ gave His all to bear our sins to be judged by a Holy God – who, the writer of Hebrews reminds us, is "a consuming fire" of holiness (Heb. 12:29).

Seventh, cedar wood, hyssop, and scarlet wool were put into the fire with the heifer (v. 6). Each of these articles was associated with the ceremonial purification of a cleansed leper in Leviticus 14:1-9. Keil and Delitzsch describe what each of these items signifies:

> But in order still further to increase the strength of these ashes, which were already well fitted to serve as a powerful antidote to the corruption of death, as being the incorruptible residuum of the sin offering which had not been destroyed by the fire, cedar-wood was thrown into the fire, as the symbol of the incorruptible continuance of life; and hyssop, as the symbol of purification from the corruption of death; and scarlet wool, the deep red of which shadowed forth the strongest vital energy (see at Lev 14:6) so that the ashes might be regarded "as the quintessence of all that purified and strengthened life, refined and sublimated by the fire" (Leyrer).[86]

The fire not only consumed the entire heifer, but to its ashes were added multiple scriptural symbols of purification. This compound expression then further extols God's means of purifying man's uncleanness, which is ultimately found in *"Jesus Christ, who gave*

Refining and Reminding

Himself for us, that He might redeem us from every lawless deed and purify for Himself His own special people, zealous for good works" (Tit. 2:13-14). Anyone experiencing the Lord's cleansing was also enabled to offer up good works to God, just as those purified by the ashes could also present offerings to the Lord again. Because Christ's cleansing is powerful and complete, we can agree with David's request, *"Purge me with hyssop, and I shall be clean; wash me, and I shall be whiter than snow"* (Ps. 51:7).

Eighth, while Jewish tradition records that nine red heifers were slaughtered from Moses to the destruction of the Herod's temple (Mishna: *Parah* 3:5), there were always some of the original ashes from this first heifer in subsequent burnings. This pictures that complete efficacy of Christ's sacrifice and priesthood to meet every need of the believer to remain in communion with God forever. There will never be a need for Him to be offered again because His shed blood is eternally able to cleanse the guilty conscience at regeneration, and defilement from our hearts in an ongoing way afterwards.

For this reason, the writer of Hebrews reiterates several times that the perfect sacrifice of Christ will never be repeated (Heb. 9:26, 28, 10:12, 14, 18). The basis for all purification is Christ's shed blood which was presented to God in heaven and was fully accepted at that time:

> *But Christ came as High Priest of the good things to come, with the greater and more perfect tabernacle not made with hands, that is, not of this creation. Not with the blood of goats and calves, but with His own blood He entered the Most Holy Place once for all, having obtained eternal redemption. For if the blood of bulls and goats and the ashes of a heifer, sprinkling the unclean, sanctifies for the purifying of the flesh, how much more shall the blood of Christ, who through the eternal Spirit offered Himself without spot to God, cleanse your conscience from dead works to serve the living God?* (Heb. 9:11-14).

The work accomplished at Calvary and Christ's continuing priesthood are able to meet every need for the believer to remain holy unto God! *"For by one offering He has perfected forever those who are being sanctified"* (Heb. 10:14). "Perfected forever" speaks of who we are positionally in Christ, whereas "being sanctified" identifies His continued work in us to make us like Himself – holy and pure. God's grand prerogative for all His people is that they be conformed to the moral image of His Son (Rom. 8:29).

Ninth, the heap of ashes, stored in a clean place, presents a twofold testimony. First, it was a witness of God's holiness and that He could not tolerate uncleanness in His people. Second, it testified of God's hatred of sin and provided a means of removing its defiling influence from His people. The ramifications of ignoring His provision for cleansing resulted in that person being cut off from the commonwealth of Israel (vv. 13, 20).

Tenth, it was *"a statute forever to the children of Israel and to the stranger who dwells among them"* (v. 10). There was no end to God's provision for cleansing away defilement. It was always to be available for anyone who wanted to be "clean" again in order to enjoy God's presence. Praise the Lord!

The Provision of Purification (vv. 11-22)

Anyone touching a corpse would be unclean (v. 11). The solution was to remain in separation for a week and to apply the water of purification on the third and seventh days to become clean again (vv. 12-13). The same procedure pertained to those dwelling in the same tent with someone that had died – all the people and things in the tent (unless a covered vessel) were considered unclean (v. 14). Those touching a dead body, whether in an open field or in battle, even a human bone or a grave, would also become unclean (vv. 15-16).

Given God's judicial decree at Kadesh-Barnea, the entire population of those twenty years of age and older would die before entering Canaan forty years later. That works out to be about 85 funerals a day on average, which meant the Jews were having regular contact with dead bodies and graves, all of which made them ceremonially unclean. The resolution for defilement was simple and available at all times: Those unclean...

> *shall take some of the ashes of the heifer burnt for purification from sin, and running water shall be put on them in a vessel. A clean person shall take hyssop and dip it in the water, sprinkle it on the tent, on all the vessels, on the persons who were there, or on the one who touched a bone, the slain, the dead, or a grave. The clean person shall sprinkle the unclean on the third day and on the seventh day;*

Refining and Reminding

> *and on the seventh day he shall purify himself, wash his clothes, and bathe in water; and at evening he shall be clean* (vv. 17-19).

The water of purification was available for anyone who wanted to be cleansed of defilement and be able to offer sacrifices again at the tabernacle. However, anyone not taking advantage of the waters of purification was to be cut off from Israel (v. 20). Why such a harsh penalty? To pretend to be a servant and a worshipper of God, while willfully ignoring the defiling effects of sin, is to provoke God's anger. It is an insult to His holiness. Offerings presented with unclean hands would be putrid to Him and would defile His sanctuary (e.g., Mal. 1:6-14). Moses then reminds the people that even if someone did not touch a dead body, coming into contact with someone who did would transfer his or her uncleanness (vv. 21-22). In such cases, individuals were to wash their clothes and sprinkle the water of purification on themselves with hyssop and be unclean until evening.

The reality of the matter is that believers cannot have close association with the world without being affected – we have been yoked with sin in the past and we still have a nature within us that gravitates to sin. The reference to all in the tent of the deceased being defiled also indicates that even believers, in the flesh, have a defiling effect on those closest to them. However, with that said, those who do not open themselves up to such carnal influences, as seen in the covered vessels in the tent, are not contaminated by those acting in the flesh.

This requires the Christian to test everything: the influence of secular philosophies, carnal pleasures and amusements, and also the behavior of others with whom we associate (1 Cor. 15:33). For example, Proverbs warns us not to keep close company with fools or with angry people, lest we become like them and suffer the consequences (Prov. 13:20, 22:24). Further understanding of what defilement is should then prompt us to keep short accounts with God through confessing sin, lest we prompt His parental chastening (Heb. 12:6). The water of purification in this chapter symbolizes these two ongoing qualities of spiritual cleansing available in Christ to all believers today.

First, by the washing of the Word, believers learn to recognize and think of filth as God does. Paul refers to this ongoing ministry of the Lord Jesus to sanctify His Church:

> *Christ also loved the church and gave Himself for her, that He might sanctify and cleanse her with the washing of water by the word, that He might present her to Himself a glorious church, not having spot or wrinkle or any such thing, but that she should be holy and without blemish* (Eph. 5:25-27).

The washing of the Word enables believers to identify and repudiate thoughts, motives, and behavior which do not have the Lord's approval. Paul tells us that *"to be carnally minded is death ... the carnal mind is enmity against God ... So then, those who are in the flesh cannot please God"* (Rom. 8:6-8). What exposes the depravity of the carnal mind? The answer is the conviction of the Holy Spirit through exposure to God's Word.

The seven-day period of resolving uncleanness after touching a dead body indicates that there is often a process for believers to first recognize and then repudiate uncleanness in what they have done in the flesh. For an example, a believer may feel grieved in their conscience after doing or saying something without understanding what it is all about. Yet, through continued exposure to God's Word, seeking the Lord's wisdom in prayer (Jas. 1:5), and the conviction of the Holy Spirit, believers are enabled to better understand what God disapproves of and to reject it. On this point, C. A. Coates writes:

> The period of uncleanness typifies a believer who has sinned by allowing some working of the flesh, and the period of seven days indicates that, in such a case, purification can only be brought about by a moral process which takes time. I do not mean that we are to take the "seven days" literally, but they evidently represent a completed exercise, whether the actual time be long or short. And it is to be noted that responsibility to use the means of purifying rests, in the first place, on the unclean person.[87]

The second phase of cleansing is to confess and repent of known failures which have been exposed by God's Word and morally understood (Jas. 1:21-23). True repentance is repentance that should not be repented of (2 Cor. 7:10). It is more than telling God, "I know this is wrong, I am sorry – please forgive me." True repentance includes an aspiration to, by the grace of God, not repeat the same offense.

Refining and Reminding

As soon as one is conscious of sin, the sin should be confessed – in so doing we effectively sprinkle the ashes of the red heifer on ourselves: *"If we confess our sins, He is faithful and just to forgive us our sins, and to cleanse us from all unrighteousness"* (1 Jn. 1:9). Of course, God desires His children not to sin (1 Jn. 2:1) so that He can walk together with them in the light of divine truth (1 Jn. 1:6-7). But when we do sin (venture into darkness), there is an immediate solution – His cleansing! This is why Eleazar sprinkled the blood of the heifer before the entrance of the tabernacle and did not smear it on the horns of the Bronze Altar. This symbolized the means of cleansing, the path, if you will, back to God. This provision permits the Christian life to be one of ongoing separation from the world while still permitting evangelical connections in the world.

Today believers can rejoice that Christ has delivered them not only from consequences of their sins, but also from sin's present claims and influences. Christ's provision of purification permits heaven-bound pilgrims to journey through our sin-defiled world as heavenly-minded strangers. This is what the water of purification from the ashes of the red heifer pictures for us in Numbers 19.

Meditation

> Christian reader, let us never forget that, when we look at the death of Christ, we see two things, namely, the death of a victim, and the death of a martyr — a victim for sin, a martyr for righteousness — a victim, under the hand of God, a martyr, under the hand of man. He suffered for sin, that we might never suffer. Blessed be His name forevermore! But then, His martyr sufferings, His sufferings for righteousness under the hand of man, these we may know. *"For to you it is given, in the behalf of Christ, not only to believe on Him, but also to suffer for His sake"* (Phil. 1:29). It is a positive *gift* to be allowed to suffer with Christ. Do we esteem it? In contemplating the death of Christ, as typified by the ordinance of the red heifer, we see not only the complete putting away of sin, but also the judgement of this present evil world. *"He gave Himself for our sins that He might deliver us from this present evil world, according to the will of God and our Father"* (Gal. 1:4).[88]
>
> — C. H. Mackintosh

Miriam Dies and Moses and Aaron Err
Numbers 20:1-13

Commentators have differing opinions of the timing of the previous four chapters. The challenges to leadership, the affirmations of the priesthood, and the laws of purification contained in chapters 16-19 seem to stand alone without marking a progression of time. As the content in these chapters is foundational to the continuance of sacrifices and offerings, it seems reasonable to place them early in Israel's wilderness experience.

Numbers 33 contains a detailed listing of Israel's itinerary from Egypt to the border of the Promised Land. We know their wanderings began when they departed Kadesh-Barnea for Hazeroth (12:16), which is also mentioned in 33:17. In this chapter, we find the Israelites at Kadesh in the desert of Zin, which is also mentioned in 33:36. The next verse tells us that they moved from Kadesh to camp at Mount Hor, located near the boundary of Edom (33:37). This is where Aaron dies (vv. 14-21) and the timing of his death is stated in 33:38, *"in the fortieth year after the children of Israel had come out of the land of Egypt, on the first day of the fifth month."* This means that all the events of this chapter occurred during the final year of the Israelites' forty-year stay in the wilderness.

Miriam Dies (v. 1)

The Israelites returned to Kadesh in the first month of the fortieth year since their Egyptian exodus. They will enter Canaan on the tenth day of the first month in the following year (Josh. 4:19). Miriam died and was buried at Kadesh (v. 1). The voice and tambourine of the one who led the women in jubilant praise after the great victory at the Red Sea were now silent; Miriam retired into God's rest. The narrative has not mentioned her name since she was punished thirty-eight years earlier with leprosy. Though still the sister of Israel's leaders, the

Refining and Reminding

shame of that event no doubt clung to her the remainder of her life and evidently limited her ministry during her autumn years.

As we will soon see, Miriam, Aaron, and Moses will all die within the space of one year. Miriam, Moses' eldest sibling, lived a long life; she was likely between 127 and 130 years of age at her death. Interestingly, she would have been approximately the same age as Abraham's wife Sarah was when she died.

Moses and Aaron Err (vv. 2-13)

Thirty-nine years earlier the Kadesh oasis had an abundance of water; however, that was not the case now. In fact, the Israelites found no water at Kadesh, which prompted the congregation to bitterly complain to Moses and Aaron (v. 2):

If only we had died when our brethren died before the Lord! Why have you brought up the assembly of the Lord into this wilderness, that we and our animals should die here? And why have you made us come up out of Egypt, to bring us to this evil place? It is not a place of grain or figs or vines or pomegranates; nor is there any water to drink (vv. 2-5).

We have not heard such strife against God's leaders since Korah's revolt in Numbers 16. Numbers is a book about testing and refining. At their first arrival at Kadesh, the Lord tested the Israelites to expose their unbelief, but the purpose now is to cause them to further value the priesthood, which God had established to administer grace to them. For thirty-nine years, God's faithfulness has been demonstrated. Moses will later tell his countrymen that they *"lacked nothing"* during their wilderness wanderings (Deut. 2:7).

What the people discerned about the place was correct; Kadesh was not a place for growing crops, for planting grape vines, or fig and pomegranate trees, as there was no water. However, instead of beseeching the Lord through the priesthood for help, they complained against God's leadership and assumed the worst was going to happen – that they were all going to die there. Why would God preserve them in every way for thirty-nine years and then permit them to perish on the eve of fulfilling His promises? This is not reasonable, but it is natural for carnal flesh to belittle the benefits of divine grace.

Apparently, this was the Israelites' first test in a long time and it quickly revealed a need that they could not provide for themselves. But instead of seeking the Lord's help through the priesthood, they chose to complain. How often the Lord's people today commit this same error despite knowing God's past faithfulness. Some test (trial) reveals our need for God's grace, but instead of seeking our Great High Priest for the help needed, we instead complain to others and to the Lord about our situation. Such doubting of God's goodness will always trouble our souls and will often lead to contention with others. All of this is a warning that we are trying to alleviate the trial in our own strength and wisdom.

Paul had learned to be joyfully content in the Lord, despite his outward circumstances. He knew that God had endorsed every test in his life for his good and to increase his capacity to serve. He tells the believers at Philippi what he has learned to better equip them for future challenges also:

> *I know how to be abased, and I know how to abound. Everywhere and in all things I have learned both to be full and to be hungry, both to abound and to suffer need. I can do all things through Christ who strengthens me. ... Indeed I have all and abound. I am full, having received from Epaphroditus the things sent from you, a sweet-smelling aroma, an acceptable sacrifice, well pleasing to God. And my God shall supply all your need according to His riches in glory by Christ Jesus* (Phil. 4:12-13, 18-19).

However, the Israelites at Kadesh were not content, but doubted God's goodness and boldly confronted His leaders. The people's statements against Moses and Aaron were hurtful for several reasons. First, they were rejecting their leaders after their thirty-nine years of faithful service. Second, the complainers were of the new generation and they had observed firsthand the consequences of doubting God's faithfulness. Third, Moses and Aaron were quite elderly at this time and deserved the respect of the younger people, not their disdain (Lev. 19:22; Job 32:7; 1 Tim. 5:1-2). Moses was 119-120 and Aaron, 122-123 (Ex. 7:7, 33:39), and it is not likely that anyone standing before them was over sixty years of age.

Although offended by the people's accusations, they wisely did not respond because they did not know the mind of God on the matter. This demonstrates the wisdom Scripture often associates with the hoary

Refining and Reminding

crown (Job 12:12; Prov. 16:31). Moses and Aaron went to the tabernacle to seek the word of the Lord and His glory appeared to them (v. 6). The urgent need was water, so the Lord told Moses:

> *Take the rod; you and your brother Aaron gather the congregation together. Speak to the rock before their eyes, and it will yield its water; thus you shall bring water for them out of the rock, and give drink to the congregation and their animals* (vv. 7-8).

These instructions were patently clear. Moses took the rod, a symbol of God's authority, and he and Aaron led the people to a particular rock (v. 9). The rod that Moses carried was not his own rod, but Aaron's fruitful rod that had been residing in the most holy place for thirty-eight years. Regrettably, what Moses said to the people was not what God had told him to say: *"Hear now, you rebels! Must we bring water for you out of this rock?"* (v. 10). Then we read that *"Moses lifted his hand and struck the rock twice with his rod; and water came out abundantly, and the congregation and their animals drank"* (v. 11). Since Moses was speaking for God and had a symbol of God's authority in his hand, the Lord brought water from the rock despite Moses' disobedience.

Moses and Aaron Punished (vv. 12-13)

Although the life-threatening situation for the Israelites was instantly alleviated, the consequence of disobedience for their leaders was not. The Lord spoke to Moses and Aaron: *"Because you did not believe Me, to hallow Me in the eyes of the children of Israel, therefore you shall not bring this assembly into the land which I have given them"* (v. 12). Nothing more was said. Israel's prominent leaders did not argue with the Lord about their punishment; rather they accepted it as just recompense for their foolishness.

We might think that God was too harsh with Moses and Aaron. Does not years of faithfulness count much more in God's estimation than one mistake about striking a rock instead of speaking to it? The Lord would still reward Moses and Aaron for their faithfulness, but their disobedience and pride, especially while representing the Lord, had to be sternly reprimanded. When God assigns responsibility to His servants, they also are under greater accountability (e.g., Luke 12:48;

Jas. 3:1). Although Moses and Aaron received a measure of mercy in this matter, they were punished for at least four reasons.

First, they had misrepresented both the word and character of God in what they said to the people. F. B. Hole explains:

> What God had to say to the people came through his lips, since he came from God to them. Aaron as priest was commissioned to go from the people to God, and was not God's spokesman, so angry words from his lips would not have been so grave a matter. The failure of Moses was precisely at that point which was most important of all, as giving the word from God.[89]

To believe God's word and obey Him is to hallow Him before others, but instead, Moses and Aaron misrepresented God's character to the people. God wanted to show mercy to His people, not to display anger towards them.

Second, Moses and Aaron's actions distorted what God wanted to teach His people about how to obtain His grace when they were distressed and in need. As mentioned previously, the rod to be used in executing the miracle was Aaron's priestly rod that had been before the Lord in the most holy place (v. 9). Moses, however, did not portray the priestly ministry of speaking to the rock to receive grace, but instead struck the rock in anger with "his rod" (v. 11). Whether "his rod" was actually Moses' rod representing the authority of the Law or a vague reference to Aaron's priestly rod cannot be positively ascertained grammatically. However, the use of either rod in this manner did not reflect what God wanted His people to learn about obtaining grace through priestly intercession. Hence, because it is a more striking contrast, it seems most likely that Moses struck the rock with Aaron's fruitful priestly rod.

If Israel's leaders had done what they were told to do, Israel would have witnessed God's bountiful provision of grace without any display of reproach or anger. Merely speaking to God in the presence of the staff (to illustrate His authority) would have resulted in the satisfaction of everyone's urgent need. But Moses and Aaron did more than this and the lovely picture of receiving tender-mercies through heavenly intercession was ruined. On this point, C. A. Coates draws an important application for us to consider:

Refining and Reminding

> "Take the staff" was a word which should have dismissed from the minds of Moses and Aaron all thought of what the people were, and should have filled them with thoughts of the grace in which Jehovah had set up a priest on their behalf. This was the great thing, the vital matter of witness, the appropriate expression of divine glory, at that moment. Jehovah would magnify "the staff" and all that of which it was the token. To miss this was to miss all that really mattered. ... All must be of grace that is really for divine glory, and grace would not be grace if it were measured by what God's people deserve.
>
> Let us ponder "the staff"! The people of God, when tested, often speak the language of unbelief. But are God's thoughts towards them, and His ways with them, according to this, or are they according to the blessed fact that Christ is before Him as Priest on their behalf? Thank God! the latter is the case; would that we took in the greatness and reality of it! In regard of entering the land, all must be of grace.[90]

Third, in saying, *"Must we bring water for you out of this rock?"* they were presenting themselves as the doers of the miracle instead of exalting the Lord in the matter. They did not lead the people into having higher contemplations of God, but used the miracle to elevate themselves. No doubt they felt slighted and unappreciated by the criticism. Certainly, they wanted their countrymen to hold them in higher esteem. However, when the Lord's servants die to their reputations and to the praise of men, they become numb to human criticism and more attentive to God's honor. Such servants are more profitable to the Lord and are more likely to be used by Him for His glory.

Fourth, Moses' action of striking the rock twice was a profound offense against God because it ruined the typology that God was impressing into Scripture to illustrate the future redemptive work of His Son. Israel's most admired servant failed to accurately represent God's bountiful grace in Christ that had been so wonderfully displayed earlier in Aaron's blooming rod.

Recall that not long after departing from Egypt, the people came to Rephidim, but there was no water there. The need was desperate, and being commanded of the Lord to do so, Moses struck a particular rock with his rod and water gushed out from it (Ex. 17:1-7). Paul tells us in 1 Corinthians 10:4 that the One who supplied the water was with His people: *"For they drank of that spiritual Rock that followed them, and that Rock was Christ."* This meant that the rock at Rephidim and the rock at Kadesh, though separated by many years and miles, were reckoned as the same in the mind of God. Each rock typifies Christ, but represents a different aspect of His ministry.

The water gushing from the rock that Moses struck in Exodus 17 pictures what became available to men after Christ went under the rod of God at Calvary. The Lord Jesus spoke of this rock and tied the water from it to the blessings of the Holy Spirit that would result from His completed work at Calvary (John 7:37-39; Acts 2). After drinking from the rock at Rephidim, the Israelites, for the first time, had the wherewithal to enter into battle against the Amalekites (who symbolize the flesh in Scripture). As a result, they were able to revel in the victory secured by God's power. Likewise, by faith believers can be victorious in a sin-cursed world because Christ has already conquered the prince of this world (John 12:31-34, 16:11), sin of the flesh (Rom. 6:6), and the world (John 16:33; 1 Jn. 5:4).

This is likely the reason the Lord told Moses in Exodus 17 to smite the rock with the rod that He had previously used to strike the Nile to turn its waters into blood. Egypt, the strongest nation on earth at that time, represented the world and the rod which struck Egypt with death is the same rod that struck the Rock to shed His blood and bring living water to give life.

Yet, for believers to continue living out the victory gained at Calvary, they must continue to draw spiritual wherewithal from the victorious Rock. The Rock never needs to again go under God's rod, for the benefits of Calvary are eternal. Christ shall never be judged again for man's sin, but man must continue to rely upon Christ's heavenly priesthood to draw strength in times of temptation and need (e.g., Jas. 4:6-8). This is accomplished by humbly speaking to the Rock in prayer:

> *Seeing then that we have a great high priest, that is passed into the heavens, Jesus the Son of God, let us hold fast our profession. For we have not an high priest which cannot be touched with the feeling of our infirmities; but was in all points tempted like as we are, yet without sin. Let us therefore come boldly unto the throne of grace, that we may obtain mercy, and find grace to help in time of need* (Heb. 4:14-16).

Refining and Reminding

Therefore, having been once smitten, speaking to the Rock in prayer suffices to receive God's grace!

Indeed there were reasons for the Lord to be angry with Moses and Aaron at Kadesh, but we must understand, their behavior was already foreknown and anticipated in the providential workings of God. From a typological standpoint, it was fitting that Moses should die before the Israelites entered the Promised Land (Deut. 34) and that the Joshua should lead the Israelites into Canaan (Josh. 1).

Moses brought the Law, which could never bring spiritual life or produce vitality; the Law only condemned the Jews because they could not keep it. Consequently, Law-keeping, which centers in human effort alone, can never result in victorious living, which depends solely on God's infusing power. Joshua pictures Jesus Christ of the New Testament; both of their names mean "Jehovah is salvation" or "Jehovah saves." Israel's trip through the Jordan River symbolizes the reception of the resurrection life of Christ. It is only by this pervading power that a believer can have victory over the enemy, lay hold of spiritual possessions, and please God.

Additionally, Aaron, the high priest of the Law of Moses, could only atone for sin; he could not minister life to lost sinners. Hence we will see that Aaron had no place in Canaan either. Hebrews tells us that a better High Priest and Mediator has come; He brought a better sacrifice into a better sanctuary and secured a new and eternal covenant that could provide propitiation for sin and bestow life on the basis of righteousness and grace. Israel could not obtain God's promises of goodness in the Promised Land on the basis of law-keeping and neither can we. We all need God's unmerited favor available through Christ's death, burial, and resurrection. This is later pictured when the Jews followed Joshua through the Jordan River to enter Canaan.

Regardless of the typology and personal ramification of Moses and Aaron's sin for themselves and others, there are several practical lessons from this narrative that become painfully obvious. First, it shows the agonizing repercussions that just one wrong act done in the flesh can cause God's people. Second, leaders need to be careful how they respond to wayward sheep who are being contentious, *"for the wrath of man does not produce the righteousness of God"* (Jas. 1:20). Third, sheep would be wise not to put their leaders into needless situations which might provoke carnal outbursts, as that would benefit no one (Heb. 13:17). Any complaints worthy of their attention should be evaluated by Scripture, be free of personal ambition and insults, and be submitted in the spirit of love and truth (Eph. 4:15; 1 Tim. 5:19).

Meditation

> When Satan, my foe, shall come in like a flood,
> To drive my poor soul from the Fountain of good,
> I'll pray to the Savior who meekly did die;
> Lead me to the Rock that is higher than I.
>
> — John Price

Stubborn Edom and Aaron Dies
Numbers 20:14-21

No Passage Through Edom (vv. 14-21)

Moses sent messengers east from Kadesh to the king of Edom to receive permission to pass northward through Edom. The Edomites were the descendants of Jacob's twin brother Esau, who settled in the region south of Moab and just south and east of the Dead Sea. Moses appealed to the king to remember and renew the past kindness that existed between their forefathers, Esau and Jacob – twin brothers (Gen. 33:1-17):

> *Thus says your brother Israel: "You know all the hardship that has befallen us, how our fathers went down to Egypt, and we dwelt in Egypt a long time, and the Egyptians afflicted us and our fathers. When we cried out to the Lord, He heard our voice and sent the Angel and brought us up out of Egypt; now here we are in Kadesh, a city on the edge of your border. Please let us pass through your country. We will not pass through fields or vineyards, nor will we drink water from wells; we will go along the King's Highway; we will not turn aside to the right hand or to the left until we have passed through your territory"* (vv. 14-17).

The king of Edom declined to permit the Israelites passage through Edom, even though Moses had promised not to damage the land or take any provisions (including water) from it. The king threatened to attack the Israelites if they set foot in his territory (v. 18). Perhaps there had been a misunderstanding, so Moses clarified that their intentions were to use the King's Highway and they were willing to pay for any water that the livestock or people drank while passing through Edom (v.19; Deut. 2:6). The King's Highway was a thoroughfare running from the Gulf of Aqaba in the south, through or near Edom's cities of Teman, Sela, and Bozrah to Damascus in the far north.

The king of Edom responded by bringing out his army to bar Israel's way. There were several narrow passes through the mountains on the King's Highway that were quite defensible. To push through Edom would cause much needless bloodshed. Additionally, Edom was not the enemy God intended His people to war with. The Lord had commanded Moses not to meddle with or harass the Edomites, Moabites, and Ammonites while journeying to Canaan (Deut. 2:5, 9, 19). Because these nations originated in Abraham and Lot, they were distant kin to Israel. Moses decided to lead the Israelites around Edom, which added many more miles to their route.

Although Jacob and Esau were able to put their differences behind them in their autumn years, that would not be the case for their descendants. Edom became a heathen nation that loathed the Jews, their fraternal brothers (Ezek. 35; Obad. 15-16). Edom now has a long history of hostility toward the Jewish nation (e.g., 1 Sam. 14:47; 1 Kgs. 9:26-28; 2 Kgs. 8:20-21), which commenced in this chapter when the Israelites were journeying to Canaan.

Aaron Dies (vv. 22-29)

The burial and mourning for Miriam and the ambassadors going to and coming from Moab kept the Israelites at Kadesh for more than three months. Edom's defiance forced Moses to lead his people east-northeast to Mount Hor before turning south-southeast, then east and finally north to avoid Edom. They arrived at Mount Hor on the western boundary of Edom *"in the fortieth year after the children of Israel had come out of the land of Egypt, on the first day of the fifth month"* (33:38).

After arriving at Mount Hor, the Lord informed Moses and Aaron that it was time for Aaron to be gathered to his people (v. 23). The Lord reminded Aaron that he had already been told that he would not enter Canaan because he rebelled against His word *"at the water of Meribah"* at Kadesh (v. 24).

The actual location of Mount Hor has been much debated. Josephus identified Mount Hor as *Jebel Nebi Harun,* which means "the Mountain of the Prophet Aaron" in Arabic.[91] It is a twin-peaked mountain 4780 feet above sea level located on the east side of the Jordan-Arabah Valley near Petra. Albert Barnes writes that "this striking mountain, rising on a dark red bare rock is remarkable far and near for its two summits, on one of which is still shown a small square building, crowned with a dome, called the Tomb of Aaron."[92] However, this traditional site of Aaron's tomb cannot be correct, as in the next chapter the king of Arad became alarmed by the Israelites' northeasterly march from Kadesh and attacked them.

The Canaanite city of Arad was situated about 45 miles northeast of Kadesh and 25 miles southeast of Hebron, so an east-northeast movement by the Israelites to Mount Hor from Kadesh would have been interpreted as a threatening advance. There is a high chalk-looking, steep-sided hill a few miles northeast of Kadesh, called Jebel Maderah. Jebel Maderah is just outside Edom's western boundary and meets all the conditions of the narrative, but Jebel Nebi Harun, 45 miles to the southeast and deep into Edom, does not. Jebel Maderah is likely Mount Hor, where Aaron died.

It was time for Aaron to depart. The Lord commanded Moses to take Aaron and Eleazar up into the mount, so that all the people could see them (vv. 25-27). Moses did so, and with the nation watching, he stripped Aaron of his priestly garments and put them on his son Eleazar. The priestly office was represented by the holy garments, which meant that Eleazar was Israel's new high priest. This was the first time that the priesthood had been transferred, so it was done in a public way so that there would be no challenges to it, as in the past.

After the priestly garments were on Eleazar, Aaron immediately died: *"Aaron was one hundred and twenty-three years old when he died on Mount Hor"* (33:39). What a stirring scene this must have been for Moses, Aaron's brother, and Eleazar, his son, to climb up into the mount knowing that Aaron would not be coming back down with them. They did not touch Aaron after his death or bury him, as that would have made them unclean for a week, but rather they returned to camp (v. 28). As we have already seen, God did not punish Aaron as He did Miriam with leprosy to ensure that the ministry of the priesthood would not be interrupted. Such was the situation now. The high priest could not be defiled by a corpse; therefore, we can assume that the Lord took good care of Aaron's body.

Aaron did not suffer in death (Heb. 7:23), nor had he been plagued with declining health, for he was able to climb up into the mount without assistance. He had served the Lord faithfully, he had run his course, and now it was time to depart into God's eternal rest. The nation mourned the death of Aaron for thirty days (v. 29). In about seven months they would mourn the death of Moses for thirty days also

(Deut. 34:5-8). However, the death of these men did not stop the work of the Lord, for it must continue until all the purposes of God are accomplished. We close our study of this chapter with a timely reminder from John J. Stubbs on the reality of this truth:

> There comes a time when a man's ministry must recede either through sickness or age, or death itself brings it finally to an end. Another, or others, must continue God's appointed work. Until the Lord Jesus Christ has come, this fact must ever be borne in mind. The question is, "How is the thought that one's ministry must be passed on to another received in the heart?" Aaron may have had his misgivings and regrets, but he can be commended for his humility in accepting God's will for him without a murmur. Whatever special work God has given, it is a good thing to continue in it in the knowledge that the time will come when it must be given up. Being constantly aware of this should help all to be diligent in the work God has given. It should also help the preacher, the elder, the servant, and all involved in God's work to accept graciously that its continuation does not depend upon us, but rather upon God. One thing is certain, God's work must go on and it will, even though His servants must pass on.[93]

Meditation

> The bitterest tears shed over graves are for words left unsaid and deeds left undone.
>
> — Harriet Beecher Stowe

God buries His workmen but carries on His work.

— Charles Wesley

The Serpent on the Pole
Numbers 21

Canaanites at Hormah Defeated (vv. 1-3)

Being prevented from entering Edom, Moses led the Israelites east-northeast on the road to Atharim; he then planned to turn south to the Gulf of Aqaba. The king of Arad interpreted this as a hostile advance and attacked the Israelites and captured some of them (v. 1). Arad was a Canaanite city located about 15 miles northeast of Beersheba and some 25 miles southeast of Hebron. Since Arad was situated about 45 miles northeast of Kadesh, the east-northeast movement by the Israelites from Kadesh to Mount Hor on the road to Atharim was viewed as an Israelite invasion of Canaan.

Moses promised the Lord that, if He would return those taken prisoner, they would destroy the Canaanite cities in that region. The Lord granted Moses' petition and the Israelites utterly vanquished the Canaanites. Thirty-eight years earlier the Israelites had engaged these Canaanites without the Lord and were soundly defeated. The Canaanites had routed them all the way to Hormah (14:44-45), a Canaanite city located just a few miles southwest of Arad. Now it was the Israelites who drove the Canaanites back to Hormah, probably 35 to 40 miles north of their position on the road to Atharim. This was the first major confrontation against the Canaanites and the Israelites were victorious this time because the Lord was with them. Thirty-eight years later Hormah reaped the meaning of its name, "cursed for destruction."

The Bronze Serpent (vv. 4-9)

Although encouraged by their astounding victory over the Canaanites, it was not yet God's timing or the location for His people to enter the Promised Land. It was necessary for them to first experience the spiritual ramifications of what was to be typified in crossing the Jordan River under Joshua's leadership.

The death of Aaron, moving away from the Promised Land, and then seeing the difficult rolling mountainous and arid terrain ahead of them soured the Israelites. We read:

> *Then they journeyed from Mount Hor by the Way of the Red Sea, to go around the land of Edom; and the soul of the people became very discouraged on the way. And the people spoke against God and against Moses: "Why have you brought us up out of Egypt to die in the wilderness? For there is no food and no water, and our soul loathes this worthless bread." So the Lord sent fiery serpents among the people, and they bit the people; and many of the people of Israel died* (vv. 4-6).

The Israelites had become completely dissatisfied with God's provision of manna. Whenever God's provision of spiritual sustenance is loathed, a believer's inner man (i.e., his or her spirit) quickly withers. This permits the carnal nature within to have its way without restraint. This is why Paul identifies a spiritually healthy person as one whose *"inward man is being renewed day by day"* (1 Cor. 4:16). The enjoyment and satisfaction of reading and meditating on God's word as one engages in spontaneous prayer and personal reflection is the same as feasting on God's manna. The Lord Jesus Christ and His Word is God's bread of life for us today (John 6:35, 47-51). We may be tempted not to feed on God's manna when we are busy or tired, but the outcome of that decision will never be favorable – that is when we need God's provision the most.

The Israelites had lost this perspective, so the Lord brought fiery serpents among them to further test them. The serpents would be effective in unmasking the true character of their discontent and in bringing them to self-judge their sin. Trials expose aspects of carnality in our hearts, which we may not have previously been aware of, but must be identified and self-judged nonetheless. Thankfully, the Israelites benefitted from this fiery trial.

The serpent's bite resulted in death! The correlation the Israelites were to learn was that the root of sin in them also had repercussions – death. C. A. Coates explains that God cannot bring us into what His love proposes to give us without first teaching us this profound truth:

> This visitation of God [the fiery serpents] brought home in a sharp and terrible way that the naughtiness of the flesh is really satanic in

origin. It is a poison introduced by Satan himself. ... Can we wonder that it is directly and positively adverse to God? It is a terrible thing to contemplate, but there is no full conviction of sin until this is brought home to one experimentally. The bite of the fiery serpent is the divine conviction of what the flesh truly is in the very source of its being. ... We shall never understand what life is as the gift of God until we realize that we are death-stricken, and deservedly so, and we can do absolutely nothing to extricate ourselves from that state or its consequences.[94]

Understanding their desperate need, the Israelites came to Moses and acknowledged: *"We have sinned, for we have spoken against the Lord and against you; pray to the Lord that He take away the serpents from us"* (v. 7). Dear believer, be thankful that the Lord loves you too much to leave you the way you are. God's Spirit will continue to probe and work in your heart and mind to effect change in how you think and in what you do – this is God's work of progressive sanctification.

Moses, immediately interceded on behalf of the people and God responded with a solution to avoid death: *"Make a fiery serpent, and set it on a pole; and it shall be that everyone who is bitten, when he looks at it, shall live"* (v. 8). Moses did as the Lord said and explained to the people that all they needed to do to survive the serpent's venom was to "look and live" (v. 9). Anyone bitten by a serpent, and who wanted to live, could look at the bronze serpent on the pole and be healed. Neither the Lord nor Moses forced anyone to take advantage of this life-saving provision. Those bitten, who wanted to live, looked by faith at the bronze serpent and those who refused were responsible for their own demise.

The Lord Jesus used this historical event to teach His audience the essence of His gospel message. Soon, He would be lifted up on a cross to become the object of faith by which eternal life could be received: *"As Moses lifted up the serpent in the wilderness, even so must the Son of Man be lifted up, that whoever believes in Him should not perish but have eternal life"* (John 3:14-15). The provision of the bronze serpent on a pole in Numbers 21 has its ultimate fulfillment in Christ hanging on the cross.

In Scripture, bronze speaks of "fiery" judgments, while the serpent itself is a symbol of sin, and the lofty pole, as just discussed, prefigures Christ's cross. The imagery is astounding. God positionally condemned sin in the flesh (the energy of lawlessness) through the death of His Son on the cross. As a result, Paul tells us that "the Old Man" (i.e., what we were in Adam by nature) was crucified and died when Christ died, so that we are no longer slaves to sin (Rom. 6:6). Because Christ rose from the grave, those trusting in Him receive eternal life in Him and the ability to overcome sin through the power of the Holy Spirit (John 3:16; Rom. 8:13).

From a practical standpoint, all of us were born snake-bitten (i.e., spiritually dead in Adam; Rom. 5:12). Although many will never admit that they are dying because of sin, those who do realize their hopeless condition can escape eternal condemnation and experience the full love of God by trusting in Christ for healing. As C. H. Mackintosh explains, God had much more for the Israelites (and us too) than just escaping death; He wanted them to experience His love:

> When Israel murmured, the serpents' bite was the answer. When Israel confessed, God's grace was the answer. In the one case, the serpent was the instrument of their wretchedness; in the other, it was the instrument of their restoration and blessing. ... It is a very common error to view the Lord Jesus rather as the averter of God's wrath, than as the channel of His love. That He endured the wrath of God against sin is most preciously true. But there is more than this. He has come down into this wretched world to die upon the cursed tree, in order that, by dying, He might open up the everlasting springs of the love of God to the heart of poor rebellious man.[95]

Mount Hor to Moab (vv. 10-20)

> *Now the children of Israel moved on and camped in Oboth. And they journeyed from Oboth and camped at Ije Abarim, in the wilderness which is east of Moab, toward the sunrise. From there they moved and camped in the Valley of Zered. From there they moved and camped on the other side of the Arnon, which is in the wilderness that extends from the border of the Amorites; for the Arnon is the border of Moab, between Moab and the Amorites* (10-13).

These verses illustrate what happens when people properly apprehend the death of Christ by faith (look at the serpent on the pole) – they are spiritually enabled to "move on" in the things of God. The children of Israel left Mount Hor by way of the Red Sea (v. 4) and arrived at the Arnon River which empties into the eastern mid-portion

Refining and Reminding

of the Dead Sea (v. 13). In the short space of a few verses, the Israelites covered more ground than at any other time in their journey from Egypt to Canaan – nearly 150 miles.

The Israelites arrived at the northern boundary of Moab and the southern border of the Amorites, who had invaded and settled in the plains of Moab north of the Arnon River. The Israelites rejoiced at the bubbling brooks of the Arnon River valley (vv. 14-15). From there they traveled to Beer where the Lord showed Moses a well of water for the people (v. 16). The sight of this well caused the Israelites to burst into jubilant song: *"Spring up, O well! All of you sing to it – The well the leaders sank, dug by the nation's nobles, by the lawgiver, with their staves"* (vv. 17-18). Apparently, the leaders had to initially dig out some of the dirt, so that the well would be unblocked and the water made available for all to drink. Likewise, leaders today, knowing where the soul's needs can be satisfied, should labor to lead others to the place where they can drink of Christ also.

This is the third time that Scripture records the Israelites singing during their journey. They first sang Moses' song of redemption after being delivered from Pharaoh at the Red Sea (Ex. 15). Here they sang a song of deliverance from the fiery serpents and their enjoyment of being with the Lord. As mentioned previously, this pictures the believer's deliverance from the enslaving power of sin in the flesh. Later in this chapter the Israelites will sing a taunting song of victory (vv. 27-30). However, between Moses' song of redemption and that of deliverance in this chapter is the incident of them singing naked about the golden calf (Ex. 32:18). This illustrates to what depths of depravity man can quickly sink without God's life-sustaining provisions for the soul. Indeed, God is the deepest and sweetest well of satisfaction.

Peter mentions a "well," for the final time in Scripture, when he warns against false teachers. *"These are wells without water, clouds carried by a tempest, for whom is reserved the blackness of darkness forever"* (2 Pet. 2:17). False teachers offer falsehoods, which culminate in false hopes. There is no bubbling fountain of refreshment in them, only a dry hole awaiting its condemned occupant. However, the Lord Jesus is God's messenger of truth, who offers an abundant life of joy despite circumstances (John 10:10). When one embraces the Savior, a fountain of refreshing spiritual drink is brought to the believer by the Holy Spirit (John 7:39). The abundant life of Christ is thus enjoyed, and like Israel in the midst of the wilderness, we, too, can sing to the Well, *"Spring up, O well."*

This is why the Spirit of God included dual types of Christ in the chapter. F. B. Hole explains the tie between the bronze serpent and the springing well:

> Both realities of these two types – the brazen serpent and the springing well – are brought together in this one chapter, just as the realities typified are found together in the opening verses of Romans 8. Only there the order is reversed. Verse 2 speaks of the Holy Spirit as *"the Spirit of life in Christ Jesus,"* and verse 3 of the condemnation of *"sin in the flesh,"* that is, of the old life "in Adam." There is no more important lesson for a believer to learn than that his old life as a child of Adam has been condemned in the cross of Christ, and that the Holy Spirit indwelling him is the power of that new life which is his in Christ, and upon which no condemnation can ever rest.[96]

From Beer the Israelites pushed further north to Pisgah, which is east of the Jordan River and northeast of the Dead Sea (v. 19). From this location the Israelites gained their first view of the Jordanian valley. Moses would later climb up the heights of Pisgah to view the Promised Land from Mount Nebo before his death. Mount Nebo may be the highest peak among the Pisgah summits on the far western edge of the Transjordan Plateau.

King Sihon and the Amorites Defeated (vv. 21-32)

Because the Amorites controlled the plains of Moab between the Rivers Arnon and Jabbok, Moses asked permission to pass through their territory on the King's Highway (v. 21). Moses promised that the Israelites would not take anything from the land to eat or drink the water while passing through (v. 22).

King Sihon did not answer Moses' request by an envoy. Rather, he gathered his full army and attacked the Israelites. This battle resulted in the slaughter of the Amorites all the way north to Ammon's border at the Jabbok River (vv. 23-24). Afterwards, the Israelites claimed the Amorite cities and possession for themselves, including its capital city of Heshbon about 25 miles east of Jericho (vv. 25-26). This was all poetic justice because King Sihon had previously invaded Moab and brutally seized the region and rebuilt the cities for the Amorites to dwell in. Sihon's achievement was commemorated in poetry (vv. 27-30). However, the song that had once been proudly sung by the Amorites was now satirically caroled by the Jews in celebration.

After the major confrontation was over, Moses sent men to investigate Jazer, a smaller city about 15 miles northwest of Heshbon. The Amorites found at Jazer were also expelled (v. 32). In the end, the region between the Jabbok and Arnon Rivers was free of Amorites, meaning the Israelites could safely dwell there before continuing their journey north.

King Og of Bashan Defeated (vv. 33-35)

Not only had the Amorites taken much of what previously had belonged to Moab, but they also took Gilead and Bashan which belonged to Ammon. The Amorites had pushed the Ammonites eastward into the mountains. When King Og of Bashan heard of his brethren's defeat in Moab, he also gathered his forces against the Israelites.

The Lord encouraged Moses to confront Og: *"Do not fear him, for I have delivered him into your hand, with all his people and his land; and you shall do to him as you did to Sihon king of the Amorites, who dwelt at Heshbon"* (v. 34). The battle between Og and the Israelites occurred at Edrei located on western edge of Bashan about 30 miles east of the Sea of Galilee.

The Israelite defeated Og and all of his people; there were no survivors (v. 35). Again the Jews claimed the conquered land as their own. They now controlled a vast region of the Transjordanian plain from Mount Hermon in the north (Deut. 3:8), to the Moabite border in the south (i.e., the Arnon River), and eastward to the region of the Ammonites. They now could move westward across the Jordan River into Canaan without any threat of an enemy approaching from their rear.

Meditation

> Life is offered unto you, hallelujah!
> Eternal life thy soul shall have,
> If you'll only look to Him, hallelujah!
> Look to Jesus who alone can save.

Devotions in Numbers

"Look and live," my brother, live,
Look to Jesus now, and live;
'Tis recorded in His word, hallelujah!
It is only that you "look and live."

I will tell you how I came, hallelujah!
To Jesus when He made me whole –
'Twas believing on His name, hallelujah!
I trusted and He saved my soul.

— William A. Ogden

Balaam, a Donkey, and the Angel of the Lord
Numbers 22

The Israelites have been unstoppable in their northern march through the plains of Moab, where they will safely encamp through the remainder of Numbers (v. 1). We find out in the book of Joshua that the inhabitants of Canaan knew all about the defeat of the Amorite kings and were terrified that they would be conquered next (Josh. 2:10-11). This widespread fear among various people groups in the region sets the stage for the plotting of the Midianites and Moabites against the Israelites in chapters 22 through 25.

Balak Sends for Balaam (vv. 2-21)

Balak, the king of Moab, was alarmed at both the size and the military feats of the Israelites (vv. 2-3). Balak contacted the elders of Midian in an attempt to form an alliance against their common threat who had now settled in the plains of Moab (v. 4). This included soliciting the help of a well-known prophet named Balaam from Pethor to come and curse the Israelites (v. 5). We learn in the next chapter that Balaam's homeland was far north in Aram (23:7; Deut. 23:4). The kingdom of Aram (modern-day Syria) once stretched from the Lebanon mountains eastward across the Euphrates and northward to Assyria. It seems likely that Pethor was located near the Euphrates River (v. 5). This means that the two trips to fetch Balaam to Balak's location in the following verses would have required several weeks to accomplish.

Balak, whose name means "waster," thought that if Balaam cursed the Israelites, his forces would then be able to drive them from the land (v. 6). Interestingly, Balaam's name means "a devourer of the people" or "confuser of the people" which describes the painful effect his doctrine later would have on the Israelites in Numbers 25.

As previously mentioned, God had already instructed Moses not to meddle with or harass the Edomites, Moabites, and Ammonites while journeying to Canaan (Deut. 2:5, 9, 19). This is why Moses trekked around Edom and Moab before turning west into the plains of Moab to confront the Amorites. The Moabites did not actually have anything to worry about, which should have already become apparent to them.

Elders from Moab and Midian departed with a "diviner's fee" to solicit Balaam's assistance (v. 7). Peter likens the carnal, greedy disposition of false teachers in his day to that of Balaam: *"They have forsaken the right way and gone astray, following the way of Balaam the son of Beor, who loved the wages of unrighteousness"* (2 Pet. 2:15). Balaam was pursuing the "wages of unrighteousness" and later would reap its wages – death (Rom. 6:23). The Lord always pays a fair wage.

After Balaam heard Balak's proposition, he told the princes, *"Lodge here tonight, and I will bring back word to you, as the Lord speaks to me"* (v. 8). And the princes did so. We might be tempted to think that Balaam was a prophet of Jehovah since Balaam mentions to his constituents that he would wait to hear from Jehovah before answering them. Commenting on Balaam's craftiness, F. B. Hole writes:

> If we glance at verses 8 and 18, we discover that Balaam managed to cover his enchantments, which were, of course, of the devil, with the appearance of reverencing Jehovah as his God. Balak hoped to bring a curse on the people of God by enlisting the help of this professed prophet of God, who was really a servant of Satan. An attack of that kind is marked by exceeding subtlety.[97]

Balaam may have been a Midianite, as he perishes with them later (31:8). The Midianites, who were fathered by Abraham, would have initially held to a monotheistic worldview, as evidenced by Jethro's declarations in Exodus 18 to Moses, his son-in-law. However, we learn that the Midianites associated with Balak worshipped at the same pagan altars. So even if Balaam believed in one god or even a more supreme god among other gods, it did not mean that he had exercised faith in the true God. This seems obvious, as Balaam was a prophet for hire and well-known in a region inundated with paganism. This suggests he had some knowledge of supernatural things which he could profit from, but he did not know Jehovah personally, nor did he previously have authority to speak for Him.

In Old Testament days, when God had a message for a particular person or collective of people, He normally sent an angel to deliver it directly or He opened the mouth of a prophet to speak it on His behalf.

Refining and Reminding

On other occasions, where a direct verbal message was not advantageous, the Lord communicated through dreams and visions to convey His will or to call His servants into ministry. The prophets Isaiah, Daniel, Ezekiel, and Zechariah all saw the Lord through visions, and many others, such as Samuel, Elijah, and Jeremiah, spoke personally with the Lord. On rare occasions, the Lord Himself (as we shall soon see) entered the realm of time and space to appear and to speak to someone. These appearances were usually to faithful Old Testament characters central to accomplishing God's sovereign purposes. The Lord did not normally appear to those who were perishing in unbelief; His interaction with Balaam in the next three chapters is the exception.

The Lord already knew who was visiting Balaam, but He asks Balaam who they were to test him (v. 9). Balaam answers the Lord accurately: *"Balak the son of Zippor, king of Moab, has sent to me, saying, 'Look, a people has come out of Egypt, and they cover the face of the earth. Come now, curse them for me; perhaps I shall be able to overpower them and drive them out'"* (vv. 10-11). The Lord's response was terse: *"You shall not go with them; you shall not curse the people, for they are blessed"* (v. 12). Although Balaam wanted to profit from the opportunity, to his credit, he told the contingency from Balak to return to the king to tell him that the Lord had refused to let him come (v. 13).

After hearing this news, Balak decided to send a greater number of more honorable princes to Balaam to again seek his assistance (vv. 14-15). These men journeyed to Pethor and delivered Balak's message to Balaam: *"Thus says Balak the son of Zippor: 'Please let nothing hinder you from coming to me; for I will certainly honor you greatly, and I will do whatever you say to me. Therefore please come, curse this people for me'"* (vv. 16-17). Balaam responded to this offer: *"Though Balak were to give me his house full of silver and gold, I could not go beyond the word of the Lord my God, to do less or more. Now therefore, please, you also stay here tonight, that I may know what more the Lord will say to me"* (vv. 18-19).

We might commend Balaam for this reply, but what he says is not founded in submission, but greed. Balaam already knew what the will of God was in this matter (v. 12), so for him to say that he would seek the mind of the Lord only exposed his inherent lust for honor and riches. This explains why the Lord gave Balaam permission to go with

Devotions in Numbers

the men the next morning (v. 20). God was going to teach Balaam the price of cloaked rebellion, but at the same time He would publicly extol His people through him. John J. Stubbs advises that God's dealings with self-willed Balaam are a warning to believers not to behave the same way:

> There is a lesson in this for believers, for very often open profession is made of wanting to do God's will, but sadly all the time the desire is to want one's own way. Balaam was eventually dealt with by God. He not only, under compulsion from God, had to speak His word, but was finally punished by perishing among the Midianites. Sometimes God allows even His children to have their own way and deals with them for their own foolishness. It is always foolish to push forward with selfish desires and ambitions, for if these are not in harmony with God's will, it can spell spiritual disaster for the believer. When Balaam went back with the men, he did not carry divine approval with him, and he suffered the consequences.[98]

The next morning we read that *"Balaam rose in the morning, saddled his donkey, and went with the princes of Moab"* (v. 21). C. H. Mackintosh observes, "Satan knew his man, and the price at which he could be purchased."[99] However, whatever personal ambition Balaam had for going was to be overruled – he would be able to speak only what God put into His mouth.

Balaam, the Donkey, and the Angel of the Lord (vv. 22-41)

What happened to Balaam on the way to Balak is one of the most bizarre encounters between God and a man recorded in Scripture:

> *Then God's anger was aroused because he went, and the Angel of the Lord took His stand in the way as an adversary against him. And he was riding on his donkey, and his two servants were with him. Now the donkey saw the Angel of the Lord standing in the way with His drawn sword in His hand, and the donkey turned aside out of the way and went into the field. So Balaam struck the donkey to turn her back onto the road. Then the Angel of the Lord stood in a narrow path between the vineyards, with a wall on this side and a wall on that side. And when the donkey saw the Angel of the Lord, she pushed herself against the wall and crushed Balaam's foot against the wall; so he struck her again. Then the Angel of the Lord went further, and*

> *stood in a narrow place where there was no way to turn either to the right hand or to the left. And when the donkey saw the Angel of the Lord, she lay down under Balaam; so Balaam's anger was aroused, and he struck the donkey with his staff* (vv. 22-27).

Why was God angry with Balaam, if He had given Balaam permission to return with the princes to Balak? The Lord knew what was in Balaam's heart, where resided the hidden longing to injure the very people that God loved (Deut. 23:5). The Lord foreknew how Balaam's doctrine would corrupt the Israelites and hence how its future outcome would injure His own heart.

We then read that the Lord enabled the donkey to speak to Balaam, *"What have I done to you, that you have struck me these three times?"* (v. 28). Balaam, apparently forgetting that he was speaking to an animal, answers the donkey's question, *"Because you have abused me. I wish there were a sword in my hand, for now I would kill you!"* (v. 29). The donkey replied, *"Am I not your donkey on which you have ridden, ever since I became yours, to this day? Was I ever disposed to do this to you?"* (v. 30). Although the wise speech of the donkey is amazing, it shadows in comparison to Balaam's obstinate foolishness. He was so enraged that he thought nothing of his donkey talking with him, nor the sound reasoning that she employed. Perhaps, as a pagan diviner, he had witnessed such things before, but it is quite evident that he felt outwitted by his donkey, for he answers her final question with a subdued "no."

C. A. Coates suggests that Balaam's folly was of the worst sort:

> Jehovah saying, "they are blessed," should have settled the matter definitely, but these words evidently did not take out of Balaam's mind the thought that perhaps, after all, it might be possible to curse them, and to earn the wages of unrighteousness which he loved. …The Angel of Jehovah set Himself in the way as an adversary against Balaam, and he had a threefold warning that the way in which he was moving was for his ruin. He was really blinder and more foolish than his ass, and God used the ass to forbid his folly. No folly could be greater than for Satan or for men to think that they can defeat God, and bring a curse where He has put a blessing.[100]

Immediately after Balaam answered his donkey's final question, the Lord opened Balaam's eyes. Balaam became speechless and fell flat on the ground as soon as he saw the Angel of the Lord standing before him with His sword drawn (v. 32). The Angel of the Lord reproved Balaam:

> *Why have you struck your donkey these three times? Behold, I have come out to stand against you, because your way is perverse before Me. The donkey saw Me and turned aside from Me these three times. If she had not turned aside from Me, surely I would also have killed you by now, and let her live* (v. 33).

As it turns out, Balaam's donkey saved her master's life three times, by either turning out of the way of danger or just laying down under Balaam, as in the final scenario. She received a thrashing from her master each time after doing so. In pondering this last instance, William MacDonald suggests that the frustrated "donkey, a symbol of stubbornness, knew when to quit, but not the stubborn, willful prophet!"[101]

Realizing the grave situation he was in, Balaam humbly replied to the Angel, *"I have sinned, for I did not know You stood in the way against me. Now therefore, if it displeases You, I will turn back."* The Angel of the Lord, knowing the lustfulness of Balaam's heart, permitted him to continue his journey, but with a warning: *"Go with the men, but only the word that I speak to you, that you shall speak"* (v. 34). So Balaam went with the princes of Balak.

We might wonder why the Lord permitted Balaam to go on with the princes rather than commanding him to return home. However, the latter option would have interfered with what Balaam really wanted to do and the lesson he would learn about the consequences of pursuing what God does not approve of. God's plans had not changed, for He was determined to bless His people despite what Balaam would do. F. B. Hole reminds us that God does not change what He is determined to do, although the way we come to realize this depends on what we do:

> We must remember that God does not change **His purpose.** If, knowing this, we persist like Balaam, God may change **His dealings** with us, as He did with Balaam, and permit us to go so that in His discipline we may reap the bitter result of our own way. Even so, as with Balaam, He will give us ample warning of what lies before us.[102]

Notice that the Angel of the Lord is the Lord Himself, for both had a divine posture before Balaam in Pethor and en route to Balak and

Refining and Reminding

both issued the same command to Balaam. When God appeared to someone in the Old Testament, the event is referred to as a *theophany*, which means "God appearance." At such times, the Lord usually appeared as a normal-looking man, but on certain occasions He took other forms to accentuate His message. For example, the Lord spoke to Moses from a bush that appeared to be burning (Ex. 3), and to the Israelites from within a pillar of cloud (Ex. 13). The Israelites watched Mount Sinai visibly burn and quake at God's presence, though He Himself was concealed by thick, ominous clouds. Each of these unusual presentations conveyed the holiness of God to those who witnessed the spectacle.

Whether in human form or in some unusual depiction, the One appearing was normally referred to as "the Angel of the Lord." The title is unique and should not be confused with the expression "an angel of the Lord," which may refer to the appearances of one of many holy angels. Contextual observation confirms that appearances of "the Angel of the Lord" were *theophanies*. A theophany is a pre-incarnate visit of the second person of the Godhead to the earth as His Father's messenger. The Lord Jesus stated that no one had ever personally seen God the Father (John 6:46). The Lord also said that anyone who had seen Him had seen the Father (John 14:9). This means that God the Father did not appear to anyone in Old Testament times, but rather the only One who could perfectly represent Him. For this reason, some refer to these supernatural Old Testament appearances as *Christophanies*, or literally, "Christ appearances."

In addition to the title of "the Angel of the Lord," the context of Scripture can be used to identify a theophany, which has the following characteristics. The Angel of the Lord is rightly worshipped as God by others (Josh. 5:14; Judg. 6:18-20). The Angel of the Lord initiates covenants and promises that only God can keep (Gen. 16:10, 22:16-17). In most occurrences, the Angel of the Lord clearly identifies Himself as God (Gen. 31:11-13; Ex. 3:2-6).

Evidently, Balaam had not yet discerned in his previous communications with Lord how much He loved His people and was determined to bless them. The Angel of the Lord, however, illustrated this holy fervency in this matter – by standing in Balaam's way. Three times the Lord warned Balaam through inexplicable circumstances that he should not take money from those intending to harm God's people. Yet, grace was shown to Balaam in that the Lord permitted Balaam's

Devotions in Numbers

donkey to see the threat, thus sparing Balaam's life. Despite the pagan prophet's greed, the Lord would use him to publicly bless His people and to confound and shame Balak.

When Balak heard that Balaam was approaching, he met him on the border of Moab near the Arnon River (v. 36). Put out by Balaam's delay, Balak scolds Balaam: *"Did I not earnestly send to you, calling for you? Why did you not come to me? Am I not able to honor you?"* (v. 37). Balaam then informed Balak, that though he had come as requested, he would not be able say anything against Israel, unless permitted by God to do so (v. 38). Balak took Balaam to Kirjath Huzoth where he offered oxen and sheep (probably to Baal), and set meat before Balaam and the princes that were with him (vv. 39-40).

The next day Balak took Balaam up into the high places of Baal, that he might see the far extremity of the Israelite camp (just the end portion) – the people he wanted Balaam to curse (v. 41). In the coming days, the Lord would teach Balaam much about the wages of unrighteousness. Balaam would never return to his home to enjoy the riches and honor he sought. He was slain by the very people he was requested to curse (31:8). God was determined to bless His people regardless of what Balak and Balaam did, but they would reap the consequences of willfully rebelling against what God had sovereignly decreed.

Meditation

> How blest the righteous are, when they resign their breath!
> No wonder Balaam wished to share in such a happy death.
>
> "Oh! let me die said he, the death the righteous do;
> When life is ended, let me be found with the faithful few."
>
> But Balaam's wish was vain, his heart was insincere:
> He thirsted for unrighteous gain, and sought a portion here.
>
> He seemed the Lord to know, and to offend Him loath;
> But Mammon proved his overthrow, for none can serve them both.
>
> May we, O Lord, most high, warning from hence receive,
> If like the righteous we would die, to choose the life they live.

— John Newton

Balaam's First Two Prophecies
Numbers 23

After arriving at the high places of Baal and observing a portion of the Israelite camp in the distance, Balaam hoisted his true colors. He commanded Balak to build seven altars for him and to prepare seven bulls and seven rams to sacrifice (v. 1). There can be no doubt now – the man who professed himself to be a prophet of Jehovah is really in league with the powers of darkness. He even used heathen enchantments in an attempt to invoke Jehovah's attention (24:1). Balaam may have believed that Jehovah was foremost among other gods, but not the only supreme God who created and controls all things. If he had, he would not have requested the erection of altars in the high places of Baal.

Balaam's First Oracle (vv. 2-12)

After the seven altars were built, Balak offered the fourteen animals on them (v. 2). Balaam instructed Balak to *"stand by your burnt offering, and I will go; perhaps the Lord will come to meet me, and whatever He shows me I will tell you"* (v. 3). Balaam departed from Balak to seek a better place to see the Israelites. There, God did appear to Balaam, who immediately touted the seven altars and sacrifices on the altars as a ploy for the Lord to rethink His determination to bless the Israelites (v. 4, 22:12).

The Lord responded by putting His word in Balaam's mouth and telling him to return to Balak and to declare the message that he has received (v. 5). So Balaam returned to the location of the altars and declared God's oracle to Balak and the princes of Moab (v. 6):

> *Balak the king of Moab has brought me from Aram, from the mountains of the east. "Come, curse Jacob for me, and come, denounce Israel!" How shall I curse whom God has not cursed? And how shall I denounce whom the Lord has not denounced? For from the top of the rocks I see him, and from the hills I behold him; there!*

A people dwelling alone, not reckoning itself among the nations. Who can count the dust of Jacob, or number one-fourth of Israel? Let me die the death of the righteous, and let my end be like his! (vv. 7-10).

It is evident that in Balak's first attempt to curse the Israelites, he did not want Balaam to see too much of the camp so that he would have a diminished appraisal of Israel. But the Lord ensured that the truth came out in the prophecy *"Who can count the dust of Jacob, or number one-fourth of Israel?"* (v. 10). Although Balaam saw just one-fourth of the camp, he responds by saying, in effect, if this part is so much, what must the whole be? So despite Balak's attempt to limit Balaam's view of the Israelites, from "the top of the rocks" Balaam received a heavenly sense of them, that is, he saw them as God did.

His first poetic oracle reflects this divine vantage point. Besides declining to curse the Israelites, Balaam declared God's assessment of His people and His determination to bless them. First, Balaam acknowledged their separation to God from among all other nations. Second, God had multiplied the seed of Jacob into a great nation. Third, they were beautified with righteousness, speaking of their justification, which guaranteed them a long and glorious standing before God even after death (perhaps speaking of Israel during the Kingdom Age). Israel's justification will be again stressed in Balaam's second prophecy.

God has already shown that He can speak His word through a donkey which has no natural capacity to formulate human speech. He now speaks by the mouth of a pagan prophet who has no spiritual understanding of what is important to God. Balaam will later die during an Israelite attack, meaning the only way that Moses could have learned the details of these chapters was through divine inspiration, which consequently proves that God spoke through Balaam, and the donkey, for that matter.

Balak, not expecting Balaam's betrayal, immediately reviled his babbling prophet, *"What have you done to me? I took you to curse my enemies, and look, you have blessed them bountifully!"* (v. 11). Balaam simply confirmed what he had already told Balak – he could only speak to him what the Lord put in his mouth (v. 12). C. H. Mackintosh assesses the scene before us:

Balak and Balaam with "all the princes of Moab" may assemble to hear Israel cursed and defied; they may "build seven altars," and "offer a bullock and a lamb on every altar"; Balak's silver and gold may glitter under the covetous gaze of the false prophet; but not all the powers of earth and hell, men and devils combined, in their dark and terrible array, can evoke a single breath of curse or accusation against the Israel of God.[103]

Balaam's Second Oracle (vv. 13-26)

Not satisfied with the outcome of his first attempt, Balak suggested to Balaam that they go to a different and loftier position to curse the Israelites (v. 13). This location was a field on the summit of Pisgah, which was nearer the Israelites, but yet would still prevent Balaam from seeing their entire camp. Again, Balak built seven altars and offered a bull and a ram on each altar (v. 14).

Balaam tells Balak to stand by the altars while he separates himself a short distance to see if the Lord would speak a word to him (v. 15). The Lord did meet with Balaam and did put a word in his mouth, which he rehearsed in the ears of Balak and the princes of Moab (vv. 16-17):

Rise up, Balak, and hear! Listen to me, son of Zippor! God is not a man, that He should lie, nor a son of man, that He should repent. Has He said, and will He not do? Or has He spoken, and will He not make it good? Behold, I have received a command to bless; He has blessed, and I cannot reverse it. He has not observed iniquity in Jacob, nor has He seen wickedness in Israel. The Lord his God is with him, and the shout of a King is among them. God brings them out of Egypt; He has strength like a wild ox. For there is no sorcery against Jacob, nor any divination against Israel. It now must be said of Jacob and of Israel, "Oh, what God has done!" Look, a people rises like a lioness, and lifts itself up like a lion; it shall not lie down until it devours the prey, and drinks the blood of the slain (vv. 18-24).

In receiving the first oracle, the narrative states that "God" (Elohim) met with Balaam, but in their second meeting, God's proper name is used, "the Lord met Balaam." The God Israel worships, Jehovah, the great I AM, the self-existing God who is eternal and therefore always keeps His promises and does not change his mind, was the One speaking to Balaam! The Author of Balaam's second message may have been shocking to Balak – as it would be obvious that Israel's God was speaking through his prophet.

The Israelites, with all their murmurings, shortcomings, and past failures, were still God's chosen people, no matter what. Because Jehovah had redeemed them and brought them out of Egypt, they were positionally justified in His presence. The high ground from which Balaam views them reflects, not man's thoughts of Israel, but God's heavenly estimation of them in Christ.

Despite all their spots and wrinkles, from God's lofty station above the earth, the defects of His people were hidden from view. Not once in any of his prophecies does Balaam even hint of Israel's past failures or sins. Their justification before God ensured His protection of them and their success over their enemies. Accordingly, the reference to the shout of the King among them refers to the Lord, as a Warrior, leading His people into triumph over their adversaries.

Israel's blessed position and security on earth was certainly not achieved in themselves, but because of God's faithfulness to accomplish what He promised Abraham (Gen. 12:1-3). For this reason, there was no sorcery or power that could impede God's plans for His people.

So when Balaam declared *"Oh, what God has done!"* – He was speaking of God's justification and separation of Abraham's descendant unto Himself. There was a coming day when the nations would be astounded at Israel, but they would not say, "Oh, look at what Israel has done!" but rather realize God's determination to bless them above all other nations. The higher Balaam went up to observe the Israelites, the more beautiful God's people became in his sight. He could not curse what God had blessed!

Although God's promises towards Israel are unique, all those justified in Christ can rejoice to say, "Oh, what God has done!" Paul often described the blessings achieved in Christ through justification so that others would appreciate their standing in Christ. For example, to the church at Rome, Paul wrote:

> *If God is for us, who can be against us? He who did not spare His own Son, but delivered Him up for us all, how shall He not with Him also freely give us all things? Who shall bring a charge against God's elect? It is God who justifies. Who is he who condemns? It is Christ who died, and furthermore is also risen, who is even at the right hand*

of God, who also makes intercession for us. Who shall separate us from the love of Christ? Shall tribulation, or distress, or persecution, or famine, or nakedness, or peril, or sword? ... For I am persuaded that neither death nor life, nor angels nor principalities nor powers, nor things present nor things to come, nor height nor depth, nor any other created thing, shall be able to separate us from the love of God which is in Christ Jesus our Lord (Rom. 8:31-35, 38-39).

Balak was furious after hearing Balaam commend Israel again; Balak charged his prophet to *"neither curse them at all, nor bless them at all!"* (v. 25). It grieved him to hear that the seed of Jacob was the outcome of God's wondrous grace and work. But there was much more that Balak had to learn about the blessings God purposed for those justified in His sight. Balaam merely answered Balak as he had previously, *"Did I not tell you, saying, 'All that the Lord speaks, that I must do'?"* (v. 26).

Unwilling to concede the quest, the pagan king took Balaam to a high summit situated above the town of Beth Peor. Balak thought that if he offered sacrifices at the higher elevation of Pisgah, God surely would grant him his request (vv. 27-28). However, Balak was mistaken on two counts. First, there was nothing Balak could do in his own wisdom or efforts to impress God or to earn His favor. Second, Jehovah was not going to curse those He had promised to bless.

God, speaking through Balaam, had already declared: *"God is not a man, that He should lie, nor a son of man, that He should repent. Has He said, and will He not do?"* (v. 19). God cannot sin and does not deceive anyone (Jas. 1:12), though at times He may not fully reveal a particular truth until He deems it necessary to do so (1 Cor. 2:8-9). But, concerning Israel, He had declared what He would do and He always does what He says He will do.

Twice Jehovah had flatly rejected Balak's efforts to curse His people, yet the powers of evil never rest from trying to undermine God's sovereign plans for His people. So, another seven altars were erected on a mountain above Peor and a bull and a ram were again offered on each one (vv. 29-30). From this location Balaam was able to see, for the first time, the full beauty and tribal order of the Israelite camp.

Meditation

On May 24, 1844, Samuel Morse, who invented the telegraph system and Morse Code, sent the very first telegraph from Washington, D.C. to Baltimore, Maryland. This message consisted of a brief quotation from Numbers 23:23: "What hath God wrought!" (KJV) or "Oh, what God has done!" (NKJV). Samuel Morse boldly testified to what everyone should understand: design demands a designer and the chief architect of all things is God. Balaam should have recognized God's handiwork in Israel's existence, order, beauty, and military success. Sadly, many today commit Balaam's foolish error when they think of Israel.

Balaam's Last Two Prophecies
Numbers 24

Balaam's Third Oracle (vv. 1-14)

Although Balaam's heart was corrupt and, if possible, he still wanted to see Israel cursed, a change in his disposition was noticed at Peor. First, he had learned that *"it pleased the Lord to bless Israel"* (v. 1), meaning that there was no satanic power that could change what Jehovah had determined to do. This meant that Israel was invincible.

Second, Balaam no longer used sorcery to try to manipulate the situation or to change what he knew he could not. Although he had told Balak that he was leaving the previous altars to speak to the Lord, we now learn that he did so to privately invoke enchantments. This shows the power of God's word to examine the thoughts and intents of the heart and to effect change (Heb. 4:12). Balaam therefore chooses not to leave the location of this third set of altars.

Third, in the first two oracles, Balaam was an unwilling instrument compelled by God to speak his messages. So, though the prophecies in Numbers 23 were inspired, God spoke through an unwilling and mostly unlikely instrument, much like He spoke through Balaam's donkey. But after learning the truth, Balaam became more accepting of what God would do and hence became a willing instrument. He now admitted that his eyes were wide open and he fell down before the will of God (vv. 3-4). For this reason, the Spirit of God temporarily came upon Balaam and took possession of him to express the last two prophecies (v. 2).

God spoke through Balaam a third time:

> *The utterance of Balaam the son of Beor, the utterance of the man whose eyes are opened, the utterance of him who hears the words of God, who sees the vision of the Almighty, who falls down, with eyes wide open: How lovely are your tents, O Jacob! Your dwellings, O Israel! Like valleys that stretch out, like gardens by the riverside, like aloes planted by the Lord, like cedars beside the waters. He shall*

pour water from his buckets, and his seed shall be in many waters. His king shall be higher than Agag, and his kingdom shall be exalted. God brings him out of Egypt; he has strength like a wild ox; he shall consume the nations, his enemies; he shall break their bones and pierce them with his arrows. He bows down; he lies down as a lion; and as a lion, who shall rouse him? Blessed is he who blesses you, and cursed is he who curses you (Num. 24:3-9).

Balaam's first prophecy highlighted Israel's separation from the nations to Jehovah. His second oracle centered in Israel's justification before God and the security and power that standing affords the Jewish nation. In Balaam's third oracle, he will declare how God has beautified them with honor and victory. Balaam's prophetic disclosure here was a direct answer to Moses' prayer recorded in Psalm 90: *"Let the beauty of the Lord our God be upon us, and establish the work of our hands for us"* (Ps. 90:17).

The chief benefit of God's beautification is captured in verse 5: *"How lovely are your tents, O Jacob! Your dwellings, O Israel!"* Although they are without a home and still dwelling in the wilderness, the Israelites are fully satisfied in being in the Lord's presence. Yet, God fully intended to set them in the Promised Land where He would prosper them (vv. 6-7) and ensure that they triumph over their enemies (v. 8). This included Agag (v. 7) – probably a royal title among the Amalekites (1 Sam. 15:8), much like Abimelech was among the ancient Philistines (Gen. 20:1-2). When established by God, Israel's kingdom would be a blessing to those who would honor the Jewish nation as God intended, or an instrument of punishing those who do not (v. 9).

In summary, the third prophecy first declares the fruitfulness and beauty of the nation as associated with the land God was going to give them, and then their supremacy over all their enemies in that land.

Balak was fit to be tied after listening to Balaam's third blessing for Israel. He struck his hands together in anger and indicted the prophet: *"I called you to curse my enemies, and look, you have bountifully blessed them these three times! Now therefore, flee to your place. I said I would greatly honor you, but in fact, the Lord has kept you back from honor"* (vv. 10-11). However, Balaam is quick to defend himself against Balak's protest:

Did I not also speak to your messengers whom you sent to me, saying, "If Balak were to give me his house full of silver and gold, I could not

> *go beyond the word of the Lord, to do good or bad of my own will. What the Lord says, that I must speak?" And now, indeed, I am going to my people. Come, I will advise you what this people will do to your people in the latter days* (vv. 12-14).

The words, "I will advise you what *this* people will do to *your* people in the latter days" had to send chills down Balak's spine. Not only had he listened to Balaam bless his enemies three times, but now he was going to learn that instead of the Israelites being cursed by God and defeated by him, it would be his people that would be defeated by the Israelites!

Balaam's Fourth Oracle (vv. 15-25)

Balaam's fourth prophecy contained four separate predictions that revealed not only Israel's future but also what will happen to surrounding nations when God exalts Israel. Pagan though he was, his eyes had been opened to the marvelous realities of God's doings (v. 15). Balaam saw the vision of *The Almighty*, he heard the words of *God*, and he had knowledge of *The Most High* – thus being fully inspired by the Holy Spirit, Balaam spoke the mysteries of God (v. 16).

Balaam begins by foretelling that *"a Star shall come out of Jacob"* and *"a Scepter shall rise out of Israel"* (v. 17). The star refers to Christ's first advent, and the scepter to His second. The coming Messiah would be born a Jew and when He arrives to establish His kingdom, none will be able to oppose Him (vv. 18-19). Edom and Moab are identified as being under Israel's rule. Even after Moses showed grace to Edom and Moab on their journey to Canaan by not attacking them, these two people groups, generally speaking, would be in constant opposition to Israel throughout their history (Ezek. 35; Obad. 15-16; 1 Sam. 14:47; 2 Kgs. 8:20-21).

No descendant of the Edomites can be identified today. They were ruled over by the Babylonian and Medo-Persian Empires. The latter pushed them from their homeland into the southern hill country of Judah. In 126 B.C. the Jews conquered the Edomites remaining in their land and forced them to convert to Judaism. Many Moabites were displaced from their homeland by Babylon in the sixth century B.C. and later by the Arabians from the east (Ezek. 25:10). For the most part, the Moabite people lost their identity and were assimilated into other societies. However, Jeremiah tells us that Christ will show mercy to a remnant of the Moabites during the Kingdom Age (Jer. 48:47).

Through Israel's coming Messiah, Balaam further predicts the fall of the Amalekites (v. 20), the Kenites (vv. 21-22), and then Asshur and Eber (vv. 23-24). The Amalekites opposed the Israelites soon after coming out of Egypt when they were weak and tired. The Lord said that His people would continue to war with the Amalekite until the time He removed all remembrance of them (Ex. 17:14-16).

Amalek was the grandson of profane Esau, *"who for one morsel of food sold his birthright"* (Heb. 12:16). Consequently, both Esau and Amalek are used in Scripture to picture lusting flesh which continues to war against God's people. Likewise, the new nature of the believer received at regeneration cannot sin (1 Jn. 3:9) and therefore also continually wars against the flesh nature: *"For the flesh lusts against the Spirit, and the Spirit against the flesh; and these are contrary to one another, so that you do not do the things that you wish"* (Gal. 5:17). There is nothing in the old nature that can please God (Rom. 8:8) – only when our vessels are under God's control do we have the capacity to please Him. Thankfully, after our future glorification, the flesh nature will be obliterated in believers forever. The Amalekite in us will be gone forever and all will be in submission to Christ.

Moses' father-in-law Jethro was a priest in Midian (Ex. 2:15), and also called a Kenite (Judg. 1:16, 4:11). The origin of the Kenites is unknown, but they appear to be related to the Midianites, at least often choosing to dwell with them. Historically, the Kenites, beginning with Jethro, always behaved favorably towards Israel (Judg. 4:17; 1 Sam. 5:6). Most of the Kenites were carried away by Assyria into captivity in the eighth century B.C., as prophesied by Balaam (v. 22). However, centuries later, descendants of the Kenites through Hemath, the Rechabites, earned Jeremiah's praise for faithfulness to authority and were acknowledged even then as being a nomadic tent-dwelling people. The Kenites likely represent Israel's allies who are to continue on their pilgrim journey until they can rejoice with Israel in Christ's Kingdom.

Lastly Balaam spoke of the ships of Kittim which would destroy Asshur (Assyria) and Eber. Eugene H. Merrill explains the prophecy:

> Many scholars think that Kittim refers not only to Cyprus specifically but also to all western Mediterranean maritime powers generally, particularly Rome (Jer. 2:10; Ezek. 27:6; Dan. 11:30). This

remarkable prophecy found fulfillment in the overthrow of Asshur, which represented Mesopotamia and Persia, and Eber, which was the original name for the Hebrews, or Israelites. Later Rome did indeed incorporate the vestiges of the Assyrian Empire as well as Israel within its universal domination.[104]

Eber, in this prophecy, probably refers to non-Jewish descendants of Eber, a forefather of Abraham. The ships of Kittim may refer to the maritime exploits of Alexander the Great in the region, which occurred prior to the Grecian Empire falling to Rome. What is clear in this complex prophecy is that when the Scepter of Israel comes, He will remove all those who oppose His exaltation of Israel.

C. H. Mackintosh summarizes Balaam's previous three oracles before pondering God's final message to Balak through Balaam:

> In the first parable we see the absolute separation of the people; in the second, their perfect justification; in the third, their moral beauty and fruitfulness; and, now, in the fourth, we stand on the very summit of the hills – on the loftiest crag of the rocks, and survey the wide plains of glory in all their length and breadth, stretching away into a boundless future. We see the Lion of the tribe of Judah crouching; we hear his roar; we see Him seizing upon all His enemies, and crushing them to atoms. The Star of Jacob rises to set no more. The true David ascends the throne of His father, Israel is preeminent in the earth, and all His enemies are covered with shame and everlasting contempt.[105]

Balak was done with Balaam and God was finished with him too, so we read that *"Balaam rose and departed and returned to his place; Balak also went his way"* (v. 25). "Returned to his place" does not mean his far north homeland of Aram, but returned to his old occupation of a prophet for hire. We learn in the next chapter of the devilish counsel Balaam provided the Moabites and Midianites which caused Israel's corruption and subsequent chastening. Later, when these offenders were punished by an Israelite invasion, Balaam perished among the Midianites (31:8).

So Balaam ignored the truth he had been given and sided with the enemies of God's people, and, as a result, never made it back to Aram. Considering the wonders that God revealed through Balaam, F. B. Hole suggests that Balaam is "a solemn example of what good things a man may utter while he himself remains in 'the bond of iniquity,' like Simon the sorcerer in Acts 8."[106]

Meditation

There shall a Star from Jacob come forth,
And a Scepter from Israel rise up,
And dash in pieces princes and nations.

As bright the star of morning gleams,
So Jesus sheds glorious beams
Of light and consolation!

Thy Word, O Lord, radiance darting,
Truth imparting, gives salvation;
Thine be praise and adoration!

— Christian Charles Josias von Bunsen

The Doctrine of Balaam
Numbers 25

Before reviewing the narrative, we briefly pause to consider Balaam as the whole of Scripture represents him. Any doubts we may have about Balaam's true character and disposition towards Jehovah are answered in the New Testament by Peter, Jude, and John.

Peter refers to the *"way of Balaam"* as an indictment against the false teachers of his day who pursued the *"wages of unrighteousness"* (2 Pet. 2:15). Like covetous Balaam, these false teachers were attempting to represent God for financial profit. While God did choose to speak through Balaam to Balak, he was nonetheless an impure vessel in God's hands. Peter highlights the true character of Balaam as like other false teachers who use religion as a cover for their self-seeking. The outcome of their teaching is all the same – to lead God's people into sin and away from Him, instead of drawing them nearer to Him (31:16; 2 Pet. 2:14).

Jude speaks of *"the error of Balaam,"* which wrongly assumed that God had to judicially curse His people on the basis of their spiritual and moral failure. Balaam understood neither God's merciful character, nor His means of righteously judging sin through a substitution. Blood atonement in the Old Testament pictured God's ultimate means of propitiation for human sin that would be achieved by the sacrifice of His Son.

Finally, John records the last mention of Balaam's name in Scripture, when Christ refers to *"the doctrine of Balaam"* in his letter to the church at Pergamos:

> *But I have a few things against you, because you have there those who hold the doctrine of Balaam, who taught Balak to put a stumbling block before the children of Israel, to eat things sacrificed to idols, and to commit sexual immorality* (Rev. 2:14).

Devotions in Numbers

As we soon will see, Balaam instructed Balak to seduce the Israelites to commit idolatry and immorality with the daughters of Moab, so that God would be forced to punish them. While *"the way of Balaam"* speaks of his corrupt motives and *"the error of Balaam"* his wrong assessment of God's character and ways, *"the doctrine of Balaam"* refers to the willful teachings to purposely cause the corruption of God's people.

Of course the Lord hates every bit of it, so Balaam, a corrupt false prophet who did not know the true God, eventually reaped what he had sowed and perished among the very people whom he sought to assist. Interestingly, Balaam's name does not appear in this chapter, but the devastating evil which he instigated does.

Harlotry and Its Judgment (vv. 1-9, 14-18)

While the Israelites were camped at Shittim (just east of the Jordan River; Josh 2:1), some Jewish men engaged in sexual immorality with Moabite women (v. 1). The woman slain later by Phinehas was a Midianite. The Midianites and Moabites worshipped at the same pagan altar and both were conspiring together to solicit Jewish men to come there. Hence this fraternization resulted not only in immorality, but also in idolatry, as the Canaanite fertility rituals incorporated both sensual and religious aspects (Deut. 23:17-18). The result of Balaam's doctrine then was that some Jewish men began to sacrifice and bow down to the gods of Moab with their feminine consorts (v. 2). Israel's joining with Baal of Peor greatly angered the Lord (v. 3).

The Lord instructed Moses to *"take all the leaders of the people and hang the offenders before the Lord, out in the sun, that the fierce anger of the Lord may turn away from Israel"* (v. 4). In turn Moses commanded the judges to purge out of Israel by death anyone who had worshipped Baal of Peor (v. 5). Matthew Henry comments to the outcome of the doctrine of Balaam in this chapter:

> The friendship of the wicked is more dangerous than their enmity; for none can prevail against God's people if they are not overcome by their inbred lusts; nor can any enchantment hurt them, but the enticements of worldly interests and pleasures. Here is the sin of Israel, to which they are enticed by the daughters of Moab and Midian. Those are our worst enemies who draw us to sin, for that is the greatest mischief any man can do us. Israel's sin did that which all

Balaam's enchantments could not do; it set God against them. Diseases are the fruits of God's anger, and the just punishments of prevailing sins; one infection follows the other. Ringleaders in sin ought to be made examples of justice.[107]

Given what the Israelites had witnessed of the Lord's holiness and power over the last forty years, it was nothing less than arrogant folly for a Jewish man named Zimri to bring a pagan prostitute into the camp, especially in plain view of Moses and others gathered at the tabernacle (v. 6). The scene is disturbing. Those who loved the Lord the most were weeping before Him over this terrible sin, while those who loved Him least were attempting to solicit their counterparts into sin and away from the Lord.

The entire exploit was intolerable for a righteous person, and Aaron's son Phinehas rose up in holy zeal to uphold God's honor: *"Now when Phinehas ... saw it, he rose from among the congregation and took a javelin in his hand; and he went after the man of Israel into the tent and thrust both of them through, the man of Israel, and the woman through her body"* (vv. 7-8). His zeal for God was demonstrated in his righteous action which pleased the Lord. Because of Phinehas' righteous judgment of evil in the camp, the plague that was sweeping through the camp, which had already killed 24,000 people, was stayed (v. 9).

Moses provides the name of the Jewish man killed, Zimri, a leader in the tribe of Simeon (v. 14), and also the name of the Midianite woman who perished at the end of Phinehas' javelin, Cozbi (v. 15). Scripture rarely records the names of pagan Gentile women, but in this instance it was to show the utterly desperate ploy of the Moabites to stop Israel, as Cozbi was the daughter of Zur, a leader among the Midianites. Cozbi's appearance in the Israelite camp was not by chance, but reveals the effort of Midianites to lead Zimri and others astray at any price.

The sharp decline in the size of the tribe of Simeon in the second census (i.e., from 59,300 in 1:23 to 22,200 in 26:14) indicates that many of the guilty slain in the plague were Zimri's kin. No other tribe experienced such a huge reduction in numbers. This indicates how powerful invitations of the world can be, even to those older in the faith who have served the Lord faithfully for many years. Commenting on this point, C. A. Coates suggests that friendliness of the world is to be feared more than its curses:

> It must not be supposed that it is only young believers who are exposed to the world's snare. For it comes in at the end of the wilderness, as acting upon those who have, typically, made a good deal of spiritual progress, and who have known something of the good of the indwelling Spirit, both for inward satisfaction and as power to get the victory over enemies. The fact that persons have come distinctly into view as subjects of divine working makes it a definite object with Satan to seduce and corrupt them. And sometimes it becomes sorrowfully manifest that those who have successfully resisted persecution fall before what appeals to fleshly gratification. How often the friendliness of the world, and even an appeal to the lowest lusts of the flesh, have succeeded in casting the people of God down from their excellency! It is not to little children, but to young men – who are strong, and who have the word of God abiding in them, and who have overcome the wicked one – that the warning is addressed, *"Love not the world, nor the things in the world"* (1 John 2:15).[108]

Beside the corruption of Israel's leaders, who should have known better, the other sorrowful outcome of Balaam's doctrine is that it also brought God's wrath upon the Midianites. The Lord commanded Moses: *"Harass the Midianites, and attack them; for they harassed you with their schemes by which they seduced you in the matter of Peor and in the matter of Cozbi, the daughter of a leader of Midian, their sister, who was killed in the day of the plague because of Peor"* (vv. 16-18). While the women of Moab contributed to Israel's corruption, we sense from these verses that it was the Midianites who took the lead in plotting against God's people. The Moabite women may have indulged in what was to them nothing more than customary sensual practices to honor their deity.

The Israelites had obeyed the Lord and had passed by the Moabites, but both the Moabites and Midianites had needlessly provoked the Lord by attempting to lure His people away from Him through moral and religious corruption. Because the Lord told Moses to attack the Midianites, their judgment would be immediate as Moses' death was imminent. The judgment of the Midianites, Balaam, and likely some Moabites too is recorded in Numbers 31. Phinehas will finish what he

Refining and Reminding

started by leading 12,000 Jewish soldiers into battle *"with the holy articles and the signal trumpets in his hand"* (31:6).

The sin of the Moabites against Israel sets a painful course for the nation for centuries to come. For example, the Moabites greatly oppressed the Israelites under the reign of King Eglon early in the era of the judges, but then they were severely punished by Jehovah for doing so (Judg. 3:12-30). Later, Isaiah, Jeremiah, and Ezekiel all prophesy against the Moabites (Isa. 15-16; Jer. 48; Ezek. 25). Although at times the Moabites were more friendly to Israel than other nations, their overall long conflict with the Jews is traced back to Numbers 25, where it needlessly began.

The Reward of the Faithful (vv. 10-13)

The Lord was pleased with Phinehas, who promptly took action against that which dishonored His name: *"Phinehas the son of Eleazar, the son of Aaron the priest, has turned back My wrath from the children of Israel, because he was zealous with My zeal among them, so that I did not consume the children of Israel in My zeal"* (vv. 10-11). Notice that Phinehas did not act in his own name, in his own power, or for his own glory; rather, the Lord said that *"he was zealous with My zeal."* In this respect Phinehas lived up to the meaning of his name, "a mouth of brass." Brass results from a superheated amalgamation of copper with tin and speaks of divine judgment in Scripture.

Phinehas was not a soldier, but a priest, but he acted as a warrior to uphold the Lord's honor.

> As a priest, Phinehas would have the censer in his hand in Tabernacle service. In chapter 31 the trumpet was in his hand ready to be blown, but on this occasion the javelin was in his hand to execute swift and unsparing judgment upon the sinning pair (Ps. 106:30). ... While the congregation, Moses and Aaron among them it would seem, stood before the Tabernacle weeping with much sorrow, Phinehas had other feelings too. They were feelings of a passion of zeal for God and a righteous anger that an Israelite should have the awful effrontery to commit such a deed. When Phinehas stood up and performed his act with the javelin, he was a young man. His seniors stood by and did nothing, merely watching as the man and woman went into the tent. Perhaps they were numb with sorrow and their weeping caused them to hesitate, but Phinehas, jealous for the Lord his God, had no hesitation.[109]

God viewed his zealous act of judging the wicked as an atonement of sorts, that is, the shed blood of Zimri and Cozbi appeased His wrath over Israel's sin. C. H. Mackintosh extols the zeal of Phinehas and highlights what was accomplished because of his faithfulness:

> God's glory and Israel's good were the objects that ruled the conduct of the faithful Phinehas on this occasion. It was a critical moment. He felt there was a demand for the most stern action. It was no time for false tenderness. There are moments in the history of God's people in the which tenderness to man becomes unfaithfulness to God; and it is of the utmost importance to be able to discern such moments. The prompt acting of Phinehas saved the whole congregation, glorified Jehovah in the midst of His people, and completely frustrated the enemy's design. Balaam fell among the judged Midianites; but Phinehas became the possessor of an everlasting priesthood.[110]

God honors those who honor Him; therefore, God entered into a covenant of peace with Phinehas and promised him an everlasting priesthood (vv. 12-13). Previously, the Lord had made a covenant with Aaron and his son (Ex. 29:9) and then chose Eleazar to replace Aaron as high priest in Numbers 20. The Lord now bestows on Phineas and his descendants the honor of being Israel's future high priests.

Two points of application from this chapter are pertinent for us to consider in the Church Age. First, though the leaders of God's people may not engage in a particular sin as Zimri did, they will still be judged by God for condoning it (v. 4; Heb. 13:17).

Second, Phineas demonstrates that remaining silent when sin is apparent and God's name is being disgraced is sin. God's people must be zealous for Him and be willing to act appropriately in His strength for His name's sake. Paul exhorted the church at Ephesus, *"have no fellowship with the unfruitful works of darkness, but rather **expose them**"* (Eph. 5:11). Carnality in the Church or civil edicts that disdain the name of Christ or oppress His Church should cause us to do more than to sorrow privately before the Lord. Believers should be willing to expose the unfruitful works of darkness and to beseech the Lord openly to act against what is known to be corrupt. May the Lord help us in these things!

In this chapter, we saw that Balaam was successful in corrupting the Israelites by leading them into idolatry through seductive Midianite women. Balaam understood that no human army could defeat the

Refining and Reminding

Israelites because God had blessed them. However, he also knew that Jehovah was a holy and jealous God and He would be moved to punish His people if they provoked Him to do so. The unregenerate man cannot pursue the things of God, but as we have just witnessed, God's people still have a nature within them that can go the way of the unregenerate! The lesson for us today is clear: If we want God's blessing in our homes and in our local churches, we had better learn to practice separation from all that would defile us and grieve the heart of God.

Meditation

> He that takes truth for his guide, and duty for his end, may safely trust to God's providence to lead him aright.... Truth is so obscure in these times, and falsehood so established, that, unless we love the truth, we cannot know it.
>
> — Blaise Pascal

The Second Census
Numbers 26

The Israelites, encamped just east of the Jordan River across from Jericho, were poised to enter the holy land. God had accomplished a number of wonderful feats in the forty years since delivering His people from Pharaoh. First, as evidence of His unabated love for His people, Jehovah had sustained them and safely brought them to Canaan as promised. Second, He had accomplished His decree at Kadesh-Barnea, in that, except for Joshua, Caleb, and Moses, all those twenty years of age and older, at that time, had perished in the wilderness (vv. 63-65). Third, Jehovah introduced Himself to the Israelites at Sinai, and since that time He had taught them about Himself and given them His Law which they had to keep to benefit from His presence. Fourth, He had tested and refined the faith of His people to prepare them for the arduous task of warfare and conquest ahead of them. Fifth, the surrounding nations had been made aware of Israel's awesome and powerful God, Jehovah.

The Census (vv. 1-51, 57-62)

After the plague subsided, the Lord commanded Moses and Eleazar (61 to 62 years Moses' junior) to number the people again as he had done at Sinai in the second year of their journey from Egypt (vv. 1-3). This chapter records this census. One of the delightful aspects of this account is that we learn that the sons of Korah did not perish in judgment with their insolent father (vv. 9-11). We also learn that Shelah (Judah's son that was supposed to marry the widow Tamar, but did not), did later marry and have children (v. 20).

The tally of each tribe is mentioned in the same order as in the earlier census in Numbers 1, except that Manasseh precedes Ephraim. As both were tribes of Joseph, this is likely due to the fact that Manasseh was now the larger of the two tribes. The following table shows the numbers of the tribes at each census (vv. 4-51):

Refining and Reminding

Tribe	Census at Sinai	Census at Plains of Moab
Reuben	46,500	43,730
Simeon	59,300	22,200
Gad	45,650	40,500
Judah	74,600	76,500
Issachar	54,400	64,300
Zebulun	57,400	60,500
Manasseh	32,200	52,700
Ephraim	40,500	32,500
Benjamin	35,400	45,600
Dan	62,700	64,400
Asher	41,500	53,400
Naphtali	53,400	45,400
Totals	**603, 550**	**601, 730**

Comparing the two census totals, we find that there was a small decrease in the total number of Israelites at the end of their forty-year wilderness journey. It is noteworthy that if the Midianites and Moabites had not sought to corrupt God's people, there would have been 22,000 more Israelites than when they began their journey. The census result is a clear example that when God's people disobey – they cease to grow. However, remember that the oldest Israelite in this group, less Moses, Caleb, and Joshua, is fifty-nine years old. This means that though slightly smaller in number, the overall population actually had more youthful vitality than it did at Sinai.

The sharp drop in numbers for the tribe of Simeon is best explained by the judgment on their tribe in the previous chapter (25:14). Sadly, the sin of Simeon's leaders would drastically reduce the tribe's inheritance in Canaan also – meaning the entire tribe would suffer for their forefather's sin for centuries to come.

The tribe of Manasseh enjoyed the greatest gain. Reuben's decline in numbers may have been partly due to the rebellion and subsequent judgment of their leaders Dathan and Abiram, and those following them in Numbers 16.

The Levite males, one month of age and older were also counted as in Numbers 3, except the individual tallies of Levite sects are not recorded in Numbers 26. The total number of male Levites increased by 1,000 to 23,000 (probably a rounded number) during the time since the last census (vv. 57-62). The Levites were numbered separately at Sinai because they were not to be counted as soldiers in Israel's army. They are counted separately again because this census was to determine land allotments in Canaan. Although the Levites were not to obtain a region of land for a possession, they would be given specific cities to reside in. The Lord and serving Him was their inheritance.

Division of Land (vv. 52-56)

One of the chief purposes of the Census was to ensure that Canaan was fairly divided among the tribes as an inheritance – larger tribes would get larger portions of land (vv. 53-54). We also learn that the method of distributing the land to each tribe would be by lot (vv. 55-56). About seven years into the future, after the Israelites had conquered most of Canaan, we find Joshua and Eleazar overseeing the land disbursements as determined by the drawing of lots (Josh. 14:1-2). Jewish tradition states the name of a tribe was drawn from one urn while the associated land allotment was drawn simultaneously from another urn.[111]

The Lord used a variety of ways to direct His covenant people through the centuries. He had provided the Urim and the Thummim, two stones in the High Priest's breastplate, to answer questions asked of Him by the High Priest (Ex. 27:21). He also used the casting of lots by the hands of a priest or recognized prophet to direct His people. So Israel understood that Jehovah was guiding the distribution process, and the proceedings left nothing to chance (Prov. 16:33). Furthermore, it would be evident to all that the Lord was guiding the process because it would fulfill the prophetic utterance made by Jacob centuries earlier. This confirmed that a sovereign God was in full control of the distribution process, which should alleviate any assertion of unfairness or favoritism.

Refining and Reminding

The Sons of Korah

Although there are several other references to the sons of Korah later in Scripture, we first learn in Numbers 16 that they did not perish with their father during his overthrow attempt. Korah and his wife, and his household (apparently including servants and children), were swallowed alive by the earth (vv. 27, 32). Jude tells us that Korah perished because of his rebellion against God (Jude 11).

However, his sons were not self-assertive and chose to side with the Lord, rather than with their father when the call of separation came. Perhaps Korah's sons begged their father not to rebel against the Lord, but in the end he would not listen. This then led to the gut-wrenching decision of each of Korah's sons to depart from him and stand with Moses. This decision not only saved them from death, but is also honored in the Psalms. David wrote twenty of the psalms in Book 2 (Psalms 51-70) and seven of these are ascribed to or dedicated to "the sons of Korah" (Psalms 42, 44-49).

Understanding what happened in Numbers 16 gives much more meaning to Psalm 84:10: *"For a day in thy courts is better than a thousand. I had rather be a door keeper in the house of my God than to dwell in the tents of wickedness."* Indeed, descendants of Korah's sons Assir, Elkanah, and Ebiasaph went on to serve the Lord in the tabernacle and then at the temple in Jerusalem (1 Chron. 6:22-30). David actually appointed some of Korah's descendants as musicians to sing before the tabernacle once the ark rested in Jerusalem until the temple was built almost forty years later (1 Chron. 6:37).

Paul instructs children to honor and obey their parents *"in the Lord"* (Eph. 6:1-4). The stipulation phrase, *"in the Lord,"* implies children are to serve their parents as unto the Lord in matters of righteousness, but not in matters of sin. The sons of Korah chose to stand with the Lord, rather than side with their father who was rebelling against God's expressed will and, for that reason, they were spared judgment and then honored by the Lord.

Meditation

> Fare ye well, fare ye well, I will not go with you to hell,
> I mean with Jesus Christ to dwell, let me go!

> — Unknown

Inheritance Laws and a New Leader
Numbers 27

This chapter is quite refreshing to the soul after wading through so many chapters highlighting Israel's unbelief and corruption, and the consequences of those sins. It begins with the genuine faith of the daughters of Zelophehad who knew that Canaan would be taken as God had promised and they wanted an inheritance in their father's name. Their names are recorded three times in Scripture as a testimony of how God rewarded their faith: *"But without faith it is impossible to please Him, for he who comes to God must believe that He is, and that He is a rewarder of those who diligently seek Him"* (Heb. 11:6). Lastly, we have the humility of Moses exemplified in obediently handing over the mantle of leadership to a younger man named Joshua, who had already proven himself as a man of integrity and faith.

The Daughters of Zelophehad (vv. 1-11)

Zelophehad was from the tribe of Manasseh. He had died with the older generation in the wilderness, but had taken no part in the rebellion of Korah (v. 3). He had five daughters, but no sons: Mahlah, Noah, Hoglah, Milcah, and Tirzah (26:33). Claiming the promises of God for their own, the daughters of Zelophehad came to the doorway of the tabernacle to appeal to Moses, Eleazar, and Israel's leaders (vv. 1-2):

> *Our father died in the wilderness; but he was not in the company of those who gathered together against the Lord, in company with Korah, but he died in his own sin; and he had no sons. Why should the name of our father be removed from among his family because he had no son? Give us a possession among our father's brothers* (vv. 3-4).

In faith the daughters of Zelophehad prized what had not yet been secured in Canaan, their possession in the Promised Land. Their testimony stands in sharp contrast to the unbelief and corruption of

Refining and Reminding

their countrymen, as recorded in the previous chapters. They did not want their father's name to be forgotten, nor did they want to live in Israel's inheritance without having a part in it. Laws of inheritance previously delivered by Moses did not address their situation, so Moses took the matter to the Lord for a ruling (v. 5).

The gracious God of heaven sided with the daughters of Zelophehad (v. 6):

> *The daughters of Zelophehad speak what is right; you shall surely give them a possession of inheritance among their father's brothers, and cause the inheritance of their father to pass to them. And you shall speak to the children of Israel, saying: "If a man dies and has no son, then you shall cause his inheritance to pass to his daughter. If he has no daughter, then you shall give his inheritance to his brothers. If he has no brothers, then you shall give his inheritance to his father's brothers. And if his father has no brothers, then you shall give his inheritance to the relative closest to him in his family, and he shall possess it"* (vv. 7-11).

The Lord said, *"the daughters of Zelophehad speak what is right."* When God's people speak unprejudiced words of faith, they always speak right in God's estimation. God is obliged to honor such requests fostered in genuine confidence in Him. Consequently, God gladly sided with the daughters of Zelophehad. C. H. Mackintosh explains why God did so:

> Their words are words of faith, and, as such, are always right in the judgment of God; it is a terrible thing to limit "the Holy One of Israel." He delights to be trusted and used. It is utterly impossible for faith to overdraw its account in God's bank. God could no more disappoint faith than He could deny Himself. He can never say to faith, "You have miscalculated; you take too lofty — too bold a stand; so lower down, and lessen your expectations." Ah! no; the only thing in all this world that truly delights and refreshes the heart of God is the faith that can simply trust Him; and we may rest assured of this, that the faith that can trust Him is also the faith that can love Him, and serve Him, and praise Him.[112]

Indeed, God's own heart is refreshed when we count His promises as good as done and choose to earnestly wait for the blessed outcome of our faith. The book of Joshua records that when the land was being divided among the tribes, these women of faith received a portion for their inheritance: *"the daughters of Manasseh received an inheritance among his sons; and the rest of Manasseh's sons had the land of Gilead"* (Josh. 17:5-6). The language of the text is beautiful and upholds the authority of Joshua and Eleazar, who were speaking for the Lord in the matter of allotment, and also the corporate authority of the tribe in conferring grace to the family of Zelophehad.

Some today think that family order trumps church authority in managing the affairs of life. Let us remember that while husbands and fathers are accountable to God for the wellbeing of their own families, church elders are also accountable to God for those under their care in the local assembly. This is shown to us in the terminology of administrating an inheritance in Joshua 17 – it was *"the daughters of Manasseh"* who received a tribal portion, not the daughters of Zelophehad. They enjoyed what the entire tribe cherished and was blessed by God with. Likewise, believers should not neglect the meetings of the Church, nor serving each other within the Body of Christ. All believers are joint heirs with Christ and thus we, all together, share the riches of His inheritance. On this important distinction, C. A. Coates exhorts:

> In Numbers 36 the chief fathers of Manasseh stood for the principle of maintaining each tribe's inheritance in its integrity as distributed by lot. Some are inclined to make the family principle everything. But it is as essential to inherit in tribal character as it is to inherit family-wise. Indeed the holy affections and mutuality that belong to family relations will only be safeguarded and developed as we respect the divine ordering and sovereign distribution which pertains to the assembly. The five daughters of Zelophehad secured an extended territory to Manasseh … but they had to recognize that they held the inheritance subject to the limitations which divine sovereignty imposed. They had to own that there was a tribal order which they must not transgress; they were not at liberty to do as they pleased in Israel. They could only hold the inheritance family-wise as they respected the tribal assignment of it by lot. The lesson of this for us is that we must accept the divine order which is set up, and which is to regulate things with particular reference to how we walk together in local assemblies (1 Cor. 14:37).[113]

Refining and Reminding

Accordingly, the daughters of Manasseh would therefore receive the blessing they requested, but they also had to abide by God's limitations concerning this possession and the tribal authority in administering it (36:1-12). If they married, they must take husbands of the tribe of their father to ensure that no tribal inheritance would be lost at the time of Jubilee.

The Law of Inheritance was expanded to ensure that all confusion was eliminated in passing inheritance from generation to generation. The inheritance protocol was first to sons, but if no sons, then daughters; but if no daughters, then brothers; if no brothers, then uncles; if no uncles, then closest kin. This Law would ensure peace among God's people and that nothing was lost of God's goodness to each of the tribes.

In summary, the daughters of Zelophehad were rewarded for their faith which was rooted in God's revealed truth, but in such a way to also ensure tribal interests were safeguarded. We see this same pattern in the New Testament, as individuals are given to the Church by Christ for its general edification, rather than for mere personal benefit (Eph. 4:11-12). May the Lord's people always act in truth-based faith for the good of others. The believer's spiritual blessings in heavenly places in Christ (Eph. 1:3) are not for self-focused doings, but for selfless Christ-exalting ministry, which, of course, will benefit the serving believer also.

A New Leader (vv. 12-23)

The Lord told Moses that it was time for him to be gathered to his people (i.e., to die; v. 13). Moses was instructed to climb up in the mountain range of Abarim so that he could behold the vista of the Promised Land to the west before he died (v. 12). The specific summit in this range we later learn was Mount Nebo (Deut. 32:49).

Then the Lord reminded Moses of his failure to obey Him and to honor Him before the people a few months earlier at Kadesh in the Wilderness of Zin (v. 14; 20:12). After the incident at the waters of Meribah, Moses had been informed that he would not enter the Promised Land with the Israelites, but that he would be able to see it. Moses did not beg the Lord to reconsider His punishment, nor did he ask to live a little longer. Rather, he accepted the Lord's decision and made the following request on behalf of his countrymen:

Let the Lord, the God of the spirits of all flesh, set a man over the congregation, who may go out before them and go in before them, who may lead them out and bring them in, that the congregation of the Lord may not be like sheep which have no shepherd (vv. 16-17).

Moses' unselfish request in the matter of appointing a successor is a mark of a true leader, one who possessed a superb spirit of self-surrender. He did not seek a monument to be remembered by after his death, nor did he ever seek fame or fortune after meeting Jehovah forty years earlier. He had gone on with the Lord and spiritually matured into a man sold out for the glory of God and for the good of His people – marks of a true leader.

When God first summoned Moses to deliver His people from bondage and from Egypt, Moses rejected the idea. He argued that the Israelites would not believe that he was from God, that the Egyptians would not release their slave force, and that, beside all this, he was not an eloquent speaker. A few moments later, after God demonstrated His power and affirmed Aaron as his helper, Moses surrendered to God's call.

Over the following years Moses' faith in and devotion to Jehovah steadily grew. After Moses' death, Joshua recorded sixteen times in his book that Moses was "the servant of the Lord." In fact, the New Testament attributes a special honor to Moses' service to the Lord. The Greek word *therapon*, translated "servant" in Hebrews 3:5, is used to describe the type of servant Moses was. *Therapon* is not the typical word used in the New Testament to describe a servant or a slave. This word conveys the idea of a voluntary servant who is motivated by devotion for his superior. At first, Moses was hesitant to accept the call of God for his life, but when he did, he did so of his own free will.

The Lord had already selected Moses' successor, but what a lovely display of humble leadership is recorded for us to observe by permitting Moses to intercede for those he loved. The Lord answered Moses' request:

Take Joshua the son of Nun with you, a man in whom is the Spirit, and lay your hand on him; set him before Eleazar the priest and before all the congregation, and inaugurate him in their sight. And you shall give some of your authority to him, that all the congregation of the children of Israel may be obedient. He shall stand before Eleazar the priest, who shall inquire before the Lord for him by the

Refining and Reminding

> *judgment of the Urim. At his word they shall go out, and at his word they shall come in, he and all the children of Israel with him -- all the congregation* (vv. 18-21).

Joshua's years of serving Moses not only prepared him for his own ministry of leading the Israelites, but also pointed to it. Even before Joshua's confirmation in this chapter, we see indications of his future ministry during the years he faithfully served Moses. For example, Joshua first appears in Scripture as a young man leading the attack against the Amalekites in Exodus 17. The scene is glorious: Moses, on the mount, holding up the rod of God over the battlefield, pictures Christ's intercessory power for His people from the throne of grace in heaven. But while Moses intercedes above, Joshua wields the sword victoriously below. This sight portrays Christ's unrestrained power in the believer's life as he or she uses the Word of God (the sword of truth, Heb. 4:12) and fully relies on the strength of the Holy Spirit.

Next, Joshua is seen at the base of Mt. Sinai waiting for Moses to descend with the Word of God; he stood apart from the idolatrous clamor within the camp of Israel (Ex. 32:17). Likewise, in behavior the Lord Jesus was separate from sinners and longed only to do God's will (John 5:30). Joshua would again demonstrate faithfulness when, months after leaving Mt. Sinai behind, he was one of the twelve spies sent by Moses into Canaan on a reconnaissance mission. They brought back a pledge of the fruit of that land which was their promised inheritance. Ten of the spies doubted God's faithfulness, but Joshua, along with Caleb, resolutely withstood them (Num. 13 and 14). Much of the Lord's ministry was centered in confronting those who would deny God's faithfulness to His word.

The above events were a foretaste of Joshua's later ministry; he had been chosen by God to subdue the nations of Canaan and then to divide their land for an inheritance for His people. As is often the case before one comes into the fullness of his or her divine calling, Joshua's accomplishments cast their shadow beforehand. He was a man of courage, tenacity, conviction, and holiness – a proven leader among his peers. In God's plan, the young Joshua of the wilderness had forty years of preparation before becoming the victorious Joshua of the Promised Land.

Yet, we learn in verse 21 that Joshua's interaction with Jehovah would not be as personal as what Moses had enjoyed in the wilderness.

Joshua would be more dependent upon Eleazar the high priest, who had the Urim and the Thummim, to understand the counsel and judgments of God.

Moses obeyed the Lord and set Joshua before Eleazar and the congregation to publicly recognize him as Israel's new leader. By laying his hands upon Joshua, Moses identified himself with him and hence his appointment was confirmed before the people. After this event, there is little narrative pertaining to the Israelites encamped in the plains of Moab until after Moses' death, which is recorded at the end of Deuteronomy. The remaining pages of Numbers and the book of Deuteronomy are mainly occupied with further legislation and with moral instruction.

The best leaders are those who would rather be followers, but the need of the hour is so great that they must rise up to serve. This would certainly be true of Moses, of whom Scripture says, he *"was very humble, more than all men who were on the face of the earth"* (12:3). When God called Moses to lead His people out of Egypt, Moses said, *"O my Lord, I am not eloquent, neither before nor since You have spoken to Your servant; but I am slow of speech and slow of tongue"* (Ex. 4:10). Yet God patiently dealt with His servant, even bringing Aaron alongside to assist him in his calling, which he fulfilled. And in the end, after forty years of communing with and working with the Lord, Moses probably knew Jehovah better than any man before him.

Meditation

A leader is one who knows the way, goes the way, and shows the way.

— John C. Maxwell

A true and safe leader is likely to be one who has no desire to lead, but is forced into a position of leadership by the inward pressure of the Holy Spirit and the press of the external situation.

— A. W. Tozer

Various Offerings
Numbers 28

The next two chapters reaffirm the offerings required daily, on the Sabbath, each month, and during the Levitical feasts described in Leviticus 23. One outstanding feature of each of these sections is the prominent place of the sin offering whether in worship, thanksgiving, or celebration. The sin offering is mentioned thirteen times in Numbers 28 and 29. Thirteen is the number of rebellion in Scripture. It seems likely then the text is symbolically showing that an appropriate sin offering is necessary to appease God's anger over man's rebellious ways. Man is a sinner, a natural rebel, and therefore cannot do anything to please God until his sin has been dealt with.

Of course, this all points to Christ's once-for-all propitiation at Calvary, which permits believers to interact with God in worship, prayer, thanksgiving, etc. However, with that said, dealing with sin is not the focus of this chapter; rather, God's delight in His Son is. C. H. Mackintosh explains:

> There are seventy-one verses in the entire section; and, out of these, thirteen allude to the sin offering, and the remaining fifty-eight are occupied with sweet savor offerings. In a word, then, the special theme here is God's delight in Christ.[114]

Daily Offerings (vv. 1-8)

The Lord instructed Moses: *"Command the children of Israel, and say to them, 'My offering, My food for My offerings made by fire as a sweet aroma to Me, you shall be careful to offer to Me at their appointed time'"* (vv. 1-2). The Lord referred to these sacrifices as *"My offering,"* *"My bread,"* and *"My sacrifices"* to claim His right to them – they were not optional but demanded! Commenting on verse 2, F. B. Hole writes:

Nothing was left to the discretion or feelings of the people; rather, God was to be acknowledged and honored according to His pleasure. In this we see a principle of importance. We draw near to God today and worship Him in another order of things. Later in Israel's history one of their prophets said, *"Receive us graciously; so will we render the calves of our lips"* (Hos. 14:2); thus recognizing that something coming out of their hearts through their lips would be more acceptable than the mechanical presentation of an animal.[115]

John J. Stubbs explains why it was so important to God that He have His portion from His worshipping people:

All the offerings God demanded to be brought speak of Christ. The fact that God could use the pronoun "My" with regard to them shows that He delighted in all these presentations which spoke of His lovely Son. If this was the case then with these sacrifices from the Jewish people, how much more is it true in this present age when believers in assemblies gather to worship. Now that Christ, who is pictured in these offerings, has come, lived, died, and risen again, what a joy it is to delight the heart of God with His own Son. God has always delighted in His Son and will continue to do so for all eternity. His heart feeds upon Him and He is refreshed and satisfied. What a precious thought this is with which to begin the chapter. In worship the Christian approaches God in occupation with Christ. He is the great theme of worship. It is a precious exercise therefore to speak to God in worship about His Son.[116]

The daily offerings Moses mentions had already been legislated at Mount Sinai more than thirty-eight years earlier and had been practiced since that time (Ex. 29:38-46). There were to be two items presented with the lamb at each daily burnt offering: a meal and a drink offering (vv. 3-4). The meal offering consisted of one-tenth of an ephah of flour mixed with one-fourth of a hin of pressed oil, and the drink offering of one-fourth of a hin of wine which was to be poured out before the Lord (v. 5; Ex. 29:40).

The priests could not enter the tabernacle to serve the Lord without putting a sacrifice upon the Bronze Altar; to do so would result in death. God permitted the priests to enter the tabernacle twice a day after offering a lamb each morning and evening as a burnt sacrifice (vv. 6-8). Thus, the priests and the people would be reminded each morning and again at the end of each day that without sacrifice there was no

Refining and Reminding

acceptance with God. The Israelites had the immense privilege of having God dwell among them, but the smoking altar testified that the entire arrangement was tentative, strictly dependent upon the continuation of holy sacrifices to deal with their unholiness.

All that was consumed upon the altar ascended up to God as a sweet aroma; thus its continuous smoke was a testimony of God's utter delight and infinite satisfaction in the death of His Son in obedience to His will. It was only in this ascending fragrance that Israel had acceptance before God, and it is none the less true for the Christian today, less the fire and smoke, for now our Altar is Christ and He is before God in heaven and we are accepted in Him (Eph. 1:3-6).

In the same way that the daily offerings of Israel were a perpetual sweet savor to God, we have been accepted in the Beloved as a continual sweet savor offering unto God. Logistically speaking, the fire on the Bronze Altar was occasionally extinguished and the sweet savor before God ceased for a time, but through Christ's redemptive work, all believers are made a sweet savor unto God forever!

The daily sacrifices, therefore, allowed God to tabernacle among His people and to communicate His will to them through Moses. Through the daily sweet-savor sacrifices the tabernacle could continue to be "the tent of meeting." The billowing smoke was a continual testimony that their acceptance with God was due to the burning sacrifices. Unless Jehovah was moving the camp site, the absence of smoke from the Bronze Altar meant that the Israelites had no acceptance before God; the priests could not enter the tabernacle. This meant there would be no worship offered to God, and no communication or fellowship with God.

Sabbath Offerings (vv. 9-10)

The Sabbath Day had been consecrated for the Lord at Mount Sinai (Ex. 20:8-11). The people were to cease from working, to reflect on the Lord, and to dedicate themselves afresh to Him. For this reason the burnt offerings were to be double on every Sabbath (i.e., double the lambs, grain, and drink offerings). The Sabbath typified the rest that God had for His people in Christ. Thus, one day in seven was set aside to show double appreciation for the Lord. As God delights in His Son, it should be our aspiration to present to the Father that which delights and refreshes His heart.

God has displayed a pattern in which we should rest one day in seven (Gen. 2:1-3), yet this is not commanded. It seems logical that periodic rest would help remedy physical fatigue and emotional strain. The Law commanded the Jews to keep the Sabbath, which they miserably failed to do. The Lord issued no such command to the Church, as individual believers can worship God anytime and anywhere as believer priests (John 4:23-24). In the dispensation of grace, men must *"go forth, therefore, to Him outside the camp, bearing His reproach"* to be saved (Heb. 13:13). The writer of Hebrews informed the Jews that they were no longer under the Law but under a new covenant of grace that was established by Christ. The pattern of the early Church was to gather corporately, not on Saturday, but on Sunday – the first day of the week, which was Christ's resurrection day (1 Cor. 16:2; Acts 20:7). On Sunday, believers gathered to worship their Savior, not to keep the Law. This is why John refers to Sunday as "the Lord's day" (Rev. 1:10).

Monthly Offerings (vv. 11-15)

Earlier the blowing of the silver trumpets at the New Moon festival was commanded (10:10), but this is the first time that a monthly offering has been mentioned. On the first day of each month the Jewish nation was to present additional burnt offerings besides the daily offerings. These included two young bulls, one ram, and seven yearling male lambs; all were to be without blemish (vv. 11-12). Also drink and grain offerings were to accompany the burnt sacrifices (vv. 13-14). Lastly, *"one kid of the goats"* was required as a sin offering (v. 15).

Although the goat, the sin offering, was mentioned last, it is most likely that it was presented first before the Lord, as that would be the normal procedure of obtaining acceptance of what was offered afterwards (Ex. 29; Lev. 5; 8; 9; 14; 16). The sin offering was for sins of ignorance once realized, but here the monthly sin offering was commanded as a catch-all for sins of ignorance not personally dealt with.

Passover Offerings (vv. 16-25)

Every Jewish male was required to present himself before Jehovah three times a year at The Feast of Unleavened Bread, The Feast of Weeks, and The Feast of Ingathering (Ex. 34:18-23). In all, seven feasts were to be observed: Passover, Unleavened Bread, Firstfruits, Weeks

(Pentecost), Trumpets, Day of Atonement, and Tabernacles. The first three feasts ran together in the spring, Pentecost followed fifty days afterwards, and the three remaining feasts were separated by only a few days in the fall. Each feast was to be a *"holy convocation"* or, literally, a "sacred calling together" before the Lord (v. 18). Like the Sabbath day, these feast days were set aside solely for Jehovah; it was a time for worship and reflection, not for labor (Lev. 23:2-3).

The feasts were to be observed *"before the Lord,"* which initially meant at the tabernacle, but later at the temple in Jerusalem. Each of the three seasons of festivals was tied to the Jewish agricultural calendar. The Feast of Unleavened Bread occurred in March/April and related to the barley harvest. The Feast of Weeks occurred during the wheat harvest (about seven weeks after the barley was reaped) and marked the end of the spring harvest time. The Feast of Weeks is also referred to as Pentecost (Acts 2:1, 20:16), the Day of Firstfruits (28:26), and The Feast of Harvest (Ex. 23:16). The Feast of Ingathering, also known as The Feast of Tabernacles, occurred at the end of the agricultural year in September or October.

The Passover Feast and The Feast of Unleavened Bread were both instituted in Exodus 12. The annual Passover Feast was to remind the Israelites of their deliverance from Egypt and their restoration to Jehovah through redemption. Through the sacrifice of an innocent substitute (a yearling male lamb without blemish) and the application of its blood, the firstborn of each house was saved from the tenth plague. But beyond this, the entire Jewish nation obtained a new beginning and a new life with God at this time. The Hebrew calendar was to align itself with this event marking *"the beginning of months"* (Ex. 12:2); Passover was held on the fourteenth day of the first month in the Jewish calendar.

Year by year the Passover meal would serve as a memorial feast of what God had accomplished through blood redemption in Egypt; however, it has its culmination in the ultimate redemptive work of Christ at Calvary. Just hours before His death the Lord Jesus instituted the Lord's Supper to commemorate in the hearts of believers for centuries to come what He would accomplish through the sacrifice of Himself (Luke 22:19-20). The Passover Feast then pictures Christ on the cross; this was the day the Passover lambs were slain and was also the day when the Lamb of God was slain for the sins of the world (1 Cor. 5:7).

The Passover Feast was to be held on the fourteenth of the first month, The Feast of Unleavened Bread on the fifteenth day, and The Feast of Firstfruits on the following day (vv. 16-17). The Feast of Unleavened Bread was to last seven days, meaning the total duration of the first three spring feasts was to be eight days.

Both The Passover and the last day of The Feast of Unleavened Bread were to be holy convocations to the Lord, which required the people to cease from laboring (vv. 18, 25). Each day of Unleavened Bread was to be marked by burnt offerings of two young bulls, one ram, and seven yearling male lambs; all were to be without blemish. These were in addition to the daily offerings (v. 23). There were also special drink and grain offerings to accompany the burnt sacrifices (vv. 20-24). Additionally, a goat was required to be offered as a sin sacrifice to atone for sin which permitted the other offerings to be accepted (v. 22).

Feast of Weeks Offerings (vv. 26-31)

The Feast of Weeks occurred seven weeks and one day (i.e., 50 days) after the waving of the barley sheaf before the Lord in the Feast of Firstfruits (two days after The Passover). This celebration occurred towards the end of the wheat harvest in late spring or early summer.

The sacrifices for The Feast of Pentecost, in addition to the daily sacrifices, included: two young bullocks, one ram, and seven yearling lambs for a burnt offering, one kid of the goats for a sin offering, and two yearling lambs for a peace offering (vv. 26-27; Lev. 23:18-19). The sweet savor offerings were to be accompanied by a meal offering and a drink offering (vv. 28-31).

Although not mentioned in Numbers, the more specific instructions in Leviticus included an unusual meal offering of two leavened loaves composed of ground grain from the recent wheat harvest (Lev. 23:16-17). While portions of other unleavened meal offerings were burnt on the Bronze Altar, nothing with leaven could be offered to the Lord in this way (Lev. 2:11). The two wave loaves were to be waved before the Lord and then eaten by the priests (Lev. 23:20).

This was the only time throughout the entire year that leavened bread was presented to the Lord. Although not specifically stated, it is assumed that oil was mixed into the leavened dough before baking, as all meal offerings were to be anointed with oil before being burned on the altar, or to have oil mixed within before they were baked (Lev. 2:1-

16). Olive oil is a symbol of the Holy Spirit in Scripture, but what is the significance of the leaven in the meal offering, especially since leaven represents an evil influence? Understanding more about how the dough was leavened before being baked will be helpful in answering this question. L. Duane Lindsey describes the process:

> The bread was leavened by placing in the dough a lump of leaven (i.e., sourdough) from bread of the preceding barley harvest, thus reemphasizing the close connection between the barley and the wheat harvest, and the festivals associated with them.[117]

The resurrected Lord Jesus was represented before the Lord in the barley wave sheaf at The Feast of Firstfruits. The grain from this sheaf was later ground and used to create sourdough. Fifty days later, a lump of the barley sourdough was placed into the freshly ground wheat flour to create the two wave loaves. Thus, the wave sheaf and the wheat harvest that followed are connected in the two loaves. Obviously there is no leaven in Christ, the Wave Sheaf, but believers united with Him (the Church) still have a leavened nature within them. L. M. Grant further explains the symbolism of this unique meal offering of the two loaves.

> The two wave loaves picture the acceptance of both Jewish and Gentile believers, who are seen in 1 Corinthians 12:13 to be joined together in one body by *"the baptism of the Spirit."* As the waving of the sheaf of firstfruits is typical of the ascension of the Lord Jesus to heaven, so the waving of the two loaves pictures the Church as being *"raised up together"* and made to *"sit together in the heavenly places in Christ"* (Eph. 2:6). This could not be applied to Israel, for Israel is God's earthly people, but the Church is identified today with Christ in heaven. Wonderful grace!

> These wave loaves are said to be "the firstfruits to the Lord." This does not contradict the fact that the wave sheaf (offered 50 days earlier) was the sheaf of firstfruits, typical only of Christ raised and glorified. From this viewpoint Christ stands alone. But when the people are considered, the firstfruits from among mankind focuses upon the Church, which is the first result of the work of Christ. So James 1:18 tells us, "Of His own will He brought us forth by the word of truth, that we might be a kind of firstfruits of His creatures." This

has taken place before the general harvest which will involve Israel and the nations.[118]

The two wave loaves represent the spiritual body of the Church composed of both Jews and Gentiles. The Law imposed a wall between these two groups, but the efficacious work of Christ has pulled down that barrier and has eternally united them in the bonds of divine love and peace (Eph. 2:14-16). This explains why only burnt offerings were required at The Feast of Firstfruits, but a sin offering (one kid of the goats) and a peace offering (two yearling lambs) had to be presented at Pentecost. As this feast pictures the acceptance of all believers in Christ, a sin offering of the substitutionary goat was imperative. Since the peace offering typifies the fellowship of believers with God through the Lord Jesus Christ, the two lambs had to be offered also.

As The Feast of Firstfruits speaks of the Lord Jesus being alone in His resurrection and ascension, only a burnt offering was required to show God's acceptance of all that had been accomplished. But Pentecost, as seen in Acts 2, involves the blessing and acceptance of those whom the Lord calls His "beloved" and His "brethren" – His Church (2 Thess. 2:13; Heb. 2:1).

Meditation

O child of God, there is for thee
A hope that shines amid the gloom,
A gladsome hope that thou shalt see
Thy Lord, for He will surely come.

Exalted now to Heaven's throne,
The Savior there of sinful men;
His loving heart yearns over His own,
And for them He will come again.

Then joy unmingled will be thine,
Earth's tears and trials all forgot;
So cheer thy heart, no more repine,
His word is sure: He'll tarry not.

— Thomas D. W. Muir

Offerings at the Feasts of Jehovah
Numbers 29

As mentioned in the previous chapter, seven annual feasts were to be observed by the Jews: Passover, Unleavened Bread, Firstfruits, Harvest (Pentecost), Trumpets, Day of Atonement, and Tabernacles. The first three feasts ran together in early springtime, Pentecost occurred fifty days after the Firstfruits observance, and the three remaining feasts were separated by only a few days in the beginning of autumn (this would normally correspond to our month of September). This created a long interim between these and the spring feasts, which typify Christ's death (Passover), burial (Unleavened Bread), resurrection (Firstfruits), and the creation of the Church (Pentecost).

From a prophetic viewpoint, the gap between the spring and fall festivals pictures the Church Age, and the fall feasts themselves picture God's future dealings to restore a remnant of Israel to Himself. These include The Feast of Trumpets, The Day of Atonement, and The Feast of Tabernacles, and collectively these were later referred to by the Jews as "the High Holy Days." These three feasts mark the conclusion of the religious year (i.e., there were no more biblical feasts until Passover the following spring).

Moses directed that The Feast of Trumpets should be observed on the first day of the seventh month; however, sometime after the Babylonian exile, the Jews began to commemorate this feast on the first day of Tishri; Tishri is the first month of the Babylonian calendar. Over time the Jews adopted the Babylonian calendar, including the Babylonian names for the months of the year in association with the Feasts of Jehovah. Thus, the first day of the seventh month became known as the first day of Tishri and The Feasts of Trumpets soon was referred to as *Rosh Hashanah*, which literally means "the head of the months." In fact, today the Jews continue to celebrate The Feast of Trumpets as a New Year festival; this means Passover no longer marks the start of the Jewish calendar as God intended. The ancient rabbis believed God initiated the creation of the world on this very day – The Feasts of Trumpets. This celebration began a period of time known as the "Ten Days of Repentance," a time of personal reflection, leading up to *Yom Kippur*, the Day of Atonement.

Feast of Trumpets Offerings (vv. 1-6)

The feast is not specifically titled in Scripture, but is identified by the phrases *"a memorial of blowing of trumpets"* (Lev. 23:24) and *"a day of blowing the trumpets"* (v. 1). Since the blowing of the trumpets became the distinguishing characteristic of the day, it became known as The Feast of the Trumpets. The feast was a holy convocation to the Lord (v. 1).

The animals to be sacrificed as burnt offerings were a young bullock, a ram, and seven young lambs and each group of animals was to be presented on the altar with a meal offering and drink offering (vv. 2-4). A kid from the goats was also to be offered as a sin offering (v. 5). These burnt offerings were in addition to the normal daily burnt offerings and those routinely presented at the first of each month (v. 6). Jewish tradition considered this feast to be a preparatory call of the people to stand before God in judgment, which would occur ten days later on the Day of Atonement.

Another mysterious aspect of this feast is that the text does not specifically state what is to pierce the silence of this special day. The Hebrew word *teruah* is translated "blowing of trumpets" in both Leviticus 23:24 (where *teruah* first appears in Scripture) and Numbers 29:1. *Teruah* literally means "a clamor" and by implication "an acclamation of joy," "a loud noise," or "an alarm." The word is tied with the sounding of a silver trumpet as an alarm in Numbers 10:5-6, and the blowing of a ram's horn, the *showphar,* in the year of Jubilee (Lev. 25:9). It is also used to speak of "a shout of joy" by people (Ezra 3:11-13), the noise of musical instruments (Ps. 33:3), and even the clang of a cymbal (Ps. 105:5). In summary, the exact meaning of *teruah* is indeed indefinite and what was to initiate the joyful clamor is unknown. All this to say, we are not told the specifics of "the clamoring" that was heard on this feast day. Jewish tradition favors the blowing of the ram's horn, the *shophar,* instead of the silver trumpets, but in reality, all that is practiced presently during The Feasts of Trumpets is developed tradition.

Refining and Reminding

Today, a series of one hundred *shophar* blasts, consisting of four different types of tones and various repetitions, is sounded to announce the convening of God's courtroom of judgment. The final blast is a longer and louder unbroken sound, *Tekiah Gedolah*, which supposedly signals a final invitation before *Yom Kippur* to receive repentance and atonement from the King who sits on the heavenly throne. Hence this feast symbolizes the future blast of a trumpet at the end of the Tribulation Period to announce the gathering of all Jews back to Israel (Matt. 24:31). This was one of the purposes for sounding the trumpet in Exodus 19 – the assembling of the Jewish nation together before the Lord. This Jewish feast is not associated with "the last trump" Paul refers to, which relates to the rapture of the Church from the earth (1 Cor. 15:51-52; 1 Thess. 4:13-18). That trump call is for Christ's Gentile bride and will occur just prior to the Tribulation Period and will end the Church Age. From a symbolic standpoint, then, The Feast of Trumpets pictures the future calling of the Jewish people back to Israel.

Day of Atonement Offerings (vv. 7-11)

The Day of Atonement had special significance among the seven feasts of Jehovah and took place on the tenth day of the seventh month (Lev. 23:27). The specific details of this feast are recorded in Leviticus 16. As referenced in verse 7 and three times in Leviticus 23:27-32, this feast day was a day for afflicting one's soul; the Jews understood this to mean a time of fasting and reflection. As with all the feasts, this was a "holy convocation," meaning there was to be no normal work done this day; in fact, God promises destruction upon anyone who did (Lev. 23:30).

In addition to the daily offerings, the same burnt offerings as described for other feast days were to be presented on the Day of Atonement also (i.e., a young bullock, a ram, and seven young lambs). Each group of animals was to be presented on the altar with a meal offering and drink offering (vv. 8-10). A kid from the goats was also to be offered as a sin offering, in addition to the sin offerings specified in Leviticus 16 (v. 11).

Only on the Day of Atonement was the high priest permitted to enter the Most Holy Place of the tabernacle, there to apply the blood of a bull and of a goat on and before the Mercy Seat. This atoned for (covered) all the sins the nation committed the previous year. It was also a unique occasion because the high priest put off his normal glorious attire and wore a plain white linen garment while applying the blood of atonement. This feast was an annual reminder of the ongoing problem of sin and that the blood of animals did not satisfy God's anger over sin, nor did it purge the sinner's guilty conscience. Rather, the entire feast pointed the Jewish nation to God's vital provision in Christ. From an eschatological viewpoint, this feast represents a future day during the latter part of the Tribulation Period when the Jewish nation accepts Jesus Christ as their Messiah and receives the Holy Spirit (Zech. 12:10).

Feast of Tabernacle Offerings (vv. 12-40)

Five days after The Day of Atonement came The Feast of Tabernacles, falling on the fifteenth day of the seventh month in the Hebrew calendar (Lev. 23:34). The feast lasted a total of eight days; the first and the eighth days (Lev. 23:35-36) were declared a "holy convocation," a high Sabbath day (vv. 12, 35; Lev. 23:39). In contrast to the "affliction of souls" that took place on The Day of Atonement, this feast was a time of thanksgiving and rejoicing. With harvest complete and the barns and storehouses full, it was time for everyone to gather to express their gratitude to Jehovah. Hence, this festival was sometimes referred to as "The Feast of Ingathering" (Lev. 23:39).

The burnt offerings for this feast were extensive: on the first day thirteen young bulls, two rams, and fourteen lambs in their first year were to be offered to the Lord in association with meal and drink offerings (vv. 13-15). A kid from the goats was also to be offered as a sin offering (v. 16). Then each of the next six days these burnt and sin offerings were to be repeated (less one bull for each day; vv. 17-34). On the final day of the feast a single bull, a single ram, and seven yearling lambs were presented as burnt offerings with their associated meal and drink offerings (vv. 35-37). The standard sin offering of a goat was also sacrificed with its associated meal and drink offerings (v. 38). Moses conveyed all the details of the offering to the Israelites and warned them to obey what the Lord expected of them (vv. 39-40).

Although not described in this chapter, Leviticus 23 informs us that each Jewish family was to cut down branches from various leafy trees, such as willows and palms, and to erect makeshift booths to dwell in for the seven nights and eight days of this festival (Lev. 23:40-43). This activity was to remind the Jews of how God delivered them from bondage in Egypt and that they dwelled with Jehovah in the wilderness

Refining and Reminding

while residing in tents. The booths, then, were a memorial of what God had accomplished for His people. Jehovah did not want them to forget that He was their beginning. For this reason, The Feast of Tabernacles was to be an annual event throughout their generations.

This feast pictures the glory of the Jewish nation after they are purified and restored to Jehovah at the end of the Tribulation Period (Rom. 9:27, 11:25-27). During the Millennial Kingdom, the Jewish nation will come into all the fullness of the Abrahamic covenant; thus, The Feast of Tabernacles forms a lovely and fitting close to the entire series of Jehovah's feasts. In recognition of its prophetic meaning, William Kelly notes the significance of the eight-day duration of The Feast of Tabernacles:

> The feast was the shadow of coming glory. God thus shows us, by this remarkable introduction of the eighth day here, the connection of the earthly blessing with the heavenly glory of resurrection. Resurrection points to heaven, and can never satisfy itself except in heavenly places; and therefore a link is here intimated with glory on high, whilst there is the fullest possible recognition of a day of rest and blessedness for the earth and the Jewish people. As we are told here in the latter part of it, they were all to keep this feast with gladness and joy. The eighth day is evidently brought in in a mysterious way – not now pointing to those who may be a testimony for God where all seemed to be removed from the earth, as we saw in the notice of the harvest at the end; but now, when we have the fullness of the witness of glory here below, this finger, so to speak, points upward, showing that in some way not developed in this chapter there will be the connection of the resurrection and heavenly glory with the day of Jehovah for the earth.[119]

As demonstrated when God saved Noah and his family (a total of eight souls) from judgment in the ark to start anew in the world, the number eight in Scripture is tied with new beginnings. For example, the Lord Jesus was raised up from the dead on the first, or eighth, day of the week – Sunday. The Jewish nation will experience the fullness of joy, peace, and blessing after being infused with the resurrected life of Christ. At the Lord's Second Coming to the earth, He will identify with His covenant people again and they will accept Him, the One they previously crucified, as their Messiah (Zech. 12:10). Spiritual fruit such as joy, peace, and love can only be produced through spiritual rebirth, which coincides with the Holy Spirit being poured out upon the Jewish nation at the end of the Tribulation Period. From that day forth, the Jewish nation will enjoy a wondrous new beginning with Jesus Christ, their Messiah (Joel 2:25-3:21; Zech. 12:10-13:1).

Had the Jews understood the prophetic meaning of The Feast of Tabernacles, it is doubtful they would have been so careless as to its observance through the centuries. In the days of Nehemiah, the Jews knew nothing about it until the Law of Moses was read to them (Neh. 8:14-17), even though the nation observed this feast some eighty years earlier under Zerubbabel's leadership (Ezra 3:4). This is one of many historical examples that illustrates man's natural propensity to forget those things which are important to the Lord. The Church would do well to remember that every part of the spiritual life suffers when Christ ceases to be at the forefront of our mediations and contemplations!

Meditation

> When you cease from labor, fill up your time in reading, meditation, and prayer: and while your hands are laboring, let your heart be employed, as much as possible, in divine thoughts.
>
> — David Brainerd

> In place of our exhaustion and spiritual fatigue, God will give us rest. All He asks is that we come to Him...that we spend a while thinking about Him, meditating on Him, talking to Him, listening in silence, occupying ourselves with Him – totally and thoroughly lost in the hiding place of His presence.
>
> — Chuck Swindoll

Vows
Numbers 30

We pass from what was compulsory in the last chapter to what was optional – the expressing of vows to the Lord. The necessity of vows is not imposed in Scripture, but if anyone did make a vow to the Lord, it was binding unless disallowed straightaway by male headship. For this reason, vows were not to be made impulsively (Prov. 20:25).

Moses first instructed the men: *"This is the thing which the Lord has commanded: If a man makes a vow to the Lord, or swears an oath to bind himself by some agreement, he shall not break his word; he shall do according to all that proceeds out of his mouth"* (vv. 1-2). It was much better not to vow at all than to do so and not honor it. Associating God's name with a falsehood would be insulting to Him.

So vows were to be honored if uttered; the vow of a wife (vv. 6-8, 10-14) or of a daughter living at home (vv. 3-5), however, was subject to their husband's or father's approval, respectively. If he rejected the vow within a day, it was not binding, but if he said nothing, it was. If he did reject the vow for carnal reasons or initially said nothing but later disavowed it, then he, not his wife or daughter, would be responsible to the Lord for the consequences (v. 15). This probably meant that he would either have to make atonement for the guilt of the offense by a sin and trespass offering or be punished by the Lord.

A vow of a widow or divorced woman was binding, as she was not under male authority in her home (v. 9). Moses closed the chapter by summarizing, *"These are the statutes which the Lord commanded Moses, between a man and his wife, and between a father and his daughter in her youth in her father's house"* (v. 16).

"Between a man and his wife" and *"in her father's house"* affirms biblical headship of the man in his home. We also see from verse 15 that where God gives authority, there is also accountability. This authority is also seen in the guiding of children into the uttering of wedding vows.

Devotions in Numbers

While it is recognized that some women will not marry, God's general design for the family is that the woman will always be provided for and protected by male authority. As sons mature, they will leave their father's house to establish and head a new family, and daughters will be given by their fathers in marriage (Ps. 78:63). A son, having approval, will leave his parents (Luke 20:34) and then cleave to his wife. In this way, she experiences a transfer of authority (from her father's authority to her husband's).

This transition of authority is clearly seen in this chapter in that a father could nullify a vow to God made by his daughter (living under his authority), or a husband could nullify a vow to God made by his wife. This transfer of authority may explain why, when Paul explains divine order in 1 Corinthians 11:3, the wife is nestled between Christ and the man for her protection. Unfortunately, the proper care and respect afforded to the feminine gender in Scripture has been mostly lost in our modern culture. When man devalues what God places a premium on – neglect and abuse always follow. Many of our society's problems would be resolved if, under Christ's headship, men wholeheartedly pursued biblical manhood and women sought to virtuously fulfill the roles God created them for.

Vows in the Old Testament might be to abstain from something (Ps. 132:2-5), or to promise things or services to the Lord (Lev. 27). For example, in the last chapter we read: *"These you shall present to the Lord at your appointed feasts (besides your vowed offerings and your freewill offerings) as your burnt offerings and your grain offerings, as your drink offerings and your peace offerings"* (29:39). So a Jew might propose to offer the Lord a peace offering in recognition of some favor He granted to the offerer (Lev. 7:16). Such offerings ministered to the offering priest and enriched the communion and fellowship of the saints (who were clean) before the Lord. The fulfillment of such vows then became the substance of things prompting common joy among God's people; thus David wrote, *"I will pay my vows before them that fear Him"* (Ps. 22:25). And Psalm 116:14 reads, *"I will pay my vows to the Lord now in the presence of all His people."* As the Church is not under Law, how may we apply this principle now?

First, the Lord Jesus forbids us from making vows today (Matt. 5:33-37), as we cannot promise what we may do in the future. James warns, *"Instead you ought to say, 'If the Lord wills, we shall live and do this or that'"* (Jas. 4:15). While a vow may be viewed as a

Refining and Reminding

legitimate expression of one's devotion to God, it would be better to express one's aspiration to serve God in prayer and through pursuing a consecrated life, rather than committing to some particular vow which may not be within one's control.

Second, the idea of a free-will gift to the Lord (but not through a pledge) to benefit the fellowship and communion of God's people is commendable. May each of us view our fellow brethren in our local assembly with such high esteem that we are prompted to give to the Lord in order to enhance the body-life and to bless others. This is really the idea of the Jewish peace offering that was often vowed – enjoying the Lord while together in His presence.

Meditation

> Take my life, and let it be consecrated, Lord, to Thee.
> Take my moments and my days; let them flow in ceaseless praise.
> Take my hands, and let them move at the impulse of Thy love.
> Take my feet, and let them be swift and beautiful for Thee.
>
> Take my will, and make it Thine; it shall be no longer mine.
> Take my heart, it is Thine own; it shall be Thy royal throne.
> Take my love, my Lord, I pour at Thy feet its treasure store.
> Take myself, and I will be ever, only, all for Thee.
>
> — Frances R. Havergal

Midianites Punished and Plundered
Numbers 31

While most of the remainder of Numbers and nearly all of Deuteronomy pertains to affirming legislation, the narrative of Israel's journey to Canaan is briefly resumed in this chapter. Before they can move forward into Canaan, they must first move backwards to inflict vengeance on the Midianites, as the Lord commanded Moses. It was not the war that they had been preparing for, but rather resulted through their own unfaithfulness to Jehovah by philandering with pagan women and bowing down to their gods.

God's desire was for Israel to pass peacefully through the land of the Moabites and Midianites to enter into the Promised Land. But their failure as God's pilgrims, through the purposeful solicitation of the Midianites (primarily) to do evil, invoked God's wrath against them. We in the Church Age would do well to remember that, as strangers in this world, our normal course as Christians is to be inoffensive pilgrims while journeying heavenward. If we get sidetracked by carnal lusting and secular amusements, these will war against our soul needlessly and cost us precious time in pursuing those things important to the Lord.

Vengeance on the Midianites (vv. 1-11)

The Lord commanded Moses: *"Take vengeance on the Midianites for the children of Israel. Afterward you shall be gathered to your people"* (vv. 1-2). Moses responded by sending a thousand men from each tribe into battle with the Midianites and putting Phinehas the priest in charge of the attack (vv. 3-5):

> Then Moses sent them to the war, one thousand from each tribe; he sent them to the war with Phinehas the son of Eleazar the priest, with the holy articles and the signal trumpets in his hand. And they warred against the Midianites, just as the Lord commanded Moses, and they killed all the males. They killed the kings of Midian with the rest of

Refining and Reminding

> *those who were killed ... Balaam the son of Beor they also killed with the sword* (vv. 6-8).

The Israelites were completely victorious over the Midianites and their secret adversary Balaam, but we might wonder about two aspects of this engagement. First, why did the Lord not assign Joshua, Israel's new leader, to confront the Midianites? Second, why did Moses select Phinehas, a priest, to lead Israel into battle, as priests were not soldiers in Israel's army?

As to the first question, other than rehearsing the Law in the ears of the people, this endeavor is Moses' final act of his official life, though his personal story does not finish until Deuteronomy 34. The failure of the Israelites with the Midianites happened on Moses' watch, so he was responsible for retribution.

C. H. Mackintosh provides an answer to the second question as to why Phinehas, and not Joshua, was called upon to lead Israel's army:

> On the contrary, it is to Phinehas, the son of Eleazar the priest, that the conduct of this expedition is committed; and he enters upon it "with the holy instruments and the trumpets." All this is strongly marked. *The priest* is the prominent person; and *the Holy instruments,* the prominent instrumentality. It is a question of wiping away the stain caused by their unholy association with the enemy; and therefore, instead of a general officer with sword and spear, it is a priest with holy instruments that appears in the foreground. True, the sword is here; but it is not the prominent thing. It is the priest with the vessels of the sanctuary; and that priest the selfsame man who first executed judgment upon that very evil which has here to be avenged.[120]

So although Joshua had been duly appointed to succeed Moses, the cleansing of the lingering stain, the damage and offense of the sin committed by the Midianites against God, was a priestly matter. Phineas had initiated this cleansing when he thrust a javelin through a Jewish man and a Midianite woman in Numbers 25. He now is called on to thoroughly judge the evil, to ensure it would never occur again.

The Midianite women and their young children were enslaved, and the Israelites took the cattle, flocks and goods as spoil (v. 9). Besides killing the adult males, they also burned the Midianite cities and fortifications (vv. 10-11).

Returning From War (vv. 12-24)

However, when the Israelite soldiers returned to camp with the spoils of war and many captives, Moses was angry with them for keeping the women alive, for they were the ones Satan had used to lure the Jewish men to Baal (vv. 12-16). Moses ordered every captured Midianite to be slain, except for young virgin girls, who would not pose a spiritual threat (vv. 17-18). The virgins spared numbered 32,000 (v. 35). This drastic measure was necessary to ensure every aspect of what had contaminated Israel was eradicated. C. H. Mackintosh describes the plain and practical moral of this for Israel:

> The Midianites furnish a type of that peculiar kind of influence which the world exerts over the hearts of the people of God – the fascinating and ensnaring power of the world used by Satan to hinder our entrance upon our proper heavenly portion. Israel should have had nothing to do with these Midianites; but having, in an evil hour – an unguarded moment – been betrayed into association with them, nothing remains but war and utter extermination.[121]

Such extreme measures to remove what incites the flesh to sin are amplified in the New Testament. But believers in the Church Age have an advantage over the Israelites of old in living for God, because His Spirit dwells within them and He is able to refute carnal thinking and mortify the deeds of the flesh: *"If by the Spirit you put to death the deeds of the body, you will live"* (Rom. 8:13).

Positionally speaking, co-crucifixion took place at the cross and became effectual for a believer at his or her conversion (Rom. 6:6). In Adam, we were *"made subject to vanity"* (Rom. 8:20). At the cross, the old man, the man in Adam, the man that we once were, the man who was dominated and controlled by the flesh, died with Christ. Paul conveys the practical aspects of this positional truth to the Galatian believers: *"Those who are Christ's have crucified the flesh with its passions and desires"* (Gal. 5:24). The purpose of crucifixion was to end the life of someone, though death itself would occur sometime later. Practically speaking, the believer has been crucified with Christ so that his or her craving flesh will eventually die (i.e. there should be a diminishing influence of the old nature in the believer's life as he or she matures in Christ).

Furthermore, Paul commanded the saints at Colosse to *"put to death your members which are on the earth: fornication, uncleanness, passion, evil desire, and covetousness, which is idolatry"* (Col. 3:5). In addition to the believer's lusting flesh eventually dying (ultimately this occurs at glorification) and the need to mortify its deeds whenever observed until then, Paul told the believers at Colosse not to feed (strengthen) the nature of the old man, but rather to put him off (Col. 3:9). The ungodly longings of the flesh (some of which are listed in Col. 3:5) should not be strengthened through sinful behavior or by wrong thinking, but rather these should be starved so that they lose their strength and can be "put off" from the believer's conduct completely. If not fed, these ungodly longings lose their hold on the believer's life and die out more quickly – though ultimate freedom will not be achieved until glorification. Paul conveys this same fundamental truth to the believers at Rome: *"But put on the Lord Jesus Christ, and make no provision for the flesh, to fulfill its lusts"* (Rom. 13:14).

Mortification or gratification are the only two things the flesh understands, but if we choose to gratify the flesh, even a little, it will want more the next day because the flesh is never satisfied – *"The eye is not satisfied with seeing, nor the ear filled with hearing"* (Eccl. 1:8; KJV). The only spiritual recourse in dealing with the lusting of the flesh is to inflict it with a deadly blow and then to keep mortifying its deeds day after day – this is God's will for every believer. This is why the Midianites were so harshly treated; there would never be another opportunity for them to entice Israel – they were completely mortified.

It seems likely, given that females fifteen years of age and under compose roughly twelve percent of a normal population, that about a quarter million Midianites perished in this assault. The Midianites learned the hard way just how much Jehovah loathes anything that corrupts His people.

Yet, this judgment pales in comparison to the all-encompassing judgment the entire world faces at Christ's second advent. He will then shake everything unclean and every wicked person from the earth to establish His kingdom (Heb. 12:27-29). Israel will despoil the nations at that time. The Lord will then be among His covenant people again and He will ensure that nothing corrupt will influence them, which, in type, is the situation of Numbers 31. For this reason, it is fitting that this is Moses' last official act as Israel's leader. The scene before us is what God desired all along while in the wilderness with His people and it is what He will eventually enjoy with the restored Jewish nation in a coming day.

Those Jewish soldiers who had avenged the Lord against the Midianites were told to remain outside the camp and to go through the seven-day ceremonial purification required after touching a dead body (vv. 19-20). Furthermore, because the spoil coming from the Midianites was unclean, metals were to be purified by fire and everything else was to be washed with water before it was brought into the camp and distributed (vv. 21-24). The testing of fire and the washing away of filth from all that comes out of the world pictures the diligence believers are to have in judging everything we come in contact with in the world during our heavenly pilgrimage. Whatever has the possibility of corrupting holy living must be utterly repudiated.

Dividing the Spoil (vv. 25-54)

Once the spoil had been purified, it was to be divided among the people, after the appropriate amount was contributed to the Lord in support of His servants, the Levites. There were 337,500 sheep, 36,000 cattle, 30,500 donkeys, and 32,000 young female slaves to distribute among the Israelites (vv. 30-47). This was done by first splitting the spoil in half and designating one half to those who fought and the remaining half to those who did not (vv. 25-27). But before anyone received a share of the spoil, one-five-hundredth of the spoil from the soldiers' portion and one-fiftieth of the spoil from the non-soldiers' portion was given to the Lord (vv. 28-29).

The captains of the army took a count of the soldiers and it was discovered that not one warrior had been lost in the conflict (vv. 48-49). This meant that all could celebrate the victory, as not one family in the camp would be in mourning. The captains were so elated that the Lord had preserved them in such a miraculous way that they brought free-will offerings of gold to the Lord (v. 50). These were various ornaments (i.e., armlets, bracelets, rings, earrings, and necklaces) that had been confiscated from the Midianites. Moses and Eleazar received their gifts, the total weight being 16,750 shekels (about 421 U.S. pounds).

This massive gift was brought into the tabernacle as a memorial of God's faithfulness to His people (vv. 51-55). Previously, some of them had left Jehovah's presence for carnal reasons and had paid a terrible price, but now they experienced God's grace in an incredible way and were delighting in Him alone.

Refining and Reminding

Meditation

Marvelous grace of our loving Lord,
Grace that exceeds our sin and our guilt!
Yonder on Calvary's mount outpoured,
There where the blood of the Lamb was spilled.

Grace, grace, God's grace,
Grace that will pardon and cleanse within;
Grace, grace, God's grace,
Grace that is greater than all our sin!

Sin and despair, like the sea waves cold,
Threaten the soul with infinite loss;
Grace that is greater, yes, grace untold,
Points to the refuge, the mighty cross.

— Julia H. Johnston

Two and a Half Tribes
Numbers 32

The tribes of Reuben and Gad possessed large herds and flocks and, because the Transjordan plateau east of the Jordan River was rich in pastureland, they desired it for a possession rather than what God had for them in Canaan (vv. 1-5). A number of captured cities north of the Arnon River were mentioned to define the specific areas they wanted (most of these were on or near the King's Highway). Reuben and Gad especially desired the land of Gilead and Jazer, south of Bashan. They reasoned that this was good grazing land for their cattle and flocks, and, since it had been conquered by Israel, it should be settled by Jews.

While it is true that the Eastern Plateau was within the overall boundaries God had bestowed to Abraham and his descendants, it was God's design for them to first possess the heart of that land and to secure the one place in all the earth where Jehovah had chosen to place His name – Jerusalem. Canaan formed a land-bridge between three continents and therefore was the perfect location for Jehovah to dwell among His people and for Israel to be a beacon of light to the nations. Therefore, it was Canaan that was given to Israel to possess at that time. This alone had been the expressed reason they had been delivered from Egypt: to come into and to possess Canaan through conquest. Canaan would be God's beachhead in the region for establishing His own name, but Reuben and Gad (and a half-tribe of Manasseh; v. 33) were more interested in the welfare of their cattle than in establishing His name in the land.

After first hearing their proposal, Moses was appalled. He thought Reuben and Gad wanted to settle the Transjordan area without crossing the Jordan to assist their brethren with the conquest of Canaan: *"Shall your brethren go to war while you sit here? Now why will you discourage the heart of the children of Israel from going over into the land which the Lord has given them?"* (vv. 6-8). Moses warned them of again angering Jehovah with a repetition of the same sin of "unbelief"

Refining and Reminding

that the ten spies had committed some thirty-nine years earlier at Kadesh-Barnea (vv. 9-15). These spies entered the Promised Land, verified that God had brought them to a land flowing with milk and honey, but then discouraged their brethren from venturing in to possess it. The Lord's anger was kindled and He smote the ten spies with a plague and they all died (14:37). Moses rehearsed this history lesson as a warning to Reuben and Gad – doubting the faithfulness of God to keep His promises has severe consequences.

Moses must have been relieved to hear that Reuben and Gad had fully intended to join their brethren in the conquest of Canaan before settling the Transjordan region. Their plan was as follows:

We will build sheepfolds here for our livestock, and cities for our little ones, but we ourselves will be armed, ready to go before the children of Israel until we have brought them to their place; and our little ones will dwell in the fortified cities because of the inhabitants of the land. We will not return to our homes until every one of the children of Israel has received his inheritance (vv. 16-18).

While this was honorable, Reuben and Gad were still pursuing what they wanted – rich pastureland, instead of the purposes of God which had been declared to Moses: *"For we will not inherit with them on the other side of the Jordan and beyond, because our inheritance has fallen to us on this eastern side of the Jordan"* (v. 19). These tribes did not object to entering Canaan and laboring with their brethren to conquer it; they just did not want the land God desired to give them for an inheritance, and that is the issue C. H. Mackintosh notes:

When people are not simple, not truehearted, they get into circumstances which give rise to all sorts of questions. It is a great matter to be enabled, by Divine grace, to pursue a line of action, and to tread a path so unequivocal as that no question can be raised. It is our holy and happy privilege so to carry ourselves as that no complication may ever arise. The secret of so doing is to walk with God, and thus to have our conduct wholly governed by His word. But that Reuben and Gad were not thus governed is manifest from the entire history. They were half-and-half men; men of mixed principles; mere borderers; men that sought their own things, and not the things of God. Had these latter engrossed their hearts, nothing would have induced them to take up their position short of the true boundary line. It is very evident that Moses had no sympathy with their proposal.[122]

Indeed, serious damage is done to the testimony of Christ when those professing His name deny their heavenly calling and character, and act as though they were still citizens of this world. Moses eventually conceded to their request with the stipulation that they fulfill their word to cross the Jordan and fight with their brethren to take Canaan; otherwise they would have a possession in Canaan (vv. 20-30). C. A. Coates suggests that God is a perfect Gentleman; He does not force His ways or blessings on those who think they have a better way:

> If any of us deliberately prefer to stay on the eastward side of Jordan, we need not expect that God will make us go over. He allows many things to stand which come very short of what is in His mind for His people. His ways with His saints are not arbitrary; He allows things to be tested out. If we take lower ground than that which His love proposes we should take, He may allow us to occupy it. If we do not want Canaan He may allow us to remain in Gilead. But we may be assured of this, that when our choice is tested out we shall be found to have suffered immense and irreparable loss, because not even eternity will ever give us back the privilege of inheriting the land over Jordan in the way in which it can be possessed and enjoyed now.[123]

On the positive side, the two and a half tribes did heed Moses' warning about not reneging on their commitment to enter into the Canaan Conquest: *"Be sure your sin shall find you out"* (v. 23). However, there are always long-term consequences when God's people settle for what is less than His best. A few centuries later they would reap the consequences of lusting for what was merely permissible, instead of what God wanted them to possess.

During the days of King Ahab in the mid-ninth century B.C., Ramoth in Gilead was controlled by the Syrians. Also, the Reubenites settled in the cities of Nebo, Heshbon, and Kiriathaim (vv. 37-38; Josh. 13:19). These cities and others in the region were later captured by the Moabites, which caused both Isaiah and Jeremiah to prophesy against them. However, the Moabites were later displaced from these cities by the Assyrians in the late-eighth century B.C., and that is when the two and half tribes were also exiled from the Transjordan region. They were the first Jews to be evicted from their inheritance. In the same way, earthly-minded Christians will be the first to be taken captive by the spirit of this world.

Refining and Reminding

A short time after pledging their support to Moses, the two and a half tribes did affirm with Joshua that they had not forgotten their promise to Moses and intended to honor it. In fact, Joshua placed them at the head of the column – they would be the first wave of Jewish troops into Canaan (Josh. 1:14). Perhaps this is because they were not encumbered with the task of moving families, livestock, and personal belongings as the congregation ambled into the Promised Land.

Seven years later Joshua gave Reuben, Gad, and a half-tribe of Manasseh an inheritance east of the Jordan River because they did fulfill their pledge to Moses (Josh. 13). The specific towns and regions of their inheritance are listed by Moses in verses 33-43. Manasseh settled in northern Gilead (east of the Sea of Galilee), Gad in southern Gilead, and Reuben further south in the plains of Moab (from Heshbon and Bezer west to the Jordan River and south to Aroer and over to the Dead Sea).

Meditation

> When we crossed the river Jordan, in the land we found:
> Wine and oil and milk and honey, richest fruits abound;
> Sparkling fountains, and the showers come upon the ground;
> We are able, Hallelujah! Let God's praise resound.
>
> — Kittie L. Suffield

From Egypt to the Plains of Moab
Numbers 33

Moses kept a detailed record of Israel's forty-year journey from Egypt to the plains of Moab (vv. 1-49). Although forty-two locations are listed, it seems doubtful that this is a comprehensive list of every encampment location, but rather an overview of Israel's journey from the Exodus to Canaan. To maintain good sanitation the camp would require frequent movement and many wilderness campsites would not be named. Most of the ancient places that Moses mentions cannot be identified with certainty today. Archeological and historical evidence does provide a high degree of validation of some locations, such as Kadesh.

The Forty-Year Journey (vv. 1-49)

The Israelites departed from Rameses, encamped at Succoth and then Etham heading south, before briefly turning back north to encamp at Pi Hahiroth and this is where they crossed the Red Sea. From there they moved southeast to cross the wilderness of Shur (camping at Marah) and then traversed the wilderness of Sin (camping at Dophkah, and then Rephidim) and entered the wilderness of Sinai. They remained at Mount Sinai for eleven months and a few days before journeying north into the wilderness of Paran and making numerous stops whose whereabouts are unknown today. They arrived at Kadesh in the wilderness of Zin, but then turned back south away from Canaan after God judged their unbelief to enter the Promised Land.

Their final journey back to Kadesh thirty-eight years later picks up at Ezion Geber, a northern port city on the Gulf of Aqaba. Miriam was buried at Kadesh, and Aaron four months later at Mount Hor east of Kadesh. After their victorious battle with the Canaanites and being barred to pass through Edom, the Israelites made the long journey south to Punon and again to Ezion Geber. From there they turned east and north along the desert road to Moab that circumvented Edom's eastside.

Refining and Reminding

They camped at Iye Abarim on the border of Moab before moving north to Dibon Gad and then Almon Diblathaim to arrive at the Abarim range and Mount Nebo. Israel's last encampment before crossing into Canaan was at Shittim just across the Jordan River from Jericho. The following is a map of Israel's journey described above.[124]

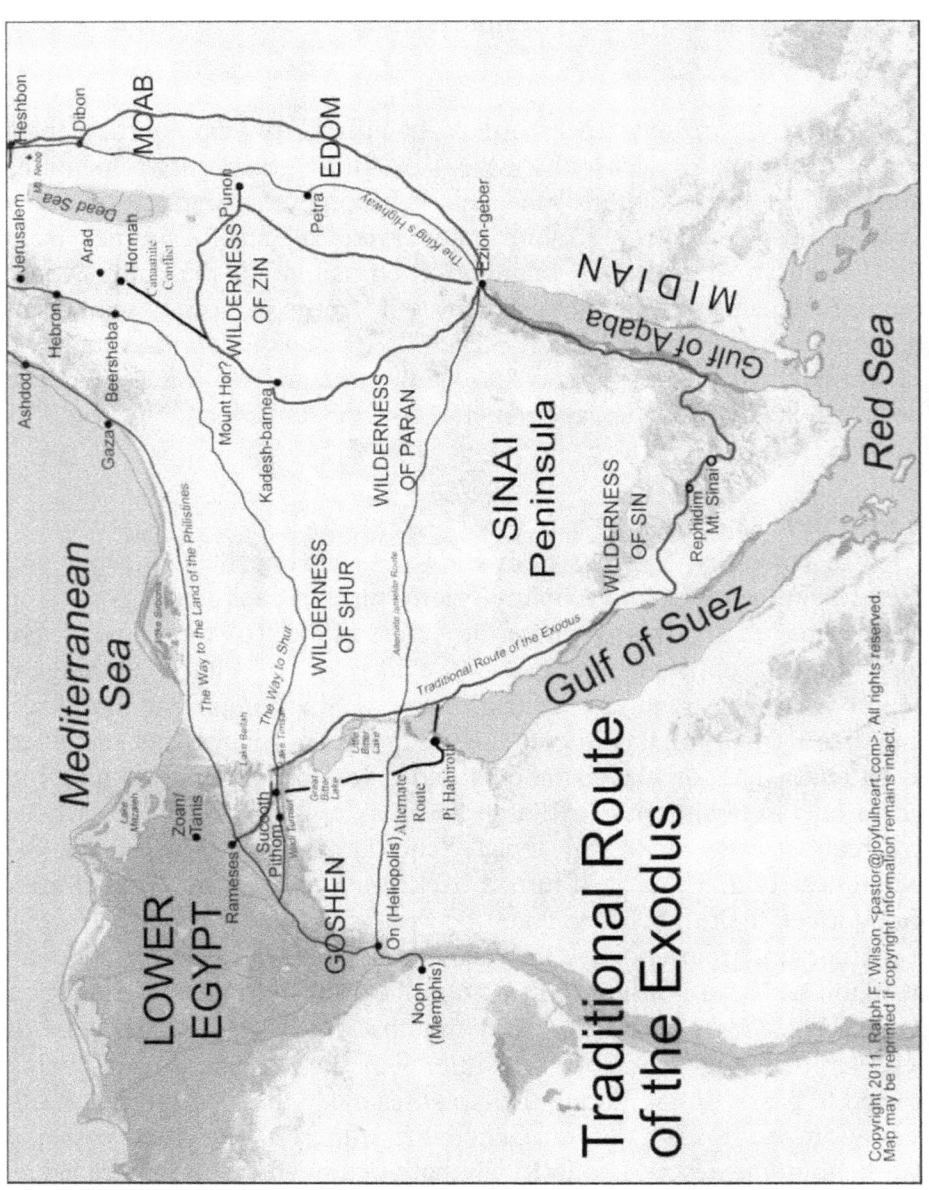

C. A. Coates suggests a practical lesson for us to glean from this journal of movements from one wilderness experience to another:

> It is a comfort to know that there can be a wilderness history in which God finds pleasure. Such a history is marked by movement, each encampment having its distinctive experience and education. We may be sure that Caleb and Joshua learned something more of God at every encampment, and having learned it they were ready to remove to the next. From the time that the tabernacle was set up, all their movements had reference to it; they were the movements of the divine testimony. We are apt to think of the wilderness as a place of trials and difficulties, and a place where the flesh is tested and exposed, and also where we experience divine resources and care. All this is true, but the lovers of Jehovah would think of it above all as the place where they are privileged to accompany "the tabernacle of testimony." It has pleased God to have a testimony here, and to have His people identified with it.[125]

We also learn from this travel journal that the ten Egyptian plagues, pronounced by Moses on God's behalf, were specifically designed for the purpose of proving I AM's superiority over the Egyptian gods (v. 4). Through the onslaught of plagues, Jehovah would be glorified, the gods of Egypt and the Egyptians themselves would be punished, and the faith of the Jews would be strengthened. J. N. Darby highlights God's faithfulness to be with His people every step of the way during their exhausting forty-year journey and now to see them conquer Canaan for a possession:

> If God numbers His people name by name, He shows, at the same time, His government and His faithfulness; for, though He had kept them, as a people, yet there were none of the first numbering left, save Caleb and Joshua. He remembers, also, all their long journey through the wilderness; each stage is before His eyes and in His memory; and now He lays down, in principle, the possession of the land by the people, and the total destruction of the inhabitants, who were to be entirely driven away and not to abide in the midst of Israel: else those who were left would be a torment for the people, and God also would do unto Israel as He had done to those nations.[126]

Refining and Reminding

Instructions for the Conquest of Canaan (vv. 50-56)

In his final message of the book (verse 50 through the end of Numbers), Moses addresses his countrymen as having already crossed over the Jordan into Canaan. To obtain the possession God has for them, they must kill or drive out the inhabitants of Canaan, and destroy all their idols and pagan high places (vv. 50-53). Only after the land is cleansed should it be divided among the tribes according to their size and as determined by lot (as previously described in Numbers 26). Moses then warns of what will happen if Israel does not purge the heathen from the Promised Land:

> *But if you do not drive out the inhabitants of the land from before you, then it shall be that those whom you let remain shall be irritants in your eyes and thorns in your sides, and they shall harass you in the land where you dwell. Moreover it shall be that I will do to you as I thought to do to them* (vv. 55-56).

Under Joshua's leadership, Israel did have a prosperous seven-year campaign in which all major cities and fortifications in Canaan were conquered (Josh. 12). A summary of what happened during that time is recorded in Joshua 11:23, *"So Joshua took the whole land, according to all that the Lord had said to Moses; and Joshua gave it as an inheritance to Israel according to their divisions by their tribes. Then the land rested from war."* This generalization seems to contradict what the Lord said to Joshua at the onset of chapter 13: *"there remains very much land yet to be possessed"* (13:1).

Joshua did destroy the cities and all who were in them; however, many Canaanites chose to hide in rocky formations, caverns, and caves in the vicinity and then they returned to their homes after the Israelites had passed. Though conquered, the inhabitants were not completely removed. This fulfilled the prophecy of Moses who predicted the Lord would remove the inhabitants of Canaan *"little by little"* (Deut. 7:22). This would prevent wild beasts from multiplying in the area and keep the farmland from falling into neglect during the years of conquest.

So, while it was true that there were pockets of resistance remaining in Canaan (Josh. 13:2-5), the Lord decreed that the land had been sufficiently conquered to be divided among His people as an inheritance. If the Jews would remain faithful to the cause, Jehovah promised to continue to help each tribe or clan drive out the remaining inhabitants from their possession (13:6). Although Judah and Simeon had several successful battles in the south (Judg. 1), most of the tribes sought to profit from the remaining inhabitants instead of driving them out.

In time, what Moses said would happen if the Israelites permitted some residents to remain (vv. 55-56) – happened. As the book of Judges verifies, Israel was afflicted by various people groups in Canaan and many Israelites eventually lost their God-given inheritance. Most of the tribe of Dan, for example, had to later resettle far north of the other tribes because the Amorites drove them out. Disobedience to God's word always has a sad consequence for His people!

Meditation

> When we walk with the Lord in the light of His Word,
> What a glory He sheds on our way!
> While we do His good will, He abides with us still,
> And with all who will trust and obey.
>
> Not a shadow can rise, not a cloud in the skies,
> But His smile quickly drives it away;
> Not a doubt or a fear, not a sigh or a tear,
> Can abide while we trust and obey.
>
> — John H. Sammis

Boundaries and Officials Dividing the Land
Numbers 34

The remainder of Numbers assumes that the Israelites have crossed over the Jordan River and have victoriously taken the land. This chapter specifies the borders Israel should have and the leaders who will oversee the division of the land once the Canaanites were conquered.

It would be good for us to recall that the Israelites' conquest of Canaan is a fulfillment of Noah's prophecy in Genesis 9. Noah spoke against his son Ham after learning that Ham had dishonored him while in a drunken state. Ham's son, Canaan, would be a servant of his brothers; Japheth would be greatly enlarged and enjoy fellowship with Shem, and Shem would enjoy a close relationship (religious privileges) with his Creator, the Lord God. The descendants of Ham's son were the Canaanites. They were an immoral and perverse people deserving judgment (Lev. 18:3, 27).

Boundaries (vv. 1-15)

The Lord told Moses ahead of time what the boundaries of the nation of Israel were to be (vv. 1-2). The southern boundary (vv. 3-5) would start at the border of Edom on the south side of the Dead Sea, and go southwest through the wilderness of Zin (just south of the Ascent of Akrabbim) to just south of Kadesh-Barnea (about 65 miles southwest of the Dead Sea). From there the border would run northwest, by Hazar Adda and Azmon to the Brook of Egypt (Wadi el-Arish). The border would follow the Wadi northwest to the Mediterranean Sea about 50 miles southwest of Gaza.

The western boundary (v. 6) was the Mediterranean Sea.

The northern boundary (vv. 7-9) ran from Mount Hor (probably Ras Al Shaka) near the Mediterranean Sea (obviously not the location where Aaron died) eastward to Lebo Hamath, then another 30 miles further east to Zedad, then ten miles southeast to Ziphron and then further southeast to Hazar Enan (about 70 miles northeast of Damascus).

The eastern boundary (vv. 10-12) of Israel ran southwest from Hazar Enan to Shepham and then to Riblah before turning south along the eastern shores of the Sea of Galilee, the Jordan River, and the Dead Sea. This meant that Israel proper did not include the land given to the two and a half tribes settling in the Transjordan region (vv. 14-15). No specific boundaries are given here for the other nine and a half tribes that would settle Canaan, as that would be decided by lot later (v. 13). The next chapter will specify cities for the Levites and cities of refuge for the manslayer on both sides of the Jordan River.

The boundaries in this chapter are for Israel proper, which is only about 145 miles in length and about 60 miles across on average. However, the land promised to Abraham in Genesis 15:19-21 and confirmed again in Joshua 1 was much greater; Canaan was merely the first portion to be possessed for an inheritance (Josh. 1:4, 6). God would fulfill his promise to Abraham by giving his descendants the land in stages, as determined by their faithfulness and willingness to conquer and possess it in the years that followed (Deut. 19:8).

Historically speaking, the Jewish people have never fully possessed all that was promised to Abraham. Even during the glorious reigns of kings David and Solomon, Israel never occupied more than about a tenth (approx. 30,000 square miles) of the land that God bestowed to Abraham according to Genesis 15:18-21.[127] The western boundary of this land was the Mediterranean Sea and the eastern boundary was to be the Euphrates River, which runs through central Iraq today. The land was to extend from the mountains of Lebanon in the north to the southern wilderness of Paran.

The following map indicates Israel's boundaries as defined in Numbers 34 and also during the Kingdom Age defined later by Ezekiel (Ezek. 47).[128]

Refining and Reminding

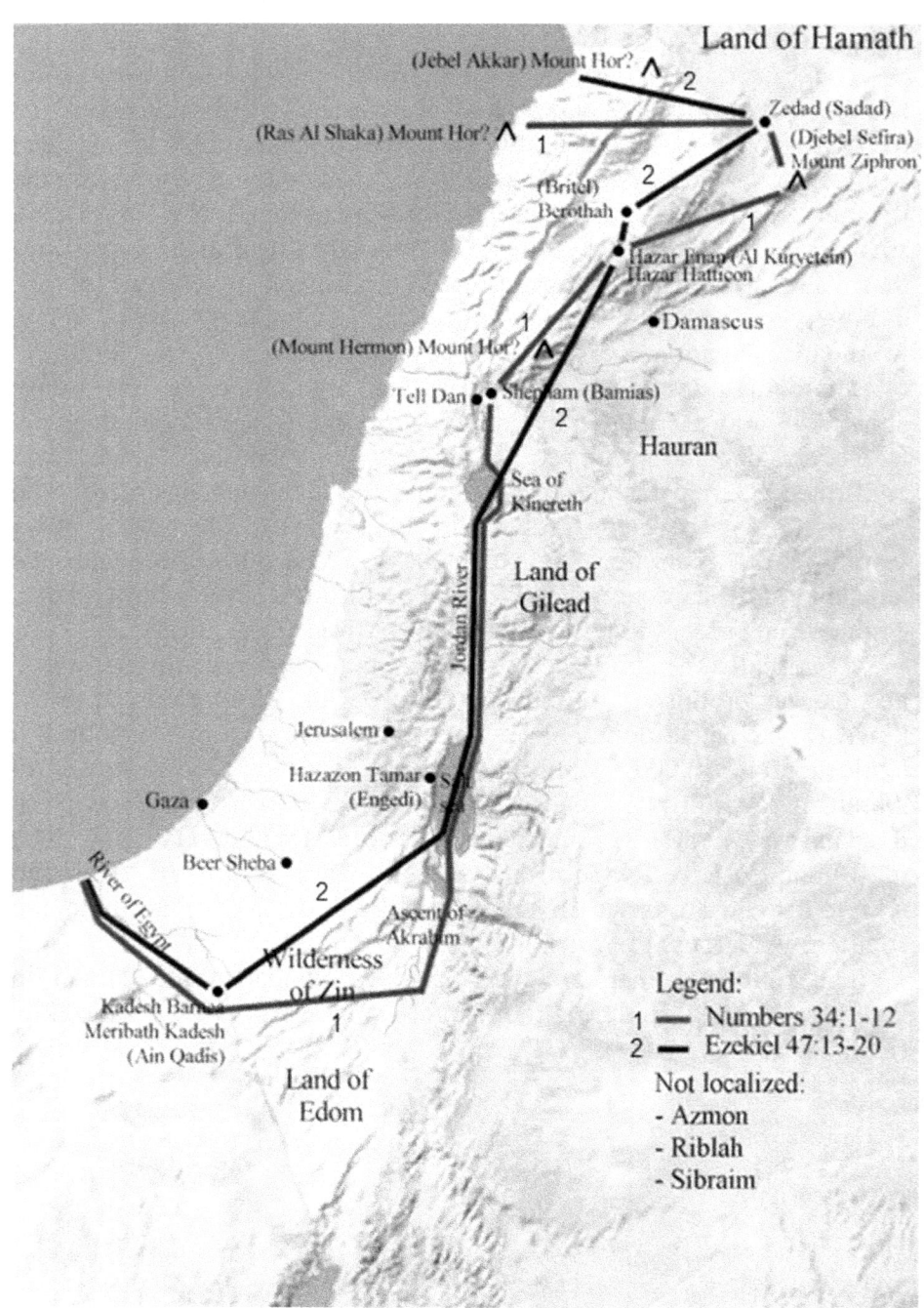

Officials Dividing the Land (vv. 16-29)

Joshua and Eleazar would be responsible for overseeing the land disbursements in Canaan. They chose a representative from each tribe to assist them. Of the twelve men listed in Scripture, only Caleb is known to us; the other men are from the new generation (less than sixty years old).

In the book of Joshua, we learn that Joshua had performed a detailed survey of Canaan prior to the land disbursements being determined by drawing lots (Josh. 14:1-2). This method of distribution had been previously commanded by Moses (Num. 26:55). Jewish tradition states the name of a tribe was drawn from one urn while the associated land allotment was drawn simultaneously from another urn.[129] It was understood that Jehovah was guiding this process, and that nothing would be left to chance (Prov. 16:33). This confidence would alleviate any assertion of unfairness or favoritism, for they would know God's will in the matter and that was all that mattered.

Meditation

> There are no "ifs" in God's world. And no places that are safer than other places. The center of His will is our only safety – let us pray that we may always know it!
>
> — Corrie ten Boom

> And shall I pray Thee change Thy will, my Father,
> Until it be according unto mine?
> But, no, Lord, no, that never shall be, rather
> I pray Thee blend my human will with Thine.
>
> I pray Thee hush the hurrying, eager longing,
> I pray Thee soothe the pangs of keen desire –
> See in my quiet places, wishes thronging –
> Forbid them, Lord, purge, though it be with fire.
>
> — Amy Carmichael

Levitical Cities and Cities of Refuge
Numbers 35

Levitical Cities (vv. 1-8)

The Levites were not to have a particular region of Canaan as a possession, but rather forty-eight cities distributed among the twelve tribes according to the tribes' census tally (vv. 6-8). The majority of this chapter deals with the distribution of these cities to the Levites.

Each Levitical city was to include a portion of outlying pasture land measuring 750 feet from the city wall in each direction (vv. 2-5). The city itself would be 1,500 by 1,500 feet, meaning the entire area of each city with pasture lands would be about 207 acres. This meant that although the Levites would not get a specific region of the Promised Land for an inheritance, they would receive nearly 10,000 acres of residential real estate. Six of the forty-eight cities were to be designated as Cities of Refuge (v. 6).

After Canaan was conquered and the tribes received their land allotments, Joshua and Eleazar assigned these cities (Josh. 21). Thirteen southern cities, nine in Judah and Simeon and four in Benjamin, were assigned to the priests (Josh. 21:8-19). Ten more cities in Ephraim, Dan and Manasseh were designated for the remaining Kohathites (Josh. 21:20-26). Hebron, the city Caleb seized from the Anakim, would also be a City of Refuge, though Caleb would keep the surrounding villages and land (Josh. 21:12-13).

The Gershonites received thirteen cities within the tribal lands of Manasseh, Issachar, Asher, and Naphtali (Josh. 21:27-33). Two of these cities, Golan in Bashan (on the eastern side of the Jordan) and Kadesh in northern Galilee, were selected to be Cities of Refuge.

The Merarites received twelve cities in the territories of Zebulun, Reuben, and Gad (Josh. 21:34-40). Bezer in the eastern pasture lands of Reuben would also be a City of Refuge. In Gad, Ramoth-Gilead was to be a City of Refuge.

About seven years after Numbers 35 was penned, Joshua and Eleazar would faithfully execute the Lord's plan to disperse the Levites evenly among His people. No Jew would need to travel more than a day's journey to a Levitical city to seek counsel from God's word. Hence, the structure and content were in place to ensure His covenant people remained in communion with Him. The Levites were to teach the people (e.g., Ezra 8:9) and parents were in turn to teach their children (Deut. 6:6-9). Unfortunately, it did not take long for the Jewish nation to neglect this perfect administration of His Word; in fact, it took only one generation (Judg. 2:8-12).

Cities of Refuge (vv. 9-34)

God gave mankind the basis for capital punishment after the flood when He commanded Noah, *"Whoever sheds man's blood, by man his blood shall be shed; for in the image of God He made man"* (Gen. 9:6). In the Law, Moses later provided the specifics regarding the implementation of this decree, as well as affirming the solemnity of the offense in the sixth commandment of the Law, which states: *"You shall not murder"* (Ex. 20:13). Although some translations render the Hebrew word *rasah* as "kill," "murder" (the premeditated act of ending another person's life) is a better translation. One may kill a sheep without breaking this commandment, but sheep cannot be murdered; thus, the Law prohibited the unwarranted ending of human life by another human.

The Law also protected the life of the accused until proven guilty. To ensure this protocol was adhered to, Joshua was to assign six cities of refuge as temporary sanctuaries where the accused could reside in safety until his or her case was formally tried (vv. 9-15). One might wonder why the number of cities of refuge was set at six. Throughout the Bible the number six is associated with human imperfection; it is man's number, which falls short of seven, God's number of completeness. If someone was suspected of falling short of the sixth commandment, there would be six cities to uphold God's righteousness and keep the land from being defiled by innocent blood (i.e., the murderer would be condemned to death and those not guilty of a crime would be pardoned).

Moses commanded that six cities be designated as Cities of Refuge. Three of the six were in Canaan; the others were located among the two and a half tribes who settled in Transjordan (vv. 6, 13; Deut. 19:2). As

Refining and Reminding

just mentioned, Joshua did so after the conquest. The three in Canaan included: Kadesh in Galilee, Shechem in Mount Ephraim, and Hebron in the mountains of Judah. The Cities of Refuge east of the Jordan River are also listed: Bezer in the plain of Reuben, Ramoth in Gilead, and Golan in Bashan. If the Israelites remained faithful and obedient, Jehovah promised to enlarge their borders; at that time the Jews were to add three more cities of refuge (i.e., to the three already associated with Canaan) for a total of nine (Deut. 19:8-10).

All six cities were evenly spread from north to south on both sides of the Jordan River. All six cities were to uphold the righteousness of God in the land and the path to justice was to be readily found. The gates to the Cities of Refuge were always to be open, so that every manslayer might find protection until justice could be determined (Deut. 19:3). F. B. Meyer further notes the Jewish provisions to assist a fleeing fugitive:

> The manslayer who had killed any person unwittingly and unawares might flee from the pursuit of the next of kin. The roads were kept in good repair; clearly written directions at the crossways indicated the route; and, according to Jewish tradition, runners learned in the Law, were stationed at various stages to direct and help the fugitive.[130]

When someone sought refuge in a City of Refuge, no retaliation by the relatives of the deceased was permitted. Appointed judges would then hear the case in the public place of decision – the gate of the city (Josh. 20:4). All the inhabitants of the city were to uphold the ruling of the judges (Josh. 20:6).

If the slayer was found guilty of premeditated murder, he or she was put to death; a lesser penalty was required for accidental deaths or those caused by a non-premeditated act of violence. Under the Law, certain types of crimes carried the death penalty:

1. Premeditated murder (Ex. 21:12).
2. Murdering one's parents (Ex. 21:15).
3. Kidnapping (Ex. 21:16).
4. Cursing or rebelling against one's father or mother (Ex. 21:17).
5. Injuring a pregnant woman and causing her unborn child to die (Ex. 21:22-23).

6. Allowing a bull, known for "pushing," to kill someone (both the bull and the master were to die; Ex. 21:29).
7. Adultery (Deut. 22:22-25).
8. Intrusion into the priestly office (Num. 18:7).

Moses provided specifics for determining if someone had committed premeditated murder and deserved the death penalty (vv. 16-21) or had acted "suddenly without enmity" and would be spared death, though still guilty of *manslaughter* (vv. 22-25). If the accused was found innocent of intentional manslaughter, he or she could dwell within the confines of that city without the threat of familial revenge. Upon the death of the high priest, all who had been found innocent of murder were allowed to return to their inheritance without any further threat of retaliation (vv. 26-28). However, if the guilty party left their City of Refuge before the high priest died, then he was not protected: *"If the manslayer at any time goes outside the limits of the City of Refuge where he fled, and the avenger of blood finds him outside the limits of his City of Refuge, and the avenger of blood kills the manslayer, he shall not be guilty of blood"* (vv. 26-27).

The section closes with Moses reminding his countrymen that God was righteous and therefore His law for upholding justice in the land should be obeyed (v. 29). No person should be condemned to death by a single witness (v. 30). No bribes or ransoms should be paid by the wealthy to escape justice (v. 31), nor could a guilty party pay a ransom to shorten his or her stay in a City of Refuge while waiting for the high priest to die (v. 32). To void God's law in this matter would pollute the land with innocent blood, which He would not tolerate (v. 33). The Lord desired to dwell with His people in an undefiled land that represented His holy and just character (v. 34).

The writer of Hebrews tells believers today that they enjoy God's communion by ceasing to work to earn salvation and by receiving His rest through the finished work of Christ (Heb. 4:1-5, 10). Christ is the City of Refuge for all believers. Through spiritual baptism we become one with Him and become safe and secure in Him forever. The writer of Hebrews also explains the eternal security believers have because of their union with Christ:

Thus God, determining to show more abundantly to the heirs of promise the immutability of His counsel, confirmed it by an oath, that

Refining and Reminding

> *by two immutable things, in which it is impossible for God to lie, we might have strong consolation, who have fled for refuge to lay hold of the hope set before us* (Heb. 6:17-18).

While we wait to enter our heavenly abode with Him, the Lord Jesus Christ is our Refuge. At His coming our earthly sojourn will conclude and our bodies will experience glorification – the finale of our salvation. In this spiritual sense, believers, who are also spiritual priests, are safe in their City of Refuge until they can come into their final rest (2 Cor. 5:8; 1 Pet. 2:5, 9).

Today, the Cities of Refuge represent the gracious ongoing work of God to bring condemned sinners into a safe and secure resting place to escape judgment. Those who openly admit their guilt before a Holy God can flee to a refuge far safer than any available from the avenger of blood – Christ Himself. The Lord Jesus Christ has already suffered for the condemned and in Him alone do we find divine forgiveness and peace with God.

The hope of the manslayer, incarcerated in a city of refuge, was for the death of the high priest, but the believer's hope in Christ today is much better. Our High Priest will never die, and when He comes again in glory, we will be liberated from a world ruled by the god of this age!

Meditation

> Justice Gray of the U.S. Supreme Court once said to a man who had appeared before him in one of the lower courts and had escaped conviction by some technicality: "I know that you are guilty and you know it, and I wish you to remember that one day you will stand before a better and wiser Judge, and that there you will be dealt with according to Justice and not according to law."[131]

Marriage of Female Heirs
Numbers 36

The earlier request to Moses by the daughters of Zelophehad had resulted in the ruling that the inheritance of a man who dies without sons should then go to his daughters (27:1-11). If the man had no daughters, then the inheritance would go to his brothers; if he had no brothers, then to his uncles; if he had no uncles, then to his closest kin.

Although the law was understood, the heads of the tribe of Manasseh wanted to preserve their tribal allotment appointed by God in the event the daughters of Zelophehad should marry into other tribes (vv. 1-4). Specifically, the elders were concerned that Manasseh would lose land in the year of Jubilee if a daughter of Zelophehad married outside the tribe. Bringing the matter before Moses was a wise precaution that would eliminate contests and quarrels later if the situation arose.

The Jews had already been commanded by Moses not to marry outside of the Jewish community after arriving in Canaan (Ex. 34:11-16; Deut. 7:1-4). Now, it was determined that the daughters of Zelophehad (and others in a similar situation) should marry within their respective tribes as necessary to preserve their tribal distinction and inheritance (vv. 6-9).

The book closes by recording the obedience of these women who had so wonderfully demonstrated God-honoring faith before the entire Jewish nation – a nation which in times past had frequently doubted God's word:

> *Just as the Lord commanded Moses, so did the daughters of Zelophehad; for Mahlah, Tirzah, Hoglah, Milcah, and Noah, the daughters of Zelophehad, were married to the sons of their father's brothers. They were married into the families of the children of Manasseh the son of Joseph, and their inheritance remained in the tribe of their father's family* (vv. 10-12).

Refining and Reminding

For their faith and obedience, these five women have their names recorded in Scripture three times – God delights in honoring those who honor Him! They were true children of Manasseh because they desired to preserve their tribal inheritance and to show love towards their brethren by marrying within their tribe.

Paul tells us that true children of God also have an interest in their heavenly inheritance in Christ: *"The Spirit Himself bears witness with our spirit that we are children of God, and if children, then heirs – heirs of God and joint heirs with Christ"* (Rom. 8:16-17). C. A. Coates summarizes what the daughters of Manasseh teach us by their example concerning the proper perspective of one's inheritance:

> The Apostle reasons, "And if children, heirs also" – as much as to say, If you are children, the inheritance must have a great place in your thoughts. I suppose the children of God come to light in three ways: (1) by practicing righteousness; (2) by loving the brethren; and (3) by having interest in the inheritance. Zelophehad's daughters had proved themselves to be true children of Joseph by their interest in the inheritance.[132]

May we live every day in expectation of our great and eternal inheritance in Christ, for He promises: *"he who overcomes shall inherit all things, and I will be his God and he shall be My son"* (Rev. 21:7).

The final verse states that God gave all the commands in Numbers through Moses to Israel: *"These are the commandments and the judgments which the Lord commanded the children of Israel by the hand of Moses in the plains of Moab by the Jordan, across from Jericho"* (v. 13). The New Testament frequently affirms Moses' authorship of the Pentateuch (Mark 21:19, 26; Luke 2:22, 16:29, 20:28, 24:27; John 1:45). Paul reminds us that these things were recorded for our benefit: *"Now all these things happened to them as examples, and they were written for our admonition, upon whom the ends of the ages have come"* (1 Cor. 10:11). Indeed, Numbers is full of many practical lessons for God's people in how to live as pilgrims and strangers while trekking through successive wilderness experiences in life.

Obviously, the wilderness experience of believers in the Church Age is different than what Israel experienced. Israel's wandering years resulted from rebellion. Additionally, the nation did not experience spiritual regeneration and baptism into Christ, as the Church has. However, the pattern of victorious living in Canaan is similar: One must first cross the Jordan (i.e., be associated with the death, burial, and resurrection of Christ), then be willing to be circumcised (i.e., to have no confidence in the flesh), then be willing to engage the enemy (i.e., to go on with the Lord in faith). In doing so believers today (like the Israelites did after entering Canaan) practically lay hold of their inheritance (i.e., heavenly blessings in Christ) and by doing so gain His peace and rest.

In Numbers, the Israelites are suffering discipline for doubting God's Word and goodness. They are approaching the Jordan River and their new beginning with Jehovah. At Gilgal, He will roll away their reproach and shame, and then lead them triumphantly into conquest. One of the most astounding features of Numbers then, is God's faithfulness and merciful disposition to go on with His people despite all their failures. He will refine those He loves and bring them into all that He has purposed to do for them. The same is true for believers today. As we see in the book of Joshua, the Israelites will come in to Canaan and they will receive the inherence God has provided for them – just as He promised!

Meditation

> It may be at morn, when the day is awaking,
> When sunlight through darkness and shadow is breaking,
> That Jesus will come in the fullness of glory
> To receive from the world His own.
>
> It may be at midday, it may be at twilight,
> It may be, perchance, that the blackness of midnight
> Will burst into light in the blaze of His glory,
> When Jesus receives His own.
>
> Oh, joy! Oh, delight, should we go without dying;
> No sickness, no sadness, no dread and no crying.
> Caught up through the clouds with our Lord into glory,
> When Jesus receives His own.
>
> — H. L. Turner

Deuteronomy

Overview of Deuteronomy

The Author
Both Jewish and Christian tradition credit Moses with being the author of the Pentateuch. The Lord Jesus affirmed that Moses was the author of the books of the Law (Luke 24:27, 44). Moses led the Israelites out of Egypt and was then the principal human instrument God used to communicate with His people and guide them through several wildernesses to the border of Canaan. Moses spoke directly with the Lord and was an eyewitness of all the events occurring during this forty-year period.

Being well educated in Egypt, Moses would have been able to complete such a writing task (Acts 7:22). Moses was given the Law on Mount Sinai and told by Jehovah to record it (Ex. 17:14, 34:27). At the end of his life, Moses entrusted God's written word to the priests who placed the "Book of the Law" in the Ark of the Covenant for safekeeping (31:9, 26). David, Ezra, and the Lord Jesus also affirm that Moses wrote the five books of the Law (1 Kgs. 2:3; Neh. 8:1; Mark 7:10, 12:26).

After delivering his final message, Moses climbed to the summit of Nebo to view the Promised Land. This is where the Lord's servant died. The Lord buried Moses' body in a secret grave in the valley below. The brief epilogue of chapter 34 was added sometime later. The writer is unknown, but some believe Joshua wrote the first eight verses shortly after Moses' death and Ezra wrote the last four verses several centuries later.[133] Josephus claims Moses wrote chapter 34 prophetically prior to his death.

Date
Biblical scholars have placed the date of the Exodus from as early as 1580 to as late as 1230 B.C. Archeological evidence has been used to bolster various dates in this range. Recognizing that the Exodus occurred 480 years before Solomon began constructing the temple (1

Refining and Reminding

Kgs. 6:1) and that the temple work was initiated in about 960 B.C., a date in the mid-fifteenth century B.C. for the Exodus seems appropriate. Note: The 1 Kings 6:1 reference may include the 93 years in which Israel was in service to foreigners during the era of the judges (Acts 13:18-21). An Exodus date of 1446 B.C. is approximate.[134] The completion date of the book of Deuteronomy (less the last chapter) would be approximately forty years later, just prior to the death of Moses, or 1406 B.C.

Theme

This book commences with the Israelites poised just east of the Jordan River on the Plains of Moab across from Jericho. The older Israelites who had heard God's Law at Sinai were now all gone. If the younger generation was to be victorious in Canaan and to seize their possession, Jehovah must go with them into Canaan and fight for them. For that to happen, Moses had to first thoroughly review God's covenant with the new generation and they had to agree to renew it with unconditional obedience.

This is the focus of the book of Deuteronomy, which means "second law." It was dispensed by God to ensure that the new generation of Israelites both knew Him and would not forget Him or His laws after they inherited the Promised Land. *"You shall remember"* is repeated seven times in Deuteronomy. This tone stresses that Deuteronomy is not merely repeating the contents of Exodus, Leviticus, and Numbers, but is calling the nation to covenantal renewal. When God reiterates some truth in Scripture, it is not for the sake of preserving the truth through redundancy, but rather for emphasis.

Moses, under God's authority, had delivered his countrymen from slavery in Egypt and then led them faithfully for forty years in the wilderness. He now teaches again that which is necessary for Israel to continue experiencing the joy of God's covenantal love. Where Numbers was filled with types and practical lessons, Deuteronomy lays out wise practical instructions.

Perhaps this is why Christ quoted more from Deuteronomy during His earthly ministry than from any other Old Testament book, except for Psalms. In fact, Deuteronomy is the third most referred to Old Testament book in the New Testament. There are eighty-three quotations from or allusions to Deuteronomy in the New Testament; only the books of Psalms and Isaiah have more.

"Possession" is a key word in Deuteronomy. After the Israelites cross the Jordan, Joshua connects seizing one's possession in obedient faith to obtaining God's rest. However, Moses cannot speak of entering God's rest now because the Israelites have not yet crossed the Jordan. This event spiritually typifies the death, burial, and resurrection of Christ – the starting point of having divine power in living the victorious life of faith. Before we can understand the practical meaning of divine rest, we first must understand how we acquire our divine inheritance – through Christ alone (Eph. 1:3).

For this reason, the English words "possess," "possessed," and "possession" are found sixty-five times in Deuteronomy, which is more than double the references in any other book in the Bible. Sixty-three of those references are translated from the Hebrew word *yarash* (or a variant), which means "to occupy by expelling the previous tenants." This is why *yarash* is sometimes translated "to drive out," or "to displace" as well as "to possess." Altogether *yarash* (or a variant) occurs seventy-eight times in Deuteronomy. Besides reaffirming the precepts of the Law in Deuteronomy, Moses is also highlighting throughout the book that conflict is necessary for Israel to possess the land that God has for them to inherit. It is no surprise then that "land" is mentioned frequently (187 times in the book) to denote this emphasis on inheritance.

Likewise, we learn in the New Testament that spiritual warfare is a necessary aspect of a believer's development and is inevitable on this side of heaven; it is the means of learning Christ and of more intimately identifying with Him. Believers are to stand fast on the triumphant ground of Calvary, where Christ won the victory over Satan. Yet, we also understand that the Kingdom of God advances as believers live for Christ by utilizing their spiritual blessings in heavenly places – in this sense there is much ground to be gained. Israel must go into the Promised Land to get their possession, but the Jews must first renew their covenant with God to have success in Canaan! No covenant renewal – no land!

It is observed that the English word "love" appears sixteen times in Deuteronomy, which is more than in any other book in the Pentateuch, and also more than in any other historical or prophetic book in the Old Testament. Deuteronomy is really God's book of reminders accentuating His covenantal love. The Lord wants His people to do well, so that they can enjoy the full benefits of His presence. He has

Refining and Reminding

reserved Israel for Himself and no other nation. Deuteronomy 10:12-13 affords a concise summary of what the Lord expected of His people:

> *And now, Israel, what does the Lord your God require of you, but to fear the Lord your God, to walk in all His ways and to love Him, to serve the Lord your God with all your heart and with all your soul, and to keep the commandments of the Lord and His statutes which I command you today for your good?*

Outline

The bulk of the book is composed of three messages. The first addresses gleaning from past failures (chps. 1-4), the second, living for God in the present (chps. 5-29), and the third, having confidence in the Lord for the future (chps. 30-34). A simple outline for the book is as follows:

Historical Prologue (1:1-4:43)
Covenant Obligations (4:44-26:29)
Covenant Blessings and Curses (27:1-29:1)
Covenant Claims (29:2-30:20)
Moses' Departure (31:1-34:12)

Devotions in Deuteronomy

Israel's Refusal to Enter Canaan
Deuteronomy 1

Introduction (vv. 1-4)

Before reviewing Israel's history, Moses identifies the nation's present location (vv. 1, 5) and the date (v. 3). We learned in Numbers 25:1 that Israel's encampment was at Shittim, which was just east of Jericho and the Jordan River. Deuteronomy commences with Moses addressing the entire nation: *"These are the words which Moses spoke to all Israel on this side of the Jordan in the wilderness"* (v. 1). He delivers to the younger generation those statutes and instructions they must remember and obey after entering the Promised Land. His first of five oracles is a four-chapter historical prologue (Deut. 1-4).

In verse 2, Moses states that the 130- to 150-mile journey from Mount Sinai (Horeb) to Kadesh along Edom's western border required only eleven days. This short interval to arrive at Canaan initially is contrasted with the nearly 38-year interlude required for the Israelites to return to Canaan the second time. The long delay resulted from their disobedience. Moses' implied message is blunt: Do not provoke God's wrath again by unbelief – be obedient and invade the land He has given to you.

Moses began delivering his sermons shortly after the defeat of the two Amorite kings (v. 4; Num. 21), on the first day of the eleventh month in the fortieth year since departing Egypt. Since Israel will later mourn Moses' death for thirty days (34:8) and Joshua led the Israelites (after three days of preparations) across the Jordan on the tenth day of the first month (Josh. 4:19), we surmise that Moses delivered the entire contents of Deuteronomy over the course of one week.

Refining and Reminding

The Failure and Consequences of Unbelief (vv. 5-46)

The historical prologue spanning the next four chapters begins in verse 5: *"On this side of the Jordan in the land of Moab, Moses began to explain this law."* The Hebrew word *ba'ar* is rendered *"to explain"* and literally means "to dig." By implication, Moses was digging down into God's Word to make His instructions clear and understandable for His people. "Law" is a key word in Deuteronomy; it is found twenty-four times. Only the book of Psalms with thirty-eight has more occurrences in the Old Testament.

Another noticeable distinction of Deuteronomy is observed in verse 6: *"The Lord our God spoke to us in Horeb."* The expression *"the Lord our God"* is found ninety-two times in the Bible, and Deuteronomy has more occurrences than any other book, with twenty-three. The frequency of this expression and the prevalent occurrences of the words "law," "love," "land," and "possession" (as discussed in the Overview section) combine to declare Deuteronomy's central message: Through faithful obedience to God's Law, the Israelites would properly recognize Jehovah as their God among the nations and likewise Jehovah's love for them would be evident to the nations when Israel miraculously possessed Canaan as His inheritance for them.

Moses had already revealed the boundaries in Canaan that the Israelites would initially have (Num. 34:1-15); however, he also notes that God had promised to the descendants of Abraham, Isaac, and Jacob much more land (vv. 7-8; Genesis 15:18-21, 26:3-5, 28:13-15). Deuteronomy contains indications that the Lord would continue to enlarge Israel's borders if His people chose to go on with Him in faith and obedience. However, to date, the Jews have never fully possessed this region which extends to the mountains of Lebanon in the north, to the Euphrates River in the east, and to the wilderness of Paran in the south.

Having just mentioned God's covenant with the patriarchs to give their descendants a special land, Moses acknowledges what the Lord had already done as part of that covenant – He had increased their descendants' numbers as *"the stars of heaven"* (v. 10). This was mentioned for two reasons. First, Israel's significant enlargement showed that God had kept His promise to Abraham (Gen. 15:5, 22:17), and therefore He should be trusted to make good on the remaining aspects of that covenant. Second, the nation had grown so significantly that Moses did not feel he could adequately govern the people: *"I alone am not able to bear you"* (v. 9). But then he provided the reason he felt inadequate to lead them: *"How can I alone bear your problems and your burdens and your complaints?"* (v. 12). As C. H. Mackintosh observes, if Moses' brethren had been joyfully walking with the Lord, instead of operating in the flesh, Moses would not have felt encumbered and burdened by them. Thus, there would have been no need to appoint more leaders and judges:

> Here lies the secret of much of the "encumbrance" and the "burden." They could not agree among themselves; there were controversies, contentions and questions; and who was sufficient for these things? What human shoulder could sustain such a burden? How different it might have been with them! Had they walked lovingly together, there would have been no cases to decide, and therefore no need of judges to decide them. If each member of the congregation had sought the prosperity, the interest and the happiness of his brethren, there would have been no "strife," no "cumbrance," no "burden." If each had done all that in him lay to promote the common good, how lovely would have been the result![135]

Human character has not changed during the past three millennia; how much easier would the job of church elders be today if all the sheep in their care were controlled by the Holy Spirit! This is why the writer of Hebrews exhorts believers to: *"Obey those who rule over you, and be submissive, for they watch out for your souls, as those who must give account. Let them do so with joy and not with grief, for that would be unprofitable for you"* (Heb. 13:17). In a coming day, each of us will give an account to the Lord for belittling, disrespecting, or rebelling against those ministers of His authority (Rom. 13:1-2).

At this juncture, Moses could not present a joyful report of Israel to the Lord. In fact, their stubborn and carnal disposition made it necessary for him to appoint administrators and judges to handle all their squabbles and complaints. These men were in addition to the seventy elders appointed by God to judge the nation. Moses worked with the various tribes to appoint wise men of sound character and good reputation to assist him in serving the people (vv. 11-18). These leaders and judges were to be honest and just, showing no partiality in executing their office.

Moses then recounts the failure of the people to enter Canaan almost thirty-nine years earlier (vv. 19-46). This occurred after the

Refining and Reminding

Lord delivered them safely through the wilderness of Paran (a region without water) to Kadesh (vv. 19-21). The Lord had honored His word and had brought them safely to the threshold of the Promised Land, His inheritance for them. Moses told the Israelites, *"Look, the Lord your God has set the land before you; go up and possess it"* (v. 21). However, that is not what happened.

We learn something from Deuteronomy that was not revealed in Numbers: It was actually the people's idea to send spies into Canaan to assess its fortifications, population, and agricultural wherewithal (v. 22). Afterwards, the Lord gave Moses permission to send the spies, but the notion originated with the people (Num. 13:1). Albert Barnes summarizes the matter:

> The plan of sending the spies originated with the people; and, as in itself a reasonable one, it approved itself to Moses; it was submitted to God, sanctioned by Him, and carried out under special divine direction. The orator's purpose in this chapter is to bring before the people emphatically their own responsibilities and behavior. It is therefore important to remind them that the sending of the spies, which led immediately to their complaining and rebellion, was their own suggestion.[136]

Instead of entering Canaan in faith based on God's promise and on Moses' command, they wanted to venture forward by human sight. As we all know, sight-based faith is a deficient faith that cannot please God (Heb. 11:6). This means that the disaster at Kadesh-Barnea actually began the moment the spies entered Canaan, not when they returned.

The Lord Jesus stated it was the unrighteous who wanted to see a "sign or a wonder" in order to believe in Him. He called these "sign seekers" an evil generation and spiritually adulterous (Matt. 12:38-39). Even those people that witnessed the miracle of the feeding of the 5000 were pestering the Lord the very next day: *"What sign will You perform then, that we **may see it and believe** You?"* (John 6:30). Did they not recall the miracle of the day before? Had they not filled their bellies with a boy's multiplied sack lunch? The Israelites saw miracles every day in the wilderness for forty years, yet it did not increase their spirituality – for they constantly murmured against God and His leadership.

Peter shows us that true faith in God opens our eyes to understand the things of God. When the Lord asked His twelve disciples if they, too, would turn away from Him, as many had done, Peter responded, *"Lord, to whom shall we go? You have the words of eternal life. Also we have come to **believe and know** that You are the Christ, the Son of the living God"* (John 6:68-69). The unrighteous want a sign to believe, but the righteous believe, and then understand. Instead of seizing in faith what God had provided for them, the Israelites wanted proof that Canaan was as good as the Lord said it was, and to assess whether they could take it. Consequently, sending the spies into Canaan showed the Israelites' doubts in the Lord and needlessly delayed the nation's entrance into their inheritance.

Moses apparently did not discern the folly of sending a spy from each tribe into Canaan (vv. 23-24). The spies returned forty days later to give their report (Num. 13:35) and to present samples of the land's fruitfulness. They confirmed that the Lord had kept His promise: *"It is a good land which the Lord our God is giving us"* (v. 25).

However, ten of the spies convinced the people that they would not be able to overcome the Canaanite fortifications or the Anakim (the giants) in Hebron. Sadly, the congregation put their confidence in what the spies *saw* in Canaan rather than what the Lord *said* He would do for them in Canaan. Instead of proceeding forward in faith, they lingered in their tents and murmured against the Lord, even accusing Him of hating them and of wanting to destroy them in the wilderness (vv. 26-28).

Moses encouraged the people not to be afraid of the taller Canaanites because the Lord would fight for them and would carry them on to victory. Was not the Lord stronger than the Canaanites? Moses then reminded them of how God had mercifully delivered them from Egypt and had tenderly cared for them in the subsequent wilderness experiences. But reviewing God's past evidences of faithfulness did not displace the people's unbelief; they truly doubted God's ability to conquer Canaan (vv. 29-33).

Moses then reminds the younger generation in front of him of the consequences of Israel's rejection of Jehovah at Kadesh: those twenty years of age and older would perish in the desert, except for Caleb and Joshua, who stood with the Lord against the ten spies and their evil report (vv. 34-38). Joshua and Caleb would lead the next generation into the Promised Land to take it.

Refining and Reminding

Indeed, the book of Joshua records that these two men did just that. It took seven years to sufficiently conquer Canaan in order that the land could be divided among nine and a half tribes. Before the land is divided, Caleb will remind Joshua of Moses' promise to him (Josh. 14:36). He had already spied out the region in which the fortification of Hebron was located and he wanted that to be his possession, even though the powerful Anakim resided there (9:2).

Moses concludes the chapter by reminding the people how their forefathers, now all dead, further rebelled against the Lord by not accepting His punishment for them (vv. 39-46). Instead of going on with the Lord in the wilderness as He commanded, they decided to attack the Amorites without Him and were soundly beaten. Because they were in rebellion, the Lord did not heed their cries; rather, He kept them at the oasis of Kadesh for many days.

God's people would not go up when Jehovah commanded them to, and then when He bid them to turn back, they disobeyed the Lord and went forward. They even said, *"We have sinned against the Lord; we will go up and fight, just as the Lord our God commanded us"* (v. 41). William Kelly points out the solemn lesson for us to consider in serving the Lord: "There may be a thorough spirit of disobedience at the very time that people talk of doing whatever God is pleased to command."[137]

Not everyone who calls Jesus Christ "Lord" or who even does wonderful things in His name is a child of God; rather, the Lord supplies us the real test of authenticity: *"Not everyone who says to Me, 'Lord, Lord,' shall enter the kingdom of heaven, but he who does the will of My Father in heaven"* (Matt. 7:21). Humble submission and faithful obedience is the wisdom that God values in our lives. And this is why Moses rehearsed Israel's past failure in the ears of the younger generation: those who refuse to learn from the mistakes of others are doomed to repeat them.

Caleb's Example

As just mentioned, Caleb and Joshua were the only ones from the previous generation who were permitted to enter Canaan. Seven years after Moses' last message, the Israelites finished conquering Canaan. Before Joshua began to divide the land among the tribes, Caleb stepped forward to make a bold request of his life-long friend: *"Now therefore, give me this mountain of which the Lord spoke in that day; for you heard in that day how the Anakim were there, and that the cities were great and fortified. It may be that the Lord will be with me, and I shall be able to drive them out as the Lord said"* (Josh. 14:12). Caleb had waited forty-six years to receive his inheritance in Hebron which Moses had promised him. Joshua bestowed on Caleb the city of Hebron, the fortification of giants.

There was no question of Caleb mistrusting the Lord; rather, he mistrusted himself. As H. L. Rossier explains, Caleb understood that if there were any obstacle to the Lord's being with him, it originated with himself:

> *We realize strength in proportion as we mistrust self,* and these two things surely go together. It is thus that we go from strength to strength. Isaiah 40:28-31 beautifully expresses the same truth: *"Even the youths shall faint and be weary, and the young men shall utterly fail."* This is the end of man's best strength, but *"the everlasting God, the Lord... faints not, neither is weary."* Our confidence is in Him, and more: *"He gives power to the faint; and to them that have no might He increases strength."* He communicates His strength to the feeble; it is made perfect in weakness. Then he adds: *"But they that wait upon the Lord shall renew their strength; they shall mount up with wings as eagles; they shall run, and not be weary; and they shall walk, and not faint."* Such was the case with Caleb. He walked in the consciousness that his strength was in and with God.[138]

Caleb is a great example to us in our present day of weakness and complacency. His character upholds the finest virtues to be found in soldiers of the cross today: one who is sold out for the Lord and yet mistrusts self. He exhibited unabated divine strength because he lacked self-confidence. His humility and continued dependence on God were unrelenting. H. F. Witherby suggests that Caleb's testimony should inspire every true believer to rise above the doldrums of earthly existence to experience real spiritual vitality:

> *"If so be the Lord will be with me, then I shall be able to drive them out, as the Lord said."* How this noble possessor shames the feeble, nerveless soul! To have lived for thirty-eight years in a very chorus of murmurings and yet still to sing "the Lord is my strength and my song" is a miracle indeed, and a miracle it was, as Caleb owned, *"And now, behold, the Lord hath kept me alive, as He said." "As He said";* three great words, greater than the accumulated murmurings of all Israel for eight and thirty years. *"As He said,"* for Caleb had not

Refining and Reminding

dropped down like other men of war and died. Few soldiers of Christ can so speak. Too many an aged Christian soldier seems to regard his long term of service as a plea for immunity from that hourly dependence on God, which at the first won him his victories; and "if the Lord be with us" becomes exchanged for the vainglorious and the degenerate, *"I will go out as at other times before, and shake myself"* (Judg. 16:20).[139]

Caleb understood that his dependence on the Lord infused him with divine power; thus, it did not matter to him that his possession was a fortification occupied by giants. Hebron, which the Anakim called Kiriath-arba, was his inheritance and he wanted to bravely claim it for God. This city had special significance for the Jewish nation as Abraham and Sarah were buried there (Gen. 23:19, 25:10). Even though he was eighty-five years of age, he knew the Lord was with him and therefore he had confidence that he would drive the Anakim from his inheritance.

Later, Caleb, in the strength of the Lord, did drive out the giants and claimed Hebron as his home (Josh. 15:13-14). Hebron would become both a City of Refuge and a Levitical City. This demonstrates the wide range of blessing that is possible to the Lord's people when just one person rises up in faith to do the impossible when empowered by God to do so!

Meditation

We cannot train ourselves to be Christians; we cannot discipline ourselves to be saints; we cannot bend ourselves to the will of God: we have to be broken to the will of God.

— Oswald Chambers

A Long Journey, but Lacking Nothing
Deuteronomy 2

Desert Wanderings (vv. 1-25)

Moses quickly passes over thirty-eight years of wilderness wandering to pick up Israel's history shortly after the death of Aaron and after turning back south to avoid confrontation with Edom (v. 1). Israel had sought passage through Edom and Moab on the King's Highway (even offering to pay for food and water required while passing through), but was denied (v. 6). Circumventing Edom added many miles to their trip, but was necessary because the Lord had commanded Israel not to meddle with or harass the Edomites (vv. 4-5), the Moabites (v. 9), or the Ammonites (v. 19). These people groups were distant kin through Esau and Lot, respectively; therefore, the Lord would not permit Israel to inherit the land He had given them.

So to avoid bloodshed, the Israelites skirted both Edom and Moab. Moses led the Israelites around Edom's western, southern, and eastern borders and then Moab's eastern border through the Zered Valley to arrive at Moab's northern boundary at the Arnon River (vv. 8-24).

It was after suffering this extra hardship of journeying through arid and rough terrain, but prior to engaging the Amorites, that Moses reminds his countrymen that they had lacked nothing during the last forty years (v. 9). Before they became inundated with the plunder of the Amorites, Moses reminds them that it was only because of the Lord's faithfulness to them during their wandering years that they would be able to enjoy the spoils of victory as they approached Canaan.

Arriving in the plains of Moab, the Israelites discovered that the Amorites had pushed the Moabites south and the Ammonites eastward from their homelands between the Arnon and Jabbok Rivers. There was no prohibition against attacking the Amorites; they were a wicked people and not distant kin.

Moses affirmed the words of the Lord after the Israelites crossed the Arnon, *"This day I will begin to put the dread and fear of you upon*

Refining and Reminding

the nations under the whole heaven, who shall hear the report of you, and shall tremble and be in anguish because of you" (v. 25). Then, in the remainder of this chapter and the beginning of the next, Moses recorded how the Israelites had vanquished the Amorites as they moved northward through the Plains of Moab. A few months later, Rahab (a Canaanite residing in Jericho) will acknowledge the fulfillment of verse 25. The various people groups in Canaan were alarmed at how the Amorite armies and cities were almost effortlessly destroyed by the Israelites.

Sihon and His People Are Vanquished (vv. 26-37)

The Israelites had sought to peacefully pass northward on the King's Highway through the region controlled by the Amorites, even offering to pay for any food or water required along the way. Nevertheless, instead of answering the Israelites' request, Sihon king of Heshbon gathered his forces and attacked the Israelites, who retaliated by wiping them out and driving the surviving Amorites from the land (vv. 26-37; Num. 21:21-32).

The Israelites captured and plundered the Amorite cities. Moses informed his countrymen that the victory was God's doing, *"for the Lord your God hardened his* [Sihon's] *spirit and made his heart obstinate, that He might deliver him into your hand, as it is this day"* (v. 30). Not only would Jehovah instill fear in the hearts of the inhabitants of Canaan through this incredible triumph, and reward His people with Amorite possessions, but He was also executing justice on the Amorites for brutally invading Moab and seizing their land.

The progression of verse 31 is noteworthy for victorious living in any age: *"I have begun to give"* ... *"begin to possess."* What God has determined to give us must be possessed by faith. At present, God *"has blessed us with every spiritual blessing in the heavenly places in Christ"* (Eph. 1:3). Like the Israelites of old, God first reveals to believers what He has given us in Christ, and then He exhorts us to begin possessing these resources experientially by faith as enabled by the Holy Spirit. With each challenge, trial, and sorrow, believers learn to increasingly rest in Christ in heavenly places, for all of our resources are found in Him (Eph. 2:6). All beneficial spiritual exercise then begins with resting in Christ. We are not to resort to carnal weapons to resolve our difficulties, nor to become depressed because our expectations are not met. We understand that whatever situation we face, He also faces, and He is in full control. With our final rest still before us, let us take full advantage of the divine rest available for us today in Christ.

Several months earlier the Israelites had been victorious over the Canaanites at Arad who had attacked them unprovoked. But that victory was minute in comparison to wiping out the Amorites and taking possession of their fortified cities. The Lord was beginning to reward and build the reputation of His own people because they had chosen to trust Him. The Lord delights to show Himself strong in those who will rest in Him.

Meditation

>As men rejoice when they divide
>The spoils which they have gained,
>So shall it ever be,
>When Christ shall set them free.
>For He shall break the shoulder's staff,
>The rod of the oppressed,
>And every battle won,
>As victors we shall rest.
>
>For unto us a Child is born,
>To us a Son is given;
>His kingdom shall increase,
>And never, never cease;
>Upon the throne of David shall
>He reign forevermore,
>Till every knee shall bow
>And every heart adore.

— Grant Colfax Tullar

Victory and Spoil
Deuteronomy 3

The prologue, narrating Israel's history continues into this chapter where Moses recounts Israel's battle with Og, the Amorite king of Bashan (Num. 21:33-35). Not only had the Amorites seized much of what had previously belonged to Moab, but they also took Gilead and Bashan which belonged to Ammon. The Amorites had pushed the Ammonites eastward into the mountains. Both the Moabites and Ammonites were descendants of Lot through his two daughters.

Og and His People Are Vanquished (vv. 1-11)

After King Og heard of his brethren's defeat in the south, he gathered his forces against the Israelites, who were coming north on the King's Highway (v. 1). The Lord told Moses, *"Do not fear him, for I have delivered him and all his people and his land into your hand; you shall do to him as you did to Sihon king of the Amorites, who dwelt at Heshbon"* (v. 2). King Og and his forces engaged the Jews at Edrei located on the western edge of Bashan about thirty miles east of the Sea of Galilee. Despite their sixty high-walled cities with barred gates, the Amorites (men, women, and children) were completely vanquished; there were no survivors (vv. 4-6; Num. 21:35).

The Jews claimed the conquered land and the Amorites' livestock and goods as their own (v. 7). This meant that the Israelites now controlled a vast region of the Transjordan plain from Mount Hermon in the north to the Moabite border in the south (i.e., the Arnon River), and eastward to the region of the Ammonites (as marked by the southern course of the Jabbok River; vv. 8-10). They now could move westward across the Jordan River into Canaan without any threat of an enemy approaching from their rear.

We find out that Og was the last of the giants (the Rephaites) in that region. The Rephaites were an ancient tribe of tall people similar to the Anakim in southern Canaan; they are first mentioned in Genesis 14:5.

The Moabites call them Emim (2:11), but the Ammonites referred to them as Zamzummim (2:20).

Albert Barnes suggests that Og's bed did not pertain to Og's place of nightly slumber, but rather to his burial sarcophagus. Barnes further suggests that "the 'iron' was probably the black basalt of the country, which not only contains a large proportion, about 20 percent, of iron, but was actually called 'iron' by the Arabians."[140] Og's bed (perhaps referring to his final resting place – his coffin) measured six feet wide and over thirteen feet long (v. 11). If this was Og's nightly resting place, obviously the bed would be somewhat larger than the man and may have been so for status purposes. Based on this and other historical information concerning ancient giants, a nine- to ten-foot Og is reasonable.

Land for Two and One-Half Tribes (vv. 12-22)

Moses reviews again the land allotments for Reuben, Gad, and a half-tribe of Manasseh which were discussed previously in Numbers 32. If these tribes fulfilled their pledge to Moses to assist their brethren to conquer Canaan, then they would have their requested inheritance east of the Jordan River (vv. 18-20). The specific towns and regions of their inheritance are listed by Moses in verses 12-17 and reflect the more thorough description in Numbers 32:33-43. Manasseh would settle in northern Gilead (east of the Sea of Galilee), Gad in southern Gilead, and Reuben further south in the plains of Moab (from Heshbon and Bezer west to the Jordan River and south to Aroer and over to the Dead Sea).

After the defeat of the Amorite kings, the Lord had a special message for Joshua, Israel's appointed leader to replace Moses: *"Your eyes have seen all that the Lord your God has done to these two kings; so will the Lord do to all the kingdoms through which you pass. You must not fear them, for the Lord your God Himself fights for you"* (vv. 21-22). There was not one Jewish casualty mentioned during either of the Amorite campaigns and the Lord promised that future battles would be just as decisive, that is, as long as He was fighting for Israel.

The Lord's retaliation against the Midianites (Num. 31) had already happened before Moses rehearsed this history. Moses noted that not one Jewish soldier had been harmed during that battle either. So if you count the Canaanites at Arad, the Lord had already proven four times to Joshua that His promise was reliable. This would be a great comfort to

Refining and Reminding

Israel's new leader during the next seven years while he confronted armies many times greater in size than what he commanded. Nonetheless, the Lord was much greater than all of them combined!

Moses Again Forbidden to Enter Canaan (vv. 23-29)

Moses then publicly recounts a private conversation that he had had with the Lord. Moses first acknowledged God's greatness and mighty display of power in crushing the Amorites. He may have thought that, since the Lord had started the process of conquering the region and giving land to His people, his prohibition against entering Canaan had been rescinded. However, this was not the case. When Moses asked to cross over the Jordan to see the good land and the pleasant mountains (vv. 23-25), the Lord flatly denied his request and gave counter instructions:

> *Enough of that! Speak no more to Me of this matter. Go up to the top of Pisgah, and lift your eyes toward the west, the north, the south, and the east; behold it with your eyes, for you shall not cross over this Jordan. But command Joshua, and encourage him and strengthen him; for he shall go over before this people, and he shall cause them to inherit the land which you will see* (vv. 26-28).

Instead of journeying into the good land, Moses was to spend his final days strengthening Israel's new leader for the arduous task ahead. By referring to this conversation, Moses, for the third time, was affirming Joshua's leadership of the Jewish nation. Perhaps that is why Moses did not own his failure at this juncture (though he does later in the book), lest it be a distraction from upholding Joshua's leadership.

God would permit Moses to see the Promised Land from the summit of Nebo in the Pisgah range just before he died (34:1-4). After his conversation with the Lord, Moses noted that they would remain in the valley opposite Beth Peor until he had finished delivering his final messages (the remainder of Deuteronomy).

Moses was probably somewhat disappointed by the Lord's answer to his prayer, but he fully accepted the Lord's will for his remaining days. Moses loved the Lord, and His people, including Joshua; therefore, it would delight his soul to strengthen Joshua for the challenges ahead. Commenting on Moses' prayer and response, Matthew Henry writes:

Moses encouraged Joshua, who was to succeed him. Thus the aged and experienced in the service of God should do all they can to strengthen the hands of those who are young, and setting out in the faith. ... Moses prayed that, if it were God's will, he might go before Israel, over Jordan into Canaan. We should never allow any desires in our hearts, which we cannot in faith offer up to God by prayer. God's answer to this prayer had a mixture of mercy and judgment. God sees it good to deny many things we desire. He may accept our prayers, yet not grant us the very things we pray for. If God does not by His providence give us what we desire, yet if by His grace He makes us content without, it comes to much the same. Let it suffice thee to have God for thy Father, and heaven for thy portion, though thou hast not everything thou wouldst have in the world. ... If we have the earnest and prospect of heaven, let these suffice us; let us submit to the Lord's will, and speak no more to Him of matters which He sees good to refuse us.[141]

God would permit Moses to view the Promised Land, but not to enter it. F. B. Hole suggests that this limitation was truly a mercy of the Lord:

It is a comfort to recognize that there is not only wisdom but also an element of grace in the discipline that God imposes on His saints. Moses was spared many a heartbreak that Joshua must have suffered, owing to the failures of the people.[142]

Moses was a hundred and twenty years old and had faithfully led a stiff-necked people for forty years; it was time for him to enter God's final rest, not the long conflict looming ahead in Canaan.

As mentioned in Numbers 20, there are typological reasons why Moses could never enter Canaan; the best he could do was to point the way and deliver God's people to its border. Moses brought the Law, which could never bring spiritual life nor produce vitality. Paul tells us that the purpose of the Law was to show the Jews their sin (Rom. 3:20) and to point them to the solution – Christ (Gal. 3:24).

As a result, the Law which Moses brought only condemned the Jews because they could not keep it. Consequently, Law-keeping, which centers in human effort alone, can never result in victorious living; this depends solely on God's infusing power. Joshua pictures Jesus Christ of the New Testament; both their names mean "Jehovah is salvation" or "Jehovah saves." Israel's trip through the Jordan River symbolizes the reception of the resurrection life of Christ. It is only by this pervading power that a believer can have victory over the enemy in Canaan, lay hold of spiritual possessions, and please God.

Meditation

    O may we our doubts remove,
    Those gloomy thoughts that rise,
    And see that Canaan is for us,
    With zealous, unclouded eyes!

    To only view that glorious land,
    To merely stand where Moses stood,
    Oh how gloomy life would be,
    To not cross Jordan as we should.

                    — WAH

Take Heed to Yourself
Deuteronomy 4

Obey the Law (vv. 1-14)

Moses commences his address by reminding his countrymen that he had taught them God's Law and, if they wanted to live with God and inherit the land He had for them, they must obey it (vv. 1-2). The Law was God's and therefore should not be diminished or added to (v. 3). They had just witnessed first-hand the immense power of God to judge by the sword or a plague (speaking of the 24,000 Jewish men who perished for bowing to Baal of Peor; Num. 25). These men had defiled themselves spiritually and morally with Moabite women in pagan fertility practices. This example was to show that those who followed the Law lived, and those who did not died. This astounding judgment served as a warning to the Jews: God would not tolerate idolatry among His people. The implication was that all pagan influences (the Canaanites) had to be completely eradicated from the Promised Land (v. 4).

Indeed, Moses had taught the Israelites the Lord's commandments, which were to be the Law of the land, once they settled into Canaan (v. 5). By following His Law, it was God's desire that His people would be a beacon of truth, justice, and holiness to the nations. A sanctified Israel would not only exalt Jehovah's name among the nations, but also draw them to their Creator. As Moses concludes, such a holy and blessed nation would have the esteem of the Gentiles:

> Therefore be careful to observe them; for this is your wisdom and your understanding in the sight of the peoples who will hear all these statutes, and say, "Surely this great nation is a wise and understanding people" (v. 6).

If Israel chose to keep God's statutes (which included the Ten Commandments), that would show them to be wise and would demonstrate their understanding of the things important to God.

Refining and Reminding

However, as a nation, Israel had not yet attained to such wisdom, nor has the Church for that matter. Yet, there have been individuals who have shown such understanding down through the ages.

One such example of consecration is found in the Lord's servant Daniel. In Daniel 6 we read that King Darius had been tricked into signing a thirty-day pray-only-to-him statute. But afterwards, a faithful and righteous Jew named Daniel continued to pray three times a day to Jehovah. This meant that the king was forced to condemn to death a righteous man he greatly esteemed. Just before Daniel was lowered into the den of lions, this pagan king encouraged Daniel that "his" God whom he served continually would deliver him. William MacDonald comments on the effect that the life and convictions of a dedicated believer like Daniel have on an unregenerate soul:

> It is beautiful to see how even unbelievers will sometimes pick up on the faith and morals of consistent believers whom they observe at close hand. Only too often Christians fail their unsaved friends and relatives by not having as high standards of faith and practice as the world expects from God's people.[143]

Daniel was not such a person; he was willing to suffer loss, even to die, rather than to compromise his God-honoring convictions, and that testimony spoke volumes to the king. The Lord did protect Daniel, and in the end his accusers were fed to the lions and Daniel and, more importantly, his God were exalted throughout the Persian Empire by royal decree. Today, the Lord wants His Church to be a consecrated, holy people that obey His word in order to convey an accurate testimony of Himself and His message throughout the earth. Sadly, religious hypocrites uttering "sweet Jesus" endearments do more harm to the cause of Christ than anything else; the lost need to witness men and women whose unwavering devotion to the Lord Jesus is shown by obedience to His expressed will without reservation.

Moses then asked two rhetorical questions to punctuate the necessity of the Jewish nation to continue in God's Law:

> *For what great nation is there that has God so near to it, as the Lord our God is to us, for whatever reason we may call upon Him? And what great nation is there that has such statutes and righteous judgments as are in all this law which I set before you this day?* (vv. 7-8).

Devotions in Deuteronomy

There was only one people group on the entire planet that God had chosen to reveal Himself to and make a covenant with – Israel. Jehovah wanted to enjoy a special relationship with the Jewish nation. This initial meeting occurred at Horeb (Sinai) where Israel saw the awesome nature of God displayed on a quaking, thundering, and fiery mount covered with darkness (vv. 9-10). They did not see God's form, but they did hear His voice thundering like a trumpet and they did receive His Law on two stone tablets there (vv. 11-12). Having witnessed God's holiness firsthand and having received His Law through Moses, the Jews should fear Jehovah and honor Him by both obeying His Law and teaching it to following generations (vv. 13-14). God's Law was to be the Law of the Promised Land – it should never be forgotten!

Avoid Idolatry (vv. 15-40)

Moses then reminds the congregation that because they saw no distinct form of God at Sinai, they should not attempt to represent Him through any formed image (v. 15). It was customary for pagans to create and worship idols patterned after various creatures, or terrestrial or celestial forms, but this was forbidden because it honored the creature and not the Creator (vv. 15-19; Rom. 1:20-25). To express the eternal, self-existing, transcendent Creator in such a limiting fashion would be intensely insulting to an omnipotent, omniscient, omnipresent God. Even if one meant to worship Jehovah, idolatry misrepresents God and demeans Him. It would be an offense far more insulting than likening a king or the president of a great nation to bacteria.

Moses then prompts them to compare where they came from with what God was offering them now. Jehovah had brought them out of *"the iron furnace, out of Egypt, to be His people, an inheritance, as you are this day"* (v. 20). They should never forget that Jehovah specifically delivered them out of slavery to be His special inheritance. So although the Law-giver would not be overseeing them in the Promised Land, it was imperative that they continue to honor the Law of Him who would be dwelling with them and avoid idolatry (vv. 21-23). Moses punctuates this imperative by reminding them of what they had witnessed at Mount Horeb: *"the Lord your God is a consuming fire, a jealous God"* (v. 24).

Despite his pungent warnings, Moses foreknew that Israel would not heed his exhortations and would eventually forsake the Lord for the gods of Canaan, thereby provoking Jehovah's anger: *"When you beget*

Refining and Reminding

children and grandchildren and have grown old in the land, and act corruptly and make a carved image in the form of anything, and do evil in the sight of the Lord your God to provoke Him to anger" (v. 25). Prophetically speaking, he then foretold that the Lord would punish them for their idolatry with captivity and dispersion of the nation (vv. 26-28). Though this was a tragic consequence of Israel's unfaithfulness, it was not the end of the story – *"in the latter days,"* God's dispersed people would sincerely cry out to the Lord and be purified and restored to Him:

> *But from there you will seek the Lord your God, and you will find Him if you seek Him with all your heart and with all your soul. When you are in distress, and all these things come upon you in the latter days, when you turn to the Lord your God and obey His voice (for the Lord your God is a merciful God), He will not forsake you nor destroy you, nor forget the covenant of your fathers which He swore to them* (vv. 29-31).

Jacob uses the expression *"the last days"* (its first appearance in Scripture) while blessing his sons (Gen. 48-49). This same clause is also translated in various locations in the Bible as "the latter days" and "the last times." In general context and given the precedence of Genesis 49, these terms all describe a period of time in which God will draw together that which is necessary to conclude His purposes for a nation or people. For the nation of Israel, this expression is synonymous with the yet future conclusion of Gentile authority over Israel. Moses tells us that this period of time will also include Israel's final rebellion against God (also see 31:29) and, consequently, God's judgment upon His adulterous wife (Israel) during the Tribulation Period (Ezek. 36:17-19).

Although speaking to a future rebellious people, Moses' promise, *"you will seek the Lord your God, and you will find Him if you seek Him with all your heart and with all your soul,"* wonderfully shows God's desire to be one with those who will seek Him. Those who seek God – will find Him! Scripture repeatedly offers man an opportunity to search out and commune with God if man will yield to what God wants him to understand and obey: *"You will seek Me and find Me, when you search for Me with all your heart"* (Jer. 29:13). *"Now set your heart and your soul to seek the Lord your God"* (1 Chron. 22:19). *"The Lord is near to all who call upon Him, to all who call upon Him in truth"*

(Ps. 145:18). God provides abundant mercy to those who humbly seek Him with empty hands, which He promises to fill with blessings:

> *I love those who love Me, and those who seek Me diligently will find Me. Riches and honor are with Me, enduring riches and righteousness. My fruit is better than gold, yes, than fine gold, and My revenue than choice silver. I traverse the way of righteousness, in the midst of the paths of justice, that I may cause those who love Me to inherit wealth, that I may fill their treasuries* (Prov. 8:17-21).

As the Lord Jesus confirmed, God richly blesses those who seek His love and forgiveness (Matt. 11:28-30, 19:28-30).

Having spoken of Israel's future departure from the Lord, her chastening, and final restoration, Moses changed the discussion from the latter days to past days (vv. 32-40). He reminded them, through rhetorical questions, that God had chosen them to be His unique people, for no other nation on earth could claim to have heard God's voice from the midst of the fire and lived (vv. 32-33).

To further substantiate this point, Moses asked, *"Or did God ever try to go and take for Himself a nation from the midst of another nation, by trials, by signs, by wonders, by war, by a mighty hand and an outstretched arm, and by great terrors, according to all that the Lord your God did for you in Egypt before your eyes?"* (v. 34). It was all true! They had seen the signs and wonders that God first worked in Egypt and then throughout their wilderness journey: the Egyptian plagues, the parting of the Red Sea, the water gushing out of dry rocks, the manna from heaven, the constant pillar of cloud and fire, the piles of quail in the camp, the opening of the earth to swallow rebels, and more recently the powerful defeat of the Amorites and Midianites (vv. 35-36). They knew more than any nation just how strong God's arm was; therefore, they should not fear to conquer Canaan, for the Lord would be with them.

Lastly, Moses reminded his countrymen that, because of God's love for their forefathers, He chose to deliver their descendants out of Egypt and bring them into an inheritance, Canaan (vv. 37-38). Having warned the Jewish nation against idolatry, affirming their election and great privileges as Jehovah's people, and foretelling their future infidelity, Moses concludes his first of five oracles with this charge:

Refining and Reminding

> *Therefore know this day, and consider it in your heart, that the Lord Himself is God in heaven above and on the earth beneath; there is no other. You shall therefore keep His statutes and His commandments which I command you today, that it may go well with you and with your children after you, and that you may prolong your days in the land which the Lord your God is giving you for all time* (vv. 39-40).

This is the first of nine occurrences in the book of the expression, "that it may go well with you," or "that it may be well with you." Moses' grand point is this principle: one typically enjoys a long and blessed life by choosing to follow God and to obey His Law, but pursuing sin results in misery which usually shortens one's life. As a general rule, this code of conduct still rings true today!

Having been introduced to, chosen by, and blessed by the one true God, what greater delight could Israel have than to show their appreciation to Him through faithful obedience? C. H. Mackintosh surmises that the real crux of being a faithful servant to the Lord relates to how much we appreciate our privileged responsibility of delighting His heart:

> But, above and beyond His moral claims stands the marvelous fact that His heart is gratified, His spirit refreshed by our keeping His commandments, and doing those things that are pleasing in His sight. Beloved Christian reader, can anything exceed the moral power of such a motive as this? Only think of our being privileged to give pleasure to the heart of our beloved Lord! What sweetness, what interest, what preciousness, what holy dignity it imparts to every little act of obedience to know that it is grateful to the heart of our Father! How far beyond the legal system is this! ... The difference between the legal system and Christianity is the difference between death and life, bondage and liberty, condemnation and righteousness, distance and nearness, doubt and certainty.[144]

To do something so as to avoid punishment is childish in comparison to yearning to do nothing that would injure God's heart. Because we are self-focused in our lusting, we often forget the monstrous face of sin which God witnesses every moment of every day. Simply put, avoiding sin pleases God and that alone should inspire us to be a holy and obedient people. Indeed, this is what God desired for Israel and why Moses summarizes fundamental principles of God's covenant with Israel in this treatise: God, who is spiritual in nature, chose Israel to be His people, He has an exclusive right to their allegiance, and He has deep hatred of idolatry in every form.

So although the chapter break is still nine verses away, a panorama of the dispensation of the Law has been displayed before us. It began with divinely spoken and written words delivered through Moses, followed by man's departure from God's Law and the sorrowful consequence of doing so, and, finally, the restoration made possible because of God's faithfulness and willingness to show mercy. That, beloved, is why Israel, despite their failings, was permitted to live in the inheritance God had for them and it is why we can have immense confidence in Him also. He will always do what is best for us. He is a good God and we are indebted to His mercy!

Transjordan Cities of Refuge (vv. 41-43)

With the Amorite cities conquered throughout the Transjordan region, Moses names three cities to which an unintentional manslayer might flee to get a fair trial and be protected from the kin of the deceased. He lists the cities from south to north: *"Bezer in the wilderness on the plateau for the Reubenites, Ramoth in Gilead for the Gadites, and Golan in Bashan for the Manassites"* (v. 43). See Numbers 35 for further details concerning the Cities of Refuge.

Introduction to God's Law (vv. 44-49)

This introduction is better placed in the next chapter, where Moses launches into a review of the Ten Commandments: *"Now this is the law which Moses set before the children of Israel"* (vv. 44). As Moses again confirms the timing of his message – Israel had vanquished the Amorites and was on the edge of the wilderness poised to enter Canaan (vv. 45-49) – it seems likely that he is starting a new message.

Meditation

> Just as a servant knows that he must first obey his master in all things, so the surrender to an implicit and unquestionable obedience must become the essential characteristic of our lives.
>
> — Andrew Murray

Refining and Reminding

This is none other than a satisfied life. The Christian cherishes nothing but God; henceforth he is satisfied with His will.

— Watchman Nee

A Holy God and Holy Commandments
Deuteronomy 5

The words *"And Moses called all Israel, and said to them"* in verse 1 mark the beginning of a new message (the second of five in Deuteronomy). The third-person reference to Moses is another indication throughout the book of new oracles. Having addressed Israel's past doings and failures in the previous four chapters, the aged leader commences the longest thematic section of the book, which focuses on Israel's present need to know and observe God's statutes for them to survive and flourish. Moses' review and explanation of the Law begins in verse 5 and concludes in 26:15.

Although the Lord is speaking specifically to Israel through Moses at this junction, the instruction, in principle, is foundational if all God's people are to rightly please Him: *"Hear, O Israel, the statutes and judgments which I speak in your hearing today, that you may learn them and be careful to observe them"* (v. 1). Notice the progression: God's people are to "hear" – "learn" – "observe" (i.e., "do") what God commands.

We cannot obey what we have not learned, and we cannot learn what has not been revealed. Therefore, God initiates the opportunity for us to demonstrate love for Him through obedience by first revealing what He wants us to honor. Then, God explains what He reveals so that we understand it. Moses, the priests and the Levites were to ensure that the people understood God's Word. (This would be the role of apostles and teachers later.) Lastly, God's people are then accountable to God for obeying what they have been taught.

Moses then reminded the people that God had instituted a new covenant with them at Mount Sinai (Horeb) nearly forty years ago (v. 2). The burning, shaking, smoking, thundering mountain had incited fear in the people who backed away from Sinai and asked Moses to talk to God on their behalf, which he did (vv. 4-5). Obviously, the previous older generation was present at that time, but Moses reminded the

Refining and Reminding

people that God's covenant was meant to guide and instruct the living of Israel (future generations), not the dead (v. 3). For this reason, verse 3 reads better in the English with the word "only" inserted after "fathers" and "also" after the first "us": *"The Lord did not make this covenant with our fathers [only], but with us [also], those who are here today, all of us who are alive."*

Moses, acting on both the wishes of the people and God's command, climbed into the holy mount and spent forty days alone with the Lord. During that time God wrote His commandments on two tablets of stone and gave them to Moses to pass on to the people (v. 22). Rabbinic writings dating back to the third century A.D. place the number of commands in the Torah at 613 (Talmud Makkot 23b). The most outstanding of these, which were to guide daily Jewish conduct, are commonly referred to as "the Ten Commandments."

The Ten Commandments (vv. 6-21)

The preamble of the Law was brief; it identified Jehovah as the one true God and the Deliverer of the Israelites from Egypt and from bondage (v. 6). The foundation of the Law was then decreed in ten distinct moral commandments (vv. 7-21). God provided Moses with specific details of the Law's implementation afterwards (the next eleven months), which composes half of Exodus, Leviticus, and half of Numbers. God promised to show mercy to those who love Him and choose to keep His commandments (v. 10).

The first two of the Ten Commandments address recognizing God as Creator and not worshipping creation. The first commandment is: *"You shall have no other gods before Me"* (v. 7; Ex. 20:3). Moses explained how to obey this commandment – it is by believing in the one true God and giving Him first place in your life: *"The Lord our God, the Lord is one! You shall love the Lord your God with all your heart, with all your soul, and with all your strength"* (6:4-5). The Lord Jesus reiterated this teaching: *"'You shall love the Lord your God with all your heart, with all your soul, and with all your mind.' This is the first and great commandment"* (Matt. 22:37-38).

The second commandment is: *"You shall not make for yourself a carved image – any likeness of anything that is in heaven above, or that is in the Earth beneath, or that is in the water under the Earth; you shall not bow down to them nor serve them. For I, the Lord your God, am a jealous God"* (vv. 8-9; Ex. 20:4-5). Have you ever heard someone say, "God to me is ..."? The individual is revealing to you his or her self-concocted god, an imaginary image of a god which fits his or her liking and, therefore, will readily condone that person's moral standard of doings. In this way, holiness becomes relative; a self-manufactured god will not judge sin. This idol may not be a golden calf, but neither is it the Lord as revealed in the Bible.

God does not have varying degrees of holiness and righteousness; His character defines moral integrity, and all that does not measure up to it will be judged. When an individual replaces the true God of Scripture with a created image (whether visible or imaginary), he or she has violated the second of the Ten Commandments. To reject God as Creator is to violate both the first and the second commandments. Evolutionary teaching exalts man and demotes or denies God – it is an intellectual religion which is high on self and applauds nature's ability to do what only God can do – create life!

The first two commandments alone are sufficient to prove that each of us has offended God. Yet, if there is any doubt about this, the remaining commandments prove the point:

- Do not blaspheme God or use His name disrespectfully (v. 11).

- Put aside one day in seven (e.g. the Sabbath day) to honor the Lord; this was addressed to servants as well (vv. 12-15).

- Honor your parents (v. 16).

- Do not murder (v. 17).

- Do not commit adultery (v. 18).

- Do not steal (v. 19).

- Do not lie (v. 20).

- Do not covet (lust after what is not yours; v. 21).

If you ask people on the street if they are a good person, most will say, "Yes, I am a pretty good person." Their moral standard of reckoning, however, is all wrong, and they don't even know it. They have fabricated a self-righteous system in which they weigh their good deeds against their bad ones (sin), thinking that their good deeds will somehow offset their sins. God's standard of judgment is quite different – absolute perfection!

Coveting, for example, is a sin generally perceived to be less offensive to God than committing adultery or murder, but in God's mind coveting is a form of idolatry (Col. 3:5). To adore anything more than Him, whether by one's actions or in one's thoughts, is the same to Him as committing idolatry. In such cases, the Lord loses significance and prominence in an individual's life; this greatly grieves Him. Consequently, by His standard, coveting is a sin and is sufficient to keep anyone out of heaven (Gal. 3:10-12).

Hence, to earn heaven through Law-keeping was, and still is, an impossibility, but the offer of grace and mercy has *come near* to all, and those who will trust the Lord Jesus Christ alone for salvation receive both grace and mercy. As Paul explains, by quoting Moses, an individual does not need to search the far ends of the earth, or venture into heaven or explore Hades to learn how to be saved; God has brought the message of salvation in Christ to us (Rom. 10:5-10).

Like the Law, Christ descended from heaven, but He accomplished what the Law could not: *"Moreover the law entered that the offense might abound. But where sin abounded, grace abounded much more, so that as sin reigned in death, even so grace might reign through righteousness to eternal life through Jesus Christ our Lord"* (Rom. 5:20-21). The Law revealed the exceeding sinfulness of man's heart and decreed death upon the sinner (Rom. 7:13), but through Christ alone, the believer receives the forgiveness of sins and eternal life (Rom. 6:23). The gospel of Jesus Christ accomplished what the Law could not. Consequently, there is *"now no condemnation to those who are in Christ Jesus"* (Rom. 8:1). The love, mercy, and grace of God are fully declared and offered in Christ alone!

The Holiness of God (vv. 22-33)

Having stated Jehovah's Law for His people, Moses then affirms the holiness of Israel's God by recounting the awesome scene at Mount Sinai when God introduced Himself to His people (vv. 23-33; Ex. 19). When the day came for the nation of Israel to meet the Lord, the long blast of a trumpet signaled Moses to lead the people to the base of the mount. The mount quaked exceedingly; it burned like an overheated furnace, and thick billows of smoke ascended up from it into heaven. From the thick darkness, a deafening voice which increased in volume uttered words as if blasted from a trumpet. So overwhelmed were the people by what they heard, felt, and saw that they *"begged that the word should not be spoken to them anymore"* (Heb. 12:19) and *"they moved and stood afar off"* from the mountain (Ex. 20:18). This day would never be forgotten in Israel. Some 1,500 years later the writer of Hebrews referred to this event to epitomize the holy nature of God (Heb. 12:18-21).

Though the Israelites had cleansed themselves the best they could by washing and scrubbing, they immediately felt unclean in Jehovah's presence. The prophet Jeremiah explains why: *"'For though you wash yourself with lye, and use much soap, yet your iniquity is marked before Me,' says the Lord God"* (Jer. 2:22). This was the purpose of the Mount Sinai experience; the manifestation of Jehovah's holiness made the Israelites keenly aware of their own sinful state before Him. They understood the message and fearfully retreated from the foot of the mount and *"stood afar off"*; they also begged Moses to talk with God for them, lest they die (Ex. 19:18).

Verse 22 records how God responded to the fearful withdrawal of His people from the mount and their request for a mediator to approach Him: *"These words the Lord spoke to all your assembly, in the mountain from the midst of the fire, the cloud, and the thick darkness, with a loud voice; and He added no more. And He wrote them on two tablets of stone and gave them to me."* Barnes explains the meaning of *"He added no more"* in this verse:

> God spoke no more with the great voice directly to the people, but addressed all other communications to them through Moses. This unique and sublime phenomenon, followed up by the inscription of the Ten Words on the two tables by the finger of God, marks not only the holiness of God's Law in general, but the special eminence and permanent obligation of the Ten Words themselves as compared with the rest of the Mosaic enactments.[145]

The response of the people that day honored the Lord in two ways. First, they understood their uncleanness before a holy God. Second, they realized they could not approach Him without a mediator: *"I stood between the Lord and you at that time, to declare to you the word of the Lord; for you were afraid because of the fire, and you did not go up the mountain"* (v. 5). *"You go near and hear all that the Lord our God may say, and tell us all that the Lord our God says to you, and we will hear and do it"* (v. 27). In this chapter, we see Moses representing, in type,

Refining and Reminding

Christ's mediatorship. God, as C. A. Coates explains, appreciated the people's response to His holiness:

> Jehovah was pleased with what the people said when they felt the need for a mediator. *"And Jehovah heard the voice of your words, when ye spoke to me; and Jehovah said unto me, I have heard the voice of the words of this people that have spoken to thee; they have well-spoken all that they have spoken"* (verse 28). It very definitely suggests the mediatorship of the Lord Jesus; God wants His people to feel the necessity for Christ as the Mediator. He would have them to know that He is God, and that they are men, and that they cannot meet Him "face to face" without a Mediator.[146]

Moses did ascend the mount on their behalf, but quickly returned to again warn the people not to set foot on the mountain or they would die. Jehovah's holiness was unapproachable. This is God's way of introducing salvation throughout the Bible; God first reveals to man His holiness to awaken man to his sinful state and his need for God's cleansing. The people responded rightly to God's holiness and affirmed that they would obey His Law for them (v. 28). However, the Lord implied that He already knew that they would not be faithful to their commitment to Him despite their good intentions: *"O that there were such an heart in them, that they would fear Me, and keep all My commandments always, that it might be well with them, and with their children forever!"* (v. 29: KJV). F. B. Hole observes the alls of this verse:

> Notice also in verse 29 the words "all" and "always," or, "all the days." Obedience must be **complete and continuous.** Under law man is like a boat under strain but held in safety by a chain of many links. If every link is intact all the time, well and good. But, if at any time, just one link breaks, the boat drifts on to the rocks as surely as if every link had snapped. It is a case of all and all the time. This is again emphasized in the last verse of our chapter.[147]

God is holy and His Law is holy, and His people were to be holy also. However, the latter aspect was an impossibility during this dispensation; the Jews could not continue in well-doing. The Jews could not be baptized into Christ and indwelt by the Holy Spirit, for Christ had not yet come to the earth to suffer and die for them. He had not been raised from the grave to impart resurrection power to those who were His so that they could continue in holiness. The purpose of the Law was to show the Jews that they were not holy, they could not be holy by doing good works, and therefore they needed a Savior!

Moses described the awesomeness of God at Mount Sinai on the day He was introduced to His people. Who of us, had we been there, would have behaved any differently than those fearful Jews? Seeing the majesty of God so prominently displayed would cause anyone great trepidation. Yet, there would be a future day when an even greater display of God's holy character would take place. That day, now past, also took place on a quaking mount covered with thick darkness. God demonstrated His holy character in that when His own Son was made sin for us, God did not spare Him from judgment; sin had to be judged and the Lord Jesus Christ, engulfed by darkness, bore the wrath of God for our sins. The Law at Sinai and then the Law's righteous judgment at Calvary emphatically proved God to be a holy God!

Although the dispensation of the Law has been replaced with the stewardship of grace, the Law still declares God's moral standard for right and wrong today; the Ten Commandments show us our sin (Rom. 3:20) and affirm our need of a Savior: *"Therefore the law was our tutor to bring us to Christ, that we might be justified by faith. But after faith has come, we are no longer under a tutor"* (Gal. 3:24-25). But though God's message of salvation is different today than at Sinai, God, Himself, does not change (Mal. 3:6). He is still holy and demands holiness in His people today: *"As obedient children, not conforming yourselves to the former lusts, as in your ignorance; but as He who called you is holy, you also be holy in all your conduct, because it is written, 'Be holy, for I am holy'"* (1 Pet. 1:14-16). Christians would do well to remember the events that transpired on Mount Sinai; God is a sin-hating God and we dare not test His merciful patience by endorsing sin with compromising conduct.

Thankfully for the Christian, the veil is rent, and each believer has the great privilege of walking beyond the thick cloud of darkness into the light, for God is light, and in so doing he or she can enjoy full fellowship with God (1 Jn. 1:6-8). The writer of Hebrews refers to this as *"the new and living way"* of approaching God – a way that is now available to all who have trusted Christ as Savior:

> *Therefore, brethren, having boldness to enter the Holiest by the blood of Jesus, by a new and living way which He consecrated for us, through the*

Refining and Reminding

> *veil, that is, His flesh, and having a High Priest over the house of God, let us draw near with a true heart in full assurance of faith, having our hearts sprinkled from an evil conscience and our bodies washed with pure water* (Heb. 10:19-22).

Moses' entrance before God at Sinai was so threatening that he said, *"I am exceedingly afraid and trembling"* (Heb. 12:21). Yet, believers in the Church Age can boldly and with great confidence and assurance approach the same awesome God that Moses stood before in terror. How is this possible? Because Christ is the Mediator of the New Covenant and through the sprinkling of His own blood He has opened the way for us to approach Almighty God and call upon Him as Abba Father (Rom. 8:15; Heb. 12:24). In light of this, what exhortation does the writer of Hebrews offer to believers? *"Let us hold fast the confession of our hope without wavering, for He who promised is faithful"* (Heb. 10:23). Dear believer, be holy, for God is a consuming fire (Heb. 12:29), and hold fast to Christ – He is the means and the assurance of all good things to come!

Nearly forty years had passed since that terrifying day at Sinai, but Moses refers to it now, for the same reason God revealed His holiness then: When God's people lose sight of God's holiness, they exalt themselves and enter into sin. Thus, Moses concludes his warning with a promise of God's blessing:

> *Therefore you shall be careful to do as the Lord your God has commanded you; you shall not turn aside to the right hand or to the left. You shall walk in all the ways which the Lord your God has commanded you, that you may live and that it may be well with you, and that you may prolong your days in the land which you shall possess* (vv. 32-33).

To be mindful of God's holiness is a strong defense against engaging in sin. God will not tolerate filthiness or wickedness in His presence. God is holy and He will not settle for anything less than holiness in us. There are no degrees of righteousness and holiness with God, so His people should not be satisfied with conduct which God does not approve. To go on with God in holy conduct ensures His favor and blessing! Hence the chapter concludes with a lovely promise: Those truly living for God will enjoy the security of His love and experience His full pleasure for them.

Meditation

Is, then, the Law of God untrue, which He by Moses gave?
No! But to take in view, that it has power to save.
The Law was never meant to give new strength to man's lost race,
We cannot act before we live, and life proceeds from grace.
By Christ we enter into rest, and triumph over the fall.
Whoever would be completely blest must trust to Christ for all.

— Gadsby's Hymns

There is a danger of forgetting that the Bible reveals, not first the love of God, but the intense, blazing holiness of God, with His love as the center of that holiness.

— Oswald Chambers

Legitimate Lineage
Deuteronomy 6

The Greatest Commandment (vv. 1-9)

The Lord desired two things primarily from His people in the land that He was giving them – in fear to revere Him alone as God and to observe His commandments (vv. 1-2). By doing so they would have God's blessing in the land and would enjoy a full and long life (v. 3). As already observed in Numbers, rebels and law-breakers often suffer short lives. But those who are respectful and obedient to God's authority, generally speaking, live happier and longer than those who do not!

Who would not relish a life marked by longevity and plenty? Consequently, the Jews developed a tradition of reciting morning and evening verses 4-9 as a daily prayer called the *Shema Yisrael*, or "Hear, Israel" as drawn from verse 1. This daily prayer creed also includes Deuteronomy 11:13-21 and Numbers 15:37-41. It has been a longstanding Jewish custom for parents to end the day by reciting this prayer to their children before they go to sleep.

The first two of the Ten Commandments stated in the previous chapter relate to the subject of recognizing God as Creator and not worshiping creation. The first commandment is: *"You shall have no other gods before Me"* (5:6). Moses further explained how one obeys this – by believing in the one true God and giving Him first place in your life: *"The Lord our God, the Lord is one! You shall love the Lord your God with all your heart, with all your soul, and with all your strength"* (vv. 4-5).

The first part of this commandment was to hold fast to and to confess the unity of the Godhead. C. H. Mackintosh writes:

> This truth lay at the very foundation of the Jewish economy. So long as they maintained this, they were a happy, prosperous, fruitful people; but when it was let go, all was gone. It was their great national bulwark, and that which was to mark them off from all the

nations of the east. They were called to confess this glorious truth in the face of an idolatrous world, with "its gods many, and lords many." It was Israel's high privilege and holy responsibility to bear a steady witness to the truth contained in that one weighty sentence, "The Lord our God is one Lord."[148]

The second part of the command required Israel to be fully devoted to Jehovah, the one true God. During the final days of the Lord's earthly ministry, a lawyer tested Him with a question: *"Teacher, which is the great commandment in the law?"* (Matt. 22:36). The Lord immediately responded to this question by quoting Moses' words from this chapter: *"You shall love the Lord your God with all your heart, with all your soul, and with all your mind.' This is the first and great commandment"* (Matt. 22:37-38). Notice that the Lord added *"and with all your mind"* to the Greek Scriptures beyond the original Hebrew quotation from Deuteronomy. The New Testament puts much emphasis on strengthening, shaping, girding, and renewing the believer's mind in order to properly live for Christ.

Besides having sound minds, the Lord desires His people to have devoted hearts. When it comes to having no other god besides the Creator, it means that He has first place in our life, our thinking, our allegiance, and our affections – and there are to be no close seconds concerning our love for God (Matt. 10:37). Matthew Henry nicely summarizes both aspects of God's commandment for His people in verses 4-5:

> Here is a brief summary of religion, containing the first principles of faith and obedience. Jehovah our God is the only living and true God; he only is God, and he is but One God. Let us not desire to have any other. The threefold mention of the Divine names, and the plural number of the word translated God, seem plainly to intimate a Trinity of persons, even in this express declaration of the unity of the Godhead. Happy those who have this one Lord for their God. It is better to have one fountain than a thousand cisterns; one all-sufficient God than a thousand insufficient friends. This is the first and great commandment of God's law, that we love Him; and that we do all parts of our duty to Him from a principle of love.[149]

Moses' point was that if Jehovah is the supreme Object of our affections, obedience would naturally follow. God had shown His love

Refining and Reminding

for Israel by all that He had done on their behalf; now it was time for them to demonstrate their love for Him. This is the same line of reasoning by which John inspires believers to serve the Lord in the Church Age: *"We love Him because He first loved us"* (1 Jn. 4:19). Those who have truly experienced the love of God will want to love Him back, and the Lord Jesus said, *"If you love Me, keep My commandments"* (John 14:15). Willing obedience is the ultimate test of our love for God, and that was the message Moses was delivering to the Israelites.

Furthermore, if Israel did forget the Lord and His commandments, Moses promised that they would suffer devastation and death. For that reason the Levites were to teach the people God's Law, and parents were to teach it to their children as a part of daily living:

> *And these words which I command you today shall be in your heart. You shall **teach** them diligently to your children, and shall **talk** of them when you sit in your house, when you walk by the way, when you lie down, and when you rise up. You shall bind them as a sign on your hand, and they shall be as frontlets between your eyes. You shall **write** them on the doorposts of your house and on your gates (vv. 6-9).*

Clearly, the home is the environment God has chosen for children to learn, to meditate, and to memorize God's Word. Commenting on these verses, William MacDonald writes:

> Many Christian parents take this passage as a mandate to teach their own children, not only the faith, but also other so-called secular subjects, rather than sending them to humanistic schools. In the days of Christ, the Jews actually bound portions of the law to their hands and suspended them between their eyes (v. 8). But doubtless the Lord intended rather that their actions (hand) and desires (eyes) should be controlled by the law.[150]

God-fearing parents were to teach, talk about, and write out God's word so their children would thoroughly know it. As parents spend time with their children, endless opportunities naturally arise to apply biblical instruction and application. These teachable moments do not occur unless at least one parent is at home and the children are at home.

Devotions in Deuteronomy

Unfortunately, it did not take long for Israel to neglect the teaching of God's Law to their children; in fact, it took only one generation:

> *Now Joshua the son of Nun, the servant of the Lord, died when he was one hundred and ten years old. ... When all that generation had been gathered to their fathers, another generation arose after them who did not know the Lord nor the work which He had done for Israel. Then the children of Israel did evil in the sight of the Lord, and served the Baals; and they forsook the Lord God of their fathers, who had brought them out of the land of Egypt; and they followed other gods from among the gods of the people who were all around them, and they bowed down to them; and they provoked the Lord to anger* (Judg. 2:8-12).

After Joshua died, the Levites stopped instructing the people and parents became apathetic in teaching God's Law to their children. As a result, the next generation forsook the Lord and embraced false gods. The aftermath of Joshua's death illustrates the fallacy of depending upon any spiritual influence outside the family to maintain your family's spiritual welfare. How did God respond to His people's departure from Him?

> *Now these are the nations which the Lord left, to prove Israel by them, even as many of Israel as had not known all the wars of Canaan; only that the generations of the children of Israel might know, to teach them war, at the least such as before knew nothing thereof* (Judg. 3:1-2).

God delegated to parents the responsibility of teaching the new generation about Himself. He loves His people too much to leave them void of truth and the knowledge of His presence. What was God's instrument for making His presence known? The disciplinary rod of military invasion and conquest. Israel did not remember God's awesome deliverance from slavery and from Egypt, so God used death, invasion, and servitude to awaken them again to His presence. All this occurred because the Levites failed to teach the people, and then parents chose not to instruct the next generation in the ways of the Lord.

Refining and Reminding

Beware of Prosperity and Idolatry (vv. 10-19)

What would be the chief reasons Israel would willfully neglect teaching the younger generation God's Law? Moses warned against two – first, prosperity and second, idolatry. In the arms of affluence God's people tend to forget to cling to the Lord. When we are distressed or in need, we most eagerly call out to God for help, but how often do we neglect appreciating Him when we are full. For this reason, Moses solemnly warned his countrymen not to forget the Lord after they were settled in the Promised Land and enjoying its abundance:

> *So it shall be, when the Lord your God brings you into the land of which He swore to your fathers, to Abraham, Isaac, and Jacob, to give you large and beautiful cities which you did not build, houses full of all good things, which you did not fill, hewn-out wells which you did not dig, vineyards and olive trees which you did not plant – when you have eaten and are full – then beware, lest you forget the Lord who brought you out of the land of Egypt, from the house of bondage* (vv. 10-12).

The profusion in Canaan would be in sharp contrast to their tenure as oppressed slaves in Egypt and their modest existence in the wilderness for forty years. They were about to inherit cities and homes that they did not build, wells for water that they did not dig, farmland which they did not clear, vineyards and olive groves that they did not plant. No doubt this would all be exhilarating. Our carnal nature craves the easy lifestyle, pampering, and receiving whatever we desire. However, there is no cruise-control when living for the Lord; the child of God must beware of anything or anyone that would rob their affections for the Lord.

Jehovah is jealous over His people. He would not tolerate His people having displaced affections, especially in relation to them embracing false gods (vv. 13-14). It is from this perspective that we must understand the Lord's admonishment concerning swearing in His name alone stated in verse 13: *"You shall fear the Lord your God and serve Him, and shall take oaths in His name."* It may seem that the Lord is decreeing something through Moses concerning swearing which was contrary to Christ's later prohibition against swearing (Matt. 5:34). Albert Barnes explains why there is no inconsistency in the two statements:

The command "to swear by His Name" is not inconsistent with the Lord's injunction (Matt. 5:34): *"Swear not at all."* Moses refers to legal swearing, our Lord to swearing in common conversation. It is not the purpose of Moses to encourage the practice of taking oaths, but to forbid that, when taken, they should be taken in any other name than that of Israel's God. The oath involves an invocation of Deity, and so a solemn recognition of Him whose Name is made use of in it. Hence, it comes especially within the scope of the commandment Moses is enforcing.[151]

After just witnessing the Lord's annihilation of the Amorites and Midianites, Moses' threat in verse 15 likely carried more weight: *"For the Lord your God is a jealous God among you, lest the anger of the Lord your God be aroused against you and destroy you from the face of the earth."* But how could God make an unconditional covenant with Abraham, while also threatening the nation of Israel with extinction? The answer is that the basis for God's covenant with Abraham (Gen. 12:1-3) was unconditional grace, while the covenant at Horeb with Abraham's descendants was conditional – blessing for obedience.

Hence, having reviewed the main tenets of God's covenant with Israel in the previous chapter, Moses is highlighting in this chapter its conditional nature. As J. N. Darby explains, if they wanted God's blessing in the Promised Land, their loyalty and obedience was mandatory:

> Obedience was the basis of a regular covenant; and God here, as we have seen, governs the people in the land of promise according to their responsibility, as a jealous God. Mercy, beyond law, only comes in in chapter 30. There had been mercy (chp. 10) in giving them back the law, and placing them under sparing mercy. Still, these chapters give us the great principles of God's government in the land; chapters 12-29 the terms of it.[152]

If the entire nation failed to honor Him, the Lord said, more than once, that He would start over with Moses and make a new nation. In reality, the Lord never intended to remove Israel from the earth (though He had justification to do so on several occasions). Rather, He wanted to refine His chosen people so He could commune with them and shower them with His love. This would make the Gentile nations jealous and they too would then seek to know Jehovah.

Refining and Reminding

The Lord's warning, then, was designed to show how much He longed for His people to be faithful to Him in the Promised Land, so He could continue to bless and to honor them among the nations (vv. 16-19). Verse 16 is of special significance as the Lord Jesus quoted it when the devil told Him to cast Himself down from the pinnacle of the temple to prove He was the Son of God (Matt. 4:5-6). His perverted idea was that the angels would be forced to save the Messiah from harm based on Psalm 91:11-12. Satan's challenge, as William Kelly clarifies, is rooted in the denial of God's rule and His Word:

> Tempting God was to doubt Him, as many, all of us, are apt to do. Satan took advantage of the scripture that said that He should not dash His foot against a stone. He quotes accordingly Psalm 91, intimating to Jesus that, if He were the Son of God, all He had to do was to throw Himself from the pinnacle of the temple; and all must endorse His claims. Was not this a positive promise? God would "give His angels charge concerning Him"; and what a fine proof it would be that He was the true Messiah, if He threw Himself down from such a height, and withal the angels preserved Him! But Satan as usual tampered with the plain written word, alike with its letter and its spirit; for after "to keep Thee" he omitted "in all Thy ways." This he tried to conceal from One, all whose ways were obedience, venturing to insinuate what a noble demonstration of His Messiahship it would be. And what was the Lord's answer? "Thou shalt not tempt Jehovah thy God." The true Israelite does not need to put God to the test.[153]

Although Satan misquoted and misapplied Psalm 91, the Lord Jesus was not tricked; He simply quoted verse 16: *"You shall not tempt* (i.e., test by doubting) *the Lord your God."* The Lord's response showed that he was the Son of God, and that He did not need to respond to such rebellious inclinations from the creatures that He had created.

On the contrary, God would respond favorably to genuine devotion and faithful obedience. For that to happen, the Jews must be faithful to teach their children His Law and then also to obey it (vv. 20-24). If they did this, then they could have great confidence in the Lord to bless them: *"Then it will be righteousness for us, if we are careful to observe all these commandments before the Lord our God, as He has commanded us"* (v. 25).

What application is there for us from this chapter? Christians are not to neglect the assembling of themselves in the local church; this is where the Word of God is to be administered (1 Cor. 14:22-31; Heb. 10:25). The Lord Jesus Christ has provided the Church with teachers and with the indwelling Holy Spirit to guide believers into a deeper understanding of divine truth. Christian parents must know the Lord and His Word to properly teach their children to know and love Him too. If we neglect this duty, the Lord will impose harsher methods to ensure that He is known by our children! Children must be trained up for the Lord. Thus, the Bible should never be neglected in the home, but rather should be the rulebook for all family matters.

A Christian family is not a household of Christians, but a Christian household. It is more than Christ dwelling within the hearts of family members; it is a family that is pursuing the heart of God. If the Bible is not at the center of family life and all home affairs, that home cannot be called a true Christian home.

Untrained children, not surprisingly, remain foolish (Prov. 22:15) and predictably absorb from outside influences what seems appropriate to fill their void of understanding. Children are natural sponges – they are compelled to learn and to develop an understanding of the world in which they live. The next generation in Israel did not know God, so they embraced false gods, and God had to judge His covenant people. A bitter chastening resulted because the parents neglected to raise spiritual children.

Throughout Israel's history God repeatedly chastened His wayward people to awaken them to their deplorable spiritual condition and cause them to repent and return to the Lord through obedience. God Himself has always been the greatest threat to the prosperity of the Jewish people. Because He loves them, He cannot permit them to be ignorant of His Law or to rebel against it. This is a good reminder for us in the Church Age – without ongoing spiritual revival, all our great accomplishments can easily be negated by lethargic attitudes that will eventually result in moral decline.

Meditation

I need Thee every hour, most gracious Lord;
No tender voice like Thine can peace afford.
I need Thee every hour, stay Thou nearby;

Refining and Reminding

> Temptations lose their power when Thou art nigh.
> I need Thee every hour, in joy or pain;
> Come quickly and abide, or life is vain.
>
> — Annie S. Hawks

A Special Treasure
Deuteronomy 7

A Chosen People (vv. 1-10)

It was important to the Lord that His people not mingle with the pagan inhabitants of Canaan, the land He had given them for an inheritance. They were to drive them out or exterminate them, to ensure complete consecration to Him. There were a variety of people groups dwelling in Canaan at that time, but Moses named only the seven nations which were larger and mightier than Israel: *"the Hittites and the Girgashites and the Amorites and the Canaanites and the Perizzites and the Hivites and the Jebusites"* (v. 1). Four of these nations, the Hittites, the Girgashites, the Amorites, and the Jebusites, were descendants of Canaan, Noah's grandson through Ham (Gen. 10:15-16).

While many would consider it unethical to kill women and children, the judgment came down from the Lord, who judges all that He creates as He sees fit. Let us remember that women and children perished in Noah's flood too. These people groups were part of the human rebellion against God recorded in Genesis 10 and they had persisted against the Lord until that day and deserved to be punished (v. 10). Their iniquities had accumulated and surpassed God's merciful tolerance; there must now be the unyielding execution of divine judgment. If individuals in these people groups had repented as the Canaanite harlot Rahab did by submitting to God's will for their homeland and by seeking mercy, they too would have been spared death as she was (Josh. 2).

Jehovah wanted His people uncorrupted; therefore they were to have no covenants, no unions, no fellowship with the Canaanites of any kind, especially in marriage (vv. 3-4). This standard of purity and sanctification is upheld throughout Scripture; God's charge has always been to marry only within His people (1 Kgs. 11:4; Ezra 9; 1 Cor. 7:39). Moses sternly warns his countrymen not to provoke Jehovah to jealousy by bowing down to the pagan gods of Canaan, but rather to destroy or drive out the people from the land and then purge it of all heathen shrines, idols, and altars (v. 5).

The reason for such cleansing and consecration was that God had chosen the Jewish nation as a special treasure for Himself: *"For you are a holy people to the Lord your God; the Lord your God has chosen you to be a people for Himself, a special treasure above all the peoples on the face of the earth"* (v. 6). The Lord did not choose to set His love upon Israel because of the nation's size, might, or moral fineness. Rather, they were small, weak, and stiff-necked. In fact, they were a nation of slaves when God called them out of Egypt and instituted a covenant with them (vv. 7-8).

It was because God had chosen them as "sons of Jehovah" (14:1) that they had something more precious than their inheritance in Canaan – their relationship with One who, in love, would bestow on them an inheritance. Because they were sons of God, they would inherit the land. In a similar fashion, in the New Testament the Lord Jesus speaks of eternal life as being inherited by God's children (Matt. 19:29). This meaning was understood by those who were not yet God's children: *"Good Teacher, what shall I do that I may inherit eternal life?"* (Mark 10:17), and, *"A certain lawyer stood up and tested Him, saying, 'Teacher, what shall I do to inherit eternal life?'"* (Luke 10:25). The relationship with His children is for the satisfaction of God's own heart. The Lord Jesus explained that an individual becomes a child of God through experiencing spiritual rebirth after trusting in His gospel message:

> *But as many as received Him, to them He gave the right to become children of God, to those who believe in His name: who were born, not of blood, nor of the will of the flesh, nor of the will of man, but of God* (John 1:12-13).

In His sovereign foreknowledge, God foreknows who will be His sons inheriting eternal life in Christ (Rev. 17:8). It is mind-boggling to think that from eternity past, God has been considering how to best express the satisfaction of His own love to His children. One becomes a child of God through faith and it is only in faith that we can please the Lord (Heb. 11:6). Thus, the closing verses of Scripture proclaim this promise: *"He who overcomes shall inherit all things, and I will be his*

God and he shall be My son" (Rev. 21:7). The extraordinary part of this promise is not the inheritance received, but the reception of God's own affection in being treated like a dear son. Thus, "the land" and "eternal life" were gifts of God to His sons, but sonship itself is for the delight of God's own heart. Every child of God should be absolutely thrilled by the fact that God wants to lavish him or her with His love.

But the privilege of sonship comes with a responsibility. Christians are chosen in Christ to receive God's goodness, but it is not because of their personal righteousness that they receive God's favor. It is, however, because of their holy standing in Christ that they must be a holy people. For this reason, Paul admonishes the carnal believers at Corinth to consecrate themselves to the Lord:

> *Do not be unequally yoked together with unbelievers. For what fellowship has righteousness with lawlessness? And what communion has light with darkness? And what accord has Christ with Belial? Or what part has a believer with an unbeliever? And what agreement has the temple of God with idols? For you are the temple of the living God. As God has said: "I will dwell in them and walk among them. I will be their God, and they shall be My people." Therefore "Come out from among them and be separate, says the Lord"* (2 Cor. 6:14-17).

Likewise, being chosen and redeemed by God, the Jewish nation also received a holy standing before God that no other nation enjoyed. Such an unmerited position of favor demanded Israel's holiness to God. In his epistle to the believers at Rome, Paul addresses the privileges the Jewish nation had above all other nations by posing the question: *"Who are the Israelites?"* He then lists a number of unique privileges that the Jews had received, special revelations that the Gentiles were not given (Rom. 9:4-5):

- They were an adopted nation, a special people for God (Ex. 4:22; Deut. 7:6).

- They witnessed God's glory as connected with the tabernacle and later with the temple (Ex. 40:35).

- God made certain covenants with Israel which He will honor.

Refining and Reminding

- God gave the Jews the Mosaic Law (Ex. 19:5, 31:13).

- They were given a special service towards God: to worship Him at the tabernacle/temple (Ex. 19:6).

- God made specific promises to Jewish individuals and the Jewish nation (Josh. 1:2).

- They had patriarchs: Abraham, Isaac, Jacob, etc.

- They were given Christ as their Messiah (2 Cor. 5:16).

God chose Israel to be a testimony for Him among the nations (Ps. 67:1-7), but the Jews failed miserably (Rom. 2:24). Yet, Moses' message at this juncture is purely exhortative in nature, as it precedes their failure:

Therefore know that the Lord your God, He is God, the faithful God who keeps covenant and mercy for a thousand generations with those who love Him and keep His commandments; and He repays those who hate Him to their face, to destroy them. He will not be slack with him who hates Him; He will repay him to his face. Therefore you shall keep the commandment, the statutes, and the judgments which I command you today, to observe them (vv. 9-11).

Moses wanted Israel to understand that because the One true God had created, chosen, and redeemed them, He alone was in control of their future. Only the One true God could faithfully keep His promises for *"a thousand generations"* – an idiom for "forever." Additionally, Moses wanted to affirm that Israel would be continually blessed by God in Canaan if they continued to obey His commandments.

Verses 9-10 closely parallel the message of John 3:36 in the New Testament: *"He who believes in the Son has everlasting life; and he who does not believe the Son shall not see life, but the wrath of God abides on him."* Commenting on the text while contemplating John 3:36, C. H. Mackintosh writes:

John 3:36 not only sets forth the great truth that all who believe in the Son of God are the privileged possessors of eternal life, but it also cuts up by the roots two leading heresies of the day, namely, universalism and annihilationism. The universalist professes to believe that, ultimately, all shall be restored and blessed. Not so, says

Devotions in Deuteronomy

our passage; for those who obey not the Son, "shall not see life." The annihilationist professes to believe that all who are out of Christ shall perish like the beasts. Not so, for "the wrath of God *abides*" upon the disobedient. Abiding wrath and annihilation are wholly incompatible. It is utterly impossible to reconcile them.[154]

Verse 9 is a great comfort to the lovers of God, but verse 10 is a solemn reminder that God will deal face to face with those who hate Him! Rebellion against God carries a high price tag, as the Canaanites were about to learn; however, in all ages, obedience to God's revealed truth always pleases Him and is rewarded!

Blessings for Obedience (vv. 12-26)

If the Israelites honored the covenant Jehovah made with their forefathers, then they would experience God's love and blessing in a number of ways (v. 12). They and their livestock would multiply and they would enjoy agricultural prosperity (v. 13). In fact, Israel would be so blessed that no Jew or any Jewish livestock would be barren (v. 14). Additionally, if they obeyed His covenant and His command to cleanse the land of paganism, Jehovah promised to remove illness from among them and to afflict those who hated them with diseases (vv. 15-16).

Their obedience should overrule any fear of overcoming the inhabitants of Canaan (v. 17). If anxious, they were to remember how Jehovah had devastated Egypt to gain their release and all the signs and wonders they had witnessed since that time (vv. 18-19). If they were faithful, *"the great and awesome God that was among them"* would send the hornet to drive out those Canaanites hiding within their inheritance (vv. 20-21). At Sinai, the Lord had promised to lead them into battle and to either vanquish or drive out the inhabitants of the land through supernatural wonders such as fear, panic and swarms of hornets (Ex. 23:27-28).

The Lord revealed not only how He would assist His people to rid the Promised Land of Canaanites, but also the timing of Israel's conquest: *"The Lord your God will drive out those nations before you little by little; you will be unable to destroy them at once, lest the beasts of the field become too numerous for you"* (v. 22).

In Joshua 13 we learn that seven years after this promise the land had been sufficiently conquered so that Joshua could divide it among the Jewish tribes. At that time, the Israelites had destroyed the cities

Refining and Reminding

throughout the land, but many Canaanites were hiding in rocky formations, caverns, and caves until the Israelites had passed and then they returned to their homes. Though conquered, the inhabitants were not completely removed. This was by design to prevent wild beasts from multiplying in the area and to keep the farmland from becoming overgrown during the years of conquest. This fulfilled the prophecy of Moses in verse 22.

If the Jews remained faithful to the cause, Jehovah promised to continue to help each tribe or clan destroy or drive out the remaining inhabitants from their possession (v. 23; Josh. 13:6). Their victory would be so conclusive that the names of the kings who fought against them would be quickly forgotten (v. 24).

The chapter concludes with another stern warning against idolatry (vv. 25-26). Not only were the Israelites to abhor the idols of the Canaanites, they were not even to covet the precious metals used to overlay or forge the images. From the Lord's perspective, all that was associated with paganism was accursed. Idols of gold and silver were to be destroyed in a hot fire, but the precious metals were not to be collected later.

The first city that the Israelites would conquer in Canaan was Jericho. Because it was the firstfruits of the land, so to speak, the Lord decreed that the entire city was accursed and was to be burned by fire. Just as the wave sheaf, the firstfruits of the harvest, is the Lord's portion, so the Lord claimed Jericho for Himself. Jericho represented all of the condemned in Canaan and the Israelites were warned not to pocket anything in that city – it was entirely the Lord's. Achan did not heed this warning and took some gold, silver, and a garment for himself (Josh. 7). Moses made it clear in verse 26 that if anyone stole that which had been "devoted" to the Lord, that man would become "devoted" or "accursed" himself, which meant he must be put to death. Achan, by stealing the accursed things, became accursed himself. His unchecked lusting destroyed him and his family.

There is no middle ground when it comes to loving the Lord; our misplaced affection offends Him. We, like the Israelites, should "utterly detest" and "utterly abhor" what God hates (v. 27). Lord, help us to loathe what You loathe, to yearn for what You appreciate, to seek You above all else, and to rest in Your promises!

Meditation

Like a river glorious is God's perfect peace,
Over all victorious in its bright increase:
Perfect, yet still flowing fuller every day;
Perfect, yet still growing deeper all the way.

Trusting in the Father, hearts are fully blest,
Finding, as he promised, perfect peace and rest.

Hidden in the hollow of His mighty hand,
Where no harm can follow, in His strength we stand.
We may trust Him fully all for us to do;
Those who trust Him wholly find Him wholly true.

— Frances R. Havergal

Refining and Reminding

Remember the Lord – Your God
Deuteronomy 8

The expression, *"the Lord your God,"* occurred fifteen times in the previous chapter and is found ten times in this chapter. In this section of his book, Moses is emphasizing not only the uniqueness of Israel's God, but that He has chosen Israel from among the nations to have an exclusive relationship with Him.

If the Israelites wanted the Lord's blessing in Canaan, they had to keep *"every commandment"* they had received (v. 1). No one could pick and choose what part of the Law they would obey. All that God commanded was required of them.

Moses then explained that God was using various wilderness experiences to test them: *"And you shall remember that the Lord your God led you all the way these forty years in the wilderness, to humble you and test you, to know what was in your heart, whether you would keep His commandments or not"* (v. 2). How refreshing it is to look back over the course we have traveled as pilgrims in this life to see the faithful and wise hand of God. The Lord has carefully managed tens of thousands of turns, tests, sorrows, failures, providential interjections, and successes to get us to where we are today. C. H. Mackintosh warns that we should never contaminate this delightful exercise of appreciating God's past faithfulness by thinking of our own progress and attainments, as if somehow these were accomplished without God's help.

> In short, self-occupation, in any of its multiplied phases, is most pernicious; it is, in so far as it is allowed to operate, the death-blow to fellowship. Anything that tends to bring self before the mind must be judged and refused, with stern decision; it brings in barrenness, darkness and feebleness. For a person to sit down to look back at his attainments or his doings is about as wretched an occupation as anyone could engage in. We may be sure it was not to any such thing as this that Moses exhorted the people when he charged them to

"Remember all the way by which the Lord their God had led them."[155]

Indeed, God had led His people through subsequent wilderness experiences to test them. Obviously, God already knew what was in their hearts and what they would do, but they did not know what they would do until tested. We never know how we will respond until we are challenged by a trial. A wilderness experience then reveals where we are spiritually – either strong in the Lord, or, deficient in faith, needing refining and growth. In this sense, as Arthur Pink surmises, a wilderness trial is beneficial to a believer:

> God's purpose in leading His people through the wilderness was (and is) not only that He might try and prove them (vv. 2-5), but that in the trial He might exhibit what He was for them in bearing with their failures and in supplying their need. The "wilderness," then, gives us not only a revelation of ourselves, but it also makes manifest the ways of God.[156]

Such were God's dealings with Israel during their forty-year wilderness experience. Each time God's cloud had guided the Israelites into adversity, His grace had been sufficient to overcome it. The number forty is used in Scripture to represent *probation* and *testing*, which explains its frequent occurrence. At times, God extended the nation of Israel's forty-year probationary periods to test or prove them: the Israelites were tested in the wilderness forty years (Deut. 8:2-5), then were delivered and had rest during the forty years that Othniel, Barak, and Gideon judged Israel (Judg. 3:11, 5:31, 8:28). They enjoyed dominion during the forty-year reigns of five kings: David, Solomon, Jeroboam, Jehoash, and Joash (2 Sam. 5:4; 1 Kgs. 11:42; 2 Kgs. 12:17, 12:1; 2 Chron. 24:1). Another demonstration of forty as the number of probation and testing is found in God's dealings with Nineveh – the prophet Jonah preached that, unless the inhabitants repented, God's judgment would fall on them in forty days (Jonah 3:4).

The forty days Moses spent on Mount Sinai served not only as an opportunity for him to receive the Law, but was also a time of testing for the Israelites: would they be faithful to their newly affirmed covenant with Jehovah? They failed the test, even fashioning and bowing down to a golden calf, and were judged. However, the second time Moses was before the Lord for forty days, the Israelites remained repentant and faithful. They patiently waited for Moses (the only one who could make intercession for them) to descend the mountain and tell them whether or not they had been forgiven.

The Bible also records occasions when individuals went forty days without food or drink through the supernatural care of God: Elijah during his wilderness experience (1 Kgs. 19:8), Moses before Jehovah on Mount Horeb (Ex. 34:28), and Christ during His testing in the wilderness (Matt. 4:2). How was this possible? God completely sustained each of them. On one occasion, the disciples observed that the Lord Jesus had not eaten for an extended period of time, and they encouraged Him to eat. He responded:

> *"I have food to eat of which you do not know." Therefore the disciples said to one another, "Has anyone brought Him anything to eat?" Jesus said to them, "My food is to do the will of Him who sent Me, and to finish His work"* (John 4:32-34).

From this and from the previous examples, it would seem that there are times in which God supernaturally sustains an individual's body for the purpose of accomplishing His work. The application for the believer is that doing God's will should be the primary objective of one's life and though the temporal elements of life such as food and drink are necessary, one should not be ruled by them.

This feature of spiritual life was what God wanted the Israelites to learn through their various wilderness experiences. He was testing and refining their faith by teaching them that they had to be completely dependent upon Him or they would perish:

> *So He humbled you, allowed you to hunger, and fed you with manna which you did not know nor did your fathers know, that He might make you know that man shall not live by bread alone; but man lives by every word that proceeds from the mouth of the Lord* (v. 3).

This was the aspiration of the Lord Jesus. He quoted this verse to expose Satan's test: *"Now when the tempter came to Him, he said, 'If You are the Son of God, command that these stones become bread'"* (Matt. 4:3). Though hungry after forty days of fasting, the Lord did not think so little of God's food, His word, that He would turn stones into loaves of bread to satisfy His hunger. Instead, He quoted verse 3 to demonstrate the power of God's Word to defeat Satan's attack. The outcome of this test was that the Lord Jesus was sustained in His hunger, God was glorified, and Satan was disgraced. We experience the same type of victory when we rest on the triumphant ground of Calvary and resist Satan's traps by upholding God's word in faith.

Moses said, *"You should know in your heart that as a man chastens his son, so the Lord your God chastens you"* (v. 5). The Israelites should have known that the previous forty years of wilderness trials were God's means of maturing them, just as parents chasten their children to correct sinful behavior or wrong bents. Plainly, Moses is underscoring the loving, perfecting work of God in the lives of His people in this chapter, and not their failures. C. A. Coates observes that there is no mention in this chapter of the ways of the people, nor a reference to their unbelief or their murmurings:

> The chastening ways of God are the subject; "all the way" is viewed as the leading of Jehovah. The whole of the "forty years in the wilderness" has been divine leading, divine chastening, divine education. We have all had to feel that God's ways with us have been of a humbling character. *"To humble thee"* (verse 2); *"and he humbled thee"* (verse 3); *"that he might humble thee"* (verse 16). We may have been inclined to regard such experiences as being largely wasted time. But in the outlook of this chapter not a day of it has been wasted. There has not been a single unnecessary encampment; not a spot nor a step that we can afford to forget. There has been something of spiritual and abiding value in it all. None of it is to be forgotten in the land.[157]

Despite all their failings, God had been completely faithful to them – He had proven His love again and again. Besides refining them morally and spiritually, He had provided food and water for them, and even their garments and sandals had not worn out (v. 4).

When in human history could men testify that their clothing and shoes had lasted forty years? This was daily proof of God's presence among them, for only He could cause such a miracle. Yet the chastening mentioned in verse 5 may have dulled the Israelites' recognition of the miracle recorded in verse 4. However, F. B. Hole reminds us that we should never view God's chastening in such a way to negate the good that He does, for God chastens those He loves only to make them better:

Refining and Reminding

But even this chastening came upon them because they were a people brought into relationship with God. Men chasten their own sons and not others. This is exactly the principle applied to ourselves in Hebrews 12. So the word is, *"If ye endure chastening, God deals with you as sons, for what son is he whom the Father chastens not?"* We are further told that though no chastening is a joyful matter, it afterwards yields *"the peaceable fruit of righteousness to them which are exercised thereby."*[158]

God's correction is a proof of His love towards us and of His desire that we become more like the Lord Jesus Christ than we are now (Rom. 8:29). The Israelites had learned firsthand the painful consequences of disobedience. The Lord preferred that His people be obedient; then He would not need to discipline them.

After the Israelites had crossed the Jordan and the men of the nation had been circumcised at Gilgal, God would "roll away" (which is the meaning of "Gilgal") the reproach and shame of bygone days and would begin afresh with His people. The Lord wanted to bless them in Canaan, but they had to remain devoted to Him: *"Therefore you shall keep the commandments of the Lord your God, to walk in His ways and to fear Him"* (v. 6). If they did, the Lord promised them agricultural prosperity in a land both well-watered and full of metal deposits (vv. 7-10). Both iron and copper are mentioned in verse 9 and deposits of both metals and of gold have been discovered in the hills south of the Dead Sea.[159]

Then Moses warned them not to let their privileged circumstances in Canaan cause them to neglect their devotion to Jehovah (v. 11). This might occur for two reasons. First, it is our human tendency to call on the Lord when we are distressed and in need, but then to neglect Him when all is well again. Moses exhorts his countrymen to beware when they are full in the land, that they not forget the Lord (vv. 12-13).

Second, once the Israelites were experiencing God's wonderful blessings for them in Canaan, they should not be proud, saying, *"my power and the might of my hand have gained me this wealth"* (v. 17). Rather, they should remember where they were before Jehovah intervened on their behalf – they were slaves in Egypt (vv. 15-16). Not only had the Lord supplied all their needs since their exodus, He had also protected them in the wilderness from attack and even from *"fiery serpents and scorpions."*

In summary, all that the Israelites now had was given to them by a faithful God who had sustained them so they could receive even more – there was nothing for them to be proud about. Rather, Moses exhorts them to *"remember the Lord your God, for it is He who gives you power to get wealth"* (v. 18).

Paul reiterates this truth to the believers at Corinth: *"What do you have that you did not receive? Now if you did indeed receive it, why do you boast as if you had not received it?"* (1 Cor. 4:7). Instead of being puffed up about our affluence and accomplishments, we too should remember from where we came. We were children of the devil, on the road to eternal destruction, when God intervened with grace and mercy to bestow on us salvation and all spiritual blessings in heavenly places in Christ. We have nothing to boast about (Eph. 2:1-4)!

Let us be careful not to hold dear what we have, what we are doing, or what we have done; God could blow it all away with one puff (Hag. 1:9). Our security and our prosperity are in Him alone, not in the relationships we establish, nor in our accomplishments, in our stockpiled resources, and definitely not in the organizations to which we belong.

Moses concludes the chapter by summarizing Israel's two options for the future – to be faithful to the Lord and so to prosper, or to forget Him and so to perish (vv. 19-20). If Israel departed from Him to honor the idols of the land, He promised to destroy them just as He had vanquished the nations opposing them in the Plains of Moab. Jehovah was a jealous God and He would not tolerate in His people misplaced affections or pride – they were His alone and He wanted them for Himself. The same is true today!

Meditation

> There with what joy reviewing
> Past conflicts, dangers, fears,
> Thy hand our foes subduing,
> And drying all our tears.
>
> Our hearts with rapture burning,
> The path we shall retrace.
> Where now our souls are learning
> The riches of Thy grace.

— C.H.M.

Beware of Self-Righteousness
Deuteronomy 9

In the previous chapter, Moses warned the Israelites not to forget the Lord when they were living prosperously in Canaan. In this chapter, he warns the people three times not to attribute their achievements in Canaan to their own self-righteousness. God would give them the land because of His covenant with their forefathers and to punish the wicked inhabitants of the land.

Thirty-nine years earlier the Israelites were shocked by the Canaan reconnaissance report delivered by the twelve spies. Moses did not want the people to be dismayed again by the immensity of the task before them. It was important that they neither underestimate Canaan's military strength nor be paralyzed with fear because of it. From a tactical standpoint, Canaan's fortifications, vast armies, and giants could not be overcome by sheer determination (vv. 1-2). The Israelites needed to realize that it was impossible to conquer Canaan on their own. The only solution was for the Lord their God to go before them as a consuming fire to wipe out the enemy (v. 3).

Ten of the spies Moses sent into Canaan were terrified by the size of the Anakim. Instead of stirring up trust in the Lord to invade Canaan, these men caused their countrymen to doubt God's ability to overcome the inhabitants of the land: *"Who can stand before the descendants of Anak?"* (v. 2). Moses wanted the Israelites to know the answer to this question: "We can, when Jehovah fights for us!" Without the Lord, the Jews were helpless, but with the Lord even the giants would fall before them. This meant that any victories in Canaan were the Lord's and that all boasting should then be in Him.

Paul applies this principle to the ministry of believers in the Church Age: *"So then neither he who plants is anything, nor he who waters, but God who gives the increase"* (1 Cor. 3:7). It is natural for us to boast of our accomplishments, but this is not profitable for eternity. May we remember the lesson that the Israelites came to appreciate: if the Lord is not in the work, we are wasting our time and our resources! Conversely, when we are in the will and strength of God, we *"can do all things through Christ"* (Phil. 4:13).

Moses is presenting two ways of looking at our difficulties. We may anxiously adopt a human vantage point and be crippled by a spirit of unbelief, or we may calmly look at them from a heavenly perspective by faith and enjoy confidence in the living God. We have an example of the former in the report of the ten spies and of the latter in Moses' affirmation of God's faithfulness in this chapter. It was important that the Israelites adopt this perspective before crossing the Jordan.

Moses did not want them to be hindered by fear, but neither did he want them to later think that they had seized Canaan by their own might. His warning in verse 4 is one that all believers should heed, for, as C. H. Mackintosh explains, there is a moral danger that can arise in our hearts in every victorious circumstance:

> There is the danger of self-congratulation – a terrible snare to us poor mortals. In the hour of conflict, we feel our weakness, our nothingness, our need. This is good and morally safe. It is well to be brought down to the very bottom of self and all that pertains to it, for there we find God, in all the fullness and blessedness of what He is, and this is sure and certain victory and consequent praise. But our treacherous and deceitful hearts are prone to forget whence the strength and victory come. Hence the moral force, value and seasonableness of the following admonitory words addressed by the faithful minister of God to the hearts and consciences of his brethren, *"Speak not thou in thine heart"* – here is where the mischief always begins – *"after that the Lord has cast them out from before thee, saying, For my righteousness the Lord has brought me in to possess this land; but for the wickedness of those nations the Lord doth drive them out from before thee."*[160]

Having warned them of self-exaltation, Moses supplies two reasons the Israelites would conquer the inhabitants of Canaan (vv. 5-6). First, God had promised the land to their forefathers and He would honor His word. Second, He would use the Israelites to punish the wicked inhabitants of the land. The conclusion was obvious: *"Therefore understand that the Lord your God is not giving you this good land to possess because of your righteousness, for you are a stiff-necked people"* (v. 6). Though they enjoyed a righteous standing before God through redemption, they were not a righteous people in behavior. In fact, Moses told them, *"From the day that you departed from the land of Egypt until you came to this place, you have been rebellious against the Lord"* (v. 7).

The main emphasis of this chapter, thus far, is to ensure that the Israelites not think too highly of themselves or their accomplishments – they did not deserve God's favor and they could do nothing in Canaan without Him! If the Israelites remained humble, then God would strengthen His people against their mighty adversaries. It is for this reason that Moses reminds them of their past rebellious nature.

To further punctuate his warning not to provoke the Lord to wrath, Moses recounts Israel's failure at Horeb thirty-nine years earlier – the golden calf incident (v. 8). *"At that time"* in verse 8 refers to *"at that time"* (i.e., at Mount Horeb) in verses 1-6. Through this connection, Moses was showing that the tribe of Levi had been chosen to minister to God while the nation was still at Sinai (as an outcome of the failure he was discussing).

Just prior to this failure, Moses was alone with God on the mount for forty days to receive the Law. During that time he did not eat or drink anything (v. 9). Moses noted that God wrote His statutes in two stone tablets with His own finger. Moses was to give the tablets to Israel so they would not forget His commandments (vv. 10-11).

Regrettably, while Moses was with God on the mount, the Israelites below were dancing naked around a golden calf that Aaron had fashioned (v. 13). God was ready to destroy both them and Aaron for this offense and then to make a new nation out of Moses (vv. 14-15). Moses quickly descended the mount with the stone tablets in hand and broke them before the eyes of the people to illustrate that they had willfully broken God's Law and provoked Him to wrath (vv. 16-17). Moses vividly recalls that dark day in Israel's history so as to warn a new generation of Israelites of God's holiness:

> *And I fell down before the Lord, as at the first, forty days and forty nights; I neither ate bread nor drank water, because of all your sin which you committed in doing wickedly in the sight of the Lord, to provoke Him to anger. For I was afraid of the anger and hot displeasure with which the Lord was angry with you, to destroy you. But the Lord listened to me at that time also. And the Lord was very angry with Aaron and would have destroyed him; so I prayed for*

> *Aaron also at the same time. Then I took your sin, the calf which you had made, and burned it with fire and crushed it and ground it very small, until it was as fine as dust; and I threw its dust into the brook that descended from the mountain* (vv. 18-22).

> *Thus I prostrated myself before the Lord; forty days and forty nights I kept prostrating myself, because the Lord had said He would destroy you. Therefore I prayed to the Lord, and said: "O Lord God, do not destroy Your people and Your inheritance whom You have redeemed through Your greatness, whom You have brought out of Egypt with a mighty hand. Remember Your servants, Abraham, Isaac, and Jacob; do not look on the stubbornness of this people, or on their wickedness or their sin, lest the land from which You brought us should say, 'Because the Lord was not able to bring them to the land which He promised them, and because He hated them, He has brought them out to kill them in the wilderness.' Yet they are Your people and Your inheritance, whom You brought out by Your mighty power and by Your outstretched arm"* (vv. 25-29).

Moses faithfully interceded for his people, and God punished those guilty of idolatry that day, but spared Aaron and the nation from destruction. Intercession for those in sin is hard work; Moses fasted and prostrated himself for forty days before the Lord while pleading for mercy for the Israelites. He called God's attention to His promises to the patriarchs and to how He would be vilified by the local pagans if He destroyed His people in the wilderness. Moses did not plead for Israel on their own merit, for clearly they deserved to perish, but rather he reminded the Lord that Israel was His own inheritance by covenant.

God's intention all along was to show mercy, but a holy God cannot wink at sin; it must be identified and punished. Because of Moses' intercession, the Israelites did receive Jehovah's forgiveness, but their sin cost them dearly – thousands of Israelites died by the sword and by pestilence.

To further substantiate his claim in verse 7 that they were a rebellious people, Moses adds to the Horeb example just noted other instances of insurrection at Taberah, Massah, Kibroth Hattaavah, and Kadesh-Barnea. The latter case occurred when they refused to possess the land God had given them (vv. 22-23). Having stated the facts, Moses concludes: *"You have been rebellious against the Lord from the day that I knew you"* (v. 24). Moses had endured forty years of their defiant attitudes, which meant the Lord had too!

Refining and Reminding

The key point of this chapter is that the Israelites should remember from where they came, their past failures, the daunting task ahead, and all that they had and would have was provided by the Lord. They were not a righteous people deserving God's favor, nor were they strong enough to overthrow Canaan by themselves. They should never forget Moses' intercession to God on their behalf: *"They are Your people and Your inheritance, whom You brought out by Your mighty power and by Your outstretched arm"* (v. 29).

Likewise, let us not be carried away by our imaginations into unprofitable activities or attitudes that rob glory from the Lord Jesus Christ: *"But 'he who glories, let him glory in the Lord.' For not he who commends himself is approved, but whom the Lord commends"* (2 Cor. 10:17-18). We are spectators and recipients of God's glory, not instigators or facilitators of it. Paul reminds us of what we were when God intervened to save us through Christ:

> *But God, who is rich in mercy, because of His great love with which He loved us, even when we were dead in trespasses, made us alive together with Christ (by grace you have been saved), and raised us up together, and made us sit together in the heavenly places in Christ Jesus, that in the ages to come He might show the exceeding riches of His grace in His kindness toward us in Christ Jesus. For by grace you have been saved through faith, and that not of yourselves; it is the gift of God, not of works, lest anyone should boast* (Eph. 2:4-9).

We were all vile and condemned sinners destined for the Lake of Fire and undeserving of God's mercy. Like Israel, we should remember who we were and from where we came. We have nothing to brag about; any good we do is what the Lord accomplishes in us. So we can agree with Moses: only what God does to exalt His great name matters in eternity, and frankly, He is quite able to do what He will do without our help!

Meditation

> Almighty God, whose only Son over sin and death the triumph won,
> And ever lives to intercede for souls who of God's sweet mercy need.
> O give repentance true and deep to all Thy lost and wandering sheep,
> And kindle in their hearts the fire of holy love and pure desire.
>
> — Samuel Webbe, Sr.

New Tablets
Deuteronomy 10

The outcome of Moses' intercession of the previous chapter was that he was to hew two new stone tablets, like the previous ones, and return to the mount. We might wonder why Moses recounts again what transpired during his second forty-day stint on Horeb, since it is thoroughly recorded in Exodus. However, C. H. Mackintosh asserts that the message of this chapter fills a niche in God's ongoing work to be accomplished in Israel:

> In Deuteronomy 10, the lawgiver holds up to the hearts of the people past scenes and circumstances in such a way as to rivet them upon the very tablets of the soul. He allows them to hear the conversation between Jehovah and himself; he tells them what took place during those mysterious forty days upon that cloud-capped mountain. He lets them hear Jehovah's reference to the broken tables — the apt and forcible expression of the utter worthlessness of man's covenant. For why were those tables broken? Because they had shamefully failed. Those shattered fragments told the humiliating tale of their hopeless ruin on the ground of the law. All was gone.[161]

Indeed, all was gone, because the previous covenant had been annulled by the Lord because Israel violated it, but thankfully, as a result of Moses' intercession, God was willing to reinstitute it (vv. 1-5; Ex. 24:3). God inscribed His laws for Israel (i.e., the Ten Commandments) on the new tablets that Moses brought with him. Moses also received revelation about the Ark of the Covenant that was to be constructed to store the stone tablets in (Ex. 25:10-16). After returning from the mount and constructing the Ark of the Covenant, Moses placed the tablets in the Ark (probably after the tabernacle was dedicated in chapter 40).

The reference to Aaron's death in verses 6-9 seems to be out of place as that did not occur for another thirty-eight years. Moses

Refining and Reminding

recorded in Numbers 20:28 that Aaron died on Mount Hor shortly after the Israelites left Kadesh, but before engaging the Canaanites from Arad and encircling Edom. Just prior to his death, Aaron was stripped of his priestly attire and it was put on his son Eleazar, Israel's new high priest. Moserah mentioned in verse 6 was likely the district Mount Hor was located in.

Moses alludes to this event in retrospect to show that the Lord did regard his prayer to spare Aaron's life at Horeb and to safeguard the priestly ministry of the tribe of Levi. The Levites had a threefold function: to bear the Ark of the Covenant on their shoulders, to stand before the Lord in the tabernacle and minister to Him, and to bless His name on behalf of the nation (v. 8). As the Lord was Levi's inheritance, the tribe would not receive a regional land allotment in Canaan, but rather would dwell in forty-eight cities dispersed among Israel's tribes (v. 9). This would ensure that God's word was readily available for those seeking counsel and that His Law would be known throughout the land.

Israel undoubtedly deserved God's wrath for their failure at Horeb, but Moses reminds his countrymen that he had fasted and interceded before the Lord for forty days on their behalf. Moses did not mention this fact a second time to call attention to his mediatorship, but to highlight the perilous situation the nation was in because of their blatant disregard for the first two of the Ten Commandments. Israel should remember this near-catastrophe and avoid idolatry in the future. While Moses was on the mount, the Lord agreed to preserve the Jewish nation and to lead Israel into their inheritance in Canaan (vv. 10-11).

In the last two chapters, Moses has conclusively shown that it was impossible for Israel to conquer Canaan on their own and that their rebellious disposition deserved God's wrath, not His blessing. Despite this, God was willing to shower His people with love, mercy, and blessing if they would be devoted to Him going forward. In other words, being wholly committed to the Lord was the only way Israel could overcome the Canaanites and receive their inheritance:

> *And now, Israel, what does the Lord your God require of you, but to fear the Lord your God, to walk in all His ways and to love Him, to serve the Lord your God with all your heart and with all your soul, and to keep the commandments of the Lord and His statutes which I command you today for your good?* (vv. 13-14).

"What does the Lord your God require of you?" is a noteworthy question given the Mosaic Law commanded the people to do many things. Obviously, there was something else besides obedience that God desired from His people. Fear of consequences may cause people to do what they know they should, but as Albert Barnes surmises, the Lord longs for something more – the willing submission of His people as motivated by love for Him:

> The external observances of the Law, if need be, can be enforced. But love and veneration cannot be enforced, even by God Himself. They must be spontaneous. Hence, even under the law of ordinances where so much was emphatically laid down, and omnipotence was ready to compel obedience, those sentiments, which are the spirit and life of the whole, have to be, as they here are, invited and solicited.[162]

Because Jehovah had initiated a special relationship with Israel, and with no other people group, Israel should be inspired to return His love. Although love is shown through obedience, God's deepest desire is for His children to understand that *"he who loves another has fulfilled the law. ... Love does no harm to a neighbor; therefore love is the fulfillment of the law"* (Rom. 13:8, 10). Not stealing from a neighbor was keeping the Law, but selflessly giving to that neighbor was fulfilling the Law. God's desire is that His people not be constrained from doing good, because they are focused only on not doing what is bad. God is a God of love and He wants His children to freely express what they have experienced in Him. William MacDonald suggests that verses 12-13 summarize exactly what God wanted from His people: "to fear…to walk…to love…to serve…to keep."[163]

If the Israelites would truly dedicate themselves to the Lord, He would enable them to seize Canaan as their own possession. As Creator, Canaan was His to give to whomever He chose: *"Indeed heaven and the highest heavens belong to the Lord your God, also the earth with all that is in it"* (vv. 14-15). It was God's desire to bestow whatever was necessary to ensure Israel prospered in the Promised Land and was a witness for Him to the nations. However, because God owns everything, He could also dispossess them of their stewardship at any time if they became unfaithful.

Although they were a rebellious people deserving condemnation, God found a way of righteously forgiving them and showering them with mercy and grace – they should never get over that fact! Centuries later, God would judge His own Son for their offenses to appease His judicial anger over their sin (Rom. 3:25). Hence, their very election demanded circumcised hearts, meaning that they should *"be stiff-necked no longer"* (v. 16). The Lord required male circumcision of 99-year-old Abraham as His sign to Abraham of His covenant with him and his descendants (Gen. 17:1-14). So Abraham and all the males of his house were circumcised the very day God had commanded it (Gen. 17:26-27). Then, his descendants for thousands of years would continue this symbolic ritual to honor God and to acknowledge His covenant with them. Paul tells us in Romans 4:11 that circumcision was *"a seal of the righteousness of the faith which he had while still uncircumcised."* Circumcision was a "token" of Abraham's righteous standing gained by faith in God's promise.

Why was male circumcision given as a sign? By stripping away the foreskin from the organ that best identified an individual as a man, God was symbolizing the stripping away of an old identity and the reliance on God for a new one. The act of circumcision in Genesis 17 complements beautifully the name changes given Abram and Sarai. God was about to enact His covenant with them by giving them a son. It was only fitting that they realize their new identity as God's chosen people and as human instruments to bless the entire world. Abraham was already declared just by God before circumcision was instituted (Rom. 4:11). The "circumcised life" was something Abraham was living before God.

It is the same for the believer today. When sinners humble themselves before God and confess their need for a Savior, God responds by cleansing and regenerating them (Tit. 3:5), sealing them with the Holy Spirit (Eph. 1:13), and declaring them righteous (imputing divine righteousness to their account – Rom. 4:4-5; 2 Cor. 5:21). *"If anyone is in Christ, he is a new creation; old things have passed away; behold, all things have become new"* (2 Cor. 5:17). However, our new identity in Christ demands that we live the "circumcised life," which is the "cutting off" or "putting to death" of the desires and the will of our flesh. Paul summarizes in Romans 2:29 that it is the circumcision of the heart God wants in a believer's life, not just an outward show. This is what Moses meant when he commanded Israel (men and women) to *"circumcise the foreskin of your heart."*

In one sense, the act of *circumcision* for the Old Testament Jew is similar to the act of a New Testament Christian who follows in *believer's baptism* – water baptism. A circumcised life is one that acknowledges being dead to self and alive in Christ. In this sense physical circumcision and water baptism are alike. Yet, the similarity breaks down when comparing the fuller dispensational truth of Scripture. Under the Law, parents circumcised their baby boys without their consent, whereas believer's baptism in the Church Age was *always* after people believed the gospel message (Acts 10:47, 16:31-34).

Moses then exalts God and upholds His character as the pattern of the circumcised life to be exemplified in the Promised Land by Israel:

> *For the Lord your God is God of gods and Lord of lords, the great God, mighty and awesome, who shows no partiality nor takes a bribe. He administers justice for the fatherless and the widow, and loves the stranger, giving him food and clothing* (vv. 17-18).

Accordingly, by their actions, the Israelites were to reflect to the nations God's righteous and gracious character. To show reverence and awe for Jehovah, they were to be faithful to vows in His name, be hospitable to strangers, and to uphold justice in the land (vv. 19-20). Interestingly, "the fatherless" and the "widow" are each mentioned eleven times and "the stranger" twenty-four times in Deuteronomy. No other book in the Bible has as many references to these. This indicates how God would have His people enjoy all that His love had purposed to confer to them, that is, by demonstrating His own gracious character through practical acts of love. John put the matter this way: *"We love because He first loved us"* (1 Jn. 4:19). God's love was never meant to be hoarded by ill-will or carnal attitudes, but rather to be circulated by those who are joyfully experiencing it.

To further exalt the Lord and provoke their devotion, Moses reminds them that when Jacob came to Egypt, they numbered only seventy men, but since that time God had multiplied them into a great nation (v. 22). Therefore, having witnessed the Lord's awesome work of creating, sustaining and refining the Jewish nation to bring them to the brink of the Promised Land, they should agree with Moses: *"He is your praise, and He is your God"* (v. 21).

Refining and Reminding

Truly Jehovah is the *"God of gods and Lord of lords, the great God, mighty and awesome"*! And thankfully, He is our praise and our God too. May our hearts be bound to the Lord Himself, for who He is and because of His wondrous ways, mighty acts, and proven faithfulness.

Meditation

> Cast thy burden on the Lord,
> Only lean upon His Word;
> Thou wilt soon have cause to bless
> His eternal faithfulness.
>
> He sustains thee by His hand,
> He enables thee to stand;
> Those whom Jesus once hath loved
> From His grace are never moved.
>
> Human counsels come to naught;
> That shall stand which God hath brought;
> His compassion, love, and power,
> Are the same forevermore.
>
> — Rowland Hill

The Rewards of Love
Deuteronomy 11

In this chapter, Moses again underscores the inseparable connection between devoted love and willing obedience. Moses poses two reasons Israel should continue to love the Lord. First, His past faithfulness and mighty deeds on their behalf prove He is worthy of their piety (vv. 2-7). Second, they could not conquer Canaan and flourish there unless they were loyal to Jehovah (vv. 8-24). Verse 1 is a concise preface to the chapter – the Israelites would be wise to show their love for Jehovah by obeying His Law.

God Is Worthy of Your Love (vv. 2-7)

Moses addresses the generation who had witnessed Israel's miraculous exodus from Egypt and experienced God's superb care in the wilderness. The older generation was now gone, and many in the middle generation had also perished in the wilderness because of insurrection. Parents who had seen the wonders of the past and had survived and benefitted from the Lord's chastening in the wilderness are reminded of the importance of teaching their children what they had learned (v. 2). This included setting them a good example of compliance.

Israel's entire history in Egypt and their forty-year wilderness journey were God's training program to reveal His majesty to His people and to refine them morally and spiritually (vv. 3-7). They had witnessed God's wrath on Egypt, the opening of the Red Sea, and many life-sustaining miracles. Additionally, they had been taught, corrected, rebuked, and punished throughout their desert wanderings. The purpose of their past school days was to cause them to revere and to love the Lord their God. What better heritage could they pass down to their children!

Refining and Reminding

To Be Sustained You Must Love (vv. 8-24)

Verses 8-9 summarize Moses' main point in this section: Israel's days in Canaan would be prolonged only if they obeyed all of Jehovah's commandments. They would *"be strong"* only if they kept *"every commandment"* (v. 8). Such unreserved obedience would be possible only if motivated by love – inward affection would be outwardly displayed through willing submission to God. Moses promised that God would sustain them in Canaan, a fertile, well-watered land, flowing with milk and honey, if they remained loyal to Him (vv. 10-12).

But such blessing was contingent on the "if-then" clause in verse 13: *"And it shall be that if you earnestly obey My commandments which I command you today, to love the Lord your God and serve Him with all your heart and with all your soul, then...."* Egypt was a barren land that required irrigation to grow crops, but the Lord promised to reward Israel's obedience by providing abundant rain and plentiful harvests in the Promised Land (vv. 14-15). If their love for the Lord grew cold or if they decided to serve and worship other gods, then He promised to smite them with lingering drought so that they would perish in the good land that the Lord had given them (vv. 16-18).

To obtain God's blessing in Canaan, His Word was to be loved and lived out by His people: *"Therefore you shall lay up these words of Mine in your heart and in your soul, and bind them as a sign on your hand, and they shall be as frontlets between your eyes"* (v. 18). This meant that Scripture had to be taught regularly in the home as a guide to the daily affairs of life (v. 19). Jews would later traditionalize the meaning of this passage by the wearing of small pouches with portions of Scripture on their foreheads or hanging them in the entryway to their homes (v. 20). However, the Lord is expressing His desire that His Word would so saturate the minds of His people that it would guide all their thinking and actions. Those controlled by God's Word will reap His richest blessings. For Israel, this would mean permanence in the land, comparable to the days of the heavens above the earth (v. 21).

In verse 22, Moses transitions his focus from how to maintain fruitful longevity in Canaan to the task at hand – conquering Canaan. Both aspects of Israel's future depended upon their faithfulness to Jehovah as demonstrated through obedience. If Israel would hold fast to the Lord, He promised to drive out the inhabitants of Canaan and give them the land for inheritance (vv. 23-24). The Lord vowed that *"no man shall be able to stand against you; the Lord your God will put the dread of you and the fear of you upon all the land where you tread"* (v. 25). The two men Joshua sent into Canaan to spy out Jericho would later confirm that the Lord had honored this promise.

The Lord directed the two spies to the house of a harlot named Rahab. She told the spies, *"we have heard"* the stories of how the Israelites were delivered from Egypt, and how Jehovah had parted the Red Sea (Josh. 2:9-10). She too had learned of their victories over the Amorites on the eastern side of the Jordan. In fact, this information was common knowledge among her people, and had put them in fear and trepidation as they waited for the coming invasion (Josh. 2:11). But unlike the other inhabitants of Jericho who were fortifying themselves against Israel and rejecting God's will for Canaan, Rahab was willing to yield and to beg for mercy. She expressed her faith to the spies by the words *"I know"* and by hiding them from Jericho's king (Josh. 2:9). The two spies gladly granted her request for asylum.

After returning to Joshua, the spies relayed all that had happened to them in Jericho, including their pledge to Rahab. Thirty-nine years earlier, ten of the twelve spies Moses sent to explore the land had exhibited a lack of faith, stating: *"We are not able to go up against the people, for they are stronger than we"* (Num. 13:31). Perhaps Joshua's two spies remembered this, and the fate of the men who delivered the evil report. At any rate, their own account was very different: *"Truly the Lord has delivered all the land into our hands, for indeed all the inhabitants of the country are fainthearted because of us"* (Josh. 2:24). The message rallied the Israelites to invade Canaan, and early the very next morning Joshua moved their encampment to the edge of the Jordan River just across from Jericho. Clearly, God was keeping His pledge to strike the inhabitants of the land with terror and this inspired Israel to faithfully go on with the Lord into Canaan.

Blessings and Curses (vv. 26-32)

Verses 26-32 pose a fitting conclusion to the first section of Moses' second message that began back in chapter 5. Israel's departing leader emphasized again that Israel's future would be determined by their faithfulness to the Lord and obedience to His Law. He promised to bless them for obedience and curse them for waywardness:

Refining and Reminding

> *Behold, I set before you today a blessing and a curse: the blessing, if you obey the commandments of the Lord your God which I command you today; and the curse, if you do not obey the commandments of the Lord your God, but turn aside from the way which I command you today, to go after other gods which you have not known. Now it shall be, when the Lord your God has brought you into the land which you go to possess, that you shall put the blessing on Mount Gerizim and the curse on Mount Ebal* (vv. 26-29).

The book of Joshua records the nation's compliance to Moses' command (repeated again in 27:11-14). In fact, instead of securing the interior of Canaan after decimating Jericho, Ai and Bethel, Joshua led the Jewish nation on a spiritual pilgrimage. In obedience to the above command, all the Israelites (including women, children, and strangers) trekked north up the Jordan valley, then west, and finally southwest to a specific location between the mountains of Ebal and Gerizim. This was about a thirty-mile journey one-way. Shechem was situated in a high valley below these two mountains.

At this location, Joshua first set up great stones, plastered them together, and then chiseled the words of God's Law into the dried plaster (27:2-4, 8; Josh. 8:32). Second, Joshua erected an altar with stones which had not been modified by human instruments. He then sacrificed burnt offerings and peace offerings on this altar on behalf of the nation (v. 31; Deut. 27:5-6). Third, Joshua read *"all the words of this Law"* in the hearing of *"all the assembly of Israel"* (Josh. 8:35). Israel did renew their covenant with Jehovah that day as Moses commanded.

If the Jews wanted to commune with Jehovah and experience His love and power, they had to choose to continue in the covenant which governed their relationship with Him. If they did this, He promised to lead them into Canaan and give them the land for their inheritance (vv. 30-32). The reference to these mountains being near *"the terebinth trees of Moreh"* in verse 30 is likely an allusion to where Jacob, centuries earlier, purged his house of idols. The implication here is that Israel should follow the patriarch's example of consecration and avoid idolatry by clinging to Jehovah.

The irresistible love of God can be experienced only by answering His invitation to know Him through His revealed Word. Our understanding of God's plan and our commitment to live it out will be directly proportional to the extent that we have known and experienced

Him. The Lord Jesus said, *"He who has My commandments and keeps them, it is he who loves Me. And he who loves Me will be loved by My Father, and I will love him and manifest Myself to him"* (John 14:21). Continued submission to divine truth is the pathway to intimately experiencing and knowing God in deepening degrees. This is what Jehovah wanted for the Israelites and it is what the Lord Jesus wants for His Church today.

The Lord Jesus promised that if we obey His commandments, He will manifest Himself to us in deeper fellowship (John 14:21). In order to walk with the Lord, we must be in agreement with Him on the matter of sin. For, *"can two walk together except they be agreed?"* (Amos 3:3). Surely, light has no communion with darkness; thus, may each of us walk with God according to divine truth and in moral integrity. We read in 1 John 1:5-7 that walking with God requires walking in the light of divine truth. A willingness to walk according to revealed truth brings happy fellowship with God and with other believers. We must have light to walk safely. When we choose to walk in the dark, we are inviting injury – the chastening hand of God.

Before reiterating in the following chapters specific statutes to be obeyed, Moses wanted the Israelites to understand the inseparable connection between divine blessing and Israel's willing obedience. God would not force His people to obey Him to experience His goodness in the land, but He would certainly make sure they wished they had!

Meditation

> I find doing the will of God leaves me no time for disputing about His plans.
>
> — George MacDonald

> To know the will of God is the greatest knowledge, to find the will of God is the greatest discovery, and to do the will of God is the greatest achievement.
>
> — George W. Truett

Only One Sanctuary
Deuteronomy 12

In chapters 5-11, Moses emphasized that Jehovah would enable Israel to conquer Canaan and that they would then enjoy prolonged days of blessing in the land, if they remained devoted to Him. The tie between Israel's love and obedience with God's favor and blessing was inseparable. In the second movement of Moses' ongoing oracle, he will review the religious life of Israel (Deut. 12-16) and various laws associated with Israel's covenant with Jehovah (Deut. 17-26). These statutes reflect what Israel must heed to be blessed in Canaan. Jack S. Deere summarizes Moses' intentions in this lengthy section:

> The decrees and laws that follow in this section of Moses' speech (12:2-26:15) were not meant to be exhaustive. Moses intentionally did not repeat many of the details and laws recorded in Exodus and Leviticus. ... Moses was setting a quality of living before the nation rather than an exhaustive law code that covered every detail of life. The specific laws in this section were given to help the people subordinate every area of their lives to the Lord, and to help them eradicate whatever might threaten that pure devotion.[164]

The Law of a Single Sanctuary (vv. 2-28)

The Canaanites had pagan shrines and altars to their gods throughout the land, especially in the high places and under spreading-trees (v. 2). The Israelites were to purge the Promised Land of all pagan worship centers and paraphernalia (v. 3). Not only would this remove the opportunity for idolatry in the future, but it would also prove that the Israelites did not regard the Canaanite deities as legitimate or threatening. In short, it proved that they feared the Lord their God more than all the false gods in Canaan.

This cleansing also included burning idols and wooden fertility symbols such as Asherah poles and sacred stones (v. 4). These sacred stones symbolized male reproductive organs, which honored Asherah's male counterpart – Baal. God demanded the Israelites totally prohibit paganism in the land: *"You shall not worship the Lord your God with such things"* (v. 4).

Not only were the Israelites not to worship God through any pagan articles or rituals, they were also to worship Jehovah in one particular location in the Promised Land that He would later reveal (v. 5). This would clearly determine what God considered idolatry in the land: any worship, tithes, sacrifices, feasts, etc. not demanded by the Law and at any location other than where God chose to place His name would invoke His wrath (vv. 6-7).

The location of centralized worship in Israel would ultimately be Jerusalem; however, in the days of Joshua, and for some time after, the tabernacle was pitched at Shiloh (Josh. 18:1). Later, David brought the Ark of the Covenant to Jerusalem and made a tabernacle for it (2 Sam. 6:17) and a few years later Solomon constructed a temple there. Moses was stressing that worship at any location other than at God's central sanctuary would be considered a departure from Him. In longsuffering mercy, God had tolerated certain irregularities during the wilderness years, but that would not continue once Israel was in Canaan (vv. 8-14). On this point, C. H. Mackintosh writes:

> Moses reminds the people that from the moment they entered Jehovah's land, there was to be an end to all the irregularity and self-will that had characterized them in the plains of Moab or in the wilderness. *"Ye shall not do after all the things that we do here this day, every man whatsoever is right in his own eyes"* (v. 8). … Thus, not only in the object, but also in the place and mode of Israel's worship, they were absolutely shut up to the commandment of Jehovah. Self-pleasing, self-choosing, self-will was to have an end, in reference to the worship of God, the moment they crossed the river of death. … Things might be allowed to pass in the wilderness which could not be tolerated in Canaan. The higher the range of privilege, the higher the responsibility and the standard of action.[165]

Notice that Moses does not say that what Israel did was wrong, but rather it was not acceptable. However, because it was not God's specified order, it was not right to Him. This troubling mentality has plagued the Church for centuries. Many rituals, dogmas, and traditions have been introduced into Christendom to amplify worship or to enhance service to God, but they ignore the simplicity of order and

Refining and Reminding

beauty of Church Truth embodied in the New Testament. As inspired by the Holy Spirit, the Apostles reveal mysterious truths concerning Christ's Church which we are to appreciate, and patterns and principles of conduct that we in the twenty-first century do well to heed.

Moses is underscoring the fact that God had "chosen" a place and a way for His people to abide with Him: *"There will be the place where the Lord your God chooses to make His name abide"* (v. 11). Israel could know and approach Him only by the way God had chosen. The Hebrew word *bachar,* meaning "to select," is rendered "chosen," "chooses," or "chose" in this section of Deuteronomy. *Bachar* is found 151 times in the Old Testament and twenty of those occurrences are in Deuteronomy 12-17, which is the highest concentration of the word in any comparable portion of Scripture in the Old Testament. Its usage accentuates God's sovereignty in securing glory for His name. C. A. Coates writes: *"'To set His name there.' His 'name' indicates the way in which God has made Himself known; He is in the light of revelation, and He must be approached accordingly; it could not be pleasurable to Him to be approached in any other way."*[166]

However, the one sanctuary location in Canaan made it necessary for Moses to modify the previous law which stated that all clean animals fit for sacrifice must be slaughtered at the tabernacle. While dwelling in the wilderness, this commandment was a practical one. First, it ensured no one would offer sacrifices to Jehovah anywhere other than the tabernacle and at any other's hand than a priest's. Second, if someone wanted to slaughter a clean animal for food, they would have to bring the animal to the tabernacle and offer it as a peace offering, which gave the priests a constant supply of meat.

Now, at the end of their forty-year pilgrimage in the wilderness, it was necessary to permit the slaughter of clean animals elsewhere besides the tabernacle if the animals were not to be offered as blood sacrifices to the Lord (vv. 10-13). Logistically speaking, this law had to be modified. How could a Jew in the northwest corner of Canaan bring a cow sixty miles to be slaughtered at the tabernacle; the meat would have little value by the time it was transported back to its origin. Encamped together the law was enforceable, but not when the tribes were spread throughout Canaan and the Transjordan.

To ensure clarity, Moses again stated that any activity related to Jehovah worship must occur at the location He would choose: *"There you shall bring all that I command you: your burnt offerings, your sacrifices, your tithes, the heave offerings of your hand, and all your choice offerings which you vow to the Lord"* (v. 11). Yet, clean animals not meant for sacrifice could be butchered, cooked, and eaten anywhere (v. 15). This was already permissible for game (such as deer and gazelle). Because such animals (clean or game) were not meant for sacrifice, the ceremonial laws of clean and unclean did not apply.

However, three stipulations did still apply to the modified law. First, no one was to eat the blood (v. 16). Second, any offering associated with a Levitical requirement must be brought to the one sanctuary. Verse 17 supplies a list of examples: *"You may not eat within your gates the tithe of your grain or your new wine or your oil, of the firstborn of your herd or your flock, of any of your offerings which you vow, of your freewill offerings, or of the heave offering of your hand."* Third, since the Levites would be living among the tribes in cities, they were to be provided for (vv. 18-19).

Paul told the believers at Philippi, *"For me to write the same things to you is not tedious, but for you it is safe"* (Phil. 3:1). Given the importance of what Moses has just stated (vv. 8-19), it is relevant that he repeat the stipulation of slaughter and that all prescribed religious activities must occur at the location Jehovah chooses to place His name (vv. 20-28). After reviewing the one sanctuary law for a second time Moses pleads again with his countrymen: *"Observe and obey all these words which I command you, that it may go well with you and your children after you forever, when you do what is good and right in the sight of the Lord your God"* (v. 28).

Paganism Prohibited (vv. 29-32)

For additional emphasis, Moses repeats the prohibition against all forms of paganism, as previously stated in verses 2-7. Idolatry by those who identify with the Lord is offensive to Him at any time, but even more so after having been showered with His lovingkindness. Moses was concerned that Israel, after experiencing God's powerful grace in conquering the land, might be tempted to not follow through with their part of the covenant in purging idols from the land (v. 29). They were not to let their curiosity tempt them to get ensnared with what God hated: *"How did these nations serve their gods? I also will do likewise"* (v. 30).

Regrettably believers often know that a particular activity is inherently foolish or sinful, but still dabble in it for the sake of

Refining and Reminding

understanding it better or to tease their carnal impulses without gratification. The former exercise usually leads to entanglement, while the latter just causes frustration. This kind of behavior is a bit like a mouse nibbling on a piece of the cheese in a trap. The bit of "cheese" you might get does not justify the risk of injury, nor the devastating consequences of being caught by what should have been avoided altogether. In effect, Moses is saying, "If you destroy the trap, you will not be tempted to go near it." It is wise to rid ourselves of what can only hurt us – we do not need to understand any more about it!

If Israel would purge Canaan of all pagans and all their idols, altars, shrines, etc., then there would be no opportunity to be tempted to engage in anything detestable that would provoke Jehovah's wrath (vv. 31-32). The Canaanite fertility rituals, for example, promoted fornication, which God hated. Children were God's reward to His people, so to offer one's children to false gods would be especially despicable.

This is why Leviticus 18:21 prohibited the idolatrous practice of placing one's firstborn child alive in the white-hot arms of the false god Molech as a burnt offering. Sadly, the curiosity about evil practices in the land eventually drew Israel into widespread idolatry. Jeremiah tells us that some Jews in his day (over eight centuries later) were sacrificing their children to Molech in this pagan ritual (Jer. 32:35).

Similarly, the prophet Hosea tells us that because Ephraim had engaged in Baal fertility rituals, God's people would suffer infertility (Hos. 9:10-11). The population growth that Israel sought through paganism would not occur. In fact, the prophet promised that many Jewish women would be barren and the fortunate few who did deliver children would watch many of them die in the coming Assyrian invasion (Hos. 9:12-14).

Knowing Israel's future disregard for God's Law in the Promised Land, and the terrible consequences that would follow, we can understand why Moses repeatedly reiterated the importance of obedience. For the same reason, Paul wants those in the Church Age to learn from their example: *"Now these things became our examples, to the intent that we should not lust after evil things as they also lusted. And do not become idolaters as were some of them"* (1 Cor. 10:6-7).

Dear believer, stay clear of anything that is foolish, bad, evil, or merely permissible that would draw you into the land of misery and away from the place where God has chosen to put His name. In the

Church Age, that means, remain in happy fellowship with Lord and His people. Believers are His temple (we abide in Him) and we are called after His name – "Christians" (or Christ-ones)!

Meditation

> I think what is a better thing than "thanksgiving" is "thanks-living." How is this to be done? By a general cheerfulness of manner, by an obedience to the command of Him by whose mercy we live, by a perpetual, constant delighting of ourselves in the Lord, and by a submission of our desires to His will.
>
> — Charles Spurgeon

Walking After the Lord
Deuteronomy 13

Having affirmed the one sanctuary law and a strict prohibition against paganism, Moses turns his attention to three corrupting influences that would tempt God's people into spiritual infidelity. These are false prophets (vv. 1-5), corrupt relatives (vv. 6-11), and anarchists promoting wholesale abandonment of Jehovah (vv. 12-18).

False Prophets (vv. 1-5)

Paul warned the elders at Ephesus that false teachers would secretly come among them as wolves to devour the flock (Acts 28:15-17). Similarly, Moses warns the Israelites that false prophets and dreamers of dreams would come among them with signs and fanciful messages to deceive them. God would permit this to happen in order to test their love for Him and their allegiance to His Law: *"You shall walk after the Lord your God and fear Him, and keep His commandments and obey His voice; you shall serve Him and hold fast to Him"* (v. 4).

Notice that the Israelites were to "walk after the Lord." After Abraham doubted and stumbled in his faith in Genesis 16, God admonished him to *walk before God* perfectly in Genesis 17. A walk "before" God can only be accomplished by walking in faith. In this chapter the Israelites were exhorted to *walk after God.* We also know that previously Enoch and Noah *walked with God.* In the New Testament, those receiving Christ are *to walk in Him* (Col. 2:6). Arthur Pink provides the following observation concerning the meaning of these various phrases:

> To walk *before* is suggestive of a child running ahead and playing in the presence of his father, conscious of his perfect *security* because he is just behind. To walk *after* becomes a servant following his master. To walk *with* indicates fellowship and friendship. To walk *in* denotes union. We might summarize these varied aspects of the believer's walk as intimated by the four different prepositions thus:

we walk **before** God as *children*; we walk **after** Him as *servants*; we walk **with** Him as His *friends*; we walk **in** Him as *members of His body*.[167]

Hence, what Moses is highlighting in verse 4 is Israel's total resolution to obey and serve the Lord – they must "walk after the Lord."

Moses then provides the criteria for spotting future false prophets who would test Israel's faithfulness. It is noteworthy that Moses did not deny that these supposed messengers of God would be able to work wonderful signs and may be able to correctly predict some events. Yet, such things did not validate the origin of the message; for this reason, Moses gave the people a standard for determining the authenticity of a prophet's message.

First, a miracle did not prove truth, as Satan is capable of accomplishing supernatural feats. The people already knew this from Moses' confrontation with Pharaoh and his magicians in Egypt. For instance, when Aaron cast Moses' rod upon the ground before Pharaoh, it turned into a serpent (Ex. 7). However, Pharaoh summoned his sorcerers, who also cast down rods before Aaron and Moses. The magicians' rods were transformed by enchantments into serpents also. As Satan cannot create life, it is likely that the pagan rods were some sort of demonic illusion, which appeared to be a miraculous sign.

This contest did not last long, for Moses' rod swallowed up the rods of the magicians. A rod speaks of "power" in Scripture. Egyptian power was satanic in nature and God was going to reclaim that power to accomplish His purpose, as symbolized by Moses' rod/serpent swallowing the Egyptian rods/serpents. The point here is that Satan can mimic God's doings and can even perform supernatural feats among men, but whatever he does is merely permitted to accomplish God's sovereign purposes. Everything and everyone is under His authority.

Second, a false prophet would be identified if his message was contrary to a revelation already given by someone verified to be a true prophet of Jehovah, like Moses. The Israelites were not to be wowed by a sign, nor swayed by a silver-tongued prophet, nor misled by their emotions; everything had to be tested against God's word (Isa. 8:21). What did not agree with revealed truth was to be repudiated.

Third, whatever a true prophet of God says would happen, will always happen: *"When a prophet speaks in the name of the Lord, if the thing does not happen or come to pass, that is the thing which the Lord has not spoken; the prophet has spoken it presumptuously; you shall not be afraid of him"* (18:22). Jeremiah reiterated the same test centuries later: *"As for the prophet who prophesies of peace, when the word of the prophet comes to pass, the prophet will be known as one whom the Lord has truly sent"* (Jer. 28:9). All that God says is truth, so if anything predicted by someone speaking in His name did not occur, that proved that they were not speaking the truth and thus were not from God.

Fourth, a true prophet of God will always lead His people into repentance and humility before God, never away from the Lord. This is why Moses prescribed such a stern punishment for false prophets: *"But that prophet or that dreamer of dreams shall be put to death, because he has spoken in order to turn you away from the Lord"* (v. 5). False prophets may for a time feign humility and morality (Matt. 7:15), but they are inherently self-exalting (i.e., they compete for God's honor) and self-gratifying (often secretly immoral; 2 Pet. 2:10, 14). Such individuals will eventually lead the Lord's people away from Him, so those individuals were to be exposed and slain in the Old Testament, and rejected and avoided in the New Testament.

Peter likewise warns believers in the Church Age of false prophets and also predicts their doom:

> *But there were also false prophets among the people, even as there will be false teachers among you, who will secretly bring in destructive heresies, even denying the Lord who bought them, and bring on themselves swift destruction. And many will follow their destructive ways, because of whom the way of truth will be blasphemed. By covetousness they will exploit you with deceptive words; for a long time their judgment has not been idle, and their destruction does not slumber* (2 Pet. 2:1-3).

In responding to His disciples' question about things to come, the Lord Jesus confirmed that in the latter days of the Church Age many false doctrines would be spread. Besides mass deception, many would come claiming to be the Christ (Matt. 24:5). With the coming of the Lord nigh, His warning two thousand years ago, *"Take heed that no one deceives you"* (Matt. 24:4), could never be more critical to obey.

"No one" means well-meaning preachers (and authors) too. Paul exhorted the believers at Thessalonica to *"Test all things; hold fast what is good"* (1 Thess. 5:21). Sometimes even well-known brethren can teach what is wrong and cause believers to do what displeases the Lord. We have only to turn to Galatians 2 in our Bibles to find Paul withstanding Peter for his hypocrisy of not eating with Gentile believers. Such intrusions of darkness on the children of light come from the flesh and the devil, not the Lord. Paul did test and hold to what was good, and thankfully Peter received what was good for him too. But Peter, having been wrong and rebuked for it, later wrote in the Spirit *"our beloved brother Paul."* No doubt Peter was thankful for a brother who tested all things and loved him enough to rebuke him when he had not been diligent and careful.

Given the darkness of the hour, may we test everything according to God's Word, lest we be deceived by our God-hating adversary, who wants only to cause us harm and to degrade the name of Christ. If brethren attempt to lead us away from the truth, they must be resisted, for to leave the truth is to depart from the presence of Christ!

God Over Personal Relationships (vv. 6-11)

Moses then anticipated the most tragic and heartbreaking of circumstances which might lead some Israelites to forsake Jehovah for false gods – the influence of loved ones (vv. 6-8). Moses painstakingly included a variety of close relationships, so that everyone would understand that there were no loopholes in his decree:

> *If your brother, the son of your mother, your son or your daughter, the wife of your bosom, or your friend who is as your own soul, secretly entices you, saying, "Let us go and serve other gods"* (v. 6).

Moses commanded that if any Jew enticed another friend or family member to forsake the Lord for false gods, they were to be rejected and put to death. In fact, the one who had been solicited to do evil was to cast the first stone (vv. 9-10). This decree applied to everyone, no matter what social status they might have – Israel was to be completely free of idolatry, even if it meant the death of erring loved ones (v. 12).

Although today false teachers are to be rejected and avoided rather than stoned, we find the same high level of devotion expected from God's people. The Lord Jesus said, *"If anyone comes to Me and does not hate his father and mother, wife and children, brothers and sisters, yes, and his own life also, he cannot be My disciple"* (Luke 14:26).

Refining and Reminding

From the parallel account in Matthew 10:37, we understand that the word for "hate" expresses a comparison: our love for the Lord should be so great that any natural affection would, comparatively, seem like hate. The Lord was weary of shallow followers; He wanted true disciples. He desired quality in consecration, not a large quantity of half-hearted patriots. When it comes to misplaced affections and devotions, there is no middle ground with the Lord. This was the critical point Moses was trying to get across to his countrymen.

The Lord expects our love for Him to be so astounding that by comparison our affections for anyone else would seem like hate! To love anyone or anything more than the Lord is a form of idolatry and proves we are not worthy of Him. The same truth is conveyed in the decree of stoning a loved one who attempted to solicit family members away from the Lord. Although we are under grace in the Church Age, it is profitable for us to appreciate God's desire for His people of all ages to be totally committed to Him and to love Him above all else.

Judgment for Anarchy (vv. 12-18)

The worst example of corruption that Moses could envision was if wicked men were somehow able to persuade an entire Jewish town to abandon Jehovah to serve other gods (vv. 12-13). If Jews in another town heard about this apostasy, they were first to *"inquire, search out, and ask diligently"* to prove whether the abomination was true or not (v. 14). If confirmed, then every person and animal associated with that town was to be slaughtered by the sword and everything that pertained to the town was to be heap up and burned (vv. 15-16). Not only did the town warrant complete destruction, the site was not to be rebuilt, but to remain a pile of debris (v. 17).

Lastly, Moses warned the Lord's executioners in such a situation not to show mercy to anyone or to covet any accursed thing associated with the town (v. 18). All was under judgment and everything was to be destroyed. This would ensure the moral cleansing of the region and the spiritual renewal of the people. Although compliance with this command would be heart-wrenching, those who obeyed God's word in the matter would be showered with His mercy, compassion, and blessing in the land (v. 19).

Regrettably, the Jews did not enforce this law after they inherited Canaan. Jehovah watched from heaven as the leaven of paganism spread throughout Israel. The evil that Moses warned against first infested the Transjordan region, then the North Kingdom, and lastly the Southern Kingdom. Because His people did not expel or destroy the pagans in the land, the entire Jewish nation eventually became so debased that the Lord had no alternative but to punish His people with invasion and exile. Jehovah used the Assyrians to chasten the Transjordan tribes and the Northern Kingdom in the late eighth century B.C. and the Babylonians to punish the Southern Kingdom early in the sixth century B.C. What started with a trickle of human compromise ended with a flood of divine indignation.

If the Jews had foreknown the centuries of horror awaiting them because of their disobedience, surely they would have heeded Moses' warning. Regrettably, Israel received exactly what Moses said would occur if they deserted Jehovah for false deities (Deut. 28:24-28, 64-68). Israel's history is a sobering reminder that knowledge itself will not prompt submission to God's will; rather, submission occurs when the heart chooses to act on what God has revealed. The pertinent question for God's people in every age is, "Do we love the Lord enough to do what He says?"

Meditation

> Human beings must be known to be loved; but the divine being must be loved to be known. ... The knowledge of God is very far from the love of Him.
>
> — Blaise Pascal

A Peculiar People
Deuteronomy 14

The ordinances of this chapter illustrate how separation from the Canaanite pagan culture was demanded in every aspect of Jewish living. The Jews were God's chosen people and God had marked them out to be distinct among the nations. Hence, their mourning customs (vv. 1-2), their diet (vv. 3-21), and their giving to the Lord (vv. 22-29) were all to be consecrated to Him.

If Israel obeyed God's Law, the Jewish nation would look, act, and think differently than everyone else. Their attire (which included a blue fringe), their food, their farming methods, their slaughtering of animals, their family structure, and their system of worship all declared that they were unique among all people. Israel's appearance and customs marked them as God's singular people on the earth.

While the Church is not under the same Levitical particulars, the concepts of separation from evil and worldliness are widely upheld in the New Testament. For example, James proclaims that worldliness is enmity with God (Jas. 4:4), and Paul reminds Christians to refrain from anything that has even the appearance of evil (1 Thess. 5:22). No matter in what age or dispensation God's people find themselves, holiness and full dedication to the Lord is expected!

Improper Mourning (vv. 1-2)

The Lord did not want His people adopting the pagan burial practices of the Canaanites, who often shaved their eyebrows and the forepart of their heads or marred their bodies in various ways to express sorrow:

> *You are the children of the Lord your God; you shall not cut yourselves nor shave the front of your head for the dead. For you are a holy people to the Lord your God, and the Lord has chosen you to be a people for Himself, a special treasure above all the peoples who are on the face of the earth* (vv. 1-2).

This was not a new commandment; Moses had already prohibited the Jews from cultic grieving practices in which the body was marked with cuts or tattoos: *"You shall not shave around the sides of your head, nor shall you disfigure the edges of your beard. You shall not make any cuttings in your flesh for the dead, nor tattoo any marks on you: I am the Lord"* (Lev. 19:27-28). As God has created each individual as unique, we should be careful not to intentionally mar what He has deemed is the best representation of what He wants us to be. In the case before us, the Lord did not want His people looking like the heathen of the land at any time, including times of mourning. Holy Jehovah cherished His people, and He demanded that they remain an unmarred, holy treasure to Him.

Dietary Laws

The dietary laws listed in Leviticus 11 are more encompassing than the lists of clean and unclean meats Moses highlights in this chapter. The Jews were first prohibited from eating the fat or consuming the blood associated with sacrifices. Then, they were commanded not to eat any creature that God deemed as unclean: *"You shall not eat any detestable thing"* (v. 3). While there may be health-related reasons for abstaining from certain foods, verse 4 and Leviticus 11:44-45 indicate the primary reason for these stipulations:

For I am the Lord your God. You shall therefore consecrate yourselves, and you shall be holy; for I am holy. Neither shall you defile yourselves with any creeping thing that creeps on the earth. For I am the Lord who brings you up out of the land of Egypt, to be your God. You shall therefore be holy, for I am holy.

The Lord was using stringent dietary laws to teach the Israelites to have a disciplined thought life, as they had to be mindful of maintaining "clean" conduct throughout their daily routine. Meal times would be a regular opportunity for the Israelites to not only thank the Lord for His goodness, but also to remember His holiness and His expectations for their personal holiness. In His unbounded grace, Jehovah had chosen them to be a holy (or "set apart") people for Himself and for His purposes. The dietary laws were one distinctive which would ensure His covenant people would be a nation separate from all others.

Refining and Reminding

Accordingly, the Jews were not permitted to eat just anything that struck their fancy. Some of God's directives (i.e., those regarding moral matters) are commanded because they are right, while others are simply right because they are commanded. Since the Jewish dietary laws were lifted in the Church Age, the entire subject matter falls into the latter category (Acts 10:10-15).

Concerning these dietary laws and similar ordinances, the practical value, if any, is not always revealed. God does not need to explain Himself to be obeyed; in fact, the lack of exposition imposes a grander test of our faithfulness. Generally speaking, however, if God does not explain His rationale for what may seem like a mundane matter to us, He is not only testing our obedience but is also revealing something which is important to Him. So while there may have been health benefits in abstaining from eating certain creatures, the primary emphasis of these dietary edicts was to affirm Israel's election in the broader sense as God's peculiar and special covenant people.

Levitical dietary laws had three ceremonial classifications: sacrificially acceptable (e.g., "holy"), clean (could be eaten and touched), and unclean (could not be eaten or touched). In verses 3-21, Moses addresses the latter two categories with respect to what the Jews could eat and should not eat. The instruction is divided into three classes: land-bound creatures (vv. 4-8), creatures living in water (vv. 9-10), and flying creatures (vv. 11-20).

For land-bound creatures (vv. 4-8), there was one simple rule: animals with a cloven (divided) hoof and that chewed their cud were considered clean (edible); all others were not. To prevent confusion, a list of clean animals is given: ox, sheep, goat, deer, gazelle, roe deer, wild goat, ibex, antelope, and mountain sheep. The camel, the badger (hyrax), the rabbit, and the swine were unclean because they either did not have a cloven hoof (e.g., the camel) or did not chew the cud (e.g., the swine).

The second class of creatures addressed lived in the water (vv. 9-10). In short, only fish with scales and fins could be eaten. All other seafood was considered unclean and therefore inedible.

The final group discussed was flying creatures (vv. 11-20). Twenty types of birds and the bat (a flying mammal) were deemed unclean; most were birds of prey (e.g., the eagle, the buzzard, and the raven). In feeding directly on their prey, these birds were eating the blood of the flesh and were thus deemed unclean. Clean birds (such as sparrows, pigeons, doves, and quail) could be eaten, although these are not specifically listed in Leviticus 11 or in this chapter.

Along similar lines, various swarms of insects were unclean and should not be eaten (v. 19). However, some winged creatures (speaking of insects) were considered clean and could be eaten (v. 20). For example, Leviticus 11:20-24 specifies four varieties of locust that were permitted in the Jewish diet. The reader might recall that John, the forerunner of Christ, made locust his staple food when he dwelt in the wilderness. For many the thought of eating insects is disgusting, but at present humanity derives about one tenth of its protein from the consumption of insects.

Additionally, the Jews were not to eat the meat of any animal, bird, or insect that was found to be already dead. Moses described this limitation more fully in Leviticus 11:24-28, 39-40. Obviously, the spread of disease would be impeded by limiting the people's direct contact with bacteria present in rotting tissue. However, health ramifications were not the main focus of this restriction as the Jews were permitted to give or sell meat from an animal found dead to Gentiles (v. 21). Rather, there were ceremonial reasons for limiting contact with dead things.

First, because the animal was not properly slaughtered (i.e., it was not "bled out" properly), those eating the meat of such an animal would defy God's prohibition against consuming blood. Second, to touch any dead body or carcass would make a Jew ceremonially unclean and therefore unfit to worship the Lord.

Although not stated in this chapter, Leviticus 11 also prohibited the Israelites from eating worms, snakes, and rodents. Anyone eating these would be, ritualistically speaking, "unclean." Boiling the meat of a young goat in its mother's milk was also prohibited (v. 21). This practice was associated with a Canaanite fertility rite and was therefore forbidden. Additionally, the limitation signified a principle: what God gave to sustain life (a mother's milk) should not be used to destroy life.

While the other peoples of the world could eat what they most enjoyed, the Jews would be a nation marked by the high privilege of eating only what pleased Jehovah – thus, their separation as Jehovah's peculiar people would be plain for all to see. They could exercise free choice in their diet, but only within the limits laid out by their God.

As mentioned previously, the Jewish dietary laws were only one of many commanded peculiarities that marked them as unique – Jehovah's

Refining and Reminding

chosen people. Their attire (Lev. 19:19; Deut. 22:5), their physical appearance (Lev. 19:28), and even what they were physically permitted to touch (Lev. 11-15) were distinct. A Jew who wanted to honor Jehovah would have to be mindful every moment of every day of what was "clean" and "unclean."

These laws showed the extent to which Jehovah was jealously guarding His covenant people; He did not want them near what was unclean, lest they be tempted to defile themselves. Thus, contact of any kind with what God deemed as unclean was forbidden. As previously mentioned, the Jewish dietary laws would later be abolished by the New Covenant secured by the Lord Jesus Christ (Mark 7:14-23; Acts 10:9-13). However, God's desire for His people to remain morally clean and set apart for Him was not abolished. Much sin in the Church today would be avoided if God's people were constantly mindful of what was clean and unclean to the Lord. May God give us grace to *"abhor what is evil and cling to what is good"* (Rom. 12:9-10), and also to *"abstain from all appearance of evil"* (1 Thess. 5:22).

> Blest are the pure, whose hearts are clean,
> Who never tread the ways of sin;
> With endless pleasures they shall see
> A God of spotless purity.
>
> — Isaac Watts

Tithing (vv. 22-29)

The tithe to the Lord (vv. 22-29) was previously commanded in Leviticus 27:30-31 and Numbers 18:21-32. However, it was necessary for Moses to modify certain procedures now that Israel was about to enter the Promised Land and would soon be required to worship at the central sanctuary.

The firstfruits of the harvest were to be waved before the Lord as an offering of thankfulness to the One who had granted the increase. The Lord laid claim to one-tenth of their entire harvest; this would be His provision for sustaining the Levites and their ministry.

Likewise, one-tenth of the clean animals and the firstborn of their herds and flocks were also His. Leviticus 27 demanded that every tenth animal that passed under the shepherd's rod (the common method of counting sheep or goats) was the Lord's. The selected animals would provide the Levites with meat and would also be used in Levitical sacrifices (e.g., two lambs were to be offered each day on the Bronze altar, and even more animals were offered each Sabbath day).

But in addition to the annual tithe, Moses spoke of a second tithe to be given to the Lord every three years. This may have been in addition to the annual tithe (i.e., another ten percent of what was remaining after the first tithe), but was more likely a substitute for the first in that the second tithe required feasting locally and not at the central sanctuary before the Lord.[168] Albert Barnes clarifies the latter position:

> The tithe thus directed in the third year to be dispensed in charity at home was not paid in addition to that in other years bestowed on the sacred meals, but was substituted for it. The three years would count from the sabbatical year (see the next chapter), in which year there would, of course, be neither payment of tithe nor celebration of the feasts at the sanctuary. In the third year and sixth year of the septennial cycle the feasts would be superseded by the private hospitality enjoined in these verses.[169]

The "second tithe" was to support locally serving Levites and the needy. Widows, orphans, and the deprived sojourner are named as recipients of the second tithe which was to be laid up within the gates of the closest Levitical city (vv. 28-29). So in the first, second, fourth, and fifth years of the seven-year cycle, the first tithe would be brought to the central sanctuary and a feast would be enjoyed before the Lord there. In the third and sixth years of the seven-year cycle, the tithe was given to local Levites and feasting by all, including the poor, was enjoyed in that city, instead of at the central sanctuary. This tithe especially symbolized that all God's people should be joyfully satisfied in His presence.

Those living a considerable distance from the central sanctuary could bring a corresponding value of silver instead of their tithe. Upon arriving at the central sanctuary, they could buy an animal for sacrifice and wine, or a fermented drink similar to beer, if desired to feast before the Lord (vv. 24-26). The Levites were also invited to this celebration to proclaim the nation's joy and satisfaction in Jehovah: *"You shall eat there before the Lord your God, and you shall rejoice, you and your household"* (v. 26). Obviously their partaking would be guided by moderation. It was a time for festive rejoicing, not gluttony or

Refining and Reminding

drunkenness, which would be offensive to the Lord and to others (e.g., Deut. 21:22).

The tithe feast demonstrates the blessing and joy a congregation receives when honoring God together wherever He deems appropriate to do so. This wonderfully typifies the blessings Christians enjoyed together when assembled in the name of their Savior to remember Him through the Lord's Supper. C. A. Coates adds:

> Such a gathering involves separation from evil, for God's Name is in His assembly, and it is a holy Name. We must remember that any spiritual blessing which we have individually is to be tithed for the assembly; it is to contribute to our joy as those privileged to meet at a center common to all saints. To recognize that there is such a center, and that all saints are under obligation to regard it, is bound up with the fear of God.[170]

As with the dietary laws, the Jewish tithing requirements were also abolished in the New Testament. However, the congregational joy and fellowship around the Lord pictured in the tithe feast lives on in New Testament Church practice. Under the Law, God demanded the tithe. But in the age of grace each believer is required to regularly and proportionately give back to the Lord as God has prospered him or her (1 Cor. 16:2). In the Church Age, God makes no demands as to the specific amount we are to give back to Him; rather, we are permitted to evaluate our situation, and to freely express our love and appreciation to Him through giving:

> *He who sows sparingly will also reap sparingly, and he who sows bountifully will also reap bountifully. So let each one give as he purposes in his heart, not grudgingly or of necessity; for God loves a cheerful giver* (2 Cor. 9:6-7).

God has wonderfully shown us that true giving commences with selfless sacrifice: *"For God so loved the world that He gave His only begotten Son"* (John 3:16). The Lord Jesus affirmed *"to whom little is forgiven, the same loves little"* (Luke 7:47)! In summary, the portion that we return of what we have received from the Lord directly reflects how much we believe we have been forgiven and how much we love Him. Those who have been forgiven much, give much, because they love much!

Considering all that the Lord had accomplished for His people, the Israelites should gladly give back to Him a portion of what they had received from Him – and so should we.

Meditation

    Take my lips and let them be, filled with messages for Thee;
    Take my silver and my gold, not a mite would I withhold,
        Not a mite would I withhold.
    Take my love, my God; I pour, at Thy feet, its treasure store;
    Take myself and I will be, ever only all for Thee,
        Ever only all for Thee.

— Frances R. Havergal

Releasing Debts
Deuteronomy 15

Generosity and Debt-Releasing Expected (vv. 1-11)
　　The Jews were already familiar with the concept of working six days and consecrating the seventh day, the Sabbath, to the Lord. The Jews, their slaves, and their beasts of burden were all to rest on the Sabbath Day. The Lord imposed the same restriction on the land; it was to be worked six years followed by an entire year of rest (Lev. 17:3-7). This meant no sowing, pruning, reaping, or harvesting would be permitted during the seventh year; the fields, the olive groves, and the vineyards were to receive a full year's inactivity. Whatever grew naturally during this time could be freely gleaned by anyone, especially the poor, and anything left after that would be God's provision for the beasts of the field. However, there was to be no organized harvest or sale of what the land did produce that year.
　　The Sabbath year ensured that one year in seven all Jews would be equal; they must live off the land, or rather, live by faith that Jehovah would provide for their needs that year. Certainly, this agricultural prohibition would remind the Jews that God owned the land on which they lived and that they were merely stewards of it (Lev. 17:23). Moses now tells them that the Sabbatical Year was also the appropriate time for the canceling of debts (vv. 1-11) and the freeing of Jewish slaves (vv. 12-18).
　　Jews were not to charge other Jews interest on their debts (23:19), nor were they to be debtors more than six years – the debt was to be released in the Sabbatical year (vv. 1-2). This meant one of two things: Either that the payment of debt was released for the Sabbatical year only (to provide financial relief and equality for all), but then was resumed afterwards, or that the debt, on legal grounds, was completely erased.[171] If the latter is correct, this did not mean that borrowers should not repay their debts if released in the Sabbatical year, but, rather, that they were bound only by their conscience to do so and not a

legal contract. Keil and Delitzsch favor the former explanation of what "release" meant for the following reasons:

> As shamat (release) points unmistakably back to Exodus 23:11, it must be interpreted in the same manner here as there. And as it is not used there to denote the entire renunciation of a field or possession, so here it cannot mean the entire renunciation of what had been lent, but simply leaving it, i.e., not pressing for it during the seventh year. This is favored by what follows, *"thou shalt not press thy neighbor,"* which simply forbids an unreserved demand, but does not require that the debt should be remitted or presented to the debtor.[172]

The understanding of a one-year relief from payment does seem to be a better contextual understanding of what actually did occur in the Sabbatical release. Regardless, Moses promised that creditors who released debts would never suffer for doing so, as God would repay them for their obedience to His law.

The act of releasing debts was to prevent Jews in the Promised Land from suffering perpetual poverty for situations that were beyond their control (v. 4). In short, releasing debts was to promote the welfare of those who were weak. From this idea, F. B. Hole suggests an important principle to guide our interaction with those poor in faith today.

> Every seventh year was to be a year of release. The well-to-do Israelite might lend money to his poor neighbor, but anything not repaid when the seventh year arrived, was to be released and left in the hand of the poor man. We see therefore that the law demanded a spirit of gracious care for the poor among His people, though this arrangement did not apply to strangers among them. Should there be no poor, the rule would lapse, but in verse 11 they are plainly told that *"the poor shall never cease out of the land."* For us Christians it is equally true that there will always be found amongst us those who are "weak in the faith," who are but "babes" in Christ; and those strong in the faith must be careful lest by their "knowledge" they make "the weak brother perish, for whom Christ died" (1 Cor. 8:11). The poor and weak must be considered.[173]

Obviously, those having a bad credit history would not be able to borrow money in the future, so it was advantageous for all to repay debts, if able. It was also beneficial for the wealthy to extend mercy and assistance to the poor, as the Lord promised to reward them. Given His goodness to Israel, it was the Lord's desire that the Jews should help each other during times of hardship:

> *If one of your brethren becomes poor, and falls into poverty among you, then you shall help him, like a stranger or a sojourner, that he may live with you. Take no usury or interest from him; but fear your God, that your brother may live with you* (Lev. 25:35-37).

Although the Jews were not to exact interest from each other, they could from Gentiles (v. 3; 23:19-20). Loans to Gentiles did not have to be released in the Sabbatical year. Because God promised to reward their obedience in the Promised Land with agricultural prosperity, they should not borrow from foreigners, but they were permitted to lend to them (vv. 5-6).

Moses reminded his countrymen that *"the poor will never cease from the land; therefore I command you, saying, 'You shall open your hand wide to your brother, to your poor and your needy, in your land'"* (v. 11). God instituted slavery regulations to protect His people from abusing each other in future generations (vv. 12-18; Ex. 21:1-11). However, God's desire for them was that they assist one another in economic hardships, rather than take advantage of each other (vv. 7-9). Moses promised that those being generous to those in need would be reimbursed by the Lord:

> *You shall surely give to him, and your heart should not be grieved when you give to him, because for this thing the Lord your God will bless you in all your works and in all to which you put your hand* (v. 10).

Centuries later, Solomon would affirm the same promise: *"He who has pity on the poor lends to the Lord, and He will pay back what he has given"* (Prov. 19:17) and *"He who gives to the poor will not lack, but he who hides his eyes will have many curses"* (Prov. 28:27). Then, at the close of the Old Testament, the prophet Malachi warns his countrymen that miserliness towards the Lord is a spiritual problem, not a financial one. The prophet told the Jews to test the Lord – see if they could out-give Him (Mal. 1:10). He then implied that God would open the windows of heaven and shower upon the obedient His overflowing goodness. The Lord always provides resources for His children to worship Him and to give to others – that is, if we have willing hearts to honor Him with what He has graciously given us.

Though Christians are not under the Law, the Old Testament does highlight what God deems appropriate conduct for His people throughout all ages, that is, to rally around and help each other during times of distress: *"Bear one another's burdens, and so fulfill the law of Christ"* (Gal. 6:2). Indeed, this was the practice of the early Church. The poor, such as widows, were cared for (Acts 6:1; 1 Tim. 5:3-5).

Early Christians did not value their possessions (of which they were merely God's stewards) more than each other (Acts 4:32). As a result of this loving unselfishness, all of the Lord's people were wonderfully sustained: *"nor was there anyone among them who lacked"* (Acts 4:34). God forbid that we, who have received so much goodness in Christ, should *"oppress one another"* by withholding back our temporal possessions from our brothers and sisters in need (Lev. 25:14, 17).

Before leaving this passage on releasing debts, let us consider a personal application pointed out by C. A. Coates as to how Christians should be a releasing people. His remarks are lengthy, but well worth reading:

> There are times when our brethren come under obligation to us. A creditor is one who has a righteous claim on his neighbor or his brother for something. It is well to consider whether we have righteous claims that remain unsatisfied. Let us turn over our ledgers and see if we have any entries standing against brothers or sisters! Yes! Brother So-and-so did not treat me with the respect that was due to me; he did not show me Christian consideration or courtesy! And another brother took full advantage of my kindness, but expressed no gratitude; he made no return for all the good I have done to him! And a sister spoke unkindly of me; she even said what was not true! And another promised to do a certain thing, but he never did it! All such things as these put us in the place of creditors. Such debts as that go on piling up year after year, and the creditors get soured by thinking so long about the debts that have never been paid! God does not like to see His sons maintaining demands on one another, so He steps in to confer a great privilege on all creditors. The creditor here is the one who gains, for he shines in the glory of correspondence with God. How could you enjoy your sabbatical year if you were thinking all the time of undischarged debts due to you from your brethren! Many local difficulties are the result of old-standing accounts. There is a

> rankling sourness in the heart on account of things said and done years ago, and it is destructive of family affections and spiritual prosperity; these things show that we have not been "seven years" in the land; we have not yet acquired sufficient wealth to "make a release." If we keep up personal grievances against our brethren, we are missing the creditor's privilege in the year of release.
>
> How often people say, "But I want righteousness." They forget that righteousness now consists in acting towards others in the same way that God has acted towards us (see Matt. 18:21- 35). Certain things are due on the debtor's part, and God's work in him would lead to the acknowledgement of this, but, as we have said before, this particular scripture is not occupied with the debtor, or the relief he gets; it is the setting forth of the creditor's privilege, and of the gain which accrues to him as he takes it up. It is not even spoken of here as a release to the debtor; it is "a release to Jehovah." The creditor has an opportunity of showing how he appreciates Jehovah's gracious favor, and of reflecting it in his conduct towards his poor brother. It is poverty in our brother that has brought him into the place of a debtor. If he had been spiritually wealthy, he would never have incurred the debt; he would have undoubtedly discharged all his righteous obligations. But his poverty may furnish me with an opportunity to act as a wealthy son of God, and to make a release.[174]

Do you want emotional healing in your life? Pray for those who persecute you, forgive (release) them of their wrongs against you, and you will set a prisoner free only to realize that you were the one taken captive by your own hardened heart. The Lord taught, *"If ye forgive men their trespasses, your heavenly Father will also forgive you; but if ye forgive not men their trespasses, neither will your Father forgive your trespasses"* (Matt. 6:14-15; KJV). In light of the debt of sin we have been forgiven by God, how can we not extend to others our forgiveness for lesser offenses (Eph. 4:32)? To forgive (i.e., to release to God's control) liberates the heart for free expression of love through service again. Those who hold grudges must realize that the root of bitterness that is festering in their own heart will affect every relationship they have, including their fellowship with the Lord. This is why God demanded that "every creditor" among the Jews release their debts – and so should every believer!

Laws Pertaining to Bondservants (vv. 12-18)

There were two main reasons Jews would become slaves to other Jews: they could sell themselves into slavery in order to pay off a debt (such as for a bride's dowry or because of economic hardship) or they could be forced into slavery as a punishment (i.e., the recompense for a crime committed). In any case, God did not desire His people to be forced to serve others as slaves, but, rather, to be a liberated people who would freely serve Him. Consequently, no Jew was to be held in slavery against his or her will for more than six years, no matter what circumstances caused the servitude.

After six years of service, or at the fifty-year Jubilee if it occurred prior to the six-year tenure (Lev. 25:39-42), a Hebrew slave was to be released (v. 12). Because God had delivered His people from slavery and richly blessed them, the master was not to release a slave without a provision from his flock, his threshing floor, and his vineyard, which would sustain him or her for a time (vv. 13-15). Moses cited that hiring a laborer to do the work that a slave would do would cost the owner twice as much as it did to house and feed the slave (v. 18). Therefore, masters were to release their serving countrymen in good favor, having economically benefited from them.

However, a Jewish slave might decline release, choosing rather to remain with his master for life: *"'I will not go away from you,' because he loves you and your house, since he prospers with you"* (v. 16). If the slave made this choice, he was taken to a doorpost, his ear was placed next to the wood, and the master pushed or pounded an awl through the slave's ear. The resulting hole marked him as a bondservant for life. In the Epistles, Paul often applied this phrase to express his own love for the Lord Jesus Christ. The only reason a man would become a perpetual bondservant would be to express love for his master, or perhaps, if he had been given a wife while in slavery, love for his family (for his family would not be released if he chose to go free). A female slave was given the same choice after six years of service (v. 17).

As love for the master is mentioned first, it seems to be the primary reason a slave would be willing to enter into a lifelong commitment to his master. Certainly, the exceptional care of the master for his slave had already been experienced, otherwise the slave would not enter into a lifetime commitment; brutality would never cause a slave to make such a pledge. However, if the slave determined that he could never be happier than in serving his master, this action becomes understandable. In type, the slave's love for his master pictures the love and pure devotion of the Lord Jesus for His Father, but "there is more than this," says C. H. Macintosh:

> "I love my wife and my children." "Christ loved the church and gave Himself for it, that He might sanctify and cleanse it with the washing of water by the word, that He might present it to Himself a glorious church, not having spot, or wrinkle, or any such thing; but that it should be holy and without blemish" (Eph. 5: 25-27). There are various other passages of Scripture presenting Christ as the antitype of the Hebrew servant, both in His love for the Church, as a body, and for all believers personally. ...The apprehension of this love of the heart of Jesus cannot fail to produce a spirit of fervent devotedness to the One who could exhibit such pure, such perfect, such disinterested love. How could the wife and children of the Hebrew servant fail to love one who had voluntarily surrendered his liberty in order that he and they might be together? And what is the love presented in the type, when compared with that which shines in the antitype? It is as nothing. "The love of Christ passes knowledge." It led Him to think of us before all worlds — to visit us in the fullness of time — to walk deliberately to the doorpost — to suffer for us on the cross, in order that He might raise us to companionship with Himself, in His everlasting kingdom and glory.[175]

The slave had two options at the conclusion of his time of binding service: he could *"go out free and pay nothing"* (Ex. 21: 2), or he could tell his master, *"I will not go out free"* (Ex. 21:5). If he chose the first option, he was to be set free; he was at liberty to live his life however he chose. Likewise, since his association with his master was severed, there would be no future assistance or benefits received from him either. If the slave chose the latter option, he would be committing himself for the remainder of his life to serve his master and he would also enjoy all the blessings of that association.

Commitment entails being given over to a cause without any reservation. Such was the pledge of a slave to his master, and such should be the pledge of every child of God to his or her Master. Only after a believer has consciously made such a determination will he or she have the unwavering obedience and devotion of a true disciple of Christ. The Lord does not force us to pledge our lives to Him, but He does warn us:

If anyone desires to come after Me, let him deny himself, and take up his cross daily, and follow Me. For whoever desires to save his life will lose it, but whoever loses his life for My sake will save it. For what profit is it to a man if he gains the whole world, and is himself destroyed or lost? (Luke 9:23-25).

Like the slave when the day of freedom arrived, those who have received a new life in Christ have only two ways to live while on earth: to completely yield to Christ, thus gaining a life worth living and fellowship with God, or to live the way one wants. The latter decision results in a spiritually desolate life that knows neither the peace nor the joy of God and counts for nothing in eternity.

Firstborn Animals Were the Lord's (vv. 19-23)

By the substitutional death of the Passover lamb, the firstborn of man and beast among the Hebrews had been spared death in Egypt during the tenth plague. Since God had purchased the lives of the firstborn, He now claimed special ownership of them (Ex. 13:1-16). Whoever opened the womb for the first time (man or donkey) had to be redeemed by the life of a lamb on the eighth day after birth. The firstborn of a clean animal was not to be redeemed, but was to be consecrated to the Lord for sacrifice (v. 19). This meant that the owner could receive no benefit from the animal, for it was the Lord's (e.g., a firstborn ox could not pull a plow and a firstborn sheep could not be shorn for its wool).

As peace offerings, the meat from these firstborn animals was for the Levites and for a communal meal to be enjoyed by the family of the offerer at the central sanctuary (v. 20). This often occurred during the three annual feasts which all Jews were commanded to attend at the central sanctuary. If the firstborn was imperfect and unsuitable for sacrifice, it was to be treated like wild game – butchered and eaten at home (vv. 21-22). The only stipulation was that the blood of the animal could not be eaten; it was to be poured out on the ground like water (v. 23).

Refining and Reminding

Meditation

> My glorious Victor, Prince divine, clasp these surrendered hands in Thine,
> At length my will is all Thine own, glad vassal of a Savior's throne.
> My Master, lead me to Thy door, pierce this now willing ear once more.
> Thy bonds are freedom; let me stay with Thee to toil, endure, obey.
> Tread them still down, and then, I know, these hands shall with Thy gifts overflow,
> And pierced ears shall hear the tone which tells me Thou and I are one.
>
> — Handley C. G. Moule

Feasts in Review
Deuteronomy 16

In this chapter, Moses briefly reviews the annual feasts to be observed as commanded in Leviticus 23 and Numbers 28-29. In all, seven feasts were to be observed: Passover, Unleavened Bread, Firstfruits, Weeks (Pentecost), Trumpets, Day of Atonement, and Tabernacles. Each of the three seasons of festivals was tied to the Jewish agricultural calendar.

The Feast of Unleavened Bread occurred in March/April and related to the barley harvest. The Feast of Weeks occurred during the wheat harvest (about seven weeks after the barley was reaped) and marked the end of spring harvest. The Feast of Weeks is also referred to as Pentecost (Acts 2:1, 20:16), the Day of Firstfruits (28:26), and The Feast of Harvest (Ex. 23:16). The Feast of Ingathering, also known as The Feast of Tabernacles, occurred at the end of the agricultural year in September or October.

The first three feasts ran together in the spring and were sometimes referred to just as *"the Feast of Unleavened Bread"* which lasted seven days (v. 16). Pentecost followed fifty days afterwards, and the three remaining feasts were separated by only a few days in the fall. Each feast was to be a *"holy convocation"* or, literally, a "sacred calling together" before the Lord (Num. 28:18). Like the Sabbath day, these feast days were set aside solely for Jehovah; it was a time for worship and reflection, not for labor (Lev. 23:2-3).

The Passover Reviewed (vv. 1-8)

The Passover Feast and The Feast of Unleavened Bread were both instituted in Exodus 12. The annual Passover Feast was to remind the Israelites of their deliverance from Egypt and their restoration to Jehovah through redemption. The Passover served as a memorial of what God had accomplished through blood redemption in Egypt; however, it culminates in the ultimate redemptive work of Christ at Calvary. The

Passover Feast then pictures Christ on the cross; this was the day the Passover lambs were slain and was also the day when the Lamb of God was slain for the sins of the world (1 Cor. 5:7).

The Passover Feast was to be held on the fourteenth day of the first month, The Feast of Unleavened Bread on the fifteenth day, and The Feast of Firstfruits on the following day (vv. 16-17). The Feast of Unleavened Bread was to last seven days, meaning the total duration of the first three spring feasts was to be eight days.

Feast of Weeks Reviewed (vv. 9-12)

The Feast of Weeks occurred seven weeks and one day (i.e., 50 days) after the waving of the barley sheaf before the Lord in the Feast of Firstfruits (two days after The Passover). This celebration occurred towards the end of the wheat harvest in late spring or early summer. The first three feasts ran together in early springtime, Pentecost occurred fifty days after the Firstfruits observance, and the three remaining feasts were separated by only a few days in the beginning of autumn (this would normally correspond to our month of September). This created a long interim between these and the spring feasts, which typify Christ's death (Passover), burial (Unleavened Bread), resurrection (Firstfruits), and the creation of the Church (Pentecost).

From a prophetic viewpoint, the gap between the spring and fall festivals pictures the Church Age, and the fall feasts, God's future restoration of a remnant of Israel to Himself. These include The Feast of Trumpets, The Day of Atonement, and The Feast of Tabernacles. Collectively these became known as "the High Holy Days," and mark the conclusion of the religious year (i.e., there were no more biblical feasts until Passover the following spring).

Feast of Tabernacle Reviewed (vv. 13-15)

Five days after The Day of Atonement came The Feast of Tabernacles, falling on the fifteenth day of the seventh month in the Hebrew calendar (Lev. 23:34). Only on the Day of Atonement was the high priest permitted to enter the Most Holy Place of the tabernacle, there to apply the blood of a bull and of a goat on and before the Mercy Seat. This atoned for (covered) all the sins the nation committed the previous year (Lev. 16). This feast was an annual reminder of the ongoing problem of sin and that the blood of animals did not satisfy God's anger over sin or purge the sinner's guilty conscience.

The Feast of Tabernacles lasted a total of eight days; the first and the eighth days (Lev. 23:35-36) were declared a "holy convocation," a high Sabbath day (vv. 12, 35; Lev. 23:39). In contrast to the "affliction of souls" that took place on The Day of Atonement, this feast was a time of thanksgiving and rejoicing. With harvest season complete, and the barns and storehouses full, it was time for everyone to gather to express their gratitude to Jehovah. Hence, this festival was sometimes referred to as "The Feast of Ingathering" (Lev. 23:39).

Leviticus 23 informs us that each Jewish family was to cut down branches from various leafy trees, such as willows and palms, and to erect makeshift booths to dwell in for the seven nights and eight days of this festival (Lev. 23:40-43). This activity was to remind the Jews of God's deliverance from bondage in Egypt and that they dwelled with Jehovah in the wilderness while residing in tents. The booths, then, were a memorial of what God had accomplished for His people. Jehovah did not want them to forget that He was their beginning. For this reason, The Feast of Tabernacles was to be an annual event throughout their generations.

This feast pictures the glory of the Jewish nation after they are purified and restored to Jehovah at the end of the Tribulation Period (Rom. 9:27, 11:25-27). During the Millennial Kingdom, the Jewish nation will come into all the fullness of the Abrahamic covenant; thus, The Feast of Tabernacles forms a lovely and fitting close to the entire series of Jehovah's feasts.

Feast Attendance (vv. 16-17)

Every Jewish male was required to present himself before Jehovah three times a year for The Feast of Unleavened Bread, The Feast of Weeks, and The Feast of Ingathering (v. 16; Ex. 34:18-23). The feasts were to be observed *"before the Lord,"* which initially meant at the tabernacle, but later at the temple in Jerusalem. This did not mean that only men were to attend the feasts of Jehovah, but rather that each man should ensure that his family and servants, and those widows, orphans, and foreigners sojourning with him attended also (vv. 11, 14).

Since their gifts were an expression of thanksgiving to God, those attending were to be generous (v. 17). If each man shared as God had prospered him during the previous months, there would be plenty for everyone. Then the feasts would truly be a time of rejoicing before the Lord. In summary, each Jewish man was responsible for himself and those associated with him to attend three feasts each year before the Lord and to come with gifts reflecting his joy and thankfulness in the Lord.

C. H. Mackintosh suggests that it was remarkable how Jehovah was ever seeking to draw the hearts of His people to Himself by means of various sacrifices and both somber and festive observances:

> There was the morning and evening lamb, every *day*; there was the holy Sabbath, every *week*; there was the new moon, every *month*; there was the Passover, every *year*; there was the tithing, every *three years*; there was the release, every *seven years*; and there was the jubilee, every *fifty years*. All this is full of deepest interest. It tells its own sweet tale, and teaches its own precious lesson to the heart. The morning and evening lamb, as we know, pointed ever to "the Lamb of God which takes away the sin of the world." The Sabbath was the lovely type of the rest that remains to the people of God. The new moon beautifully prefigured the time when restored Israel shall reflect back the beams of the Sun of righteousness upon the nations. The Passover was the standing memorial of the nation's deliverance from Egyptian bondage. The year of tithing set forth the fact of Jehovah's proprietorship of the land, as also the lovely way in which His rents were to be expended in meeting the need of His workmen and of His poor. The sabbatical year gave promise of a bright time when all debts would be cancelled, all loans disposed of, all burdens removed. And, finally, the jubilee was the magnificent type of the times of the restitution of all things, when the captive shall be set free, when the exile shall return to his long lost home and inheritance, and when the land of Israel and the whole earth shall rejoice beneath the beneficent, government of the Son of David.[176]

Justice and Reverence in Canaan (vv. 18-22)

Righteous judges and officers (perhaps clerks assisting the judges) were God's provision to uphold justice in the Promised Land (v. 18). Judges were to be accessible to the people by sitting in their city's gates. Moses duly warns them: *"You shall not pervert justice; you shall not show partiality, nor take a bribe, for a bribe blinds the eyes of the wise and twists the words of the righteous"* (v. 19). The judges and their helpers were to represent the Lord's righteous character and just authority in Canaan. This meant that they were to uphold God's Law without ignoring or twisting the truth, accepting bribes, or showing favoritism. Those perverting justice in Jehovah's name would be severely punished.

Any Jew having a controversy or an offense to be judged would have never thought about bringing it before a Gentile tribunal. Rather, it was to be heard by the priests and appointed judges of Israel. Jehovah was in the midst of His people, thus it would have been insulting to Him for His people to ask Gentile pagans, who did not know Him or His Law, to judge their grievances. Paul affirms a similar protocol for believers in the Church Age. Christians were not to take each other into Gentile courts to resolve their differences; rather, they were to submit to the judgment of the wise among them and to the elders of the church (1 Cor. 6:1-9). Paul reminded the Corinthians that it was much better to be willing to be defrauded by another believer than to disdain the name of the Lord Jesus Christ in secular courts of law.

These judges were also to ensure that the land was free of any religious practices prohibited by God's Law. Moses names two examples: planting Asherah trees (poles) and placing sacred stones near Jehovah's altar at the central sanctuary (vv. 21-21; NASV). Asherah was the Canaanite fertility goddess and Baal her consort. The sacred stones symbolized male fertility organs. If the Jews wanted God's blessing in Canaan, they must ensure that proper justice and religious purity were maintained in the land (v. 20).

Meditation

The administration of justice is the firmest pillar of government.

— George Washington

Injustice anywhere is a threat to justice everywhere.

— Martin Luther King Jr.

Guidance for the King
Deuteronomy 17

The section on religious life in Israel, beginning in chapter 11 with the law of one sanctuary, concluded in the last chapter with the three feasts to be annually celebrated before the Lord at that location. The third section of Moses' second message (which concludes in chapter 26) reveals various laws associated with Israel's covenant.

Various Reminders (vv. 1-13)

Moses briefly summarizes various commandments pertaining to proper worship. No defective sacrifices were to be offered to the Lord and no detestable thing should be connected with the people's worship (v. 1). Anyone suspected of departing from Jehovah to engage in any kind of pagan practices was to be given a proper trial at the city gate and sentenced to death if guilty (vv. 2-5).

There must be two or more witnesses for someone to be condemned and the individuals exposing the wickedness were to cast the first stones to execute the guilty party (v. 6). There was to be no tolerance for paganism; such wickedness must be swiftly judged so that evil was removed from among God's people (v. 7).

As he did during the wilderness years (1:17), Moses gave the judges of the people an opportunity to appeal to a higher authority if the case was too hard for them to discern (v. 8). However, because he would soon be departing from them, they would not be able to bring such matters to him in the future. Rather, the matter was to be brought before the priests and Levites at the central sanctuary for a determination (vv. 9-10).

The Lord previously appointed, and anointed with the Holy Spirit, seventy elders to shepherd His people (Num. 11:16). These seventy leaders formed the supreme court of Israel. During New Testament times these seventy judges were called the Sanhedrin. The decisions of this court were final and had to be obeyed (v. 11). Rebellion against this tribunal was considered "contempt of court" and was punishable by death (vv. 12-13). God wanted righteousness, justice, and peace to pervade the Promised Land; therefore rebellion, wickedness, and anarchy would not be tolerated.

Guidance for Future Kings (vv. 14-20)

The Lord foreknew that in time His people would want to set a king over them to be like the surrounding nations (v. 14). There are a number of behaviors, such as slavery and polygamy, which the Lord did not approve of, but knowing the carnality of the human heart, provided predictive laws to minimize their consequences to His people. Hence, recognizing the dangers of the people appointing a king, Moses provided guidance in the matter (vv. 14-20).

The Law did not sanction the recognition of kings, because the Jews were to look to and submit to Jehovah's leadership and authority over them. So, unsurprisingly, when the Jews approached Samuel to appoint them a king five centuries later, the Lord was offended. He told Samuel: *"they have rejected Me, that I should not reign over them"* (1 Sam. 8:7). Later, when Samuel revealed Saul as their new king, the prophet informed the people: *"You have today rejected your God, who Himself saved you from all your adversities and your tribulations; and you have said to Him, 'No, set a king over us!'"* (1 Sam. 10:19). Why shouldn't the Lord be offended? The people were rejecting their almighty God and His goodness for a fallible human leader. Later, the prophet Hosea would remind the people that God appointed Saul as their king in His anger to teach them the repercussions of rejecting Him (Hos. 13:11; 1 Sam. 12:12).

Foreknowing that the people would later demand a king, God provided the following guidance for his appointment and reign:

- The king must be a Jew and appointed by God (v. 15).
- He should not multiply horses to himself, for God must be his strength (v. 16).
- He must not cause the Jews to return to Egypt (v. 16).
- He should not multiple wives or riches for himself, lest his heart turn away from the Lord (v. 17).
- The king should have a copy of this book to ensure he knows and fears God and enforces His Law (vv. 18-19).

Refining and Reminding

A king should follow the above constraints so as to remain a humble servant of the people and to guard himself from turning away from God's Law (v. 20). Such a king would have prolonged days in office, a good legacy, and posterity in the land and perhaps even a long dynasty to testify to God's faithfulness.

These mandates were given to ensure that future kings would not stray from the Lord. If the king drifted from the Lord, the people would also forsake their God. In God's grand plan of redemption, He always intended to anoint a righteous king to rule over Israel – David, who typified a descendant of His who would be the King of kings and would rule over the whole earth in righteousness. This plan is clearly seen in the promise God made to Abraham and Sarah that some of their descendants would be kings (Gen. 17:16) and One of these, the Lord Jesus Christ, would be the King of kings (Rev. 19:6)!

Meditation

> With joy we wait our King's returning
> From His heavenly mansions fair;
> And with ten thousand saints appearing
> We shall meet Him in the air.
>
> Rejoice! Rejoice! Our King is coming!
> And the time will not be long,
> Until we hail the radiant dawning,
> And lift up the glad new song.

— Ira D. Sankey

"A Prophet" Like Moses
Deuteronomy 18

Portions for Priests and Levites (vv. 1-8)

Moses reiterated that the priests and Levites would not inherit a region of land in Canaan, but would dwell in forty-eight cities within the land allocations for the twelve tribes (vv. 1-2). The priests (descendants of Aaron) were to serve at the central sanctuary and to be supported by the offerings and tithes the people brought there (Lev. 1-7, 27).

The priests received what was offered to the Lord. They were to obtain portions of meat from animal sacrifices, as well as grain, wine, oil, and wool (vv. 3-5). The Levites not serving at the one place of worship were to be sustained by the people's gifts and tithes (14:28-29; 16:10-11). J. N. Darby overviews why supporting the priests was essential to the welfare of the nation in Canaan:

> The normal condition of the people was that of being guided by the priests, and, in case of need, by judges raised up in an extraordinary way; and to abide under the keeping of God in the land, enjoying His blessing. It was, properly speaking, a theocracy. The laws of God directed the people; they enjoyed the blessing of God; and the priests settled any questions which arose, a judge being raised up in exceptional cases. The priests are introduced here in connection with that which was necessary to the enjoyment of the land, not as a means of drawing near to God. Consequently, they were there to fulfill their ministry before God, and a certain portion belonged to them. The king was only thought of in the case when the people would ask for one, in order to be like the nations; and in that case he was to remain, as much as possible, simple in the midst of Israel, that the law of God might have its full authority.[177]

If a Levite desired to sell his property in a Levitical city and to move to Jerusalem to serve the Lord in the central sanctuary, he was permitted to do so (vv. 6-7). Such a Levite would assist the priests, but

Refining and Reminding

without intruding into the office. This meant that the serving Levite was to receive a portion of the gifts and offerings designated for the priests. The fact that he had gained profit from the sale of his property was not to decrease his portion for serving (v. 8). It was recognized that what was obtained from the sale of his property would be needed to acquire accommodations for his family where the central sanctuary was located.

No Pagan Practices (vv. 9-14)

The Israelites were warned against engaging in *"the abominations of those nations,"* that is, the heathen spiritualism of the Canaanites (v. 9). Moses provides a long list of prohibitions:

- Causing one's children to pass through the fire of Moloch (v. 10; Lev. 20:2).

- Practices of witchcraft and soothsaying (v. 10; Ex. 22:18).

- Interpreting omens and sorcery (v. 10; Lev. 19:26).

- Conjuring spells, necromancy, and spiritism (v. 11; Lev. 19:31).

- Engaging in any form of soothsaying or divination (v. 14; Num. 23:23).

All these activities were an abomination to the Lord (v. 12). Therefore, with God's help the Israelites were to purge the land of such things by slaying or driving out all the inhabitants from Canaan (vv. 13-14). Hence, there were to be no child sacrifices in an attempt to foreknow or control future events, or prophecies from false gods (i.e., soothsaying), or trying to control people by spells and enchantments (i.e., by witchcraft). No one was to interpret omens in an attempt to forecast the future. A spiritualist or medium engaged in necromancy in order to gain counsel from the dead. Necromancers do not actually communicate with the souls of the deceased, but with familiar spirits – fallen angels who pretend to be what they are not (1 Sam. 28:7-8; Acts 16:16-18).

The Lord knew that if the Israelites engaged in these detestable practices, it would lead them into immorality. It would also indicate their lack of reliance on and reverence for Jehovah. Moses warned his countrymen that if they participated in these abominations, they were rejecting Jehovah's Law and His sovereign rule over Israel.

A Prophet Like Moses (vv. 15-22)

The children of Israel asked Moses to be their mediator after seeing Jehovah's awesome display on the burning and quaking Mount Sinai. The Lord was pleased with their understanding of His holiness and their need of an intercessor to approach Him.

> *The Lord your God will raise up for you a Prophet like me from your midst, from your brethren. Him you shall hear, according to all you desired of the Lord your God in Horeb in the day of the assembly, saying, "Let me not hear again the voice of the Lord my God, nor let me see this great fire anymore, lest I die"* (vv. 15-16).

This meant that Moses would serve as Jehovah's prophet to communicate crucial messages to His people. Though God would send a long line of prophets to converse with Israel in the unfolding centuries, Moses' prophetic ministry was unique in comparison (34:10). He had enjoyed extended intimate fellowship with God, he spoke for God to the people and was a mediator representing the people to God. In this sense, Moses pictured the special Prophet that God would send in a future day to bring His ultimate message of hope to Israel (vv. 17-18). Those not heeding His Prophet's message would be judged appropriately by God (v. 19).

The role of a prophet was an important ministry in Israel; the prophet had to bravely stand before the people and be a mouthpiece for God. Prophetic exercise occurred mostly when there was spiritual decline among God's people. At such times, God sent prophets to make people aware of their sin, to call them to repentance, and to warn them of forthcoming judgment if they did not repent. Such was the situation in Israel when the Lord Jesus, the Living Word of God, was sent to the earth and was born of a virgin to testify for God (John 1:1-2).

During the Lord's first advent to the earth, He entered into the office of prophet after being anointed by the Holy Spirit at thirty years of age (Luke 3:21-23). After being tested forty days in the wilderness by Satan, the Lord Jesus began His public ministry of declaring the gospel of the kingdom (Matt. 4:17). The writer of Hebrews speaks of the Lord Jesus as being "the Apostle" of God: *"Wherefore, holy brethren, partakers of the heavenly calling, consider the Apostle and High Priest of our profession, Christ Jesus"* (Heb. 3:1). As prophet (or "apostle"), He is literally the "sent One" from the Father to perfectly represent God to mankind and to reveal God's plan of salvation. For this John refers to the Son of God as "the Word" (John 1:1; 1 Jn. 1:1); the Son became a man to bring the ultimate message of God to humanity. The Lord Jesus is a living message – He embodies the message of God. All that Christ did and said on earth was the message God wanted conveyed to man. The writer of Hebrews declares that Christ is the express image of God's person:

> *God, who at various times and in various ways spoke in time past to the fathers by the prophets, has in these last days spoken to us by His Son, whom He has appointed heir of all things, through whom also He made the worlds; who being the brightness of His glory and the express image of His person, and upholding all things by the word of His power, when He had by Himself purged our sins, sat down at the right hand of the Majesty on high* (Heb. 1:1-3).

The Lord Jesus, in His person and in His message, conveyed all the goodness of God to humanity. His sinless life reproved the self-righteous and His words confounded all human reasoning and wisdom. The Jews remembered the words of Moses who foretold the coming of a special prophet that would behave like God and would speak for God perfectly (vv. 15-22). A. T. Shearman explains why this portion of Deuteronomy has an important bearing on the office of the prophet, especially in relationship to the Lord Jesus Christ:

> Here Moses outlines the kind of ministry attached to the ideal prophet. He would be raised up from among the people (v. 15); thus, he would be in touch with contemporary needs and conditions. He would stand between the people and God in His transcendence (v. 16). The words of God would be in his mouth – he would speak by divine command (v. 18). Responsibility would be upon the people to listen (v. 19). Fulfillment of the word would be the sign of authority (vv. 21-22). The words "like unto me" (v. 15) show us the character of Moses as the prophet among his people (Hosea 12, 13). It would seem that here we have the pattern for the true prophetic office.[178]

The Jews inquired of John the Baptizer whether he was this particular prophet. John said he was not, but then proceeded to point them to Christ as the One they should be looking for (John 1:21-23). Luke agrees, and makes it abundantly clear that the words of Moses pertaining to the special prophet were fulfilled by Christ (Acts 3:22-26). Christ came to be the Great Revealer of the mind of God to the lost sheep of Israel. He continued this prophetic ministry among the Jews for over three years before giving Himself as a ransom for humanity at Calvary. The Lord ended His prophetic ministry on earth when He ascended into heaven.

It was important that Israel receive accurate communication from Jehovah. Therefore, there was to be no tolerance for anyone posing as a spokesman for false deities. Those offering prophetic counsel in Jehovah's name, which He did not speak or in the name of false gods were to be put to death (v. 20). But this created a difficulty: How would the people know if someone speaking in Jehovah's name was truly His prophet (v. 21)? The answer was that whatever a true prophet of God said would happen, always did happen (v. 22). A true prophet spoke for God and not of himself.

The New Testament confirms that the ministry of the Lord Jesus completely fulfilled Moses' prophecy in verse 18: *"I will raise up for them a Prophet like you from among their brethren, and will put My words in His mouth, and He shall speak to them all that I command Him."* The Lord Jesus perfectly conveyed the message of God to Israel, and indeed to all humanity. He confirmed many times that this was the essence of His earthly ministry:

As I hear, I judge; and My judgment is righteous, because I do not seek My own will but the will of the Father who sent Me (John 5:30).

Then Jesus said to them, "When you lift up the Son of Man, then you will know that I am He, and that I do nothing of Myself; but as My Father taught Me, I speak these things. And He who sent Me is with Me. The Father has not left Me alone, for I always do those things that please Him" (John 8:28-29).

This is why the Lord Jesus said, "Do you not believe that I am in the Father, and the Father in Me? The words that I speak to you I do not speak on My own authority; but the Father who dwells in Me does the works" (John 14:10).

Refining and Reminding

John 9 records Christ's healing of a man born blind and then that man's interrogation by the Sanhedrin. The man's understanding of his Healer progressively increased throughout the chapter: a man named Jesus (John 9:11), a prophet (John 9:17), the Son of God, his Lord (John 9:35-38). At the close of the chapter, the healed blind man worshipped the Lord Jesus, not for what He had done for him, but for who the Lord was. Clearly, the Lord Jesus was the prophet that Moses foretold, but He is more than just a prophet like Moses: He is the Son of God, our Great High Priest, and the King of the Saints!

The Lord Jesus is the only one foretold in Scripture to be a prophet, a priest, and a king. Moses led the Jews out of Egypt and spoke to them as God's prophet, but he was not called to be a priest. Samuel was a priest and a prophet, but not a king. David prophesied and ruled Israel as a king, but he was not a priest. The Lord Jesus was the foretold prophet, is presently a priest, and in a future day will rule the world from His earthly throne.

Meditation

> Be Thou my Wisdom, and Thou my true Word;
> I ever with Thee and Thou with me, Lord;
> Thou my great Father, and I Thy true son,
> Thou in me dwelling, and I with Thee one.
>
> High King of heaven, my victory won,
> May I reach heaven's joys, O bright heaven's Sun!
> Heart of my own heart, whatever befall,
> Still be my Vision, O Ruler of all.
>
> — Mary E. Byrne

Cities of Refuge
Deuteronomy 19

Cities of Refuge (vv. 1-13)

Moses commanded that six of the forty-eight Levitical cities be designated as Cities of Refuge, with three of the six being in Canaan (vv. 1-2, 7); the others were located among the two and a half tribes who settled in Transjordan (4:41-43; Num. 35:6). A few years later Joshua will obey Moses' command and appoint three Cities of Refuge in Canaan: Kadesh in Galilee, Shechem in Mount Ephraim, and Hebron in the mountains of Judah (Josh. 20:7). He also designated three Cities of Refuge east of the Jordan River: Bezer in the plain of Reuben, Ramoth in Gilead, and Golan in Bashan (Josh. 20:8). All six cities were evenly spread from north to south on both sides of the Jordan River.

In Numbers 35, Moses had already given specific instructions on how manslayers should be protected in Cities of Refuge until tried. In this chapter, he merely highlights the fact that the Law protected the life of the accused until proven guilty and those found guilty of premeditated murder should die and not be shown mercy. Those guilty of accidental manslaughter (i.e., an axe head flies off the handle while chopping wood and kills someone) was not guilty of murder and should not die (vv. 3-5). Such a person was to flee to a City of Refuge to escape vengeful relatives of the deceased until the case could be heard by the elders of that city (v. 6).

If the accused was found innocent of intentional manslaughter, he or she could dwell within the confines of that city without the threat of familial revenge. Upon the death of the high priest, all who had been found innocent of murder were allowed to return to their inheritance without any further threat of retaliation (Num. 35:26-28). However, if the guilty party left their City of Refuge before the high priest died, then he was not protected (Num. 35:26-27).

If the Israelites remained faithful and obedient in Canaan, Jehovah promised to enlarge their borders; for this outcome the Jews were to add three more cities of refuge for a total of nine (vv. 8-10). If someone committing premeditated murder fled to a City of Refuge to escape punishment, as determined by the elders of his home city, then the officials at the City of Refuge were to release the convicted murder to the "avenger of blood" (a family member of the deceased; vv. 11-12). There was to be no pity or mercy shown to a condemned murderer. The shedding of innocent blood in the land must be requited for God's blessing to be received (v. 13).

Boundaries and Witnesses (vv. 14-21)

After the conquest of Canaan, Joshua would oversee the tribal allotments. Once each tribe's inheritance was distributed among clans and families, the markers (often stone pillars) were not to be moved in an attempt to gain more land by cheating others (v. 14; 27:27). Sadly, this type of theft became a widespread problem in Israel's history (Prov. 22:28, 23:10; Hos. 5:10).

Moses closes this chapter by reaffirming that the truth is best established by the testimony of many witnesses; therefore, no one was to be found guilty of a crime by the mouth of a single witness (v. 15). False witnesses (often for personal gain or to settle a vendetta) also plagued Israel's history, as observed in the story of Ahab stealing Naboth's vineyard (1 Kgs. 21). Moses said that the priests and magistrates were to carefully examine the testimony of a witness against an accused person to ensure the testifier was not lying (vv. 16-18). If the witness was found to be false, then that person was to suffer the punishment he sought to inflict on the innocent party (v. 19). Such an example would make others think twice about committing perjury in a court of law (v. 20).

Moses then affirms the guiding principle of the Law in maintaining justice in the land: *"Your eye shall not pity: life shall be for life, eye for eye, tooth for tooth, hand for hand, foot for foot"* (v. 21). In Canaan, the deterrent for wrongdoing would be the Law of Retribution (i.e., the just and equal retaliation for offenses). God was enacting strict, even-handed justice, which afforded no mercy to guilty offenders and set forth specific *equitable* punishments to right a wrong; yet, the Law did prohibit brutality.

Moses declared the Law of Retribution at Sinai thirty-nine years earlier: *"Eye for eye, tooth for tooth, hand for hand, foot for foot, burn for burn, wound for wound, stripe for stripe"* (Ex. 21:24-25). Ideally then, if an individual caused someone else to lose an eye, the offender then forfeited one of his or her eyes in retaliation for the offense. The "eye for eye" mentality applied only to the courtroom, not to personal retribution. Commenting to this verse MacDonald writes:

> It is commonly misrepresented as vindictive, but it is not. This law is not a *license* of cruelty, but a *limit* to it. In the context it refers to what kind of penalty could be inflicted upon a false witness.[179]

True, the Law did require a life for a life (if one was found guilty of murder), but typically did not condone mutilation of the guilty party for lesser offenses. (Deut. 25:11-12 would be an exception to this generalization.) There was, however, to be just compensation for the injuries and hardships caused by an offender.

The following examples from Exodus 21 illustrate this: If a slave lost his eye while working, he was to be freed. If one man's slave was gored by another man's bull, there was to be financial restitution. If an individual or his bull caused the loss of another man's livestock, there was to be restitution according to the value of the animal. If the matter involved two bulls, and there was no neglect found in pen upkeep, the living bull was to be sold and the money split between the owner of the dead bull and the owner of the living one. If someone caused, intentionally or unintentionally, a pregnant woman to prematurely deliver a surviving baby, there was restitution to be paid for the inconvenience. Edward Dennett observes that being under Retaliatory Law would cause Israel to long for a better way – grace:

> Grace is absent in the true character of law. It is eye for an eye, and tooth for a tooth, etc. Our blessed Lord especially cites these provisions to point out their contrast with grace. He says, *"Ye have heard that it hath been said, An eye for an eye, and a tooth for a tooth: but I say unto you, that ye resist not evil: but whosoever shall smite thee on thy right cheek, turn to him the other also"* (Matt. 5:38, 39). On the ground of law, an exact equivalent is demanded – no more, and no less; but grace can remit every claim; for dealt with in grace ourselves, our whole debt remitted, we must act on the same principle in our relationships with one another. Be it, however, never forgotten that the foundation of grace itself is laid deep in righteousness, and hence it reigns through righteousness (Rom. 5:21), having thus been established upon an everlasting and immutable basis.[180]

Refining and Reminding

The Law prescribed stringent justice for crimes and offenses, even if they were unintentionally committed. Its tit-for-tat restitution would satisfy the injured party's desire for vengeance, but within limits. The Law did not teach man how the divine qualities of love, grace, and mercy should govern one's judgments. Certainly, the lack of these in resolving life's offenses would cause man to be more appreciative of God's ultimate means of making restitution for both our intentional and unintentional offenses against Him – the giving and judging of His Son in our place.

The Lord Jesus Christ would be, and indeed was, the sin sacrifice for all humanity. Through Christ we don't get what we deserve (all the horrors of hell) and we do receive what we don't deserve (all the blessings of heaven); the former is God's mercy to us and the latter is His grace. Consequently, every aspect of our salvation is permeated by the sweet aroma of Christ's love. May we never get over the love of Christ and may we long for others to know it too!

Meditation

> We will love with tender care, know the love of Christ,
> Brethren who His image bear, for "the love of Christ."
> Jesus only shall we know, and our love to all shall flow,
> In His blood-bought Church below, for "the love of Christ."
>
> — William Reid

Rules of Warfare
Deuteronomy 20

During the wilderness years, Israel had engaged in few battles and usually only because they were attacked. Examples are battles with the Amalekites in the Sinai wilderness, the Canaanites from Arad, and the Amorites in the plains of Moab. Their limited warfare had been hand-to-hand combat out in the open; they had not engaged war-chariots or fortified cities. As this was about to change, Moses lays down rules of engagement and what the proper perspective should be during the Canaan conquest.

First, Moses exhorts his countrymen not to be afraid of confronting larger armies, even if they come with many horses and chariots, because *"the Lord your God is with you, who brought you up from the land of Egypt"* (v. 1). Just as Jehovah vanquished the most powerful army in the world at the Red Sea despite its elite soldiers and war-chariots, He would overcome all of their opposition in Canaan. (Later, we learn that these war-chariots did incite fear among the Israelites; Josh. 17:16; Judg. 4:3.) The Israelites were few in number in comparison to Canaan's multitudes, so no battle would be won by Israel's military tactics or strength. They had to rely on Jehovah to conquer their enemies.

Although there are similarities between the warfare Israel was to wage in Canaan and that of believers today (indeed, the same enemy still exists), the rules of warfare are quite different for believers than for Israel long ago. However, William Kelly observes a commonality between believers warring against spiritual wickedness in heavenly places today and Israel confronting the Canaanites:

> The heavenly land is for us the scene of contest with the enemy. ... The wilderness is the scene of temptation. Canaan is the place where the enemy must be fought and beaten. But there is no power by which he can be overcome but that of God. Consequently, faintheartedness would be intolerable, for it could only arise from this – that the people

Refining and Reminding

were thinking not of Jehovah their God, but of themselves or their enemies. Thus, it is impossible to win the battles of Jehovah. What secures victory is the certainty that our God calls to the fight, that it is His battle, not ours: where it is so, we are as sure of the end as of the beginning. We are calmly convinced that ... He who calls to fight will ensure that the enemy shall be vanquished.[181]

The enemy of our souls does not fear the Lord's people per se; however, he knows he cannot advance against them when they put their full confidence in their God. In the Church Age, such actions of faith result in fresh proclamations of the devil's defeat at Calvary. Satan knows that if he can move the believer from the truth of the triumphant ground of Calvary, he can gain a victory. Watchman Nee summarizes this point in his book *Sit, Walk, Stand*:

Christ's warfare was offensive; He gained the victory over the devil at the Cross. Our warfare is mostly defensive – we war against Satan only to maintain and consolidate the victory which Christ has already gained – we hold what Christ has gained against all challenges. If we fight with the concept of gaining a victory, then we lose the battle at the onset. The Christian walk and warfare draw their strength from sitting before God and resting in Him. Satan's objective is to move us from the perfect ground of triumph, thus our armor (Eph. 6) is essentially defensive. ...

Only those who sit can stand. Our power for standing, as for walking, lies in our having first been made to sit together with Christ. The Christian's walk and warfare alike derive their strength from his position there. If he is not sitting before God, he cannot hope to stand before the enemy.[182]

Satan knows that he can overcome God's people only when they compromise the truth by doubting God's ability and promises. This is why James exhorts believers to *"submit to God. Resist the devil and he will flee from you. Draw near to God and He will draw near to you"* (Jas. 4:7-8). The prophet Ezekiel informs us that before his fall, Lucifer (now referred to as Satan or "the accuser") was a beautiful, anointed cherub (Ezek. 28:11-16). He was likely the most powerful created being that God created and, thus, is a cunning and dangerous enemy that only God controls. Consequently, believers are not commanded to confront Satan, but rather to resist him by submitting to God in faith.

Moses encouraged his countrymen not to be fainthearted in challenging the hordes of Canaan, because the campaign was the Lord's and no army on earth could defeat Him. The priests were to remind Israel's army of this fact before military engagements (v. 3). Their pronounced blessing would remind the Jewish soldiers that they fought a holy war and would embolden them to engage the enemy: *"The Lord your God is He who goes with you, to fight for you against your enemies, to save you"* (v. 4). Believers today are encouraged by similar promises:

> *Yet in all these things we are more than conquerors through Him who loved us. For I am persuaded that neither death nor life, nor angels nor principalities nor powers, nor things present nor things to come, nor height nor depth, nor any other created thing, shall be able to separate us from the love of God which is in Christ Jesus our Lord* (Rom. 8:37-39).

In Christ, the believer has been eternally delivered from the clutches of the enemy, and we reign victorious! Christians today can prosper against spiritual enemies even as the Israelites did centuries ago against physical foes in Canaan. How is this possible? Believers already have the authority of God to labor with Christ in effecting His will and power, but we must choose to walk with Him in truth (1 Jn. 1:6-7). If we choose to walk the path of darkness and disobedience, we do so alone, for the Lord cannot abide with us there. At such a time, He does not leave us, but, rather, we depart from His fellowship. However, if we walk in accordance with revealed truth, we will appreciate the Lord's communion, for He has promised: *"I will never leave you nor forsake you"* (Heb. 13:5).

As the writer of Hebrews pondered the blessed solace of the Lord's abiding presence, he concluded: *"So we may boldly say: 'The Lord is my helper; I will not fear. What can man do to me?'"* (Heb. 13:6). Though conscious of our own deficiencies and the difficulties ahead, believers, resting in their divine calling, are able to move forward as overcomers. When believers know what they have been called to do and yield themselves as a channel of mercy for that cause, they become invincible until their work is done!

Refining and Reminding

While the priests were responsible for encouraging Israel's army to step forward in faith against God's enemies, the officers were to ensure that only qualified men were serving as soldiers. During the conquest years, the vast majority of Israel's men twenty years of age and older were compelled to serve as warriors. Afterwards, however, service was mostly volunteered. In either case, some men were exempt from serving as soldiers for a time to enjoy domestic privileges. This was possible because the Lord was fighting for Israel; therefore, the Jewish nation did not need to be preoccupied with war efforts or be anxious about their final victory. God was punishing the wicked Canaanites, while at the same time providing a land for His people to inherit and settle in. For this reason, the Jews could go on with life with a high degree of normalcy even though war was raging on in Canaan.

Those exempt from fighting included the newly married for one year. Of special consideration was a betrothed man who had not yet consummated his marriage and therefore did not have children to receive his family inheritance. Additionally, those who had just invested in property and lacked sufficient time to erect a house or plant vineyards and crops etc. to sustain his family in the coming year would be exempt from service (vv. 5-7). Jamieson, Fausset, and Brown suggest a practical reason for these exclusions:

> It was deemed a great hardship to leave a house unfinished, a new property half-cultivated, and a recently-contracted marriage unconsummated; and the exemptions allowed in these cases were founded on the principle, that a man's heart being deeply engrossed with something at a distance, he would not be very enthusiastic in the public service.[183]

The officers were also responsible to remove the fainthearted soldier from their ranks, lest they defect in battle and degrade the morale of other soldiers (vv. 8-9). Ranking officers were to organize Israel's army into brigades by appointing subordinates of various ranks to oversee and care for the soldiers.

Israel's war tactics were to consist of two strategies. The nations outside Canaan proper, but within the region promised to Abraham (Gen. 15:18-21), were to be given the option of surrender and servitude, before being attacked (v. 10). If a city capitulated, then its inhabitants would be spared, but would also be required to serve and pay tribute to Israel (v. 11). If the residents rejected this offer of peace, then that city was to be besieged, conquered, the men slain, the women and children enslaved, and the city plundered (vv. 13-15). Captives would be required to revere Israel's God alone. However, nations residing in Canaan (the six listed represented all of Canaan) were to be utterly destroyed or driven out of the land without mercy (vv. 16-17). This was to prevent heathen survivors from influencing Israel by their pagan ways (v. 18).

As Israel had never besieged a city before, Moses provides counsel to guide Israel's future efforts to overthrow a fortified city. Large amounts of wood were needed to build siegeworks (e.g., an elevated platform permitted archers to shoot arrows into the city), battering rams, etc. or to ignite fires against stone walls to weaken them. So while it was necessary to harvest trees for these endeavors, they were not to lay the land waste by cutting down the fruit-bearing trees (vv. 19-20). Matthew Henry suggests that a guiding principle for life is portrayed in the commandment not to hack down the fruit trees during a siege:

> God is a better friend to man than he is to himself; and God's law consults our interests and comforts; while our own appetites and passions, which we indulge, are enemies to our welfare. Many of the Divine precepts restrain us from destroying that which is for our life and food. The Jews understand this as forbidding all willful waste upon any account whatsoever. Every creature of God is good; as nothing is to be refused, so nothing is to be abused.[184]

Since Israel would be inheriting the land, why would they destroy what would benefit them with food for years to come? May we wisely learn this principle and live in such a way that we never want what we have carelessly wasted!

Meditation

> Be an overcomer, only cowards yield
> When the foe they meet on the battlefield;
> We are blood-bought princes of the royal host,
> And must falter not, nor desert our post.

Refining and Reminding

    Be an overcomer, He who stands with you
    Is a mighty One, who is always true;
    In the sorest conflict you shall win the day,
    Face the legions dark till they flee away.

                            — Charles W. Naylor

Miscellaneous Laws
Deuteronomy 21

Unsolved Murder (vv. 1-9)

This passage indicates the value that God puts on human life and also His desire that the Promised Land be free of innocent blood (i.e., murder). Verses 1-9 describe what should be done if a man was found slain (i.e., the evidence indicated that death was not from natural causes) and no manslayer or murderer could be identified. Even though individual guilt could not be established, there was still a corporate responsibility to remove the guilt of the offense from the land. God knew all about the sin in the land where He dwelt with His people, and was offended by it. A central truth that runs throughout Scripture is that sin must be judged before sin can be forgiven and the sinner justified before God. Dealing with the guilt of the sin therefore became the responsibility of the city nearest to where the slain person was found.

To display their innocence in the matter, that town's elders (the local judges) were to take a young heifer (which had not been worked) and bring it to an untilled portion of land in a valley with flowing water. They were then to break its neck and wash their hands over it. The water for this ceremony came from the stream of the area needing to have the guilt of shed blood removed. Levitical priests were to be present to witness this ritual and to pray for God's mercy. The judges were to be the guardians of righteousness in acknowledging and rectifying the offense, while the priests were to be the channels of grace assuring the removal of guilt for the offense.

The Lord Jesus fulfilled both of these critical roles at Calvary and shortly afterwards. As God's Lamb He became the sin sacrifice to provide propitiation for the offense of our sins against God's righteous character. The flowing water through the valley represents the active agency of the Holy Spirit overseeing the sacrifice of the innocent substitute (e.g., Lev. 14:5-6; John 7:38-39). Hence, we read, *"Christ, who through the eternal Spirit offered Himself without spot to God"*

(Heb. 9:14). And then afterwards, *"Christ came as High Priest of the good things to come"* (Heb. 9:11), presented the merits of His blood before God and became *"the Mediator of the new covenant, by means of death, for the redemption of the transgressions under the first covenant"* (Heb. 9:15). The Lord Jesus was man's sin sacrifice and then He became the Great High Priest who removes the guilt of sin, the sting of death, and restores life for those who will trust in Him.

The breaking the calf's neck symbolized that the crime deserved capital punishment, while the washing of the hands declared the elders' innocence in the matter. The latter aspect reflects the believer's positional innocence before God after being justified in Christ and thoroughly washed by regeneration of the Holy Spirit (Tit. 3:5).

Although the guilty party could not be identified, a man had died by violence in the land, and hence the people bore *"the guilt of innocent blood"* (v. 9). The animal sacrifice and the prayers of the elders declaring their blamelessness were offered to God to atone for the offense that had occurred against Him. Jehovah dwelt with His people in the Promised Land; therefore, there could be no defiling of the land by the shedding of innocent blood.

Family Captives (vv. 10-14)

During ancient times in the Near East, it was typical for victorious invaders to slaughter the men, rape the women, enslave women and children, and plunder the conquered region. While it was necessary to eradicate the male population to prevent a reprisal, Israelite soldiers were to handle their captives with respect – women were not to be sexually abused and captives were not to be harshly treated. This law did not apply to Canaanite women, for they were to be killed or driven from the land, but rather to women located beyond Canaan, but still within the territory bestowed on Abraham by God in Genesis 15.

If a Jewish man did see a beautiful virgin among the captives that he would like to marry, this was permitted if a procedure was followed. The protocol protected the woman's dignity and prevented the man from making a rash decision. The young woman was to be brought into the house of the soldier's family for one month. This permitted her time to mourn the death of her parents and prepare psychologically for the radical lifestyle change of becoming an Israelite. She was to be shaved and her nails cut. She also received modest clothing appropriate for a Hebrew woman. This allowed the Jewish man to see the woman for what she was to ensure that he still wanted her for a wife (i.e., no flaunting of long hair, flashy painted nails or seductive attire).

If after a month, the man remained committed to the notion of taking the woman as his wife, he could have sexual relations with her to consummate the marriage. If later he was not pleased with her, he could dissolve the marriage, but he had to set her free. She could not be sold as a slave, because the man had humbled her. Reasons for putting her away could not be trivial, but for such things as discovering that she had previously been another man's wife (hence not a virgin) or that she would not revere Jehovah and His Law for Israel. This law sought to protect women from the common abuse captives suffered in ancient times; Israel was not to ill-treat the survivors of those they conquered.

Firstborn Inheritance Rights (vv. 15-17)

Moses then affirmed the inheritance rights of the firstborn male within a family unit:

> *If a man has two wives, one loved and the other unloved, and they have borne him children, both the loved and the unloved, and if the firstborn son is of her who is unloved, then it shall be, on the day he bequeaths his possessions to his sons, that he must not bestow firstborn status on the son of the loved wife in preference to the son of the unloved, the true firstborn. But he shall acknowledge the son of the unloved wife as the firstborn by giving him a double portion of all that he has, for he is the beginning of his strength; the right of the firstborn is his* (vv. 15-17).

The birthright blessing conferred two general rights on its recipient. First, it not only delegated rule in the family, but also a leadership position within the clan and tribe. Second, the recipient secured a double portion of the inheritance (v. 17). Before the giving of the Law which established the Levitical priesthood, this blessing also acknowledged who represented the family before God in worship – who would act as the priest for the family. At this time the Lord often set aside firstborn rights to accomplish His sovereign purposes, such as, to fulfill His covenant with Abraham, or to establish Israel, or to orchestrate types of Christ and His future work of redemption. Examples of this setting aside included Isaac instead of Ishmael, Jacob in lieu of Esau, Ephraim in place of Manasseh, and Joseph instead of Reuben)

Refining and Reminding

Verse 16 does not endorse polygamy, but rather limits abuses because of it. The Lord knows the human heart, and attempts through His Law to limit the exploitations of human carnality. We have just witnessed an example of this in the treatment of captive women. Polygamy is never upheld in a positive light in Scripture; in fact, the sad complications to family life caused by polygamy can be traced throughout the Old Testament. God's design for marriage was for one man and one woman to enter into a covenant with each other and with Him for life (Gen. 2:18-24).

Children were crucial to Jewish family life. They were helpers, even protectors when older, and eventually the inheritors of tribal allotments in the Promised Land. Inheritance and clan leadership were passed to the next generation through male children. This is why Elkanah likely married Peninnah; Hannah, his first wife, could not bear him children (1 Sam. 1:1-8). At this time, men did what was right in their own eyes (Judg. 17:6). Later, kings often had multiple wives to ensure there were plenty of males who could survive if a rival tried to seize the throne by massacring the kingly line. Though much sin occurred and grieved God's heart in ancient times, many of these offenses were not imputed as transgression because God had not yet posted His Law (Rom. 4:15, 5:13).

For example, God's original plan for marriage did not allow for divorce, but because of the hardness of man's heart, God permitted it in the Law with constraints (Matt. 19:8). Likewise, polygamy was not God's model for marriage, but He only warned Israel against it and put constraints on it (v. 17, 21:15).

Through the Mosaic Law, God proved to the Jews that they were Law-breakers and thus deserving judgment. However, in the Church Age, because believers are indwelt by the Holy Spirit, they have the capacity not only to keep the Law, but also to fulfill it in love; this represents God's fullest intention for His children (Rom. 13:8-10). If a man did not cheat on his wife, he could declare that he had kept the Law, but fulfilling the Law was not just restraining from adultery, but unselfishly giving Christ-like love to one's wife! There was no possibility of fulfilling the Law in the Old Testament, and that is why the original pattern of marriage is not affirmed until Christ does so in Matthew 19:5-6, just prior to the advent of the Church Age.

The Lord Jesus clearly states that unless a marriage covenant is dissolved for the case of adultery (some see this caveat applying only to the Jewish betrothal) any man marrying another woman commits adultery with her (Matt. 19:9). The Lord Jesus reposted the original pattern for marriage, and thus prohibited polygamy in the Church Age. If a man is already married and marries another woman, he commits adultery.

The apostles, filled with the Holy Spirit, have delivered to us the deep mysteries of God to be lived out as we fulfill the Law of love. The fact that a man would be disqualified from church leadership if he was a polygamist tells us what marital pattern is important to God. The apostles had only one wife or no wife (1 Cor. 9:5) and those in church leadership or in the office of deacons could not be polygamists (Tit. 1:6; 1 Tim. 3:2, 12). Scripture records no example of any Christian engaging in the practice of polygamy; monogamy, however, is repeatedly shown to be the proper pattern for marriage (Eph. 5:31-33). By God's Spirit within believers, His best design for marriage, which He instituted from the beginning, could be restored.

The point of this law was that if a man did have two wives and favored one over the other, the first-born son of either of them was to receive the right of the firstborn regardless. The Lord had already demonstrated the appropriateness of this earlier within Jacob's growing family (Gen. 29). The Lord explained that He opened Leah's womb because she was unloved by Jacob in comparison to Rachel (e.g., v. 15). The younger and more attractive Rachel had a monopoly on Jacob's love and affection. So God had pity upon Leah and revived her soul through the gift of child bearing – not just children, but six sons – while at the same time restricting Rachel's womb! Leah's first son was Reuben, whose name means "a son"; naturally speaking, he should receive the birthright blessing from Jacob. However, because of his later immorality with one of Jacob's concubines, that right transferred to Joseph, Rachel's firstborn son.

A Rebellious Son (vv. 18-21)

The prophet Malachi reminds us that in addition to marital companionship (Gen. 2:18), one of God's purposes for marriage is to produce a "godly seed." God is not seeking just children from the union of a husband and wife, but children who will be trained to live for Him (Mal. 2:15). Verses 18-21 address the situation in which a child is unruly and continually rebellious against parental authority. Such behavior demonstrated a lack of reverence for Jehovah and a disregard

Refining and Reminding

for God's Law (e.g., the fifth of the Ten Commandments). God decreed that the bad should be removed from the good so that the family and neighboring families were not negatively influenced by the rebel. Parents were acting under Jehovah's authority to raise their children up for Him, so an insolent child was actually rejecting His sovereign rule.

The Law posed the example of a long-endured rebellious son. Having given up all hope of reform, his parents could bring their son before the local elders for judgment. The elders were to diligently inquire into the matter and issue an impartial decision. The fact that the son was not to be judged for reckless living or drunkenness indicates his adulthood. The only offense worthy of the death penalty was stiff-necked rebellion against God's authority.

If the son was found guilty, all the local men were to be involved in his stoning. This would have a sobering effect on all who heard of it. Matthew Henry surmises that the severity of this judgment indicates how offensive to God the rebellion of a child towards his or her parents must be:

> Children who forget their duty must thank themselves, and not blame their parents, if they are regarded with less and less affection. ... Disobedience to a parent's authority must be very evil, when such a punishment was ordered; nor is it less provoking to God now, though it escapes punishment in this world. But when young people early become slaves to sensual appetites, the heart soon grows hard, and the conscience callous; and we can expect nothing but rebellion and destruction.[185]

The judgment of the rebellious son affirmed just how much God hated stubborn pride among His children too. The prophet Samuel would later remind King Saul of this fact. From God's perspective, *"rebellion is as the sin of witchcraft, and stubbornness is as iniquity and idolatry"* (1 Sam. 15:23). It is important to understand that this law did not give parents the authority to abuse their children, nor was its focus a sporadic act of disrespect or dissidence; it was for deep-seated rebellion against God's authority – parents. To this end, David renders wise counsel for the saints of all ages: *"Oh, love the Lord, all you His saints! For the Lord preserves the faithful, and fully repays the proud person"* (Ps. 31:23).

A Hanged Criminal (vv. 22-23)

The many references to death by stoning in Scripture indicate it was the preferred method of executing a condemned criminal. Stoning an offender permitted "the avenger of blood" (i.e., the family of the slain victim), the witnesses in a court case, and the local authorities to all participate in the judgment. Nonetheless, sometimes death by hanging was preferred because a corpse dangling from a rope would have a sobering effect in deterring others from committing the same crime for which the felon died (v. 22). If a criminal was hung, his body was to be removed and buried before dark. Moses did provide a reason for this, *"that you do not defile the land which the Lord your God is giving you as an inheritance; for he who is hanged is accursed of God"* (v. 23). Jack S. Deer clarifies the confusion often associated with the meaning of this statement:

> Hanging a criminal on a tree was not for the purpose of putting him to death. Rather, after he was executed for a capital offense ... his body was hanged on a tree as a warning to all who saw it not to commit the same offense. The criminal was under God's curse, not because his body was hung on the tree, but because he had broken God's Law by committing a crime worthy of death. Therefore, his body was not to be left on the tree overnight.[186]

In other words, those put to death by hanging were already cursed by God for their crimes before the execution was carried out. It was not hanging from a tree that made them accursed, but rather hanging was the proof of the curse. It was God's desire that none of His people should be accursed and be put to death in the inheritance He bestowed on them. Thus, the cursed person should be buried as soon as the officials deemed that the public spectacle had served its purpose in restraining evil.

Knowing that guilty criminals hung on a tree were cursed by God is why the Jews did not want to stone Christ, but rather demanded that Pilate crucify Him. Jewish hatred for Christ's message and His person was so intense that the Greek text does not include the pronoun "Him" in association with the word "crucified"; the people cried out, *"Crucify, crucify"* (John 19:6). Those hard-hearted Jews not only wanted an innocent man to be put to death, but they also demanded that Jesus be nailed to a tree to show that He was also cursed by God.

Refining and Reminding

Unbeknown to the Jews, that was exactly what God planned to do – to make His Son accursed. After He was whipped, stripped, and nailed to a cross, God cursed His own Son on humanity's behalf (Gal. 3:13), and in so doing, nailed the death sentence that we each deserved to His cross (Col. 2:14). He did not die for His own sins, but to provide penal substitution through death and thus become the propitiation for sinners (Heb. 2:9; 1 Jn. 2:2). God used man's injustice at Calvary to work His righteous judgment of sin. As a result, God can righteously and justly offer forgiveness of sins and eternal life to those who will trust Christ for salvation!

With this understanding, J. N. Darby suggests that a typological trilogy foretelling Israel's future rebellion is contained in this chapter:

> In chapter 21 we have three interesting cases, because of the principles which apply to the ways of God with Israel: the case of the man found slain, that of the child of the hated wife, and that of the rebellious son. The land of Jehovah must be kept pure. Israel will have to make this confession in the latter days, and to clear themselves of the blood of Messiah. If the case of the two wives applies to Israel upon earth, it applies still more closely to Christ (Head of the Gentiles) and the assembly with whom He will inherit all things, although upon earth Israel be the wife beloved. However, Israel, as a rebellious son under the old covenant, is condemned and cut off; as regards the redeemed, the curse of the law has fallen upon another – Christ.[187]

Amen! Because of Christ, the guilt of innocent blood will be taken off the people and off the land! This will permit holy Jehovah in a coming day to dwell again among His redeemed and cleansed people in the Promised Land. This is His wonderful inheritance for them.

Meditation

> Nailed upon Golgotha's tree – faint and bleeding. Who is He?
> Hands and feet so rudely torn, wreathed with crown of twisted thorn.
> Once He lived in heaven above, happy in His Father's love,
> Son of God, 'tis He, 'tis He, on the cross at Calvary.
>
> Nailed upon Golgotha's tree – as a victim. Who is He?
> Bearing sin, but not His own, suffering agony unknown.

He, the promised sacrifice, for our sins has paid the price.
Lamb of God, 'tis He, 'tis He, on the cross at Calvary.

— A. P. Gibbs

Laws of Morality
Deuteronomy 22

Laws of Morality and Separation (vv. 1-12)

This chapter provides practical examples of how a Jew might fulfill Moses' previous command, *"you shall love your neighbor as yourself"* (Lev. 19:18). If someone's ox, sheep, or donkey went astray and was found by another, the animal was to be returned to its owner (v. 1). However, if the owner lived at a distance or was unknown, the animal was to be properly cared for until the owner came seeking it; then it was to be returned to its owner (v. 2). The familiar adage, "finders – keepers; losers – weepers" was never to characterize God's people. They were not to covet or steal each other's possessions, even if misplaced (e.g., a lost garment; v. 3). There was to be no thought of wrongful trespass requiring compensation for a wayward beast, but rather goodwill towards its owner, who had suffered loss during its absence (at least, time looking for it).

Furthermore, if someone observed a neighbor's ox or donkey fallen in some way (perhaps ensnared in vines or a mud bog), he was to assist the owner to free the animal: *"You shall not see your brother's donkey or his ox fall down along the road, and hide yourself from them; you shall surely help him lift them up again"* (v. 4). In other words, no Jew was to shirk their holy duty of looking after his neighbor's interests with tenacious care! C. H. Mackintosh provides this helpful point of application.

> How prone we are to think only of ourselves, our own interests, our own comfort and convenience! ... Self is too much our object and motive spring in all our undertakings; nor can it be otherwise unless the heart be kept under the governing power of those motives and objects which belong to Christianity. We must live in the pure and heavenly atmosphere of the new creation, in order to get above and beyond the base selfishness which characterizes fallen humanity. Every unconverted man, woman and child on the face of the earth is

governed simply by self, in some shape or another. Self is the center, the object, the motive-spring of every action.[188]

Indeed, being selfish by nature, man is not inherently compelled to help others bear their burdens. However, believers, understanding the tender, providential care of God, will be prompted by the Holy Spirit to help others and so we should! Foreknowing our steps in time, God has predestined good works for us to accomplish for His glory and our reward (Eph. 2:10). God's covenant people were to aid each other in times of need and distress, and so should believers today (Gal. 6:2; Jas. 1:27, 2:14-17).

The Jews were to be kind and hospitable in the land. For example, if they found a fallen nest with a mother still brooding over her young, they could take the young, but not the mother (vv. 6-7). This practice was to teach the Israelites to be forward thinking and not to live for the moment. By taking only the chicks and permitting the mother to reproduce again, they were able to receive an additional blessing in the future. In principle, this mimicked what they already practiced in the harvesting of livestock.

The Israelites were also to construct homes with a roof parapet to protect their guests from falling (v. 8). MacDonald writes:

> A parapet or railing had to be built around the flat roof of a house to prevent people from falling off. The roof was the place of fellowship. It is important to guard the communion, especially of the young and careless.[189]

Such safety features in a home would express loving concern for guests, that is, that the host actually appreciated their fellowship.

God's people were to be peculiar in their worship and lifestyle as compared to pagan nations. The Law commanded a strict diet, precise religious practices, unique attire, specific rules for farming, and restriction for the breeding and slaughtering of livestock. There were even certain animals that the Jews were not to touch. Verses 9-12 contain further examples of laws governing daily living to illustrate their practical separation from the world:

> *You shall not sow your vineyard with different kinds of seed, lest the yield of the seed which you have sown and the fruit of your vineyard be defiled* (v. 9).

Refining and Reminding

You shall not plow with an ox and a donkey together (v. 10).

You shall not wear a garment of different sorts, such as wool and linen mixed together (v. 11).

You shall make tassels on the four corners of the clothing with which you cover yourself (v. 12).

Another prohibition was wearing clothing which would confuse male and female distinction (v. 5). The practice of cross-dressing often promoted the sin of homosexuality, which God utterly detests (Lev. 18:22, 20:13). God created each gender for specific roles for family and social life and He did not want His design eroded by the confusion of the genders. Writing early in the twentieth century, C. A. Coates notes that gender confusion creates chaos in displaying the glory of God in the Church:

Divine order is ever to be observed, and it is most important to have regard to this in a day when every feature of that order is being so largely set aside. In Christianity the man and the woman each have their distinctive clothing, and are only suitably adorned as they appear in it. The whole tendency of things today is to subvert divine order, but that order is to be maintained in God's assembly.

Nature itself teaches a woman to be retiring and modest. ... Her "clothing" would represent her whole deportment and appearance, not excluding her actual dress. It is to be suitable to the place which she has of expressing in her own person how the assembly is subjected to the Christ. So Paul, representing the authority of the Lord, says, *"Let a woman learn in quietness in all subjection; but I do not suffer a woman to teach nor to exercise authority over man, but to be in quietness"* (1 Tim. 2:11-12). He also says, *"Let, your women be silent in the assemblies, for it is not permitted to them to speak; but to be in subjection, as the law also says... it is a shame for a woman to speak in assembly"* (1 Cor. 14:34-35). I have no doubt that the disordered state of the church is reflected in the uncomely behavior of women at the present time. ... It is a reproach to see women preaching, or putting themselves into prominence; it is a setting aside of their true glory – a putting on of man's apparel.

But then, on the other hand, *"neither shall a man put on a woman's clothing."* The men are not to retire from the place accorded to them;

they are to *"pray in every place* (that is, not only in the assembly, but at home, or wherever occasion arises), *lifting up pious hands, without wrath or reasoning"* (1 Tim. 2:8). The public expression of praise or prayer, the setting forth of things in ministry, and the responsibility for order and edification in the assembly, rests with the men, and it is well for all believing men to see that they do not retire from the responsible service of the house of God. It might be as uncomely for a brother to be silent in the assembly as for a sister to speak there. It is well to reflect upon this, and to see to it that we appear in the [practical] clothing for which we are suitable.[190]

Concerning the differences between men and women, the New Testament affirms it is natural for women to have longer hair than men (1 Cor. 11:14-15). Women are to actively cover their heads during times of spiritual exercise, such as prayer and teaching, while the men remain uncovered (1 Cor. 11:4-7). While women are attending to the visual ministry of the Church, men are to lead and engage in the audible ministry (1 Cor. 14:33-35; 1 Tim. 2:8, 11-12).

Let us remember that men are not just to represent the glory of God – they are the glory of God and therefore should act accordingly when believers gather in God's presence for prayer and teaching (1 Cor. 11:5-7). Likewise, women are not just to represent the glory of the man – they are the glory of the man, and man is always to be in subjection to God. Hence, the covered head of the silent woman and the uncovered head of a leading man affirm God's glory in the Church and His order for the genders.

Satan clearly has a foothold in our modern culture, which promotes homosexuality and recognizes more gender options than "male" and "female." This perverse philosophy rebels against God's created order and purposes for each gender. Some call God's biblical order for male and female "old fashioned" and "outdated." Indeed His order is old – "from the beginning" but not outdated, for God is eternal and does not change (Mal. 3:6). But God is a perfect Gentleman, so to speak; He does not force anyone to obey His design for family life; however, He does bless those who yield to His authority. Whenever we depart from God's best, we lose His rest and the painful consequences of humanistic reasoning abruptly abound. To show honor for the Creator's intentions for male and female, the Jews were not to wear clothes pertaining to the opposite gender.

Refining and Reminding

The wearing of specific clothing to represent something important to God was not an issue of morality, per se, but it was to prevent immorality resulting from the breakdown of biblical family life. This attire limitation would serve as a daily reminder that Jehovah was holy and the Jews were to be separate from other nations in their conduct and appearance. In the spiritual sense, Paul conveys a similar message of holiness and separation to the believers at Corinth:

> *Do not be unequally yoked together with unbelievers. For what fellowship has righteousness with lawlessness? And what communion has light with darkness? And what accord has Christ with Belial? Or what part has a believer with an unbeliever? And what agreement has the temple of God with idols? For you are the temple of the living God. As God has said: "I will dwell in them and walk among them. I will be their God, and they shall be My people." Therefore "Come out from among them and be separate, says the Lord. Do not touch what is unclean, and I will receive you." "I will be a Father to you, and you shall be My sons and daughters, says the Lord Almighty"* (2 Cor. 6:14-18).

Being God's temple on earth should motivate every believer to depart from sin. To do so will secure the Lord's blessed fellowship and care. In summary, the appearance and customs of the Israelites were to mark them as unique. C. H. Mackintosh reminds us that Christians must likewise be distinctive:

> The Israelite was not to plow with an ox and an ass together; neither was he to wear a garment of diverse sorts, as of woolen and linen. The spiritual application of both these things is as simple as it is important. The Christian is not to link himself with an unbeliever, for any object whatsoever, be it domestic, religious, philanthropic, or commercial, neither must he allow himself to be governed by mixed principles. His character must be formed and his conduct ruled by the pure and lofty principles of the word of God. Thus may it be with all who profess and call themselves Christians.[191]

While the Church is not bound to Levitical particulars, the concepts of separation from evil and worldliness and maintaining a distinction between the genders are again upheld in the New Testament. James proclaims that worldliness is enmity with God (Jas. 4:4), and Paul reminds Christians to refrain from anything that has even the appearance of evil (1 Thess. 5:22).

Through philosophy and deception, Satan works to confuse our minds as to the order that God has decreed for us. Just as the Israelites were not told all the "whys" for these unusual practices, neither is the Church; God just expects us to yield to and obey what He commands – thus marking us as the most peculiar people on earth!

Laws of Sexual Morality (vv. 13-30)

Another lifestyle difference from the nations would be the emphasis of pre-marital chastity, limitations on who could be married, and the moral integrity to mark marriage. Jack S. Deere identifies the purpose of the law in this chapter and how it guarded against illegitimate exploitation:

> This law was meant to endorse premarital sexual purity and to encourage parents to instill within their children the value of sexual purity. The law might be misused, however, by an unscrupulous husband against his wife for personal reasons, or perhaps to recover the bride-price he originally paid to the girl's father. If such a husband charged that his wife was not a virgin when they were married, then her parents were obligated to produce proof of her virginity. The evidence was to be a cloth, a bloodstained garment or a bedsheet from the wedding night.[192]

If a husband, after consummating his marriage with his bride, charged his wife's parents with posing their daughter as a virgin when she was not, the parents could bring the shameful charge to the local elders (vv. 13-17). The parents of the bride were permitted to publicly prove their daughter's fidelity by producing a blood-spotted cloth for examination (v. 15). The evidence either pertained to their daughter's first sexual contact with her husband (supposedly from a torn hymen) or it was proof that she had menstruated just prior to the consummation of her marriage (thus proving she was not pregnant).

MacDonald notes that "tokens of virginity" may be translated as "tokens of adolescence" and that the stained cloth produced by the parents merely proved that their daughter was not pregnant instead of being a virgin.[193] This seems to be a more reasonable understanding of the parental defense and its purpose for two reasons. First, because the young bride had been living at home prior to joining with her husband,

Refining and Reminding

the parents would have access to menstruation evidence, but not to honeymoon bed linen, per se. Second, for various reasons which will not be explained here, most virgin women do not experience bleeding after initial intercourse.[194]

If the elders reviewing the charge found the husband's claims to be erroneous, then that man was to be publicly whipped and fined 100 shekels for bring needless dishonor on the bride's family name (v. 18). The fact that the husband's fine was double the typical bridal dowry price (v. 29) suggests that beating and the fine would be a strong deterrent for carnal motives in the matter. That is, a corrupt husband would think twice before wrongly disgracing his wife and her family in an attempt to recover the fifty shekels he had paid to obtain her.

If she was found to have been a virgin, the husband could not divorce her as long as she lived (v. 19). However, if she was found not to be a virgin, meaning she had engaged in sexual relations with another man, she was to be brought to her father's house and stoned (vv. 20-21). This harsh punishment was for three reasons. First, she had been secretly lascivious. Second, she had lied about it and implicated her father in a deceptive agreement for profit. Third, a betrothed Jewish couple were under a marriage covenant, so any sexual relationships with another before the time they consummated their marriage was considered adultery and was punishable by death.

Joseph did not want to see his young betrothed wife Mary (pregnant with the Lord Jesus) stoned for apparent fornication. Being a devout man, he sought to divorce Mary privately and spare her life. However, an angel informed Joseph in a dream that the child in Mary's womb was conceived by the Holy Spirit and not through human agency; he therefore was to take Mary as his wife, which he did (Matt. 1:19-25).

As just mentioned, a betrothed virgin was considered a married woman; therefore any sexual relationship before her union with her husband was considered adultery and both parties were to be put to death (v. 22). If an illicit relationship occurred in the city, both the fornicating man and woman were to be put to death, but if in the countryside, the woman, being the weaker gender, was given the benefit of the doubt (vv. 23-27). In other words, she could have been raped, where no one could hear her screams, but this was unlikely in a city.

Under Jewish Law, rape of a married woman was considered as serious as murder and punishable by death. However, if a man forced an unbetrothed woman, he was to pay her parents the "bride's price" of fifty shekels of silver and marry her, unless the father prohibited the marriage (vv. 28-29; Ex. 22:17). If they married, the man was not permitted to ever divorce the woman that he had defiled. This was to protect the woman from being put out while possibly being pregnant and to protect her honor. It also would cause a Jewish man to think twice about having premarital relations with a virgin, as he may be forced to live with her the rest of his life!

Leviticus 18:7-14 explicitly prohibited marriage with certain relatives to avoid incest. Under the Law, you were not permitted to marry your mother, stepmother, sibling (even if a half-sibling), granddaughter, stepmother's daughter, aunt, or uncle. In this chapter, Moses merely mentions that it was inappropriate for a man to marry his stepmother after the death of his father (v. 30).

Meditation

> We have learned to live with unholiness and have come to look upon it as the natural and expected thing.
>
> — A. W. Tozer

> In reality, moral rules are directions for running the human machine. Every moral rule is there to prevent a breakdown, or a strain, or a friction, in the running of that machine. That is why these rules at first seem to be constantly interfering with our natural inclinations.
>
> — C. S. Lewis

> I say that a man must be certain of his morality for the simple reason that he has to suffer for it.
>
> — G. K. Chesterton

Congregational Purity
Deuteronomy 23

The Congregation of the Lord (vv. 1-8)

Anyone truly seeking Jehovah and willing to adopt His Law in faith would be received by the Lord. Such a proselyte would share in Israel's commonwealth and receive salvation. For example, Rahab the Canaanite prostitute will be inducted into the tribe of Judah in just a few weeks after Moses spoke this oracle because of her faith and plea for mercy (Josh. 2). Nevertheless, the Jews were to be mindful of ceremonial cleanness when gathered before the Lord for religious purposes, such as feasts. The Laws in this section provided further guidance as to who could compose the congregation of worshippers before the Lord.

No ceremonially unclean person could participate in religious gatherings at the central sanctuary (Lev. 12-15). Additionally, neither an emasculated male, nor a child born from a forbidden marriage or illicit relationship could come before the Lord (vv. 1-2). Examples of the latter limitation would be an illegitimate child, especially one born from incest or cultic prostitution. The specific prohibition against the eunuch in verse 1 may relate to a man who chose to be castrated in a pagan ritual. The restriction of children born of inappropriate unions carried forward to their descendants for ten generations.

It is important to understand that the subject matter before us is ceremonial cleanness and not positional rejection (as for a wicked person). For instance, if a Jew accidentally touched something dead, he would be barred from congregational gatherings for a time, yet their standing as one of God's redeemed was not lost. The prophet Isaiah assures us that both the children of foreigners and eunuchs can be fully accepted by the Lord and receive His salvation (Isa. 56:3-4).

The Ammonites and Moabites were also to be excluded from the congregation. If a Jew married an Ammonite or Moabite, their children, assuming Jewish ancestry afterwards, could not be a part of the assembly for ten generations (v. 3). These nations were founded through incest (unions between Lot and his two daughters).

Furthermore, both people groups had impeded Israel's journey to the Promised Land in two ways (v. 4). First, they had not been hospitable to Israel, as epitomized in the expression that they offered no *"bread and water."* Second, the Moabites hired Balaam to curse Israel. Nevertheless, Moses reminds his countrymen that God not only ignored Balaam's petition, but *"turned the curse into a blessing for you, because the Lord your God loves you"* (v. 5). But even though Balaam's curse was diverted by God, Balaam's doctrine still corrupted His people. God's anger was kindled against them, and thousands of Israelites perished in judgment. For this reason Moses commanded Israel: *"You shall not seek their peace nor their prosperity all your days forever"* (v. 6). The implication was that these nations would be characterized by continuing resistance against the Lord and Israel.

Limitations for Edomite and Egyptian ancestry were not as stringent as for the Ammonites and Moabites; they were permitted to join the congregation after three generations (vv. 7-8). The reasons given for this reduced restriction were that Edom was Israel's brother (i.e., the heads of these two nations, Jacob and Esau, respectively, were brothers) and that Israel dwelt for a long time in Egypt. Moses' account of the Egyptian exodus verified that there were already many Egyptians among them (Ex. 12:38).

With this said, it must be understood that some of God's providential doings did create unique exceptions to this general statute. For example, the Moabite Ruth married Boaz and became the great-grandmother of King David and thus was in the lineage of Christ (Ruth 4:13-22), and some of David's mighty men were from Ammon and Moab (1 Chron. 11:39, 46).

Camp Cleanliness (vv. 9-14)

Moses reminded the people that Jehovah dwelt with them and therefore their campsite should be free of defilement. Jewish warriors returning from battle were not to bring any unclean thing back into the camp (v. 9). Men having nocturnal emissions were to remain outside the camp until evening, then wash before returning (vv. 10-11). To ensure camp sanitation, the Jews were to use a shovel to bury their excrement outside the boundaries of the camp (vv. 12-13). Then, adding a bit of wit, Moses reaffirmed that Jehovah was always in their

Refining and Reminding

midst and therefore walked through the camp also (v. 14). These regulations were to be a constant reminder that a holy, omnipresent, and omniscient God was dwelling among them and He knew everything that happened in the camp (even a person's most private moments).

Miscellaneous Laws (vv. 15-25)

A fugitive slave from a foreign nation was not to be further oppressed but was permitted asylum in Israel (vv. 15-16). This would remind Israel of their own history; they too were once afflicted slaves in a foreign land, but now had found sanctuary in the Promised Land.

The previous chapter discussed the sexual purity God desired for married couples to enjoy and the capital offense of adultery. Hence, temple prostitution, a common pagan practice among ancient cultures, was prohibited; this meant that ritual prostitutes were not to be found among His people (v. 17). Prostitution in general, whether practiced by "a harlot" (a female) or "a dog" (a male), was fornication – an outrage against God's holiness. Furthermore, no vow to the Lord was to be paid with money gained through this immoral profession; that would be an abomination to Him (v. 18).

The Jews were to be a hospitable people, especially to their destitute brethren. They were not to worsen the plight of their compatriots by charging them interest on loans (v. 19). Yet, the Jews could exact interest from foreigners (v. 20). At Sinai, Moses had exhorted his brethren: *"You shall not oppress one another, but you shall fear your God; for I am the Lord your God"* (Lev. 25:17). The Lord's people should be mindful to care for each other. Given all that we have received from the Lord, it would be offensive to Him for us to take advantage of a brother or sister in the Lord suffering a hardship.

Additionally, the Lord promises to reward those who attend to the needy. *"Blessed is he who considers the poor; the Lord will deliver him in time of trouble"* (Ps. 41:1). In the Church Age, through the power of the Holy Spirit, believers are able to fulfill God's fuller intention of the Law – to demonstrate divine love for each other (Rom. 13:10). Therefore, Paul exhorts believers not only to care for each other and the poor, but also to extend compassion to those who oppose us. If our antagonists are hungry and thirsty, we are to provide them food and drink (Rom. 12:20). He explains that such kindhearted acts *"overcome evil by doing good"* (Rom. 12:21). Such conduct is a tangible and lasting testimony of Christ in our communities.

The entirety of Exodus 30 addressed the specific nature and limitations of uttering vows to the Lord. In this chapter, Moses merely highlights that vows were voluntary in nature and not compelled, but if someone made a vow to the Lord, he or she should fulfill it to avoid being punished by the Lord for fraud (vv. 21-23). The Lord always does what He promises to do, and His people should follow the same practice.

Moses had already commanded the Israelites to *"love your neighbor as yourself"* (Lev. 19:18). He then provided examples of how neighborly love should be shown (e.g., 22:1-4). Moses closes the chapter by giving another example of how to love one's neighbor. Travelers were permitted to eat grapes from a vineyard or kernels from a grain-field, but nothing was to be harvested and then carried away (vv. 24-25).

Mutual respect was to guide this gracious provision for travelers. Owners assisted those passing through but these travelers were not to abuse this hospitality. As all Israel was to appear before the Lord each year at the central sanctuary, such a custom would better enable pilgrims to make the long journey. In this sense, loving one's neighbor assisted the congregation in their worship of the Lord together. God's people were to learn that one could not truly love the Lord without expressing genuine love for each other. The same is true today.

Meditation

> O Thou, whom all Thy saints adore,
> We now with all Thy saints agree,
> And bow our inmost souls before
> Thy glorious, awful majesty.
>
> There let us all with Jesus stand,
> And join the general Church above,
> And take our seats at Thy right hand,
> And sing Thine everlasting love.
>
> — Charles Wesley

Caring for "the Defiled" and the Poor
Deuteronomy 24

Divorce and Remarriage (vv. 1-4)

The Bible does not promote or condemn slavery, but it does acknowledge its existence, and provides regulations to limit its abuses. Similarly, divorce was never God's plan for marriage – He hates it (Mal. 2:16). Accordingly, the Mosaic Law allowed for divorce, but issued rules to limit its abuse. Slavery and divorce spring from the same fountainhead – the depraved human heart (Matt. 19:8).

The Law permitted a husband to give his wife a divorce certificate detailing her fault(s) and then she would be compelled to leave the home (v. 1). The "uncleanness in her" could not be adultery, as that would have been punishable by death, not divorce. The divorce certificate was for the woman's protection, as that would permit her to remarry without the threat of being accused as an adulteress. If she did marry another man, and he later divorced her, it was not permitted for her to remarry her previous husband because he had caused her to be "defiled" by another man (vv. 2-4). For this reason, remarriage to a previous spouse after being married to another would be an abomination to the Lord. This would amount to legalized adultery and the Lord was not going to permit that. Jack S. Deere suggests that this is the reason for this divorce/remarriage limitation:

> The purpose of this law seems to be to prevent frivolous divorce, and to present divorce itself in a disparaging light. Jesus' interpretation of this passage indicated that divorce (like polygamy) went against the divine ideal for marriage (Matt. 19:3-9).[195]

Note that the same Hebrew word *tame'*, speaking of a remarried-divorced woman being "defiled," is also used to describe a woman being defiled by the act of adultery (Lev. 18:20) or a man being defiled by a sexual union with a beast (Lev. 18:23). This comparison indicates that though divorce was permitted, it was not a behavior that the Lord approved of. Albert Barnes explains:

> Moses neither institutes nor enjoins divorce. The exact spirit of the passage is given in our Lord's words to the Jews', *"Moses because of the hardness of your hearts suffered you to put away your wives"* (Matt. 19:8). Not only does the original institution of marriage as recorded by Moses (Gen. 2:24) set forth the perpetuity of the bond, but the verses before us plainly intimate that divorce, while tolerated for the time, contravenes the order of nature and of God. The divorced woman who marries again is "defiled" (v. 4), and is grouped in this particular with the adulteress (Lev. 18:20). Our Lord then was speaking according to the spirit of the Law of Moses when He declared, *"Whoso marries her which is put away commits adultery"* (Matt. 19:9).[196]

In Matthew 19, the Lord Jesus restated God's order for marriage from the beginning (Gen. 2) and why divorce was permitted by Moses for a time. However, the era of the Law ended when the New Covenant was sealed by Christ's blood. In the Church Age, believers are to stay married or live apart in peace, but they are not to divorce and remarry someone else (1 Cor. 7:10-11). Paul asserts: *"A husband is not to divorce his wife."* The provision of divorce that was permitted among God's covenant people because of the hardness of their hearts is removed in the Church Age, because believers receive a new heart through spiritual regeneration. Through the power of the indwelling Holy Spirit, believers can now enjoy God's best intentions for the marriage relationship – satisfying companionship! As Matthew Henry infers, those who marry wrongly still have the help of the Holy Spirit to love their spouse as they should, even if they are unlovely:

> Where the providence of God, or his own wrong choice in marriage, has allotted to a Christian a trial instead of a help meet; he will from his heart prefer bearing the cross, to such relief as tends to sin, confusion, and misery. Divine grace will sanctify this cross, support under it, and teach so to behave, as will gradually render it more tolerable.[197]

Verse 5 continues to emphasize the importance of marriage by forbidding newly married men to go to war. A new husband was to be

Refining and Reminding

given a one-year reprieve from warfare to *"bring happiness to his wife whom he has taken."* This would permit the man to strengthen his marriage and start a family, so that if he did die in battle, his name would not be cut off from Israel (i.e., unless a kinsman redeemer raised up a descendant for him afterwards).

The strictness of the laws in this first section not only affirms Jehovah's best intentions for marriage and His disgust for divorce, but also expresses His own yearning for Israel. Though Israel, His wife by covenant (Ezek. 16:4-14), would play the harlot with many lovers (i.e., commit spiritual adultery), God illustrates here His willingness to restore her to Himself. The prophet Jeremiah refers to this law and then emphasizes God's longsuffering love for His covenant people:

> *"They say, 'If a man divorces his wife, and she goes from him and becomes another man's, may he return to her again?' Would not that land be greatly polluted? But you have played the harlot with many lovers; yet return to Me,"* says the Lord (Jer. 3:1).

Indeed, the Lord found "uncleanness" in Israel which demanded His action. But in mercy she was put away because of her adulteries, instead of being put to death. In a coming day, His unfaithful wife will experience the full merits of His grace; in the Millennial Kingdom, Israel will be purified and restored to God in faithfulness.

Miscellaneous Laws (vv. 6-22)

An upper and lower millstone were used regularly in Jewish households to grind grain for making bread and cakes. Money lenders were not to seize one or both stones as collateral to secure a loan, as bread was a staple to sustain the family (v. 6).

Kidnapping was a profitable crime in the ancient Near East, as victims became slaves or were sold as slaves. Young women were often forced into oppressive prostitution. The prophet Amos identified three nations surrounding Israel that were involved in the slave trade: the Phoenicians, the Philistines, and the Edomites. Philistine raiding parties, for example, would later venture into Israel and capture entire Jewish communities, which were then sold to the Edomites (Amos 1:6). These captives were then sold in the slave markets of Edom and shipped all over the world. These barbaric activities broke apart families and resulted in lifelong bondage and abuse for their innocent victims. Amos pronounced judgment upon these nations for their crimes against God's covenant people. Hence, under the Law, the penalty of kidnapping was severe – death, as it robbed the victim of his or her life (v. 7).

Leprosy was a general term for various skin diseases, including the most prominent and feared, Hansen's disease. Rather than repeating the detailed procedures for identifying leprosy, the quarantining of the infected, and the ceremonial cleansing of the cured, Moses simply reminds his countrymen to obey the specifics of Leviticus 13-14 given earlier at Sinai.

Leviticus 13 identifies two main types of leprosy that infected people: leprosy of the flesh and leprosy of the head. Spiritually speaking, these relate to two classes of deadly sins. Leprosy of the flesh refers to fleshly lusts and includes gluttony, drunkenness, fornication, lasciviousness, etc. Leprosy of the head speaks of lusting in the mind which results in pride, unbelief, arrogance, envy, humanism, etc.

There are two biblical examples of proud individuals whom God smote with leprosy. The first was Miriam, the sister of Moses, who with Aaron spoke against her brother, God's chosen leader for the people (Num. 12:1-4). Because Aaron was the high priest, he was spared judgment as that would have cut off the nation from Jehovah, but Miriam was punished with leprosy and was unclean with the disease for seven days (Num. 12:9-11). Because Aaron quickly recognized the leprosy in his veiled sister, it is likely that the disease appeared on her face, thus representing the sin of pride. Now, thirty-nine years later, Moses recalled this event to warn the people of the dangers of both leprosy and pride:

Take heed in an outbreak of leprosy, that you carefully observe and do according to all that the priests, the Levites, shall teach you; just as I commanded them, so you shall be careful to do. Remember what the Lord your God did to Miriam on the way when you came out of Egypt! (vv. 8-9).

Besides Miriam, King Uzziah was also struck in the head with leprosy because of his pride (2 Chron. 26:16-21). When King Uzziah served the Lord obediently, he was blessed. Yet, when he went his own way, God humbled him. The Lord will not tolerate pride, especially in those ruling His people. Solomon reminds us that *"The fear of the Lord*

Refining and Reminding

is to hate evil; pride and arrogance and the evil way" (Prov. 8:13) and *"A man's pride will bring him low, but the humble in spirit will retain honor"* (Prov. 29:23). God hates pride (Prov. 6:16-17). God demonstrated His hatred of pride by judging both Miriam and King Uzziah with leprosy on the head. We do well to remember this valuable lesson and bestow the Lord the honor He deserves instead of trying to retain it for ourselves.

Verses 10-13 pertain to the collection of pledges in securing a loan. The Law protected the dignity of borrowers by preventing lenders from using heavy-handed tactics to collect collateral to secure loans. For example, a lender could not force his way into a home and to take whatever he wanted as a pledge; rather, the borrower was to bring it out to him (vv. 10-11). Even the very poor were to be shown loving respect; for instance, a lender must return a cloak (the loan pledge of a poor man) at nightfall so that the borrower would be able to keep warm (vv. 12-13).

The same type of courtesy was to be shown to impoverished hired servants, whether Jews or foreigners. Employers were not to oppress them by withholding wages, but were to pay full wages at the end of each workday, lest the man have nothing with which to buy food for himself and his family (vv. 14-15).

Moses then addresses the responsibility of guilt for a crime committed by someone within the family: *"Fathers shall not be put to death for their children, nor shall children be put to death for their fathers; a person shall be put to death for his own sin"* (v. 16). This decree was contrary to the other Oriental nations at that time, who commonly punished the family of a criminal also (see Est. 9:13-14).[198] Moses affirmed that the accused was entitled to a fair trial and then only those found guilty were to be punished for their crime. Notwithstanding, a guilty father may have a corrupting influence on his wife and children, which may cause them to be implicated in the crime also (5:9).

The judgment of Achan with his entire family after the failed battle against Ai is an example of this (Josh. 7). Nothing from Jericho was to be personally plundered – it all was accursed (i.e., dedicated to God). Achan rebelled against this command and took a Babylonian garment, two hundred shekels of silver, and a wedge of gold from Jericho (Josh. 7:20-21). He then hid the forbidden spoil in his tent, thus implicating his entire family in the crime and influencing them for evil. Given the offense against God and that this *national sin* resulted in the death of thirty-six Jews, a stern penalty was called for – one that would have a sobering effect on the nation for some time to come. Achan and his entire family were stoned. His animals were killed and possessions burned. All that pertained to Achan was then covered by a heap of stones in the Valley of Achor as a public testimony to the consequence of sin in the camp (Josh. 7:24).

Moses again warns his countrymen against perverting justice by oppressing a widow, an orphan, or a stranger (v. 17). Rather, they were to remember their own history (they were once poor, oppressed slaves in Egypt) and to have compassion on those unable to defend themselves (v. 18).

Moses used the same historical rationale for invoking gracious harvesting practices in Canaan (v. 22). Instead of taking advantage of the poor and adding to their misery, the Jews were not to gather all the grain, olives, and grapes at harvest time (vv. 19-21). Anything remaining in the fields, groves, or vineyards after the first pass of reaping was to be left for the needy in the land. Those landowners who abided by this command would show their thankfulness to God for blessing them, and Moses promised that God would continue to bless the work of their hands.

This was wise in two respects. First, it permitted the poor to retain a measure of dignity in that they would have to work to glean their food. Ruth was later recognized for her good work ethic as a gleaner during the barley harvest (Ruth 2). Laziness is always denounced in Scripture. Paul upholds the proper perspective believers are to maintain: *"If anyone will not work, neither shall he eat"* (2 Thess. 3:10). Second, it would lessen the irritation of having people who were able to work begging for handouts. God's desire for the Promised Land was that generosity should prevail for the helpless and that food would always be available for the needy, if they wanted to work for it.

Meditation

We praise Thee, O Lord, for the bountiful harvest,
That now has been gathered and garnered with care;
Rewarding the toil of the sower and reaper,
While all in its blessings may share.

Refining and Reminding

    We praise Thee, O Lord, for the bountiful harvest,
    We praise Thee for sunshine, the dew and the rain;
    For soft summer breezes so gracefully bending
    The bright golden billows of grain.

    We praise Thee, O Lord, for Thy wonderful mercies,
    And while to Thy glory our voices we raise,
    O Thou that regardest the prayers of Thy people,
    Accept our thanksgiving and praise.

                       — Fanny Crosby

Laws of Responsibility
Deuteronomy 25

Just but Non-Abusive Punishment (vv. 1-3)

If there was an unresolvable dispute between two men, the case was to be brought before the judges to decide (v. 1). The guilty party was then to receive punishment suitable to the crime, but no punishment was to exceed forty stripes (probably administered by a rod; vv. 2-3). The limitation against an excessive flogging protected the dignity of the guilty man to some degree. That is, he was not to be beaten senseless as one might be tempted to do with a stubborn animal (e.g., Balaam's unrestrained wrath towards his donkey).

Later, rabbinical law of the Talmud limited a flogging to thirty-nine stripes, lest the punisher go over the limitation of forty (Mak. 22a). The thirty-nine lashes also became the standard rather than the maximum number, but was lessened if the individual was not physically able to withstand the full number (Mak. 3:11). Evidently, the Jewish leaders determined Paul was strong enough to receive thirty-nine lashes on several different occasions. In all, he was whipped five times and beaten with rods three additional times (2 Cor. 11:24).

Do Not Muzzle the Ox (v. 4)

Moses then stressed the fair and kind treatment of beasts of burden: *"You shall not muzzle an ox while it treads out the grain"* (v. 4). An ox that was serving its master by trampling stalks of grain on the threshing floor in preparation for winnowing should be permitted to eat some of the stalks. Paul later refers to this verse to show that those laboring for the kingdom of God were likewise worthy of financial support from those who had benefitted from their preaching (1 Cor. 9:9).

The New Testament indicates that Church workers were employed by the Lord, not by local churches. Serving the Lord is not a career to be chosen, but a heavenly calling to be fulfilled! God enables the worker's ministry and is responsible for supporting them financially

Refining and Reminding

(Phil. 4:10-19; Col. 4:17). As He most often accomplishes this through His people, Paul emphasizes that those who had been spiritually blessed by ministry had a "duty" to support those who blessed them (Rom. 15:27). Examples of not muzzling the laboring ox in principle would include the support of:

- The evangelist (1 Cor. 9:14).
- A teaching elder (1 Tim. 5:17-18).
- A teacher in general (Gal. 6:6).
- A commended worker (1 Cor. 9:4).

Gaius provides a good pattern to follow in the care of the Lord's servants. He extended hospitality to itinerant church workers and then did not send them away empty-handed (3 John 5-8; also see Tit. 3:14). At times workers may need to engage in secular employment for financial reasons (Acts 18:3), but nowhere in Scripture do we see them making public appeals for their own financial support. Commended workers serve the Lord (Acts 14:26), and thus the Lord wants His people to freely and amply provide for them in His name. This arrangement permits His workers to do His bidding and for the Lord to endorse their efforts by attending to their daily needs.

Levirate Marriage (vv. 5-10)

In Leviticus 20, Moses detailed the penalties for forbidden sexual relationships. Most of these (e.g., adultery, homosexuality, bestiality) required the death penalty for the guilty, but some offenses resulted in lesser penalties of excommunication or barrenness. For example, if a man had sexual relations with his sister-in-law, they would die childless (Lev. 20:21). The Law also prohibited a brother from marrying his sister-in-law if she were divorced or widowed (Lev. 18:16). However, verses 5-10 permit an exception to this limitation if the widow was childless and the deceased was dwelling with his brother on the same property. This meant that both brothers had a claim to the same inheritance. For this specific situation, the brother of the deceased was bound to marry his brother's widow (his sister-in-law) and to name their first son after the deceased (vv. 5-6).

Such marital unions were called *Levirate marriages* and were necessary to ensure that family inheritances, such as land, were passed down to the next generation. If the surviving brother refused to fulfill this important responsibility, his brother's widow was to bring the matter to the local elders who were to persuade him to do so (v. 7). In the event he still declined to take his brother's widow as his wife, then, in the presence of the elders, she was to spit in his face and remove one of his sandals to publicly shame the man for his negligence (vv. 8-9). Apparently, the guilt of his refusal was to stick with him for the remainder of his life; he was to be known as *"the house of him who had his sandal removed"* (v. 10). Besides producing children in the name of the deceased, the Levirate marriage also provided protection and care for his widow.

Historically speaking, this Jewish custom existed long before Moses formalized it here. In Genesis 38, we read that Judah lived apart from his brethren for several years, for he took a Canaanite wife who bore him three sons, two of whom had matured to a marrying age. Judah took a wife named Tamar for his oldest son Er. But because Er (whose name means "enmity") was a wicked man, God slew him. Judah then gave Tamar to his second son, Onan (whose name means "iniquity"), as a wife. Judah's actions show that it was a common practice for a brother to go in to his brother's widow and father children in the name of the deceased. In Israel, this protected a family name and inheritance from being lost in the course of time.

Miscellaneous Laws (vv. 11-16)

The preceding verses highlighted the importance of fathering children to maintain the family name and inheritance in Israel. Therefore, if a wife attempted to assist her husband who was fighting with another man, by grabbing that man's genitals, she was to have her hand cut off (vv. 11-12). Typically, the Mosaic Law did not condone the mutilation of an offender; however, the severity of the woman's punishment shows just how import fathering children was in Jewish society.

Moses then affirmed that cheating one's neighbor by the use of false weights and measurements in transacting business was an abomination to the Lord (vv. 13-16). If the Jews wanted to enjoy God's blessing in the land, they were to use accurate scales, weights, and measuring containers. Nobody wants to be cheated in business dealings; therefore, each Jew was to *"love your neighbor as yourself"*!

Eradicate the Amalekites (vv. 17-19)

Amalek was the grandson of profane Esau, *"who for one morsel of food sold his birthright"* (Heb. 12:16). Consequently, both Esau and Amalek picture lusting flesh which continues to war against God's people. The Amalekites attacked the straggling Israelites who were weak and weary after leaving Egypt (vv. 17-18). This is often when the flesh gains a victory over God's people: just after a major victory when they are exhausted.

We see this was the case for Joshua, who acted in the flesh in advancing against Ai after the great victory at Jericho (Josh. 7). Because Joshua did not seek the Lord's counsel, he was unaware that there was sin in the camp which hindered Jehovah from going into battle with them. As a result, thirty-six Jewish soldiers died. Achan's sin against the Lord was then revealed and he was publicly judged for it. After the children of Israel had experienced separation and cleansing from that which had defiled them, they were ready to be used as Jehovah's agency against Ai and Bethel. This time they would not advance in human wisdom and in their own strength, but in faith and in accordance with Jehovah's plan and with His power. Joshua 8 records their whimsical victory over Ai and Bethel without any Jewish casualties. Human reasoning and fleshly vigor were to have no part in God's operation – death to all Amalekites!

The Lord desires that the same pattern be followed in the Church Age. Until an individual experiences regeneration and receives the Holy Spirit, the flesh nature is uncontrollable (Rom. 8:2-4). Even after regeneration, a child of God cannot righteously serve the Lord with sin in his or her heart. Sins in our flesh must supernaturally be put to death *"because they that are in the flesh cannot please God"* (Rom. 8:8). One cannot rightly exercise the power of God without being under His moral authority (Luke 7:6-9).

It is for this reason, then, that once the Israelites had secured Canaan, they were to relentlessly and ruthlessly war against the Amalekites until there was no remembrance of them under heaven (v. 19). In type, carnal appetites must be brought under the control of the Holy Spirit and thus be eliminated from the work of God. What the flesh controls robs honor from the Lord and harms His people!

Meditation

Day by day and with each passing moment,
Strength I find to meet my trials here,
Trusting in my Father's wise bestowment,
I've no cause for worry or for fear.

He whose heart is kind beyond all measure,
Gives unto each day what He deems best,
Lovingly its part of pain and pleasure,
Mingling toil with peace and rest.

— A. L. Skoog and Carolina Sandell

Firstfruit Offerings and Tithes
Deuteronomy 26

Leaving the various Laws of Responsibility, this chapter paints a more cheerful scene which anticipates Israel's entrance into their own land. In fact, this is the only chapter in Deuteronomy that speaks of priestly service in conjunction with the Jews worshipping Jehovah. Every family was to offer a basket of firstfruits from the bounty of their first harvest in the land (vv. 2-11). Additionally, Moses spoke of a special tithe offering in the third year after possessing Canaan (vv. 12-15). These offerings celebrated Israel's transition from being a nomadic people in the wilderness to a thriving agricultural community settled in their own land, their inheritance from the Lord (v. 1).

The Basket of Firstfruits (vv. 2-11)

Levitical Law already required the Jews to present the firstfruits of the barley harvest at the Feast of Firstfruits, which was celebrated on the sixteenth day of the first month (Lev. 23:9-14). The firstfruits of the wheat harvest were also presented to the Lord at The Feast of Pentecost, which followed fifty days later. At the Feast of Firstfruits, a priest was to wave a barley sheaf before the Lord as an acknowledgement that He was the Lord of the entire harvest. This grain was for the priests who continually served in the temple. The Jews were not allowed to personally partake of the harvest until these offerings had been presented before the Lord.

Albert Barnes clarifies that the firstfruits offering in verses 2-11 was a unique celebration and should not be confused with any of the commanded annual firstfruit offerings:

> The firstfruits here in question are to be distinguished alike from those offered in acknowledgment of the blessings of harvest (Ex. 22:29) at the Feasts of Passover and Pentecost, and also from the offerings prescribed in Numbers 18:8. The latter consisted of preparations from the produce of the earth, such as oil, flour, wine,

etc.; while those of this chapter are the raw produce: the former were national and public offerings; those of this chapter were private and personal.[199]

After settling in Canaan, the Jews were to arrange a sample of all their first year's produce in a basket and bring it to the central sanctuary with their tithe (vv. 2-3). With basket in hand, the offerer was to acknowledge before a priest, *"I declare today to the Lord your God that I have come to the country which the Lord swore to our fathers to give us"* (v. 3). This assertion recognized the Lord's faithfulness in bringing Israel out of Egypt and settling His people in the land He had promised them. The priest then (or perhaps later in the ceremony) set the basket before the Bronze Altar.

Israel's profession at the time of their firstfruits presentation is noteworthy. The Israelites did not say, "I am coming" or "I hope to come" or "I am longing to come," but "I have come" into the land. Their baskets of firstfruits would be offered to the Lord because they *were* in the land of promise and possessed it. C. H. Mackintosh derives a helpful application from this for believers to consider today:

> We must know ourselves saved before we can offer the fruits of a known salvation. We may be most sincere in our desires after salvation, most earnest in our efforts to obtain it. But then we cannot but see that efforts to be saved and the fruits of a known and enjoyed salvation are wholly different. The Israelite did not offer the basket of firstfruits in order to get into the land, but because he was actually in it. "I profess this day, that I am come." "There is no mistake about it, no question, no doubt, not even a hope. I am actually in the land, and here is the fruit of it."[200]

One must truly be saved and know they are saved to honor the Lord with spiritual fruitfulness (1 Jn. 4:18-19). The fruit of the Spirit accompanies salvation – salvation is not obtained by mimicking what only the Holy Spirit can produce from within. Works-based salvation is a spiritual hoax with shameful repercussions; furthermore, self-helps religion mocks the gospel message and undermines the redemptive work of Christ. The whole idea of "firstfruits" is that there has been a new blessing and spiritual understanding in the believer's soul that had not been previously experienced – this is what is to be brought before

Refining and Reminding

the Lord. Concerning these lovely firstfruit acquisitions, C. A. Coates suggests:

> It has not only been in the purpose of God to give it to us, but we have now got it, by His favor, in our hearts. It is in our affections and intelligence in such a way that we can bring it to His assembly for His pleasure, and we can speak to Him about it in the fresh joy of it, and not as something we have had in store a long time. We can speak, too, of the sovereign love that has wrought so wondrously to secure it to us, and to secure us for it. The instruction here is for each individual, but it is to be carried out by all, so that a coming to one center the service and worship has united assembly character. The spiritual accessions of the individual lead him in the first place, according to this scripture, to the assembly as a contributor to its worship and joy.[201]

It seems likely that the priest uttered some liturgical statement at that presentation of the offerer's basket. It is possible that the priest even handed the basket back to the offerer to prompt the offerer to recite a more lengthy account of God's past faithfulness to Israel (v. 10). The worshipper was to recall the beginning of their nation through Jacob while in Syria, then his sojourning in Egypt, the subsequent enslavement of his descendants there, and finally God's mighty deliverance in bringing the now sizeable Jewish nation to a land flowing with milk and honey (vv. 5-9). Each of these details transpired exactly as God had promised Abraham in Genesis 15 over six centuries earlier. This rehearsal of God's past faithfulness concluded with the offerer declaring: *"now, behold, I have brought the firstfruits of the land which You, O Lord, have given me"* (v. 10).

The *"Syrian ready to perish"* refers to Jacob, as he is the one who led his family (only a few in number) to sojourn in Egypt and there his descendants became a great nation. Jacob lived about twenty years with Rebekah's brother Laban in Haran located in Syria (Mesopotamia) to escape Esau's rage (Gen. 27-31). During this time out of the Promised Land, Jacob obtained two wives (Laban's daughters) and two concubines who bore him eleven sons. The twelfth son Benjamin was born after Jacob's return to Canaan. Though Jacob arrived in Syria poor and under dire circumstances, the Lord greatly prospered him there. When he returned to Canaan, Jacob was a wealthy man with a large family.

Now that Israel was in the land of their inheritance, they could look back over the years of bitter disappointments with abiding joy – God had kept His promise to Abraham, Isaac, and Jacob. Each basket of firstfruits at the central sanctuary expressed an Israelite's joy in the Lord and thankfulness for His faithfulness: *"Then you shall set it before the Lord your God, and worship before the Lord your God. So you shall rejoice in every good thing which the Lord your God has given to you"* (vv. 10-11).

Through this first-year celebration, Moses was setting a pattern for his countrymen to follow in the Promised Land: the worship of Jehovah must be given importance over everything else. *"Whoever offers praise glorifies Me; and to him who orders his conduct aright I will show the salvation of God"* (Ps. 50:23). Genuine praise glorifies God and is a fitting display of genuine salvation. God inhabits the praises of those who are His. He delights to be surrounded by hearts overflowing with the sense of His goodness and greatness. Beloved, God deserves this – may He always receive a steady stream of praise from His people!

Similarly, believers in the Church Age come together each Lord's Day to remember that they too were about to perish in their sins until God intervened by sending His Son to suffer and die in their place. On the night before His crucifixion, the Lord Jesus instituted the "Lord's Supper" as a time for the local church to corporately remember Him (1 Cor. 11:17, 20). He said to do it often, understanding our tendency to forget Him and His work. Yet the command set down no rules for how frequently Christians should gather to remember the Lord; our love for Him will determine this matter. The early church transitioned from "breaking bread" daily in Acts 2 to the established practice of remembering the Lord once a week on Sunday (Acts 20:7).

Every Christian (believer-priest; 1 Pet. 2:5, 9) should confess their sins before partaking of the Lord's Supper (1 Cor. 11:23-32), just as the Levitical priests washed their hands and feet at the Bronze Laver before entering the tabernacle with their offerings to worship God (Ex. 30:17-21). If a Levitical priest did not prepare properly to offer worship, he was in danger of dying, and Paul acknowledges that the Christian faces the same peril if he or she approaches God in worship with unconfessed sin.

When believers assemble for worship, they should do so in the beauty of holiness (having humbly confessed their sins; 1 Jn. 1:9) and with a spiritual offering ready to present to the Lord (1 Chron. 16:29). In this sense, each believer has the great privilege of arranging their own basket of praise and presenting it before the Lord each week. The Israelites had no limitations as to how big the basket was to be or what was to be put in it. The same is true for Christians preparing to worship the Lord today! Worship proceeds from the heart, so all believers should come to the Lord's Supper as prepared worshippers and with hearts full of adoration.

Just as in the Levitical offerings, God has appointed a way for the Church to offer corporate worship to Him. As seen in the example before us, the Jews could only present their individual baskets before the Lord if they were willing to obey the specific procedure and distinct roles God had instituted for the ceremony. This is true in the Church Age also.

During the Lord's Supper, the audible ministry is to be through Spirit-led men, as the man represents God when speaking (1 Cor. 11:7), and this is in accordance with the instructions given for church order (1 Cor. 14). The women are to attend to the visual ministry in the assembly of revealing God's glory by covering all competing glories: the woman, the glory of man, and her hair, the glory of woman (1 Cor. 11:7, 15). In this way, only God's glory, as represented by uncovered men, is seen by God and the angels overlooking the gathering. This pictures the scene in heaven as seraphim and cherubim cover their own intrinsic glories with their wings in the presence of God, so that God's glory is preeminent (Isa. 6:2; Ezek. 1:11). The audible ministry is used by the Holy Spirit to align everyone's thinking on a central idea. The words themselves do not make it past the backdoor; however, the worship of prepared hearts ascends as sweet incense into God's heavenly throne room. His own heart is refreshed as He breathes in the adoration that the saints have for His Son!

The Festival Tithe (vv. 12-15)

As discussed in 14:12-19, the Jews were to offer a "second tithe" known as a festival tithe every three years. It seems unlikely that this was in addition to the annual tithe, but was a substitute for it, as every three years the tithe was to go to the nearest Levitical city and not to the central sanctuary. The "second tithe" was to support local serving Levites and the needy (v. 12). Widows, orphans, and the destitute sojourner were recipients of the second tithe and were invited to a celebratory feast (derived from provisions of the tithe). All were to enjoy the various local celebrations of the Lord's goodness to the nation.

On the first occasion that the festival tithe was brought to local priests for distribution, a liturgy was to be spoken. First, there was an affirmation that the tithe had been given in obedience to God's command (v. 13). Second, with a spirit of joyfulness the offerer affirmed that the gift had been fully consecrated to the Lord. No part of it had been eaten or used in any unclean practice, not even to offset funeral-related expenses (as these were morbid, not joyful gatherings; v. 14). Third, because of the before-mentioned diligence, the offerer could with a clear conscience ask the Lord to bless his family in the forthcoming year (v. 15).

Declarations of Commitment (vv. 16-19)

These four verses draw to a close Moses' explanation of the Law that began back in chapter 5. Israel was expected to cling to the Lord and to obey His commandments tenaciously: *"This day the Lord your God commands you to observe these statutes and judgments; therefore you shall be careful to observe them with all your heart and with all your soul"* (v. 16). God had instituted a conditional covenant with His people. He had promised to bless them in the land as contingent on their faithful allegiance to Him and obedience to His Law. Israel was now acknowledging and affirming their pledge to do so (v. 17).

The Israelites recognized that they were God's special people on the earth; this meant that they had an accountability and privilege that no other nation had (v. 18). God had set aside Israel to be a holy nation that would honor Him among all nations (v. 19). Israel was to properly represent Jehovah to the nations; in so doing, they would be a beacon of His glory for all to see and to seek!

Commitment entails being given over to a cause without reservation; such should be the attitude of believers towards the Lord. Only after a believer has consciously made that determination will he or she have the unwavering devotion of a true disciple of Christ. The Lord Jesus does not force us to pledge our lives to Him, but He does warn us of the consequences of not doing so:

> *If anyone desires to come after Me, let him deny himself, and take up his cross daily, and follow Me. For whoever desires to save his life will lose it, but whoever loses his life for My sake will save it. For what profit is it to a man if he gains the whole world, and is himself destroyed or lost?* (Luke 9:23-25).

Refining and Reminding

This means that those who have received a new life in Christ have only two ways to live while on earth: completely yielding one's life to Christ, thus gaining a life worth living and fellowship with God, or living one's life the way one wants. The latter decision results in a spiritually desolate life that knows neither the peace nor the joy of God and counts for nothing in eternity.

The Lord Jesus warned that we can have no divided allegiance if we desire to live for Him: *"No one can serve two masters; for either he will hate the one and love the other, or else he will be loyal to the one and despise the other. You cannot serve God and mammon"* (Matt. 6:24). There can be no middle ground. The Lord is either the believer's first love or He is not the Master of the believer's life.

A lack of love for the Lord will be shown through an unyielded spirit and through disobedience (John 14:15). There is such an intimate tie between genuine love for the Lord and obedience to the Lord that Paul bluntly states, *"If any man love not the Lord Jesus Christ, let him be Anathema* [eternally condemned]" (1 Cor. 16:22). Dear believer, life is short, a fleeting vapor in time. Don't waste it on vanity. What you do for eternity the world cannot destroy, nor can anyone steal (Matt. 6:19-20). What is urgently needed in the Church today is for believers to be totally sold out to the Lord Jesus Christ. Only then will the Church be the beacon of light to a dark world that desperately needs to know the Lord Jesus Christ. He is humanity's Savior, the Wave Sheaf of the fruitfruits from the dead, and the satisfier of all human need!

Meditation

> Jesus, Thou art all compassion; pure, unbounded love Thou art,
> Visit us with Thine affection, enter every longing heart.
> Firstfruits of Thy new creation, faithful, holy, may we be,
> Joyful in thy great salvation, daily more conformed to Thee:
> Changed from glory into glory, till in heaven we take our place,
> Then to worship and adore Thee, lost in wonder, love and praise.
>
> — Charles Wesley

The Curse of the Law
Deuteronomy 27

Covenant Renewal (vv. 1-10)

Having thoroughly reviewed the Law of the Covenant in chapters 5-26, and having affirmed God's commitment to bless and honor Israel and Israel's commitment to revere only Jehovah and to obey His Law, Moses begins his third oracle to the Jewish nation. Besides the thematic shift of the narrative, Jack S. Deere notes the textual clues indicating a new message: "A new address is signaled by the mention of Moses in the third person (v. 1). Moses had not been mentioned in the third person since 5:1, at the beginning of his second address (5:1-26:15)."[202]

With Israel poised to enter the Promised Land, Moses sets an example for future significant events by calling Israel to covenant renewal. National calls to obedience and commitment in the future would occur at such times as the dedication of Solomon's temple (1 Kgs. 8), and during changes of leadership (Josh. 24; 1 Sam. 12). As already mentioned in 11:26-32, the next such occasion of national covenant renewal would occur after Joshua had successfully led Israel into Canaan (vv. 1-3). As Moses would not be with them, the Jewish elders joined him in affirming that this should be done.

Although Moses has explained the specifics of the Law in previous chapters, it is at this point in Deuteronomy that we sense the Law's full ferocity. We have here the curse under the Law, followed in the next chapter by God's blessings and judgments in administrating the Law. All of this should lead the nation into covenantal renewal in chapters 29 and 30.

Once in Canaan, all men, women, children, and strangers among the Israelites were to trek north up the Jordanian valley, then westward, and finally southwestward to a specific location between the mountains of Ebal and Gerizim to confirm the covenant. This location was ideal; it was in the center of Canaan and, from the twin mountain peaks of Ebal and Gerizim, much of the Promised Land could be viewed. Thus, in the

Refining and Reminding

heart of Canaan, the valley of Shechem represented the entire land; it was here that God wanted His Law prominently displayed for all to view and to appreciate.

We read in Joshua 8 that after the victories in Jericho, Ai, and Bethel, Joshua obeyed this command and led the people from Gilgal to these two mountains. There, as Moses commanded, he set up great stones, plastered them together, and then chiseled *"all the words of this Law"* into the dried plaster (vv. 2-4, 8). Also, as instructed, he erected an altar with stones which had not been modified by human instruments and there sacrificed burnt offerings and peace offerings for the nation (vv. 5-7).

After informing Joshua and all Israel what should be done to renew Israel's covenant with Jehovah in Canaan, Moses, the priests, and the Levites rehearsed what should be affirmed:

> *Take heed and listen, O Israel: This day you have become the people of the Lord your God. Therefore you shall obey the voice of the Lord your God, and observe His commandments and His statutes which I command you today* (vv. 9-10).

Joshua also heeded this command; he read *"all the words of this Law"* in the hearing of *"all the assembly of Israel"* (Josh. 8:35).

Curses From Mount Ebal (vv. 11-27)

Then Moses decreed how the twelve tribes should be positioned on this momentous occasion and what should be publicly declared (vv. 11-27). The priests would be positioned with the Ark of the Covenant in between the two mountains in order to voice their approval while Joshua read the Law (v. 14).

The larger and more prominent tribes of Simeon, Levi, Judah, Issachar, Joseph (Ephraim and Manasseh), and Benjamin were to be situated on the north side of Mt. Gerizim to hear the blessings God promised to bestow for obedience (v. 12). The lesser tribes of Reuben, Gad, Asher, Zebulun, Dan, and Naphtali were to take a position on the sterile southern face of Mt. Ebal and acknowledge by an "amen" (literally, "so be it"), each curse pronounced for disobedience (v. 13).

Moses began by first summarizing various laws which invoked God's condemnation for the disobedient:

Cursed is the one who: makes a carved or molded image, an abomination to the Lord, the work of the hands of the craftsman, and sets it up in secret ... treats his father or his mother with contempt ... who moves his neighbor's landmark ... makes the blind to wander off the road ... perverts the justice due the stranger, the fatherless, and widow ... lies with his father's wife, because he has uncovered his father's bed ... who lies with any kind of animal ... lies with his sister, the daughter of his father or the daughter of his mother ... lies with his mother-in-law ... attacks his neighbor secretly ... takes a bribe to slay an innocent person ... does not confirm all the words of this law. And all the people shall say, "Amen!" (vv. 15-26).

Interestingly, Moses issued no command in Scripture for the tribes on the fruitful slopes of Gerizim to verbally acknowledge specific blessing with an "amen." H. F. Witherby explains why the tribes on Gerizim were not to shout "amen" after each blessing was read:

The curses were read with a loud voice by the Levites, and, as each curse for disobedience sounded in Israel's ears, the hundreds of thousands, assembled upon Mount Ebal, responded with unanimous Amens. Twelve times said they "Amen" to the twelve-times-uttered curses, and the twelfth – "Cursed be he that confirms not all the words of this law to do them" – included every possible neglect or failure of which they could be capable. Blessings also were read (Josh. 8:33-34); but concerning the Amens, sounding from Mount Gerizim, Scripture is silent. It records not one responsive "So be it" to blessings earned by the obedience of fallen man (Deut. 27). Man may justly assent to all "the judgments" (Ex. 24:3) of God's law, but they who remain under the law must remain under its curse (Gal. 3:10).[203]

Israel could agree to the curses associated with violating the Law, but could lay no claims to God's blessings which depended upon their faithfulness to keep it. As much of Israel's history has been marked by declension, what brief seasons of blessing the nation did enjoy were received through unmerited grace.

Joshua did read all of the Law of God that day and the echo of a million people repeatedly shouting "amen" to the curses of God echoed off the stony-walled amphitheater and rumbled through the valley like thunder. The Law of God was also inscribed in a stone monument on Mt. Ebal for every passerby to see. There would be no excuse for future ignorance; God had posted His Law in the center of Canaan and the

Refining and Reminding

Law had been orally declared to all the people, and they had affirmed its meaning.

The last verse of the chapter then poses the stark distinction to be understood between chapters 27 and 28. Anyone who did *"not confirm all the words of this law"* was cursed (v. 26). Paul quotes this verse in the Epistle to the Galatians and then explains its application concerning God's means of salvation not just to Israel, but to Gentiles also:

> *For as many as are of the works of the law are under the curse; for it is written, "Cursed is everyone who does not continue in all things which are written in the book of the law, to do them." But that no one is justified by the law in the sight of God is evident, for "the just shall live by faith." Yet the law is not of faith, but "the man who does them shall live by them." Christ has redeemed us from the curse of the law, having become a curse for us (for it is written, "Cursed is everyone who hangs on a tree"), that the blessing of Abraham might come upon the Gentiles in Christ Jesus, that we might receive the promise of the Spirit through faith* (Gal. 3:10-14).

Deuteronomy 27 then is not looking per se at man's doings in the present life, which may be rewarded or be punished by God in real time (that is the focus of chapter 28). Rather, the point is that from a positional standpoint, the Law renders a judicial curse on man. In the sight of God, man stands condemned by the Law and deserves condemnation. The Law demands death! This is why there is no blessing mentioned in chapter 27. In chapter 28, we shall see that man, while residing on the earth, may receive God's blessings or judgments, depending on how he lives before God. William Kelly thus summarizes this important distinction between these two chapters:

> In Deuteronomy 27 it is an *absolute* and a *personal* curse; it is not in mere circumstances [Deut. 28], such is the difference. In short then in this chapter we have the profound intimation of what the law comes to in man's – the first man's – hands. Whatever may be the goodness of God, man is ruined. The consequence is that there is only a curse and no blessing. In Deuteronomy 28 we have law, not looked at in its own nature as a question between God and man, but regarded as the rule of earthly government, as having to do with the circumstances of man. And here accordingly we have the blessing on the one hand and the curse on the other. ... It is in vain to say that we receive the blessing which belongs to Deuteronomy 27. We do not [man is

condemned]. There we get the curse and no blessing [man needs God's salvation]. But in Deuteronomy 28 we get certain blessings and then curses [based on man's behavior].[204]

In chapter 28, as active transgressors of the Law, Israel would be dealt with appropriately, but in chapter 27, Israel was already condemned under the Law in principle. As C. H. Mackintosh further notes, this is why the basis, scope, and practical application between chapters 27 and 28 are wholly distinct:

> Chapter 27 is *moral* and *personal*. Chapter 28 is *dispensational* and *national*. Chapter 27 deals with the great root principle of man's moral condition, as a sinner utterly ruined and wholly incapable of meeting God on the ground of law. Chapter 28, on the other hand, takes up the question of Israel as a nation, under the government of God. In short, a careful comparison of the two chapters will enable the reader to see their entire distinctness. For instance, what connection can we trace between the six blessings of chapter 28 and the twelve curses of chapter 27? None whatever. It is not possible to establish the slightest relationship. But a child can see the moral link between the blessings and curses of chapter 28.[205]

In chapter 27, Israel was like an incarcerated murderer awaiting execution. However, in chapter 28, that same condemned criminal on death row is given certain privileges which could make his wait more pleasant if honored, or more loathsome if rejected. Thankfully, another Man, also born under the Law, yet satisfying all its demands, would take the condemned man's place in death (Gal. 4:4-5). This would permit not only the release of the guilty man, but also give him a new opportunity to enjoy God's goodness by doing what God expected of him. Later, the redeemed man will realize that experiencing some favorable circumstances in prison for good behavior was not remotely comparable to being a guilt-free liberated man who enjoys unhindered communion with God and His immense favor! Of course, Israel will not realize that part of the story until the Kingdom Age, but believers in the Church Age know its validity now!

With the Law of God inscribed on a stone monument between Ebal and Gerizim, every passerby would know the code of morality for the land and be reminded of Israel's covenant with Jehovah. From that time forward, there would be no tolerance of ignorance; God had posted His

Refining and Reminding

Law in the center of Canaan and the Law had been orally declared to all the people, who had affirmed its meaning. If the Jews wanted to commune with Jehovah and experience His love and power, they must choose to obey the Law and let it govern their relationship with Him.

Moses had thoroughly reviewed the Law to ensure that no covenant failure on Israel's part would result through ignorance. Any failure on Israel's part would be through willful rejection of what God had demanded.

Meditation

> When it comes to God's commands, the issue is not clarity; it's commitment.
>
> — Woodrow Kroll

Blesses and Curses
Deuteronomy 28

Blessings for Obedience (vv. 1-14)

In the previous chapter, Moses reviewed the curses that Israel was to rehearse during their covenantal renewal exercise later in Canaan. Moses next reviews how Jehovah will bless the nation for their obedience. The Lord promised to exalt Israel over all nations (v. 1). The entire land (cities and countryside) would abound with God's favor (vv. 2-3). The Jews would be blessed with many children, with agricultural prosperity, and their herds and flocks would multiply (v. 4). God's people would enjoy tranquility and plenty of food, with no threat of foreign oppression because they would be invincible on the battlefield (vv. 5-8).

By choosing to keep Jehovah's commandments, the nations would know and fear them as Jehovah's holy people (vv. 9-10). If Israel obeyed, the Lord would cause them to thrive in every way imaginable in the land that He had promised to their forefathers (vv. 11-13). He would provide Israel plenty of rain for growing crops, various goods to enjoy, plenty of children, proliferation of their livestock, and overall financial prosperity. However, it was crucial that Israel observe all that God commanded, including not turning aside to serve other gods (v. 14). As in all ages, faithfulness to God produces in His people happy and fulfilled lives.

Curses for Disobedience (vv. 15-48)

If Israel departed from His Law, Jehovah promised that His curses would overtake them (v. 15). Their disobedience would reverse every reward for obedience He had just promised to give them (vv. 16-19). Furthermore, the Lord promised to confound all their doings and smite them with disease, sickness, mental illness, drought, mildew, boils, tumors, skin irritations, locust plagues, and crop-destroying worms (vv. 20-29, 34-35, 39-40, 42). If they remained stiff-necked after being chastened, then He promised that they would be overcome by their enemies, resulting in widespread death, enslavement, and finally exile (vv. 30-33, 36-38). The price of Israel's rebellion is summarized in verse 29: *"You shall not prosper in your ways; you shall be only oppressed and plundered continually, and no one shall save you."*

The normal aspirations for a Jewish man – a wife, many children, a nice house, land to cultivate, a vineyard, livestock, etc. – would not be attained (vv. 30-33). The Jews would become a people of shattered dreams. Invaders would abuse a man's wife, enslave his children (v. 41), and take over his property and livestock. Many of those surviving the invader's slaughter would go mad because of the horrific things they had observed (v. 34). Many Jews would be exiled into unknown lands with unknown gods (v. 36). In these faraway places, the Jews would become a byword and the brunt of satiric proverbs (v. 37). Jews remaining in the Promised Land would be controlled and financially impoverished by foreigners (vv. 43-44). Verses 12 and 44 clearly show the contrast between the two sections: If obedient, the Jews would be wealthy, international lenders; if disobedient, they would be poor and indebted to strangers.

Moses then paused from listing the doom-and-gloom consequences of Israel's disobedience to offer a summary statement:

> *Moreover all these curses shall come upon you and pursue and overtake you, until you are destroyed, because you did not obey the voice of the Lord your God, to keep His commandments and His statutes which He commanded you. And they shall be upon you for a sign and a wonder, and on your descendants forever* (vv. 45-46).

The sweeping and long-lasting devastation to Jewish posterity, prosperity and social dignity would be a divinely orchestrated sign from God that He was against His people. Their rebellion had caused Him to move heaven and earth against them. Because they did not serve the Lord their God with joy and gladness, the Lord would permit them to serve their enemies as despairing slaves (vv. 47-48). Instead of enjoying *"the abundance of everything,"* they would be *"in need of everything"* (e.g. food, water, clothing, etc.). Verse 47 is a good reminder that the Lord wants much more than just the believer's obedience; He desires the willing submission of a joyful heart. Fear can prompt the obedience of a toddler, but jubilant compliance can arise only from mature love and genuine appreciation.

The Unknown Tongue – A Sign of Invasion (vv. 49-51)

Continuing his warning against disobedience, Moses provided his countrymen with a specific prophecy about their future invaders:

> *The Lord will bring a nation against you from afar, from the end of the earth, as swift as the eagle flies, a nation whose language you will not understand, a nation of fierce countenance, which does not respect the elderly nor show favor to the young. And they shall eat the increase of your livestock and the produce of your land, until you are destroyed; they shall not leave you grain or new wine or oil, or the increase of your cattle or the offspring of your flocks, until they have destroyed you* (vv. 49-51).

While conquerors plundering the land without concern for human casualties would be common during an invasion, there is a portion of the prophecy that is unusual: The Lord would bring a nation from afar to conquer and exile His people – so far, in fact, that the Jews would not recognize the invader's language. In the eighth century B.C., the Lord would strengthen the Assyrians to overcome much of the region, including the Northern Kingdom of Israel. Then, over a century later, He would use the Babylonians to punish wicked nations throughout the region, including the Southern Kingdom of Israel.

The sign of the unknown tongue is used throughout Scripture as a warning to the Jewish people of imminent judgment. Moses told the people that if they rebelled against the Lord, He would punish them through a nation whose language they would not understand (v. 49). This meant that God would use an army from a distant land instead of a neighboring nation. Isaiah warned idolatrous Israel by imposing this sign just prior to the Assyrian invasion (Isa. 28:11-12) and Jeremiah referenced it as a final warning to Judah of imminent judgment for the same deeply-rooted sin (Jer. 5:15). But the Jews ignored the warnings of Moses, Isaiah, and Jeremiah; the sign of the unknown tongue was issued and severe judgment ultimately came. Yet, this was not the last time God would use the sign of an unknown tongue to alert the Jews of impending judgment for their unfaithfulness.

Refining and Reminding

According to Acts 2:9-11, ten specific languages were heard in Jerusalem at the Feast of Pentecost, just after Christ's ascension into heaven. This was the day the Church Age began (Acts 2:4; 1 Cor. 12:13). The Holy Spirit came to the believers as promised by the Lord Jesus, baptized them into the body of Christ, bestowed spiritual gifts on them, and enabled them to supernaturally serve the Lord. This event served two main purposes. First, it verified in the sight of the Jews that the apostles were continuing the ministry of Christ and were doing so by His power (Acts 2:22). Second, it served as a final warning to the nation of Israel to repent and to turn to God through Christ. As a nation, they had rejected and crucified their Messiah, but as individuals, they now had the opportunity to be saved. Unavoidable judgment was coming upon the nation of Israel and trusting Christ for salvation was the only way for them to obtain God's forgiveness.

In A.D. 70, that crushing judgment came. A vast Roman army of about 70,000 soldiers was led by the soon-to-be Emperor Titus to besiege and conquer Jerusalem. The temple that had been built by the Jewish captives who returned from Babylon towards the end of the sixth century B.C. and that had then been renovated by Herod the Great some five centuries later was destroyed. There were to be no more offerings, sacrifices, Levitical priesthood, or stench of humanized religion in the nostrils of Jehovah. Even to this day, although the Jews are back in their land and are a self-governing nation, they have no temple or priesthood to reinstate what God has put away and replaced with a New Covenant (Heb. 8:7-13).

About three to five years after the writer of Hebrews explained this truth, God used the Romans to completely remove the religious practices of the Old Covenant from Israel. In reality, these had already been replaced by the New Covenant, which had been sealed with Christ's blood forty years earlier. But the Jews had rejected the terms of this covenant which required them to receive Christ as their Messiah. Through the destruction of Jerusalem and the temple, God put an end to the Levitical order established by the Old Covenant, a system that the Jews had humanized into their own religion (Gal. 1:13-14). No more ceremonial lip service would be offered to God. Given what Jehovah had already secured by the judgment of His own Son, such religious hype was offensive to Him.

Through the New Covenant, and through it alone, God would forgive the sins of Israel and Judah, would pour out His Spirit upon them, and restore them to Himself. Some Christians, like Paul, were given the sign gift of speaking in a foreign tongue to warn Israel to trust Christ and thus avoid imminent judgment (1 Cor. 14:18). This is why Paul did not forbid others who also had this sign gift from speaking in a foreign language in the Church, if there was an interpreter (1 Cor. 14:39). The unknown tongue was a sign to the lost (1 Cor. 14:22), especially to his Jewish countrymen, whom Paul greatly desired to be saved (Rom. 9:3; 10:1).

This supernatural gift apparently diminished in normalcy during the Apostolic Age, as there is no mention of it in Scripture after A.D. 60. Paul states that the gift will eventually cease and it is significant that over half the New Testament was written after this time (1 Cor. 13:8). Although the New Testament does record the names of many Jews who did turn from Judaism to Christ, Israel, as a nation, rejected Him and will continue to do so until His second advent at the end of the Tribulation Period (Isa. 11:1-16; Ezek. 36:16-38; Joel 2:18-3:21; Zech. 12:10).

Invasion, Siege, and Dispersion (vv. 52-68)

Several prophets would later declare to their brethren that they were so far away from the Lord that they did not even recognize His chastening hand (e.g., Hag. 1). It is apparent from this chapter that the Lord will continue to increase the severity of punishment until He regains the allegiance of His covenant people. Because of His unconditional covenant with Abraham, Jehovah would not wipe out the Jews for their continued rebellion against Him, but if necessary, He was prepared to punish them with invasion and exile. This chapter closes with Moses providing a painfully graphic description of how the Lord would accomplish this.

The Lord would bring invaders into the land who would lay siege to Israel's cities (v. 52). In time, starvation would result in cannibalism; people would even resort to eating their own children to survive (v. 53). Moses said that a long siege would cause even the most *"sensitive and very refined man"* among them to behave like a barbarian against his friends, wife and children (v. 54). He will even hoard the flesh of his own children for himself to eat alone (v. 55). Similarly, even the most *"tender and delicate woman"* would not share the placenta that came from her body after childbearing; she will keep it as food for herself (vv. 56-57).

Refining and Reminding

Furthermore, starvation, filthy living conditions, and the lack of clean drinking water would lead to the proliferation of various diseases among those besieged (vv. 58-60). While the Jews might survive a siege in a walled city for some time, they would not survive the various plagues God would bring upon them: *"Every sickness and every plague, which is not written in this Book of the Law, will the Lord bring upon you until you are destroyed"* (v. 61). By God's hand, the Israelites had multiplied to be as numerous as the stars in heaven, and by His hand they would perish and become very few in number (v. 62). God would be glorified in His people one way or another, either through blessing victorious faithfulness or punishing persistent rebellion (v. 63).

Moses sternly warned the Israelites not to force God to evict them from their land through disobedience. To do so would cause God to scatter them among the nations that worship false gods (v. 64). There they would be compelled to serve idols and would suffer unending days and nights of torment and anguish of soul (vv. 65, 67). Moses then summarizes their plight: *"Your life shall hang in doubt before you; you shall fear day and night, and have no assurance of life"* (v. 66). Some surviving Jews will be shipped back to Egypt (their original place of bondage); slavery will be their only option to escape starvation. However, because of their feeble physical condition, no one will want to buy them (i.e., buyers considered them to be a poor investment; they were not worth the food required to sustain them for work; v. 68).

The Jewish historian Josephus suggests that verse 68 was fulfilled during the reign of Titus after the fall of Jerusalem in first century A.D. Multitudes of Jews were transported in ships to the Nile delta, and sold as slaves. Those 17 years of age and older were dispatched to various parts of the Roman Empire, to be employed in the public works, or doomed to fight with wild beasts in the amphitheaters. Those under 17 were so numerous that the slave market was glutted with them. Thirty children were offered for a trifle, and it was often difficult to find a purchaser.[206]

While this chapter is long and grueling to read, apparently it was not blunt enough when reviewing Israel's long, sad history of chastening. God did exactly what He said He would do if His people erred from the Law and abandoned Him. While none of these stated chastisements pertain to the Church, it behooves believers today to consider these as an indication of God's hatred of rebellion and misplaced devotion. If the Lord so severely judged His covenant people for their willful idolatry and wickedness, why would He not hesitate to chasten those committing the same offenses who are but mere second benefactors of the New Covenant confirmed with Israel (Heb. 8:8)? This is the essence of Paul's warning to the Christians at Rome:

> *For if God did not spare the natural branches* [the Jews], *He may not spare you* [the wild branches grafted in] *either. Therefore consider the goodness and severity of God: on those who fell, severity; but toward you, goodness, if you continue in His goodness. Otherwise you also will be cut off* (Rom. 11:21-22).

In Paul's olive tree analogy of Romans 11, the Abrahamic covenant is the root of the tree through which all nations of the earth shall be blessed (Gen. 12:3). The olive tree represents the Lord Jesus Christ, through whom all the blessings of God flow from the root to the branches. If the Church is to be restored to a testimony of power and vibrancy, she must repent, return to the Lord, and obey His Word. The Lord Himself said, *"I am the vine, you are the branches. He who abides in Me, and I in him, bears much fruit; for without Me you can do nothing"* (John 15:5). Without abiding in Christ, the Church is powerless and nothing more than dried up branches clattering in the secular winds of humanism. Unfortunately, this is a depiction which describes much of Christendom today.

Paul and John foretold that the spiritual condition of the professing Church would be apostate, materialistic, fruitless, and loveless just before the Antichrist is revealed and the Tribulation Period begins (2 Thess. 2:3; Rev. 3:15-18). Let us have no part in it! The days before us are evil; may God enable the true Church to hold fast to Christ and His Word. The greatest of tragedies would be for us not to learn from God's stern dealings with the Jews and to willfully repeat their offenses.

Meditation

> A creature revolting against a creator is revolting against the source of his own powers – including even his power to revolt. It is like the scent of a flower trying to destroy the flower. ... There are two kinds of people: those who say to God, "Thy will be done," and those to whom God says, "All right, then, have it your way."
>
> — C. S. Lewis

The Renewed Covenant
Deuteronomy 29

Verse 1 is not an introduction to a new message, but actually belongs in the previous chapter (as in the Hebrew text) to conclude Moses' third message (chps. 27-28): *"These are the words of the covenant which the Lord commanded Moses to make with the children of Israel in the land of Moab, besides the covenant which He made with them in Horeb."* The fact that Moses is again referred to in the third person signals the commencement of a new message, his fourth (chps. 29-30). The reader should recall that the contents of this entire book were given in five distinct messages over the course of a single week, just prior to Moses' death.

The Lord's Past Faithfulness (vv. 2-9)

Moses' fourth message reiterates the previously stated covenantal provisions, but with a special focus on Israel's inheritance of land. Some refer to the specialized content of chapters 29-30 as a standalone agreement referred to as the "Palestinian Covenant." While this distinction is permissible in title, Moses is not springing something new on his countrymen in the final moments of his tenure.

Moses begins his address by mentioning the wonderful feats accomplished by God both in Egypt to secure their release and during the past forty years (vv. 2-3). But though Israel had seen many signs and wonders with their eyes, they did not really perceive the full ramifications of what God had accomplished on their behalf: *"Yet the Lord has not given you a heart to perceive and eyes to see and ears to hear, to this very day"* (v. 4). This was not to say that their rebelliousness resulted from their ignorance of God's accomplishments, but rather that their disobedience sprang from a mind that could not understand the ways of God and His purposes.

For example, in the wilderness, they had been completely sustained by God for forty years. He provided them shade from the hot sun during the day, preserved their clothing and shoes from wearing out, and sustained them with the humble diet (v. 5). He did not provide them what they desired – grain to grind for bread and wine to drink. All this was to teach the nation that joyful sufficiency was in the Lord, not in satisfying the sinful impulses of lusting flesh – but they did not understand this lesson. Furthermore, when His people fully relied on the Lord and not on themselves, they were invincible, as shown in victory over the Amorites, which provided an inheritance for two and a half tribes in the Plains of Moab (vv. 6-8).

Moses' point in verse 5 is that without divine enlightenment, God's people will remain ignorant of His wondrous ways and judgments. But just because they do not understand what God is accomplishing before them, they are not released from obeying what they do know to be true. Paul also affirms in the New Testament that without God's help we would never understand all the mysteries associated with our salvation:

> *But God has revealed them to us through His Spirit. For the Spirit searches all things, yes, the deep things of God. For what man knows the things of a man except the spirit of the man which is in him? Even so no one knows the things of God except the Spirit of God. Now we have received, not the spirit of the world, but the Spirit who is from God, that we might know the things that have been freely given to us by God* (1 Cor. 2:10-12).

Without the inspired Word of God and the Holy Spirit to enable us to understand what God has revealed, we too would be ignorant of what is important to God. This is why the lost cannot come to Christ without the convicting work of the Holy Spirit upon their conscience (John 16:7-11), nor can the believer grow in knowledge and grace without His teaching ministry (John 14:26, 16:12-13). So, while the Israelites did not understand all that God was doing (because it had not been revealed to them; v. 29), they were still accountable to obey what God had revealed to them: *"Therefore keep the words of this covenant, and do them, that you may prosper in all that you do"* (v. 9). This verse summarizes the essence of their covenant with Jehovah.

Israel's Present Faithfulness Demanded (vv. 10-28)

The entire nation, including women, children, strangers, and servants were standing with Moses before the Lord on this momentous

Refining and Reminding

occasion (vv. 10-11). It was now time to renew their covenant with Jehovah: *"That you may enter into covenant with the Lord your God, and into His oath, which the Lord your God makes with you today"* (v. 12). Twice Moses said, *"All of you stand today before the Lord your God"* (vv. 10, 15) and three times he emphasized "today" (vv. 10, 12, 15). After twenty-eight chapters of reviewing Israel's history, the specifics of God's Law, and highlighting the blessings and curses associated with the Law, it was decision time.

God had promised Israel's forefathers, Abraham, Isaac, and Jacob, that He would bring their descendants back into the land promised Abraham (v. 13). Jehovah was now ready to make good on that promise, if Abraham's descendants (those alive then, and those yet to be born) would pledge their loyalty before He brought them into it (vv. 14-15). Hence, the book rises to its apex in chapters 28-29.

Before giving them an opportunity to voice their allegiance, Moses warned his countrymen that they were not unfamiliar with the dangers of idolatry. The older generation knew the wickedness of paganism in Egypt, and the entire nation had experienced the pitfalls of idolatry in the plains of Moab (i.e., the deceitful doctrine of Balaam; vv. 16-17). They had witnessed firsthand the painful consequences on the entire nation, even when only a few had been influenced to abandon Jehovah. Israel's failure in Moab resulted because a few leaders in the tribe of Simeon had fallen prey to Moab's seduction. Therefore they were to be on guard not to let a root of bitterness poison the whole nation (v. 18).

The writer of Hebrews references verse 18, but with an application of warning God's people against bitter hearts instead of idolatry:

Pursue peace with all people, and holiness, without which no one will see the Lord: looking carefully lest anyone fall short of the grace of God; lest any root of bitterness springing up cause trouble, and by this many become defiled (Heb. 12:14-15).

What is bitterness? Bitterness is a chronic and pervasive state caused by smoldering resentment. The Greek word for bitterness is *pikria* which means acridity (especially poison). Bitterness is a lingering hostile and agitated disposition caused by a poisonous frame of mind. Bitterness causes people to agonize over hurtful events or perceived ills to the point they become repulsive and cold in demeanor. Bitterness causes depression, anxiety, pessimism, and poor mental and physical health; it wrecks relationships and hinders communion with God. Bitterness is a choice to be sidelined from experiencing God and His goodness. So, just as Israel was to guard against the evils of idolatry, the Church was warned to avoid the destructive pit of bitterness. Bitterness is the opposite of God's grace working within us! Bitterness robs us of the peace and the holiness God wants to display in us, and sadly poisons others to suffer the same fate.

As we pour out our bitterness, God pours in his peace.

— F. B. Meyer

When the root is bitterness, imagine what the fruit might be.

— Woodrow Kroll

Moses then warned those who thought they would avoid judgment by secretly practicing paganism (vv. 19-20). They could not hide their sin from God. He promised to severely punish the guilty and even to *"blot out his name from under heaven."* Besides bringing down the curses of Deuteronomy upon his own head, God would see to it that he had no male heir to continue the family name.

In summary, Moses suggested two reasons why Israel should not tolerate a single idolater in their midst. First, just one person secretly practicing paganism could be the idolatrous root that eventually poisoned the entire nation (v. 18). This very phenomenon would occur after Ahab, the king of Israel, married the wicked daughter of the king of Zidon, Jezebel (1 Kgs. 16:31). She then popularized the worship of the Canaanite fertility gods Baal and Ashtaroth in the Northern Kingdom. Under her influence Ahab *"did more to provoke the Lord God of Israel to anger than all the kings of Israel that were before him"* (1 Kgs. 16:33).

Second, God's covenant was with the entire Jewish nation, meaning all would suffer for the corruption of a few within Israel (vv. 21-22). This necessitated vigilance in Israel to take quick and decisive action against any Jew, clan, or tribe that departed from God's Law. This corporate responsibility for self-preservation is shown in the near civil war which occurred over the misunderstood pillar erected by the two and a half tribes in Joshua 22, and the near eradication of the tribe of

Refining and Reminding

Benjamin for gross immorality in Judges 20. It was *all for one and one for all* in Israel, and nobody wanted to be judged by God because of their negligence in monitoring each other, supporting the weak, and dealing with the wayward.

Moses' appeal to the entire nation here is similar to Joshua's follow-up charge after the conquest of Canaan (seven years into the future):

> *Choose for yourselves this day whom you will serve, whether the gods which your fathers served that were on the other side of the River, or the gods of the Amorites, in whose land you dwell. But as for me and my house, we will serve the Lord* (Josh. 24:15).

But though the Israelites renewed their pledge to Jehovah three times that day, Joshua knew that there were those before him practicing idolatry in secret. Regrettably, only one generation later, we read of Israel's declension; they *"did not know the Lord nor the work which He had done for Israel"* (Judg. 2:10). Israel's history shows us just how fast one bad root (a single carnal person) can poison an entire people – likewise, may the Church beware of bitterness!

If the Jews did permit the corruption to spread through the land, the Lord promised to send devastation on Israel that would render the land unfit for growing anything (v. 23). Moses cites the destruction of the wicked Jordanian cities in Abraham's time as evidence of God's resolve in the matter. If (when) that did occur, Moses says even the nations will be startled by the devastation in Israel. They will ask, *"Why has the Lord done so to this land? What does the heat of this great anger mean?"* (v. 24). The answer to this question will be unmistakable, *"Because they have forsaken the covenant of the Lord God ... for they went and served other gods and worshiped them"* (vv. 25-26). Because Moses had so plainly informed the nation of exactly what God would do against them for spiritual infidelity, everyone would understand that Israel was getting the curses of the covenant they failed to keep (vv. 27-28).

Moses then closes the chapter with a concise statement of Israel's accountability to God: *"The secret things belong to the Lord our God, but those things which are revealed belong to us and to our children forever, that we may do all the words of this law"* (v. 29). As the verse does not connect well with the discourse of the previous verses, it seems likely that verse 29 was in response to looks of astonishment by the people: How could they, God's people, ever be so wicked to deserve such punishment?

If this assessment is correct, the meaning of verse 29 would be: How the good and evil things just reviewed will take effect in the future will be according to God's determination alone; man's sphere of duty pertains only to what God has revealed. Revelation demands responsibility! Man is accountable to obey God regardless of how much he appreciates or understands the basis of what God commands. While Gentiles were not under the Law, the statement, in principle, expresses humanity's general accountability to their Creator.

God's ways are not man's ways because God and His ways are perfect (Ps. 18:30), and therefore past finding out (Rom. 11:33). Mankind has a limited understanding of himself and his world. He knows only what God has revealed to him through Scripture, his conscience, or what he has determined as truth through observing creation. Beyond this, man is oblivious to truth, and unable to comprehend it in his present fallen state. But man's limited understanding of God and creation also becomes, in itself, the very medium by which faith in God is to be exercised.

Faith is the ability of the soul to reach beyond what can be verified by the human senses to trust what he cannot confirm by his own understanding. Hebrews 11:3 reminds us that it is only by faith that we know that the visible things we see did not happen by chance from visible realms, but from the hand of the invisible Creator. This is why one must have faith to please God, *"for without faith it is impossible to please Him"* (Heb. 11:6).

Man is accountable to believe what God reveals, but not accountable to act on what God has not revealed. These seemingly contradictory aspects of God's dealing with humanity intentionally create a dichotomy in the human brain. Incomplete answers to our inadequate questions do not satisfy our searching minds, but yet these perplexing aspects of God's calling should inspire awe for God and humility before Him. There are some matters that man is not expected to understand; in these abstruse areas, being dumbfounded is the expected and God-honoring outcome. Logically speaking, a time-dependent being cannot fully understand time-independent truth – the tie between creation order and the ultimate eternal order of things rests solely in God's resolve to complete His predetermined counsel. As with

Refining and Reminding

Israel, on "this day," and the Church in our day, believers are to rest completely in the Lord.

Meditation

> Where then does wisdom come from?
> Where understanding dwell?
> God comprehends the pathway,
> He alone knows well.
>
> He views the ends of all the earth;
> He sees the world He formed.
> He has established wisdom,
> Tested and confirmed.
>
> Fear of the Lord is wisdom;
> Seek it and you will find.
> Cry out for understanding;
> Let it fill your mind.
>
> Search as for hidden treasure;
> Look for it every day.
> This is the path to wisdom;
> Follow all the way.

— Susan H. Peterson

Choosing Between Life or Death
Deuteronomy 30

Recovery After Failure (vv. 1-5)

In the last chapter, Moses passionately reminded Israel of Jehovah's past faithfulness and the severe consequences of straying from Him. He thoroughly itemized the blessings for obedience and the curses for disobedience which the Law afforded and demanded. However, knowing the fickle, stiff-necked disposition of his countrymen, Moses predicts that they will break their covenant with the Lord. He therefore encourages them to not give up hope after being exiled and dispersed for their negligence; rather, they should seek the Lord again through repentance (vv. 1-2).

If they humbled themselves and genuinely sought the Lord through contrition and obedience, He would gather them back to Israel (vv. 3-6). However, as the prophets Jeremiah, Ezekiel, and Daniel later affirmed, the Jews would still remain under foreign domination even after returning from Babylonian captivity. Daniel foretells that beginning with Babylon, Israel would be controlled by five future world empires, the last one being that of the Antichrist during the Tribulation Period (Dan. 2). At the end of that seven-year period, the Lord will intervene to destroy the Antichrist and his armies and to return every Jew to the land of Israel (Isa. 11:12; Ezek. 39:28-29).

A New Heart and Renewed Favor (vv. 6-10)

At Christ's second advent, the purified Jewish nation will receive the Holy Spirit and receive Jesus Christ as their Messiah (Joel 2:28-29; Zech. 12:10). That is when verse 6 will be fulfilled: *"And the Lord your God will circumcise your heart and the heart of your descendants, to love the Lord your God with all your heart and with all your soul, that you may live."* The Old Covenant had no provision of mercy by which to reinstate Israel after failure, but through the Lord Jesus

Refining and Reminding

Christ's work at Calvary, God instituted a New Covenant with His covenant people that could (Jer. 31:31-32; Heb. 8:8).

Jeremiah says that this would be an everlasting covenant resulting in eternal blessing to the Jews (Jer. 32:40). This promise is understood to be literal, for God will erect an eternal city where the Jewish remnant will dwell (Isa. 48:2, 52:1). The prophet Ezekiel refers to the New Covenant as a *"Covenant of Peace"* with the Jewish nation (Ezek. 34:25). Isaiah proclaimed that through this covenant, *"Israel shall be saved in the Lord with an everlasting salvation"* (Isa. 45:17). Not only was the New Covenant needed to restore Israel to God, but to also secure them forever in blessings promised to Abraham.

For example those who oppose Israel will be punished by God and those who favor Israel will be blessed by Him (v. 7), just as was promised Abraham long ago: *"I will bless those who bless you, and I will curse him who curses you; and in you all the families of the earth shall be blessed"* (Gen. 12:3). Those nations who troubled His covenant people in the past will be recompensed for their evil and no authority on earth will be permitted to harass them during the Kingdom Age.

Once Israel is finally restored to God at the end of the Tribulation Period, the Holy Spirit will ensure that they never leave Him again for false gods; instead, they will continue in His Law (vv. 7-9). As a nation, they will receive the Holy Spirit, and He will circumcise their heart. That is, He will remove what is carnal and unwanted, so the heart of the nation beats only for God. Moses told his brethren that only then would they be able to follow the Lord their God with all their heart and with all their soul (v. 10). The prophets Ezekiel and Joel refer to this as "a new heart" – the benefit of spiritual regeneration (Ezek. 36:23-28; Joel 2:27-29).

While Israel did become a Jewish nation again in May 1948, they have yet to realize the peace, the security, the prosperity, and the exaltation that awaits them in the Kingdom Age, once they are restored to God through Christ. Clearly, not all Jews in the world today live in Israel – in fact, less than half do. Additionally, God's covenant people are yet to be fully regathered to the land promised to Abraham (Gen. 15:18-21). The boundaries of this inheritance were confirmed when the Israelites entered Canaan under Joshua's leadership (Josh. 1:3-4). The Jews have yet to possess this vast region of land. All this to say, God is not finished with the Jewish nation; He must yet fulfill every promise and prophecy concerning His covenant people.

The Choice of Life or Death (vv. 11-20)

In anticipation of possible excuses for neglecting the Law, Moses reminded the congregation that the Law was not confusing or beyond their grasp to understand:

> *For this commandment which I command you today is not too mysterious for you, nor is it far off. It is not in heaven, that you should say, "Who will ascend into heaven for us and bring it to us, that we may hear it and do it?" Nor is it beyond the sea, that you should say, "Who will go over the sea for us and bring it to us, that we may hear it and do it?" But the word is very near you, in your mouth and in your heart, that you may do it* (vv. 11-14).

Jack S. Deere explains why neither ignorance nor negligence would permit Israel to disregard God's clear demands on them:

Though the Law had a heavenly origin, God clearly revealed it to Israel so there was no need for anyone to ascend into heaven to get it nor did anyone need to travel across an ocean to get it. Nor did Israel need a special interpreter of the Law before they could obey it. The Law was already written down and Israel had been familiar with its demands in the wilderness. So Moses could say that the word is very near you. They could speak it (it is in your mouth) and they knew it (it is in your heart).[207]

Paul acknowledges that God's righteousness and means of blessing had been first revealed to Israel in the Mosaic Law. However, He had now revealed His righteousness and means of salvation in a superior way – in Jesus Christ. *"But now the righteousness of God apart from the law is revealed, being witnessed by the Law and the Prophets, even the righteousness of God, through faith in Jesus Christ, to all and on all who believe. For there is no difference"* (Rom. 3:21-22). Christ sealed the New Covenant with Israel with His own blood to accomplish what the first covenant could not (Heb. 8:8).

Later in Paul's epistle to the Romans, he quotes Moses (vv. 12-14) to show that God's plan of salvation through Christ can also be easily understood and is attainable:

Refining and Reminding

> *But the righteousness of faith speaks in this way, "Do not say in your heart, 'Who will ascend into heaven?'" (that is, to bring Christ down from above) or, "'Who will descend into the abyss?'" (that is, to bring Christ up from the dead). But what does it say? "The word is near you, in your mouth and in your heart" (that is, the word of faith which we preach): that if you confess with your mouth the Lord Jesus and believe in your heart that God has raised Him from the dead, you will be saved* (Rom. 10:6-9).

God reveals Himself in many ways: in creation, through the human conscience, in His written Word, through miracles, and expressly in His Son, Jesus Christ. There is plenty of revelation near all men to lead them into truth, if they will trust it. The lost do not have to explore the heights of heaven or depths of hell to find truth. What God wants them to appropriate by faith has been revealed. Likewise, what has been rejected will govern their ultimate punishment. This was the same point Moses was making in his life-or-death appeal in this chapter:

> *See, I have set before you today **life and good, death and evil**, in that I command you today to love the Lord your God, to walk in His ways, and to keep His commandments, His statutes, and His judgments, that you may live and multiply; and the Lord your God will bless you in the land which you go to possess ...*
> *I have set before you **life and death**, blessing and cursing; therefore choose life, that both you and your descendants may live; that you may love the Lord your God, that you may obey His voice, and that you may cling to Him, for **He is your life** and the length of your days; and that you may dwell in the land which the Lord swore to your fathers, to Abraham, Isaac, and Jacob, to give them"* (vv. 15-16, 19-20).

The climax of Moses' forty-year ministry is this appeal to his countrymen to "love," to "obey," and to "cling" to the Lord. Moses wanted them to make a choice at that very moment which would guide Israel into life for generations to come. God is Israel's life; apart from Him is death (separation from life). Moses was not talking about positional justification at this juncture. Israel had been redeemed by the blood of a lamb and justified by faith at the first Passover in Egypt. Moses was speaking of a consecrated way of life which maintains fellowship and communion with God.

Devotions in Deuteronomy

Paul summarizes the biblical standard of sanctification in one verse: *"For the wages of sin is death, but the gift of God is eternal life in Christ Jesus our Lord"* (Rom. 6:23). Disobedience causes separation; obedience results in fellowship with God (1 Jn. 1:5-7). Although Israel initially committed themselves to God on the Plains of Moab and continued well during the Canaan Conquest, widespread declension will mark the nation just a few years later. Israel did not choose life, and therefore suffered the devastation of being separated from their God – their life. Thankfully, at the commencement of the Kingdom Age, the Jewish nation will choose Christ and they will experience life with God again and forever in Him.

Meditation

>Almighty God, Thy lofty throne
>Has justice for its cornerstone,
>And shining bright before Thy face
>Are truth and love and boundless grace.
>
>All glory unto God we yield,
>Jehovah is our Help and Shield;
>All praise and honor will we bring
>To Israel's Holy One, our King.
>
>— The Psalter

Israel's Future
Deuteronomy 31

Joshua to Be Israel's Leader (vv. 1-8)

Just a few weeks prior to this address, the Lord told Moses that it was time for him to be gathered to his people (Num. 27:13). When it was time for his departure, Moses was to climb the mountain range of Abarim so that he could behold a vista of the Promised Land to the west before he died (34:5). The specific summit in this range we learn in the next chapter was Mount Nebo (32:49).

At that time, the Lord reminded Moses of his failure to obey Him and to honor Him before the people a few months earlier at Kadesh in the Wilderness of Zin (Num. 27:14; 20:12). After the sorrowful incident at the waters of Meribah, Moses had been informed that he would not enter the Promised Land with the Israelites, but that he would be able to view it. Moses does not go into all the details of his failure at this juncture, but simply summarizes, *"the Lord has said to me, 'You shall not cross over this Jordan'"* (v. 3).

Numbers 27 also records Moses' request that the Lord appoint a strong shepherd to guide Israel – that man was Joshua. Moses then brought Joshua before Eleazar and the congregation to publicly recognize him as Israel's new leader by the laying on of hands.

Moses had enjoyed robust vitality in his autumn years (34:7), but now, at 120 years of age, he did not have the strength to lead Israel into battle. The Lord would not permit His servant to suffer the rigors of extended warfare; it was time for him to depart (vv. 1-2). But Moses reminded his countrymen that though he would not be crossing the Jordan with them, God would go before them (v. 3). Under Joshua's leadership they would vanquish their enemies as in the plains of Moab and secure Canaan, that is, if they would be faithful to do to the Canaanites as commanded (vv. 4-5). Moses then charges them, *"Be strong and of good courage, do not fear nor be afraid of them; for the Lord your God, He is the one who goes with you. He will not leave you nor forsake you"* (v. 6). Then Moses called Joshua forward and gave him a similar charge in front of the entire nation:

> *Be strong and of good courage, for you must go with this people to the land which the Lord has sworn to their fathers to give them, and you shall cause them to inherit it. And the Lord, He is the one who goes before you. He will be with you, He will not leave you nor forsake you; do not fear nor be dismayed* (vv. 7-8).

Thirty-nine years earlier Moses had told Joshua, Caleb, and ten other spies to *"be of good courage"* just before their reconnaissance mission into Canaan (Num. 13:20). Now, on the eve of entering the land for the second time, Moses told Israel's new leader to *"be strong and of good courage."* Moses reminded him that the Lord was with him to conquer the land and He would never forsake him. This meant that the only thing to fear in Canaan was not going on with the Lord in obedience. If Israel was faithful, then the Lord would fulfill his vow to Israel's forefathers and give their descendants the land.

A few weeks after Moses' death, the Lord Himself would meet with Joshua to encourage him to be faithful to his calling to lead His people into Canaan. At that time, the Lord promised Joshua that if he obeyed His command and led His people into Canaan to obtain their inheritance, no one would be able to withstand him. Then, after affirming His abiding presence, the Lord exhorted Joshua three times to *"Be strong and of good courage"* (Josh. 1:6, 7, 9).

The Lord had stood with Moses for forty years in the wilderness, and He extended to Joshua the same promise He had made to Moses at the burning bush (Ex. 3:12): *"I will be with you. I will not leave you nor forsake you"* (Josh. 1:5). The Lord spoke to Jacob in the same way, saying, *"Return to the land of your fathers and to your family, and I will be with you"* (Gen. 31:3). Whether the child of God is commanded "to come," "to go," or "to return," the same solace of peace is enjoyed – the communion of God's presence. The prophet Jeremiah depended on it (Jer. 1:8), as did Paul (Acts 18:10). For centuries, suffering saints have found comfort in God's abiding presence during the most arduous of times. Living for Christ in a sin-cursed world is challenging, but the believer's calling in Christ is not burdensome because he or she is yoked with the Lord (Matt. 11:28-30). It is through this vital connection that we learn that every victory is the Lord's victory and that without Him we can do nothing (John 15:5)!

This is why Moses, in his final address to his successor, could challenge Joshua to *"be strong and of good courage."* Moses had experienced God's faithfulness and abiding presence, and he encouraged Joshua to do the same. When God's will is apprehended by His people, they must also have divine strength and courage to do it; otherwise, they will be overcome by the enemy who will oppose them from every possible vantage point. Therefore, Joshua could not fulfill his divine calling without the power and presence of the Lord.

Review of the Law (vv. 9-13)

Moses then delivered to the elders and priests the Law that he had written (v. 9). He commanded that the Law should be read aloud every seven years (i.e., in the Sabbath year of release) when the congregation came to the central sanctuary to observe the Feast of Tabernacles (vv. 10-11). Israel's leaders were to ensure that everyone (men, women, children, and strangers) dwelling in the land came to hear the Law, that *"they may learn to fear the Lord your God and carefully observe all the words of this law"* (v. 12). There was to be no excuse of ignorance among the Israelites; everyone blessed in the land was to hear, to learn, and to fear the Lord (v. 13).

The Prediction of Israel's Apostasy (vv. 14-29)

The Lord then told Moses that it was time for him to depart and that he should bring Joshua to *"the tabernacle of meeting"* so that the Lord could publicly "inaugurate him" as Israel's new leader (v. 14). The tabernacle was most commonly called the "tabernacle of the congregation," or the "tent/tabernacle of meeting" because it was the appointed site for God to personally reveal His will to Moses (v. 14; Ex. 29:44; Num. 11:16). Scripture also refers to God's dwelling place among men as the tabernacle of the Lord (Num. 16:9), and the tabernacle of the testimony (Ex. 38:21; Num. 9:15). The latter term pertains to the location of the stone tables upon which the Law was written; these, as we learn in verse 26, were stored in the Ark of the Covenant in the Most Holy section of the tabernacle.

The Lord then appeared to Moses and Joshua in a pillar of cloud before the doorway of the tabernacle (v. 15). Given all of his efforts to instill God's Law into the heart of his brethren, what the Lord told Moses must have been heart-breaking, though not unexpected:

> *Behold, you will rest with your fathers; and this people will rise and play the harlot with the gods of the foreigners of the land, where they go to be among them, and they will forsake Me and break My covenant which I have made with them. Then My anger shall be aroused against them in that day, and I will forsake them, and I will hide My face from them, and they shall be devoured. And many evils and troubles shall befall them, so that they will say in that day, "Have not these evils come upon us because our God is not among us?" And I will surely hide My face in that day because of all the evil which they have done, in that they have turned to other gods* (vv. 16-18).

The Lord then told Moses to write down a song (which is recorded in the next chapter) and to teach it to the Israelites to warn them against apostasy (v. 19), for the Lord would indeed bring them into a land flowing with milk and honey as promised (v. 20). However, in time, Israel's spiritual harlotry would provoke God to chasten and remove them from their inheritance. Moses' song would then enable the Israelites to understand why they had been judged and would also prompt them to renew their covenant with Jehovah (v. 21). God's covenant with Israel was conditional – to be blessed in the land, they must remain faithful. Thankfully, God's love is not fickle. He was determined to bless His people and honor His word, even foreknowing Israel's disloyalty to Him.

Moses did as the Lord commanded and taught the song to Israel that day (v. 22). The deep tenderness of the shepherd's heart continued to swell towards his flock. And foreknowing the danger ahead, Moses never tired of pouring exhortation into the ears of his brethren.

The Lord also inaugurated Joshua and personally repeated what Moses had already affirmed to his successor: *"Be strong and of good courage; for you shall bring the children of Israel into the land of which I swore to them, and I will be with you"* (v. 23). Given the arduous task ahead of him, the Lord knew that Joshua needed to hear these words again. May we too meditate on them as we fulfill our callings in the Body of Christ!

After meeting with the Lord at the tabernacle, Moses, having completed writing down all the words of the Law, entrusted it to the priests (v. 24). They were instructed to place the book of the Law in the

Refining and Reminding

Ark of the Covenant for safekeeping (vv. 25-26). The Lord resided above the Ark in the Most Holy place of the tabernacle and from that preeminent location the Law would be *"a witness against"* Israel.

Moses' next words to the congregation were pungent: *"For I know your rebellion and your stiff neck. If today, while I am yet alive with you, you have been rebellious against the Lord, then how much more after my death?"* (v. 27). After forty years of overseeing his brethren, Moses knew his brethren's rebellious disposition all too well. He had correctly assessed their future resolve to follow the Lord – they would abandon the Lord and would provoke His anger after only a short time.

Foreknowing this outcome, Moses again summoned Israel's leaders to gather before him one last time (vv. 28-29). Moses then spoke the song (perhaps a second time) that the Lord had given him (chp. 32) and then pronounced a tribal blessing (chp. 33). The Song of Moses is included within the text of Deuteronomy to emphasize Israel's need to continually renew their covenant with the Lord (v. 30).

Meditation

"I, the Lord, am with thee, be thou not afraid;
I will help and strengthen, be thou not dismayed.
Yea, I will uphold thee with My own right hand;
Thou art called and chosen in My sight to stand."
Onward, then, and fear not, children of the day;
For His word shall never, never pass away.

He will never fail us, He will not forsake:
His eternal covenant He will never break.
Resting on His promise, what have we to fear?
God is all-sufficient for the coming year.
Onward, then, and fear not, children of the day;
For His word shall never, never pass away.

— Frances R. Havergal

The Song of Moses
Deuteronomy 32

Moses may have written other songs, but three are preserved in Scripture. Exodus 15 records the wonderful deliverance of Israel from Pharaoh's army at the Red Sea. Then there is the historical record of God's faithfulness throughout Israel's history in Psalm 90. It is noteworthy that Moses begins the final message of his ministry with a song and ends it with a blessing (chp. 33).

The song of this chapter was to assist Israel in the future to make sense of why they were suffering disaster and calamity in the Promised Land – namely for apostasy. Moses had already confirmed that in that day, this song would *"testify against them as a witness"* (31:21). Yet, Moses' song also anticipated God's grace being lavished upon Israel in a future day, despite their past failures. William Kelly writes:

> This song is grounded on the secret things of God's grace, though it also embraces the judgments of the latter day. Not ignorant of the evil, Moses looks onward to the blessing that would surely come to Israel. He deeply feels what they would do against Jehovah in their stiff-necked folly and ingratitude; but he beholds in prophetic vision what He will do for them.[208]

Albert Barnes divides the Song of Moses into three separate refrains:

> The faithfulness of God vs. the faithlessness of Israel (vv. 4-19).
> The chastisement and the need of its infliction by God (vv. 19-33).
> God's compassion upon the low and humbled state of His people (vv. 34-42).[209]

The song commences with a congregational call to listen and then a prompt to acclaim praise to Israel's just, faithful, and upright God (vv. 1-4). He is the God of truth and all His ways are perfect, unlike the

Refining and Reminding

Israelites who are foolish and perverse and whose ways are corrupt (vv. 5-6). The song then reviews Israel's history from the time of their bondage in Egypt, through their wilderness wanderings, to their establishment in the Promised Land (vv. 7–14).

So far, Moses has contrasted Israel's unfavorable character and deeds with the Lord's perfections, and then reviewed God's goodness in delivering and sustaining Israel in order to fulfill His pledge to bring them into the Promised Land. The Song then becomes prophetic in nature: Israel's future ingratitude and gross idolatry against their Father and Creator are foretold (v. 6), as are the severe judgments they will suffer for their sin (vv. 15-31). In recent chapters, Moses well delineated the curses associated with disobedience to the Law. He briefly mentions a few of these in verses 24-25: hunger, pestilence, destruction, wild beasts, poisonous serpents, and the sword. Then the song offers hope to Israel; God will show His people compassion again by avenging them against their enemies (vv. 32-42).

The song then concludes on a joyful note. Despite Israel's past failures and God's just chastening, there is a day coming when righteousness will be restored to the land, Israel will be cleansed of all defilement, and Gentiles and Jews will rejoice together in what God has accomplished. This longed-for utopia will occur in the Millennial Kingdom under Christ's rule. He is the only One who can *"provide atonement for His land and His people"* (v. 43).

> *By Him* [Christ] *to reconcile all things to Himself, by Him, whether things on earth or things in heaven, having made peace through the blood of His cross. And you, who once were alienated and enemies in your mind by wicked works, yet now He has reconciled in the body of His flesh through death, to present you holy, and blameless, and above reproach in His sight* (Col. 1:20-22).

Only Christ can reconcile both Jew and Gentile to God and only after Israel's restoration will both Jew and Gentile rejoice together in God's presence. But this blessed reality of the Kingdom Age cannot occur until "the fullness of the Gentiles" and "the times of the Gentiles" have concluded. The times of the Gentiles (i.e., Gentile rule over Israel) began when Babylon conquered Jerusalem in 586 B.C. and will conclude when Christ destroys Babylon once and for all at His Second Advent (Dan. 9:27; Luke 21:24; Rev. 11:2). Paul says that Israel's spiritual blindness will continue until the last Gentile believer is added to the Church; this will conclude the Church Age, or "the fullness of the Gentiles" (Rom. 11:25).

With all this in view, C. A. Coates provides a concise summary of the Song of Moses and why it should encourage all believers to press on with the Lord through life's difficulties:

> This song celebrates the greatness of God in stability, perfection of working, righteousness and faithfulness. He will carry through the purposes of His love in spite of everything. The reminder of this is always refreshing to faith; God becomes the Rock of the soul. Only in the light of what He is could we bear to review the terrible history of failure.[210]

While there are many aspects of this song worth contemplating, we will limit our focus to two devotional thoughts. First, the theme of God's faithfulness runs through the entire song. Four times Jehovah is referred to as "the Rock" of Israel. Despite Israel's spiritual volatility and rebel tendencies, Jehovah is completely faithful and trustworthy, a steady and unchanging source of strength and salvation (vv. 15, 18, 30-31)!

David wrote Psalm 61 during one of the greatest trials of his life – his son Absalom's rebellion. The king and a handful of his loyal subjects had quickly fled for their lives into the rocky and desolate wilderness east of Jerusalem, but their provisions were low (2 Sam. 15-16). They lodged temporarily in this wilderness until Hushai, David's spy, sent word for them to hurry across the Jordan to escape their pursuers (2 Sam. 17). The situation was bleak; they were greatly outnumbered and the people were hungry, weary, and thirsty (2 Sam. 17:29).

Perhaps David was inspecting the defenses of their temporary encampment when the Lord drew his sight upward from the surrounding rock formations to his heavenly Rock of defense. David knew there was no safer abiding place than in God's presence and he expresses his resolve to remain there forever. As David became occupied with the exalted Lord instead of his circumstances, he was refreshed in his spirit and was prompted to sing praises to God. When our hearts are overwhelmed, may we also have the faith to lift our eyes from the dismal earthly outlook *"to the Rock that is higher"* (Ps. 61:2).

Refining and Reminding

Moses also highlights the importance of unitedly resting in the Rock to accomplish His work: *"How could one chase a thousand, and two put ten thousand to flight, unless their Rock had sold them, and the Lord had surrendered them?"* (v. 30). God can use one man to defeat a thousand foes, but two men fighting as one with the Lord can defeat ten thousand! God's people have greater wherewithal to rise and conquer when they work together, rather than as individuals, with the Lord. This was God's plan for Israel's success in Canaan – resting in Him and working together as one under His authority.

Second, God uses a tender term of affection in referring to Israel; the nation was *"the apple of His eye"*:

> *For the Lord's portion is His people; Jacob is the place of His inheritance. He found him in a desert land and in the wasteland, a howling wilderness; He encircled him, He instructed him, He kept him as the apple of His eye* (vv. 9-10).

Although originating in the Old Testament, this idiom (*the apple of my eye*) is an expression of endearment still commonly used today. The *Oxford English Dictionary* states that the phrase refers to "something or someone that one cherishes above all others."[211] The pupil, or aperture, through which light passes to the retina, is the tenderest part of the eye. Because sight is the most valued of our five senses, we treasure our eyes and diligently guard them from harm. The eye is an incredible organ – even the slightest injury is most acutely felt and may cause loss of function. It is also an organ that once damaged is not easily repaired through surgery. For these and other reasons our eyes are precious to us!

Consequently, when Jehovah used the term *the apple of His eye*, He was speaking of what He cherished greatly. The idiom is used three times in Scripture to express God's love for Israel: at their national commencement (v. 10), during the darkness of their spiritual apostasy in Jeremiah's day (Lam. 2:18), and, lastly, in reference to their spiritual restoration in the Kingdom Age (Zech. 2:8).

The pupil is round, dark, and in the center of the eye. It reflects an image of what is directly in front of it. If one's love is intensely focused on another, nothing can distract it; to do so would require turning away from his beloved. Then the reflection of one's self in the eye of the beloved would be lost. Hence, the term *apple of one's eye* in Scripture is an intimate expression of God's concentrated devotion and commitment to His covenant people, the Jews. Though they might look away from Him, He would not turn His head from them. Anytime they look to Jehovah, they will instantly be aware of His love for them; they will, so to speak, see their own reflection in His eye.

In summary, Moses' Song has a prophetic purpose of predicting Israel's sorrowful future, but also a didactic intention of affirming God's faithfulness to judge sin and also to show mercy to the repentant. We learn in verse 44 that Joshua aided Moses in reciting this song. Additionally, we discover that the same day it was taught to Israel, Moses went up into Mt. Nebo and died (vv. 48-49).

Moses was told a year earlier at Kadesh that he would not be permitted to go into Canaan, but perhaps he was still hoping the Lord would show mercy to His servant. However, the Lord affirmed that His judgment against Moses for failing to honor Him at Meribah had not changed (vv. 51-52). From a conceptual point of view, it would have been impossible for the failure of Moses to be disregarded without weakening the authority of Law. Aaron had gone up into Mount Hor to die a few months earlier and now it was Moses' turn to depart the realm of sorrows and hardship to join his brother in eternal rest (v. 50).

Meditation

I want a principle within of watchful, godly fear,
A sensibility of sin, a pain to feel it near.
I want the first approach to feel of pride or wrong desire,
To catch the wandering of my will, and quench the kindling fire.

From Thee that I no more may stray, no more Thy goodness grieve,
Grant me the devoted awe, I pray, the tender conscience give.
Quick as the apple of an eye, O God, my conscience make;
Awake my soul when sin is nigh, and keep it still awake.

— Charles Wesley

Tribal Blessings
Deuteronomy 33

Moses was now ready to journey from the plains of Moab to Mount Nebo, where he would be permitted to see the Promised Land just before his death. But just before the 120-year-old patriarch leaves the camp for the final time, we can imagine him turning and raising his hands to pronounce a blessing on his brethren (v. 1). The entire scene before us is reminiscent of elderly Jacob blessing each of his twelve sons just before his death in Genesis 49.

Because Joseph received the double portion of the birthright instead of Reuben, the tribes of Manasseh and Ephraim are mentioned in the Old Testament tribal listings, while Levi is often not. This is to maintain the sense that Israel was iconicly a nation of twelve tribes. This difficulty was avoided in the book of Numbers, as Levi was not to be included in Israel's army. However, Moses does mention his own tribe of Levi in his final blessing, and therefore elects to leave out Simeon. God's judgment on the tribe of Simeon for conspiring with idolatrous Midianites reduced their size by more than half. This meant that they were now the smallest of Israel's tribes and the least favored. Their inheritance in Canaan would later be within Judah's borders and in time the Simeonites would be absorbed into the tribe of Judah.

As in his song of the previous chapter, Moses presents this prophetic blessing in poetic form. Moses began by recalling that distinct moment in Israel's history when they first met Jehovah at Mount Sinai. So spectacular was the sight that it seemed as if God soared in from the northeast (i.e., Seir is east and the Wilderness of Paran is north of Sinai) to settle on the fiery, quaking mount (v. 2). With the nation gathered before the mount below, God above gave Moses the Law – their national constitution (vv. 3-4). In God's mind they were now a nation, a collective people with a constitution, a King (the Lord Himself), and a land to reside in, though they had not yet inherited it (v. 5).

Reuben (v. 6). Moses requested that this tribe not die out, but live. Because of Reuben's sin with his concubine, Jacob had prophesied that Reuben would not excel (Gen. 49:6). Moses was likely concerned that this character deficiency in Reuben would result in the tribe's downfall. His foreboding was later validated as Reuben was one of the tribes who chose not to get involved in Israel's desperate fight against the Canaanites in the days of Deborah and Barak. The Reubenites had *"great thoughts of heart"* (i.e. sincere deliberations) but chose to remain among their sheepfolds rather than to join the conflict (Judg. 5:15-16).

Judah (v. 7). When the trumpets sounded to move the camp, Judah was the first tribe to move out (Num. 2:9). They led the column and thus would be the first into battle. Therefore, Moses prayed that the Lord would help Judah against his enemies. Jacob had already prophesied that the Jewish Messiah would come through Judah (Gen. 49:10), so it was appropriate for him to lead the nation into battle. The Lord confirmed this through the Urim and Thummim when the High Priest asked the Lord who should lead the nation into battle against the Benjamites. Although it was the wrong question, as the Lord had not endorsed the battle, He still answered the question put to Him, *"Judah shall go up first"* (Judg. 20:18).

Levi (vv. 8-11). Initially, the tribe of Levi was honored because Moses, a Levite, had been selected by God to liberate the nation from Egypt and then to lead them to Sinai to meet Jehovah. Besides the plagues he called down against Egypt, God showed His approval of Moses at Massah (also called Meribah) where Moses struck the rock of Horeb to obtain water for a parched nation (Ex. 17:1-7). Then, the Lord honored the tribe of Levi at Sinai after they sided with Moses against the rebels dancing about the golden calf (Ex. 32). The Levites would become the keepers and teachers of God's Law. They would live in cities spread out among all the tribes to ensure everyone had an opportunity to know God's will.

For matters not addressed by the Law, the High Priest could consult the Lord for wisdom by using the Urim and Thummim (Num. 27:21; Deut. 22:8-10). The High Priest's breastplate had a double fold to safely carry the Urim and Thummim stones. It is unknown how these two stones were used to determine God's will. Some suggest the Urim (which begins with the first letter of the Hebrew alphabet) represented a negative answer and the Thummim (*tummim* being the last letter of the

Refining and Reminding

alphabet) a positive answer. In any case, Moses was acknowledging that the High Priest had the authority to inquire of God and was asking that God bless him with divine enlightenment.

Benjamin (v. 12). Benjamin was Jacob's youngest son and born of his beloved wife Rachel. She died shortly after giving birth to Benjamin. Moses' request for Benjamin's security and peace as the Lord's "beloved" seems to reflect Jacob's tender heart towards his youngest son. However, this did not mean that Jacob did not foresee the tribe's weakness; in fact, he said Benjamin would be as violent in spirit as a ravenous wolf devouring its prey (Gen. 49:27). This prediction was clearly seen in the wickedness of Benjamin in Judges 19 and 20, and in their refusal to repent but rather to war against all the other Jewish tribes.

Joseph (vv. 13-17). Moses then prayed for many "precious" and "best" things for the tribes of Manasseh and Ephraim, Joseph's sons. A land well-nourished by rain and ground water, with fertile ground, and lush hills of timber were requested by Moses for Joseph. These tribes would be the largest of what later would be the Northern Kingdom. Additionally, Moses asks that they be like a charging bull or gorging horned-ox against their enemies. By mentioning Ephraim before Manasseh, and then accrediting Ephraim ten thousand to Manasseh's one thousand, Moses was affirming that Ephraim, though younger, had received from Jacob the blessing of the firstborn son (Gen. 48:17-20).

Zebulun and Issachar (vv. 18-19). Moses follows Jacob's pattern of mentioning both these tribes together (Gen. 49:13-15). These two tribes could rejoice because God would bless their livelihood. Jacob further prophesied that Zebulun would be enriched by sea trade (Gen. 49:13). Moses also highlights that both tribes would be somehow prosperous by sea trade. When the lots were cast later by Joshua to divide and distribute Canaan, both Zebulun and Issachar were given land by or near the sea. Zebulun was given a portion of lower Galilee which likely contained a strip of land through Issachar's possession that gave them access to the sea (Judg. 19:10-16). Issachar was given the fertile Jezreel valley south of the Sea of Galilee and a region that wrapped around Zebulun to span the coastal plain (Judg. 19:17-23).

Gad (vv. 20-21). Moses' blessing on Gad is difficult to ascertain. The gist seems to be that, although Gad chose what they thought was the best land east of the Jordan River, they still would be blessed because they honored their pledge to secure Canaan. In fact, they would fight as valiantly as a lion to help their brethren obtain their inheritance in Canaan, which fulfilled God's will in the matter.

Dan (v. 22). Dan's blessing is short and cryptic: *"Dan is a lion's whelp; he shall leap from Bashan."* As a lion's whelp, Dan would initially have boldness, but little strength, but with maturity they would be able to leap from Bashan. As Bashan was far from Dan's possession, Moses is likely applying a metaphoric meaning. The Bashan highlands were east of the Sea of Galilee and a region known for its lions' lairs. The meaning of this blessing can be witnessed in two ways. First is in Israel's last judge, Samson. When a young lion roared against him, the Spirit of the Lord came upon Samson and he tore the lion into pieces (Judg. 14:5-6). Second, a number of Danites (who had lost their inheritance to the Amorites) later made a bold move and traveled to the far northeast of Canaan to conquer the remote city of Leshem. They took it for an inheritance and renamed it "Dan" (Josh. 19:47).

Naphtali (v. 23). Moses foretold that Naphtali would enjoy the peace of the high hill country in Israel southwest of the Sea of Galilee: *"O Naphtali, satisfied with favor, and full of the blessing of the Lord, take possession of the sea and the south"* (v. 23; NASV). When Joshua cast the lots, Naphtali indeed received the north-central highlands for an inheritance (Judg. 19:32-39). The Sea of Galilee and the Jordan River marked the tribe's eastern boundaries. The land of Asher lay to the west and Zebulun and Issachar lay to the south. Like Ephraim, Manasseh, and Asher, Naphtali would be blessed.

Asher (vv. 24-25). As just noted, Asher would be a blessed tribe. Vast prosperity is indicated by the extravagance of dipping one's foot in oil instead of anointing it. Asher's sandals of iron and bronze (or perhaps the gates of his fortresses is meant) indicate the tribe's security resulting from its military strength. Asher inherited the coastal plain from Mount Carmel to Sidon and Tyre in the north (Josh. 19:24-31). Apparently, Asher was to guard the Israelites against sea invasions, the Phoenicians being of primary concern. Although this tribe would become insignificant in size and status, they did not lose their distinction as some other tribes did. Anna, who uttered a jubilant prophetic blessing at the sight of the infant Jesus, was from Asher (Luke 2:36-38). On that occasion she demonstrated the meaning of Asher's name, "happy."

Jeshurun (vv. 26-29). Moses concludes his blessing upon the tribes in the way he began, with praise to God (vv. 26-29). As in verse 5 and

32:15, Moses refers to Israel as Jeshurun. Jeshurun's God rode on the heavens and soared on the clouds, which meant He could arrive swiftly to wrap His everlasting arms of protection about His beloved Israel. Accordingly, if Jeshurun lived up to the meaning of his name, "upright one," the Jews would be safe and secure in Canaan.

Jeshurun worshipped a unique and incomparable God. If they obeyed His Law and remained devoted to Him, they would be an incomparably blessed people – *"Who is like you, a people saved by the Lord?"* (v. 29). Indeed, they would be a happy, blessed and honored people, for no enemy can stand against a nation whose shield and sword is Jehovah Himself!

In application, Christians in the Church Age also have a name to live up to and a calling to fulfill. A Christian is an ambassador for Christ (2 Cor. 5:20). He or she is a heavenly representative of Him on earth (Phil. 3:20). As faithfully as Christ declared the name of His Father during His earthly sojourn, the Christian is now to reveal to the world the name of the Lord Jesus Christ. This was Paul's prayer for the young believers at Thessalonica: *"That the name of our Lord Jesus Christ may be glorified in you, and you in Him, according to the grace of our God and the Lord Jesus Christ"* (2 Thess. 1:12).

Paul instructs Timothy as to what is necessary for Christians to adequately display the name of Christ: *"Let everyone who names the name of Christ depart from iniquity"* (2 Tim. 2:19). Children imitate famous musicians by lip-syncing their songs on the radio, but believers cannot pretend to be holy; their conduct will either honor a sin-hating Savior or endorse a Savior-hating system. To declare the name of Christ is a high honor, but to associate with His name is the highest call to honor Him. To be identified as "a Christian" is one and the same as acknowledging Christ's call to live as He did.

Meditation

> Nothing is more generally known than our duties which belong to Christianity; and yet, how amazing is it, nothing is less practiced?
>
> — George Whitefield

> That world outside there is not waiting for a new definition of Christianity; it's waiting for a new demonstration of Christianity.
>
> — Leonard Ravenhill

Moses Dies on Nebo
Deuteronomy 34

We have now come to the last chapter of Deuteronomy and the closing of the Pentateuch. Moses has penned all that is previous to this brief chapter. Scripture does not inform us who added this inspired epilogue to the book.

Moses was not permitted to venture into Canaan before he died, but we should not think any less of him because of this limitation. He accomplished exactly what he was commissioned to do at the burning bush forty years earlier. Jehovah summoned Moses only to deliver His people from Egypt; Moses was never told to lead them into the Promised Land (Ex. 3:10). In fact, Jehovah specifically told Moses that *He* would lead the Israelites into the Promised Land (Ex. 3:8, 17); He foreknew that Moses would not enter Canaan.

From a typological perspective it was fitting that Moses should die before the Israelites entered the Promised Land and for Joshua to be commissioned to lead the Israelites into Canaan (Josh. 1). Moses brought the Law, which could never bring spiritual life; the Law only condemned the Jews because they could not keep it. Consequently, Law-keeping, which centers in human effort alone, can never result in victorious living, which depends solely on God's infusing power. Joshua pictures Jesus Christ of the New Testament; both of their names mean "God's Salvation." Israel's trip through the Jordan River represents the receipt of the resurrection life of Christ. It is only by this infusing power that a believer can have victory over the enemy, lay hold of spiritual possessions, and please God.

Moses Views the Promised Land (vv. 1-4)

Moses had resolutely guided the Israelites for forty years in the wilderness, during which time he expounded God's Law to them, and brought them safely to the brink of the Jordan River. It was here that the life and the ministry of Moses would conclude. But before the Lord could permit His servant to die, He first had to keep His promise to show Moses the land:

> *Then Moses went up from the plains of Moab to Mount Nebo, to the top of Pisgah, which is across from Jericho. And the Lord showed him all the land of Gilead as far as Dan, all Naphtali and the land of Ephraim and Manasseh, all the land of Judah as far as the Western Sea, the South, and the plain of the Valley of Jericho, the city of palm trees, as far as Zoar. Then the Lord said to him, "This is the land of which I swore to give Abraham, Isaac, and Jacob, saying, 'I will give it to your descendants.' I have caused you to see it with your eyes, but you shall not cross over there"* (vv. 1-4).

It is apparent from the description of what the Lord showed Moses of the land that this was no normal sightseeing venture, but a supernatural look-see of the entire land. No doubt Moses was strengthened by the Lord to ascend the Pisgah range in order to reach the summit of Nebo, there to receive a wonderful vista of Jericho and the Jordan Valley. However, it would be humanly impossible to see all of Gilead to the north, the Mediterranean Sea far to the west, and Zoar far south in the area of the Dead Sea. The Lord evidently opened Moses' eyes to perceive the wonders of the Promised Land, as the Lord viewed it from heaven. On this point, C. H. Mackintosh writes:

> It was grace that brought Moses to the top of Pisgah and showed him the land of Canaan from thence. It was grace that led Jehovah to provide a grave for His servant and bury him therein. It was better to see the land of Canaan, in company with God, than to enter it in company with Israel. And yet we must not forget that Moses was prevented entering the land because of the unadvised speaking. God, in government, kept Moses out of Canaan. God, in grace, brought Moses up to Pisgah. These two facts, in the history of Moses, illustrate, very forcibly, the distinction between grace and government – a subject of the deepest interest, and of great practical value. Grace pardons and blesses; but government takes its course. Let us ever remember this.[212]

The Servant of the Lord (vv. 5-9)

At the burning bush, Moses' faith in Jehovah was in its infancy, but over the strenuous years that followed, his faith in and devotion to Jehovah grew steadily. While living, Moses was spoken of as a servant

Devotions in Deuteronomy

only once (Ex. 14:31), but the title "the servant of the Lord" is not used until after his death: *"So Moses the servant of the Lord died there in the land of Moab, according to the word of the Lord"* (v. 5).

Joshua commences his book by recounting the Lord's message to him shortly after the death of Moses: *"Moses My servant is dead. Now therefore, arise, go over this Jordan, you and all this people, to the land which I am giving to them – the children of Israel"* (Josh. 1:2). Joshua then refers to Moses as "the servant of the Lord" a total of sixteen times in his own book. Interestingly, Joshua would be given the same honorary title after his death; he also finished well (Josh. 24:29).

After Moses died, the Lord buried his body *"in a valley in the land of Moab, opposite Beth Peor; but no one knows his grave to this day"* (v. 6). No doubt, if the Jews had known where Moses' body was buried, they would have sought to make it a holy site, which would have distracted them from worshipping God at the central sanctuary as commanded. This is likely the reason that Satan sought the body of Moses which led to a contention between him and Michael the Archangel (Jude 9). Evidently, there were powerful angels involved with both the direct burial of Moses and the protection of his grave afterwards. This was to ensure no human would know where Moses' body was buried and that no one, including Lucifer, would be able to steal it.

Just as the Lord had prevented the Israelites' clothing and shoes from wearing out, the Lord sustained Moses' body through the rigors of forty years of ministry. When it was time for him to join his people, Moses' *"eyes were not dim nor his natural vigor diminished"* (v. 7). Moses was a servant who experienced day-by-day rejuvenation by the Spirit of God. This shows us that even in the Old Testament, God's servants could experience daily revival, that is, if they continued to walk with the Lord (Enoch in Genesis 5 and Caleb in Joshua 14 are other examples).

Obviously, God supernaturally maintained Moses' body to enable Moses to fulfill his unique calling. However, believers in the Church Age are not to yearn for an age-defying miracle such as Moses experienced, but rather are to long for the ongoing spiritual revival of their inner man: *"Therefore we do not lose heart. Even though our outward man is perishing, yet the inward man is being renewed day by day"* (2 Cor. 4:16).

Refining and Reminding

After his death *"the children of Israel wept for Moses in the plains of Moab thirty days"* (v. 8). After this period of mourning, Joshua, Israel's new leader, prepared the Israelites to cross over the Jordan.

The Epitaph of Moses (vv. 10-12)

Moses had a unique ministry: he was called to work many signs and wonders to demonstrate Jehovah's authority and power in Egypt and to deliver His people from Pharaoh's oppressive clutches. Moses was unlike any other Old Testament prophet, in that he was able to enjoy ongoing intimacy with God while being in His presence (v. 10). On this point, the Jamieson, Fausset, and Brown Commentary notes:

> In whatever light we view this extraordinary man, the eulogy pronounced in these inspired words will appear just. No Hebrew prophet or ruler equaled him in character, official dignity, as well as knowledge of God's will, and opportunities of announcing it.[213]

Not only was the Lord's companionship a special blessing to Moses, the Lord appreciated Moses' fellowship also: *"The Lord spoke to Moses face to face, as a man speaks to his friend"* (Ex. 33:11). It is a reminder that the Lord does not have *favorites*, but He does have *intimates*; at this very moment we are as close to the Lord as we want to be – He always wants to draw us near to Himself.

Though the best efforts of Moses failed to prevent Israel from sliding into idolatry and centuries of divine chastening, the Song of Moses still points the way for Israel to return to Jehovah. At the end of the Tribulation Period, God's covenant people of old will be refined, reborn, and restored to Jehovah forever, and in the Promised Land. Then, all the promises of God afforded in the Jewish patriarchs, as recorded in the writings of Moses, will be fulfilled!

Meditation

> From the lofty hills of Moab,
> Where thy weary feet shall stand,
> Thou shalt look across the Jordan,
> And behold the promised land;
> The land of milk and honey,
> Fertile land of corn and wine,

Devotions in Deuteronomy

The land of springs and fountains –
'Tis the land that shall be thine.

From the lofty hills of Moab,
It is sweet indeed to rise
To the higher land of promise,
To the Canaan of the skies;
The land of heavenly glory,
Land of beauty all divine,
The land of many mansions,
That forever shall be thine.

— M. Lowrie Hofford

Endnotes

1. Eugene H. Merrill and Dallas Theological Seminary, *The Bible Knowledge Commentary : An Exposition of the Scriptures* (Victor Books, Wheaton, IL; 1983-1985), pp. 104-108
2. C. A. Coates, *C. A. Coates Commentary – Numbers* (Kingston Bible Trust, West Sussex, UK), chp. 1
3. F. B. Hole, *Numbers*, STEM Publishing; Num. 1: http://stempublishing.com/authors/hole/Pent/Numbers.html
4. Albert Barnes, *Notes on the Old Testament – Exodus to Esther* (Baker Book House, Grand Rapids, MI; reprinted 1851), 2:2
5. International Standard Bible http://www.internationalstandardbible.com/N/nineveh.html [last accessed April 8, 2017]
6. C. H. Mackintosh, *Numbers*, STEM Publishing; Num. 3: http://stempublishing.com/authors/mackintosh/Pent/NUMBERS0.html
7. C. A. Coates, op. cit., Num. 3
8. J. N. Darby, *Synopsis of the Books of the Bible Vol. 1 – Genesis-2 Chronicles* (Stow Hill Bible and Tract Depot, Kingston on the Thames; 1949), pp. 177-178
9. Harry A. Ironside, *Commentary on 1 Peter* (Loizeaux Brothers, Inc., Neptune, NJ; 1985), p. 56
10. *Keil & Delitzsch Commentary on the Old Testament*: New Updated Edition (Electronic Database via Hendrickson Publishers, Inc.; 1996), Num. 4:13
11. C. H. Mackintosh, op. cit., Num. 4
12. J. N. Darby, op. cit., p. 179
13. C. A. Coates, op. cit., Num. 1
14. Matthew Henry, *Matthew Henry Commentary Vol. 1* (MacDonald Pub. Co., Mclean, VA), p. 576
15. F. B. Hole, op. cit., chp. 4
16. C. H. Mackintosh, op. cit., Num. 4
17. C. H. Mackintosh, op. cit., Num. 5
18. C. A. Coates, op. cit., Num. 5
19. Albert Barnes, op. cit., Num. 5:27
20. C. H. Mackintosh, op. cit., Num. 5
21. F. B. Hole, op. cit., Num. 5
22. Albert Barnes, op. cit., Num. 6:3-4
23. John J. Stubbs, *What the Bible Teaches – Numbers* (John Ritchie LTD, Kilmarnock, Scotland; 2015), Num. 6:1
24. F. B. Hole, op. cit., Num. 5
25. C. H. Mackintosh, op. cit., Num. 6

26 J. N. Darby, op. cit., p. 184
27 Eugene H. Merrill, op. cit., p. 223
28 Matthew Henry, op. cit., p. 588
29 C. H. Mackintosh, op. cit., Num. 7
30 C. A. Coates, op. cit., Num. 7
31 C. A. Coates, op. cit., Num. 7
32 C. H. Mackintosh, op. cit., Num. 8
33 F. E. Stallan, quoted from *What the Bible Teaches – Numbers*, op. cit., Num. 8:15-22
34 F. B. Hole, op. cit., Num. 9
35 C. H. Mackintosh, op. cit., Num. 8
36 Matthew Henry, op. cit., p. 600
37 John J. Stubbs, op. cit., Num. 10:9-10
38 F. B. Hole, op. cit., Num. 10
39 F. B. Hole, op. cit., Num. 11
40 C. H. Mackintosh, op. cit., Num. 11
41 Arthur W. Pink, *Gleanings in Exodus* (Moody Press, Chicago, IL; no date), derived from chps. 22 and 23
42 E. L. Bevir. *The Christian's Friend* Magazine (vol. 15; 1888), p. 36
43 F. B. Hole, op. cit., Num. 11
44 C. H. Mackintosh, op. cit., Num. 11
45 C. A. Coates, op. cit., Num. 11
46 Albert Barnes, op. cit., Num. 11:1
47 J. N. Darby, op. cit., pp. 194
48 F. B. Hole, op. cit., Num. 12
49 J. N. Darby, op. cit., pp. 194-195
50 Matthew Henry, op. cit., p. 616
51 C. H. Mackintosh, op. cit., Num. 12
52 John J. Stubbs, op. cit., Num. 12:15
53 C. A. Coates, op. cit., Num. 12
54 C. H. Mackintosh, op. cit., Num. 12
55 J. N. Darby, *Joshua*, STEM Publishing; intro. http://stempublishing.com/authors/darby/EXPOSIT/19027E.html
56 William MacDonald, *Believer's Bible Commentary* (Thomas Nelson Pub., Nashville, TN; 1990), p. 240
57 Warren Wiersbe, *The Bible Exposition Commentary, Vol. 2* (Victor Books, Wheaton, IL: 1989), p. 287
58 C. A. Coates, op. cit., Num. 13
59 C. H. Mackintosh, op. cit., Num. 13
60 C. H. Mackintosh, op. cit., Num. 14
61 C. H. Mackintosh, op. cit., Num. 14
62 John J. Stubbs, op. cit., Num. 14:11-19
63 C. H. Mackintosh, op. cit., Num. 14
64 C. A. Coates, op. cit., Num. 15
65 Matthew Henry, op. cit., p. 634
66 C. H. Mackintosh, op. cit., Num. 15

Endnotes

[67] John J. Stubbs, op. cit., Num. 15:38
[68] Albert Barnes, op. cit., Num. 16:1
[69] William Kelly, *Numbers*, STEM Publishing; Num. 16:4
http://stempublishing.com/authors/kelly/1Oldtest/num.html
[70] C. H. Mackintosh, op. cit., Num. 16
[71] C. H. Mackintosh, op. cit., Num. 16
[72] F. B. Hole, op. cit., Num. 16
[73] C. H. Mackintosh, op. cit., Num. 17
[74] C. A. Coates, op. cit., Num. 17
[75] C. H. Mackintosh, op. cit., Num. 17
[76] F. B. Hole, op. cit., Num. 4
[77] C. H. Mackintosh, op. cit., Num. 18
[78] John J. Stubbs, op. cit., Num. 18:10-11
[79] Albert Barnes, op. cit., Num. 18:19
[80] Matthew Henry, op. cit., p. 652
[81] C. H. Mackintosh, op. cit., Num. 18
[82] C. H. Mackintosh, op. cit., Num. 19
[83] William Kelly, *Numbers*, 19:3
[84] John J. Stubbs, op. cit., Num. 19:1
[85] John J. Stubbs, op. cit., Num. 19:1-3
[86] C. F. Keil and F. Delitzsch, op. cit., Num. 19
[87] C. A. Coates, op. cit., Num. 19
[88] C. H. Mackintosh, op. cit., Num. 19
[89] F. B. Hole, op. cit., Num. 20
[90] C. A. Coates, op. cit., Num. 20
[91] Josephus, *Antiq. 4:4:6*
[92] Albert Barnes, op. cit., Num. 20:23
[93] John J. Stubbs, op. cit., Num. 20:29
[94] C. A. Coates, op. cit., Num. 21
[95] C. H. Mackintosh, op. cit., Num. 21
[96] F. B. Hole, op. cit., Num. 21
[97] F. B. Hole, op. cit., Num. 22
[98] John J. Stubbs, op. cit., Num. 22:15
[99] C. H. Mackintosh, op. cit., Num. 22
[100] C. A. Coates, op. cit., Num. 22
[101] William MacDonald, op. cit., p. 191
[102] F. B. Hole, op. cit., Num. 22
[103] C. H. Mackintosh, op. cit., Num. 23
[104] Eugene H. Merrill, op. cit., p. 245
[105] C. H. Mackintosh, op. cit., Num. 24
[106] F. B. Hole, op. cit., Num. 24
[107] Matthew Henry, op. cit., p. 687
[108] C. A. Coates, op. cit., Num. 25
[109] John J. Stubbs, op. cit., Num. 25:6
[110] C. H. Mackintosh, op. cit., Num. 25

[111] Donald Campbell, *The Bible Knowledge Commentary Vol. 1: An Exposition of the Scriptures* (Victor Books, Wheaton, IL; 1983-1985), p. 356
[112] C. H. Mackintosh, op. cit., Num. 27
[113] C. A. Coates, op. cit., Num. 27
[114] C. H. Mackintosh, op. cit., Num. 28
[115] F. B. Hole, op. cit., Num. 28
[116] John J. Stubbs, op. cit., Num. 28:2
[117] F. Duane Lindsey & Dallas Theological Seminary, *The Bible Knowledge Commentary: An Exposition of the Scriptures* (Victor Books, Wheaton, IL; 1983-1985), p. 207
[118] L. M. Grant, *Leviticus*, STEM Publishing; Lev. 23 http://stempublishing.com/authors/grantlm/LEVITICU.html
[119] William Kelly, *Leviticus*, STEM Publishing; Lev. 23 http://stempublishing.com/authors/kelly/1Oldtest/leviticu.html
[120] C. H. Mackintosh, op. cit., Num. 31
[121] C. H. Mackintosh, op. cit., Num. 31
[122] C. H. Mackintosh, op. cit., Num. 32
[123] C. A. Coates, op. cit., Num. 32
[124] Used with permission via http://www.jesuswalk.com/moses/appendix_2-route-of-the-exodus.htm [last accessed on Dec. 23, 2017]; map was modified with additional information only
[125] C. A. Coates, op. cit., Num. 33
[126] J. N. Darby, op. cit., pp. 217
[127] James Vernon McGee, *Thru The Bible Commentary Vol. 2* (Thomas Nelson Publishers, Nashville, TN; 1983), p. 4
[128] Used with permission via https://commons.wikimedia.org/wiki/File:Map_Land_of_Israel.jpg [last accessed on Dec. 23, 2017]
[129] Donald Campbell, *The Bible Knowledge Commentary Vol. 1: An Exposition of the Scriptures* (Victor Books, Wheaton, IL; 1983-1985), p. 356
[130] F. B. Meyer, *Joshua, and the Land of Promise* (Fleming H. Revell Co., Chicago, IL; 1893), p. 181
[131] Paul Lee Tan, *Encyclopedia of 7700 Illustrations: A Treasury of Illustrations, Anecdotes, Facts and Quotations for Pastors, Teachers and Christian Workers* (Bible Communications, Garland TX), 1996, c1979
[132] C. A. Coates, op. cit., Num. 36
[133] Robert Jamieson, A. R. Fausset, and David Brown, *Jamieson, Fausset and Brown Commentary* (Electronic Database via Biblesoft; 1997), Deut. 34:1
[134] Eugene H. Merrill and Dallas Theological Seminary, *The Bible Knowledge Commentary : An Exposition of the Scriptures* (Victor Books, Wheaton, IL; 1983-1985), pp. 104-108
[135] C. H. Mackintosh, *Deuteronomy*, STEM Publishing; Deut. 1: http://stempublishing.com/authors/mackintosh/Pent/DEUT01.html#a1
[136] Albert Barnes, op. cit., Deut. 1:22
[137] William Kelly, *Deuteronomy*, STEM Publishing; Deut. 1 http://stempublishing.com/authors/kelly/1Oldtest/deutrnmy.html

Endnotes

[138] H. L. Rossier, *Joshua*, STEM Publishing; Josh. 14:
H. L. Rossier, http://stempublishing.com/authors/rossier/JOSHUA.html
[139] H. F. Witherby, *The Serious Christian Series: The Book of Joshua* (Books for Christians, Charlotte, NC; no date), p. 184
[140] Albert Barnes, op. cit., Deut. 3:11
[141] Matthew Henry, op. cit., p. 738
[142] F. B. Hole, *Deuteronomy*, STEM Publishing; Deut. 3: http://stempublishing.com/authors/hole/Pent/deuteronomy.html
[143] William MacDonald, op. cit., p. 1082
[144] C. H. Mackintosh, op. cit., Deut. 4
[145] Albert Barnes, op. cit., Deut. 5:22
[146] C. A. Coates, op. cit., Deut. 5
[147] F. B. Hole, op. cit., Deut. 5
[148] C. H. Mackintosh, op. cit., Deut. 6
[149] Matthew Henry, op. cit., pp. 750-751
[150] William MacDonald, op. cit., p. 207
[151] Albert Barnes, op. cit., Deut. 6:13
[152] J. N. Darby, op. cit., pp. 224
[153] William Kelly, op. cit., Deut. 6
[154] C. H. Mackintosh, op. cit., Deut. 7
[155] C. H. Mackintosh, op. cit., Deut. 8
[156] Arthur W. Pink, *Gleanings in Exodus* (Moody Press, Chicago, IL; no date), p. 120
[157] C. A. Coates, op. cit., Deut. 8
[158] F. B. Hole, op. cit., Deut. 8
[159] "Gold, Copper, Iron Mines Reported Discovered in Southern Israel" (Jewish Telegraphic Agency; Dec. 13, 1951)
[160] C. H. Mackintosh, op. cit., Deut. 9
[161] C. H. Mackintosh, op. cit., Deut. 10
[162] Albert Barnes, op. cit., Deut. 10:12
[163] William MacDonald, op. cit., p. 210
[164] Jack S. Deere and Dallas Theological Seminary, *The Bible Knowledge Commentary: An Exposition of the Scriptures* (Victor Books, Wheaton, IL; 1983-1985), p. 283
[165] C. H. Mackintosh, op. cit., Deut. 12
[166] C. A. Coates, op. cit., Deut. 12
[167] A. W. Pink, *Gleanings in Genesis* (Moody Press, Chicago: 1922), p. 187
[168] C. F. Keil and F. Delitzsch, op. cit., Deut. 14:28-29
[169] Albert Barnes, op. cit., Deut. 14:28-29
[170] C. A. Coates, op. cit., Deut. 14
[171] Robert Jamieson, A. R. Fausset, and David Brown, op. cit., Deut. 15:2
[172] C. F. Keil and F. Delitzsch, op. cit., Deut. 15:2
[173] F. B. Hole, op. cit., Deut. 15
[174] C. A. Coates, op. cit., Deut. 15
[175] C. H. Mackintosh, op. cit., Ex. 21
[176] C. H. Mackintosh, op. cit., Deut. 15

[177] J. N. Darby, op. cit., p. 232
[178] A. T. Shearman, *Treasury of Bible Doctrine – "Christ as Prophet"* (Precious Seed Magazine, UK; 1977), p. 135
[179] William MacDonald, op. cit., p. 218
[180] Edward Dennett, Exodus, STEM Publishing; Ex. 21 http://stempublishing.com/authors/dennett/EXODUS1.html
[181] William Kelly, op. cit., Deut. 20
[182] Watchman Nee, *Sit, Walk, Stand* (Tyndale House Pub., Wheaton, IL; 1977), p. 56
[183] Robert Jamieson, A. R. Fausset, and David Brown, op. cit., Deut. 20:5
[184] Matthew Henry, op. cit., p. 808
[185] Matthew Henry, op. cit., p. 812
[186] Jack S. Deere, op. cit., p. 301
[187] J. N. Darby, op. cit., p. 232
[188] C. H. Mackintosh, op. cit., Deut. 22
[189] William MacDonald, op. cit., p. 220
[190] C. A. Coates, op. cit., Deut. 22
[191] C. H. Mackintosh, op. cit., Deut. 22
[192] Jack S. Deere, op. cit., p. 302
[193] William MacDonald, op. cit., p. 231
[194] Sara Paterson-Brown, *Education About the Hymen Is Needed* (British Medical Journal; Feb. 7, 1998), p. 341
[195] Jack S. Deere, op. cit., p. 304
[196] Albert Barnes, op. cit., Deut. 24:1-4
[197] Matthew Henry, *Matthew Henry's Concise Commentary on the Whole Bible* (e-Sword database; 2012), Deut. 24:1-4
[198] Albert Barnes, op. cit., Deut. 24:16
[199] Albert Barnes, op. cit., Deut. 26:2
[200] C. H. Mackintosh, op. cit., Deut. 26
[201] C. A. Coates, op. cit., Deut. 26
[202] Jack S. Deere, op. cit., p. 309
[203] H. F. Witherby, *The Serious Christian Series: The Book of Joshua* (Books for Christians, Charlotte, NC; no date), pp. 148-149
[204] William Kelly, op. cit., Deut. 27
[205] C. H. Mackintosh, op. cit., Deut. 27
[206] Robert Jamieson, A. R. Fausset, and David Brown, op. cit., Deut. 28:68
[207] Jack S. Deere, op. cit., p. 315
[208] William Kelly, op. cit., Deut. 32
[209] Albert Barnes, op. cit., Deut. 32
[210] C. A. Coates, op. cit., Deut. 32
[211] *Oxford English Dictionary* (Oxford University Press, NY); 1989
[212] C. H. Mackintosh, op. cit., Num. 20
[213] Robert Jamieson, A. R. Fausset, and David Brown, op. cit., Deut. 34:10-12

www.ingramcontent.com/pod-product-compliance
Lightning Source LLC
Chambersburg PA
CBHW060447170426
43199CB00011B/1125